AUSTRO-CORPORATISM
PAST • PRESENT • FUTURE

Contemporary Austrian Studies

Sponsored by the University of New Orleans and Universität Innsbruck

Executive Editors
Erich Thöni, University of Innsbruck
Gordon H. Mueller, University of New Orleans

Editors
Anton Pelinka, University of Innsbruck
Günter Bischof, University of New Orleans

Assistant Editors	Production Editor	Copy Editor
Melanie McKay	Judy Nides	Melanie McKay
Judy Nides		
Ellen Palli		

Publication of this volume has been made possible through a generous grant from the Austrian
Ministry of Foreign Affairs and the Austrian Culture Institute in New York.
The Bank Gutmann Nfg. AG, the University of Innsbruck, and Metro College of the University of New Orleans
have also provided support.

Articles appearing in this serial publication are abstracted and indexed in HISTORICAL
ABSTRACTS and AMERICA: HISTORY AND LIFE.

Günter Bischof
Anton Pelinka

EDITORS

Austro-Corporatism
PAST • PRESENT • FUTURE

CONTEMPORARY
AUSTRIAN STUDIES

VOLUME 4

Transaction Publishers
New Brunswick (U.S.A.) and London (U.K.)

Library of Congress Catalog Number: 95-21068
ISBN: 1-56000-833-4
Printed in the United States of America

Library of Congress Cataloging-in-Publication Data

Austro-corporatism : past, present, future / edited by Günter Bischof, Anton Pelinka.
    p. cm. — (Contemporary Austrian studies ; v. 4)
    Includes bibliographical references.
    ISBN 1-56000-833-4 (paper : alk. paper)
    1. Corporate state—Austria—History. 2. Austria—Economic policy—1945- 3. Austria—Politics and government—1945- 4. Industrial relations—Austria—History. 5. Austria—Foreign economic relations. I. Bischof, Günter, 1953-   . II. Pelinka, Anton, 1941-   . III. Series.
HD3616.A93A95   1995
330.12'6'09436—dc20   95-21068
                                                          CIP

Table of Contents

Introduction   1

Topical Essays
Andrei S. Markovits, *Austrian Corporatism in Comparative
    Perspective*   5
Emmerich Tálos and Bernhard Kittel, *Roots of Austro-
    Corporatism: Institutional Preconditions and Cooperation
    Before and After 1945*   21
Randall W. Kindley, *The Evolution of Austria's Neo-Corporatist
    Institutions*   53
Hans Seidel, *Social Partnership and Austro-Keynesianism*   94
Ferdinand Karlhofer, *The Present and Future State of Social
    Partnership*   119

**FORUM: Austrian Social Partnership—
A Model for Central and Eastern Europe?**
Birgitt Haller, Introduction   147
Lubomir Brokl and Zdenka Mansfeldova, *Social Partnership in
    the Czech Republic*   151
Monika Čambáliková, *Social Partnership in Slovakia*   157
Igor Lukšič, *Social Partnership in Slovenia*   164
Sándor Kurtán, *Social Partnership in Hungary*   170

Nontopical Essays
Jonathan Petropoulos, *The Importance of the Second Rank:
    The Case of the Art Plunderer Kajetan Mühlmann*   177
David McIntosh, *In the Shadow of Giants: U.S. Policy Toward
    Small Nations: The Cases of Lebanon, Costa Rica, and
    Austria in the Eisenhower Years*   222

FORUM: The 'New Right' in Austria
Günter Bischof, Introduction - *"What's right?"*   280
Michael Gehler, *Student Corporations in Austria and the Right:
    A Historical Outline*   289
Reinhold Gärtner, *Right-Wing Press in Austria*   304
Walter Manoschek, *How the Austrian People's Party Dealt
    with the Holocaust, Anti-Semitism and National Socialism
    after 1945*   317
Richard Mitten, *The Social Democratic "mémoire volontaire"
    and Coming to Terms with the Legacy of National Socialism
    in Austria*   336
Max Riedlsperger, *The FPÖ and the Right*   351

Book Reviews

Peter Pulzer: *Handbuch des Österreichischen Rechtsextremismus,*
  Stiftung Dokumentationsarchiv des österreichischen
  Widerstandes   369
Alan S. Milward: Michael Gehler and Rolf Steininger, eds.,
  Österreich und die Europäische Integration 1945-1993.
  Aspekte einer wechselvollen Entwicklung   375
Wolfgang Krieger: Klaus Fiesinger, *Ballhausplatz-Diplomatie*
  1945-1949 and Michael Gehler, ed., *Karl Gruber: Reden*
  und Dokumente 1945-1953   379
Detlef K. Vogel: Gabriele Anderl and Walter Manoschek,
  Gescheiterte Flucht. Der jüdische 'Kladovo-Transport' auf
  dem Weg nach Palestina, 1939-1942 and Walter Manoschek,
  'Serbien ist judenfrei:' Militärische Besatzungspolitik und
  Judenvernichtung in Serbien 1941/42   385
William T. Bluhm: Ernst Bruckmüller, *Österreichbewußtsein im*
  Wandel: Identität und Selbstverständnis in den 90er Jahren   388
Erika Thurner: David F. Good, Margarete Grandner, Mary Jo
  Maynes, eds., *Women in Austria. Essays on Their Situation*
  in the 20th Century   392
Anton Pelinka: H. Pierre Secher, *Bruno Kreisky, Chancellor of*
  Austria: A Political Biography   398
Michael G. Huelshoff: Anton Pelinka, Christian Schaller, and
  Paul Luif, *Ausweg EG? Innenpolitische Motive einer außen-*
  politischen Umorientierung   400
Max Riedlsperger: Kurt Richard Luther and Wolfgang C. Müller,
  eds., *Politics in Austria: Still A Case of Consociationalism?* 404

Survey of Austrian Politics: 1994
Rainer Nick   409

List of Authors   426

Introduction

In spite of Professor Peter Gerlich's humorous dictum that social partnership "cannot be explained to a foreigner, but need not be explained to a native," we are trying to address exactly those two audiences with the topical essays in this volume. Corporatism has been one of the most significant aspects of Austrian political culture after World War II; it has also been at the center of academic discussions of Austria's political system. Corporatism/*Sozialpartnerschaft* in domestic politics and neutrality in foreign policy have been the key elements in making the Second Austrian Republic so different in character from the First Republic. These days both the corporate state and neutrality have increasingly come under attack as being outdated. Yet they still are seen as possible models for the new democracies in East Central Europe. Many foreign observers have seen Austria's social partnership as a very successful instrument for stabilizing democracy and attaining compromise and consensus in the social sphere. This may make it attractive as a model for further development in the European Union, especially if and when it will be broadened with new member states from Eastern Europe.

Social partnership, then, means a orientation towards compromise between strong employers' and employees' interest groups, with the state acting as a mediating agent. Social partnership is also part of the political culture of "consociational democracy" established by the two major political camps in post-World War II Austria—the conservative Christian democrats and the social democrats. Social partnership is a basic constituent part of postwar Austrian political culture and has come increasingly under attack from both the right (the FPÖ and its populism since 1986) and the left (the Greens which have destroyed the SPÖ monopoly on the left).

The main focus of this volume deals with the past, present and likely future state of Austria's famed *Sozialpartnerschaft*, i.e., Austro-corporatism. *Andrei S. Markovits* provides a useful introduction by giving an overall evaluation of Austro-corporatism in the larger context of European politics. He notes that not corporatism itself is unique to Austria, but the specific methods how Austro-corporatism is executed that distinguishes it from the rest of Europe in general and Germany in particular. *Markovits'* approach highlights that the Austrian case can only be properly understood and evaluated from such a comparative perspective.

Emmerich Tálos and *Bernhard Kittel* describe and analyze the deeper nineteenth century and post-World War I roots of social partnership. In both the Christian democrat and the social democrat camps special interest groups favored corporatist mediation to arrive at social peace before and after 1945. They emphasize that Austro-corporatism never has been and never will be a monolithic closed model; it rather constitutes a network of formal and informal participants and rules that can change and adapt with the transformation of historical contexts.

The young American political scientist *Randall Kindley* reflects the more theoretical American approach to corporatism and political economy and pictures Austro-corporatism as an integrated part of a more general picture of major political parties and economic interest groups cooperating in an institutionalized network of governance. This network gives Austria an unusual place among Western democracies as a nation with a clear priority for political, economic and social stabilization and a low priority for innovation and participation. Kindley shows how the economic dislocation in the two difficult postwar periods favored such corporatist mediation and stresses how the post-World War II trajectory in interest mediation led from the five post-1945 "wage-price agreements" directly to the 1957 founding of the landmark *Paritätische Kommission.*

The noted economist and former state secretary *Hans Seidel* concentrates on the economic perspective of social partnership, more specifically on the Kreisky administrations' famous experiments with "Austro-Keynesianism." He explains the specific 1970s programs of fine-tuning the macro and micro sides of the recession prone economy and the role of the corporatist state in these.

Ferdinand Karlhofer addresses the future of Austro-corporatism. Facing both 1980s-style "Reaganomics" domestically and the world of the European single market internationally, social partnership is facing an uphill battle. Reaganism, Thatcherism, and now Gingrichism, with their growing anti-statist impulses have not stopped on Austria's doorsteps and are questioning the statist traditions in Austrian political culture and the entire framework of Austro-corporatism. Ironically, the social partners themselves favored Austria's early entry into the European Union and thus have subjected themselves to these strong international trends.

In the FORUM "Eastern Europe," *Birgitt Haller* has invited specialist from four of Austria's formerly communist neighbors to the East to comment on the potential model character of Austro-corporatism/tripartism for the new democracies in East-Central Europe. Czechia, Slovakia, Hungary and Slovenia have all developed different forms of institutional tripartite employers/labor/state interest mediation. All of them looked at the Austrian model of social partnership—as well as the Scandinavian and Portuguese models—whereby the Slovenes and the Hungarians found the Austrian paradigm more useful for their purposes than the Czechs and Slovaks.

The volume continues with two long essays unrelated to the main focus of this issue—both of them emanating from scholarship originally done at the History Department of Harvard University. *Jonathan Petropoulos* presents a fascinating case study of a prominent Austrian Nazi in the second rank, whose exploits have almost fallen into oblivion. The portrait of Kajetan Mühlmann, a powerful behind-the-scenes art plunderer exemplifies the archetypical opportunist Austrian *Handlanger* of the Nazi regime, whose services made the Nazi occupation of Europe possible. The art historian Mühlmann played a crucial role during the Nazis' plundering of Europe's art treasures from private and public collections. Such second-rank Austrian Nazi operatives made the gigantic Nazi art theft work in the same manner that Adolf Eichmann and his associates from Austria made the extermination of the Jews succeed. Petropoulos poignantly concludes: "As the case of Kajetan Mühlmann illustrates, the history of these operatives tells us much about how the Nazi regime functioned and how individuals responded to the unique circumstances of the time. Ultimately, National Socialist rule would have been very different, if not impossible, without their complicity."

David McIntosh has shortened his *summa cum laude* Harvard undergraduate thesis which analyzes the Eisenhower Administration's policies towards small neutral states. He carefully shows how pragmatic American neutrality policy vis-a-vis Lebanon, Costa Rica and Austria in the 1950s evolved in the larger context of the United States' specific geostrategic interests in these various regions of the world. From such a comparative perspective the Austrian case was not as unique as

Austrian scholarship—usually ignoring such comparative and larger regional American objectives—has traditionally seen it. Among the three countries, due to the ten-year occupation after the war, Austria's relations with the U.S. were the deepest and best. As a consequence, Washington gave Austria more leeway to exercise its own political will and develop policies not always popular in the U.S. With the signing of the State Treaty in 1955, the government of Chancellor Julius Raab increasingly used this leverage to escape American tutelage.

Günter Bischof's FORUM "The 'New Right' in Austria" tries to make sense out of an extremely explosive issue. "What's right?" in Austria? The grey areas between conservatism and a growing new Right is not easy to make out, neither is the demarcation line between Haider's populism, the FPÖ with its right-wing cadres, and the more extreme Neo-Nazi Right. Given that only in February 1995 right-wing extremists killed four gypsies in Oberwart (Burgenland), on the Austro-Hungarian border, one has to ask whether a fashionable, more moderate "new Right" prepares the ground for such abominations and thus bears considerable responsibility for a political climate that makes such tragic violence possible? Of course, the Austrians' specific role in the Third Reich, the lack of denazification for which the two main parties SPÖ and ÖVP are responsible, and Austria's inability to master its World War II past provide a fertile soil for the resurgence of the new Right.

This *CAS* volume was produced at the University of New Orleans. We would like to thank Ellen Palli, our assistant editor in Innsbruck, as well as Melanie McKay and Judy Nides, our hard-working team of copy editor and production editor, for their efforts. Both Robert Dupont, the Dean of Metro College at UNO, and Professor Hans Moser, the *Rektor* of the University of Innsbruck were most supportive whenever we needed it. We continue to be most grateful to our sponsors Sektionschef Peter Marboe in the Austrian Foreign Ministry, and Wolfgang Waldner and Ernst Aichinger of the Austrian Cultural Institute in New York, for their continuing support and encouragement. We also would like to thank the *Institut für Zeitgeschichte* in Vienna and the *Rijksinstituut voor Oorlogsdocumentatie* in Amsterdam for giving us permission to reprint photographs of Kajetan Mühlmann. Our anonymous reviewers as always deserve credit for helping us improve the intellectual content of the essays.

Anton Pelinka/Günter Bischof
Innsbruck/New Orleans, March 1995

Austrian Corporatism in Comparative Perspective

Andrei S. Markovits

Introduction

Many small countries share the dubious fate of being ignored or even unrecognized by much of the world. Happily, Austria is not one of them. True enough, a few letters mailed from the United States to Austria without the geographic qualifier "Europe" find their way to Australia, thereby giving credibility to the message of an Australian-colored yellow and green T-shirt on which a smiling kangaroo is crossed out over the caption "I am Austrian, mate, not Australian." But apart from this superficial confusion with Australia, Austria does not have profile and image problems like those of many small countries. Indeed, Austria is eminently present in many different images to a diverse set of publics. To the world at large, Austria is in fact the image of Wolfgang Amadeus Mozart, the Trapp family, skiing and great food. And the different scholarly and academic publics have their own images of Austria to which they refer in their work and research.

For the health professions, Sigmund Freud is every bit the giant that Mozart has been for the world of music, or for the world *tout court*. Freud and other Viennese figures of the early psychoanalytic movement continue to remain indispensable for any proper understanding of modern psychiatry and psychology. Even though Austria lost its pre-eminence in these fields, as well as that of medicine in general, the Vienna School of Medicine still means something to historians and students of medicine. To economists, the works of Joseph Schumpeter, Eugen Boehm-Bawerk, the Menger brothers (Anton and Carl), Friedrich von Wieser and, of course, Friedrich von Hayek, maintain strong associations with Austria. Art historians continue to assign pride of place to the immense creativity of Viennese artists such as Gustav Klimt and Egon Schiele, not to mention the great collective effort of the group of artists associated with Vienna's Secession. Architects remain preoccupied with studying the progressive housing policies of "red" Vienna and the buildings of Otto Wagner, while to philosophers the writings of Ludwig Wittgenstein and the Vienna Circle of logico-positivists still represent major reference points. Mathematicians continue to respect the work of Erwin Schroedinger. Sociologists maintain their admiration for the pioneering research of Paul Lazarsfeld, Marie Jahoda and Hans Zeisel, which these scholars displayed in their classic study of unemployment caused by the Great Depression in the Marienthal region southeast of Vienna. To be sure, historians of all stripes continue to find Austria a fruitful area of study. Depending on their specialty, Austria remains as relevant to students of political history as it does to those of the military and economic variant.

Tellingly, however, Austria's continued relevance for all these disciplines remains anchored in her past. Only in political science (or the study of politics) have phenomena of Austria's present captured the imagination of key practitioners. Political scientists derive their interest in Austria solely from the post-1945 era, that is, from institutions of the Second Republic such as Austria's neutrality and its corporatism. These two closely related phenomena have furnished perhaps the most essential pillars of the Second Republic's successful stability. More important still, they lie at the core of constructing a modern Austrian identity, which has been complementary to but different from the identity offered by Austria's history. Significantly, the successful interplay of neutrality and corporatism in the formation of a modern Austrian identity helped the Second Republic gain a certain distance from the continued dominance of all things German in Austria's daily life, thereby obviating the developments which led to the tragic relationship between these two related countries during the interwar period.

Neutrality and corporatism are currently undergoing substantial changes to the point of suffering from serious erosion, though neither is in danger of disappearing completely. While to political scientists specializing in international relations, it has been mainly Austria's neutrality which offered an undeniable attraction, to students of comparative politics, political sociology and international political economy, it has been Austria's corporatism that has warranted much scholarly attention. In the remainder of this overview I will offer some comparative thoughts on Austria and its corporatism.

Corporatism in Historical and
Comparative Context

Corporatism is neither new nor exclusive to Austria. As a distinct structure of organizing interests and influencing public policy, as a particular structural link between civil society and the state, as a public representation of private interests, corporatism can not only claim a long historical pedigree but also a wide geographic presence. It was practiced by the guilds of medieval city-states whose corporatist arrangement of the *"Ständestaat"* became a major programmatic rallying point for Catholic collectivists of the nineteenth century in their counterattack against the secular and class-based collectivism of Marxian socialism. The proponents of this revived corporatism hoped that the ills of capitalism and the fragmentations of pluralist liberalism might better be countered by a vertically-arranged "organic" corporation of *"Stände"* than by the horizontally-stratified competition of classes advocated by all versions of Marxism at the time.[1] Indeed, it is not by chance that some of the most pioneering advocates of the *"Ständestaat,"* most notably Karl Vogelsang and Ottmar Spann, became, respectively, major intellectual precursors and representatives of Austria's Catholic-conservative *Lager* which, in its fascist incarnation between 1934 and 1938, practiced the corporatism of the notorious *"vaterländische* Front." But as the contribution to this volume by Emmerich Talos and Bernhard Kittel clearly demonstrates, the roots of corporatism in Austria were structurally alive and well in the nineteenth century much beyond its "black" incarnation of politicized Catholicism. Thus, collective interest organizations that claimed a certain representational hegemony vis-a-vis their members and also enjoyed some form of legal recognition on the part of the state existed in Austria from the latter half of the nineteenth century. Various chambers of commerce were installed as representative bodies of trade, industry and business. It was these institutions that were later to blossom into that quintessential trinity of Austrian corporatism, the Chambers of Business, Agriculture and Labor, respectively, which—with their compulsory membership—have rivalled in inclusiveness the sovereignty Austria extends to its citizens, a sovereignty based on participatory concepts of liberal democracy anchored in the individual. As such, these chambers have, at least formally speaking, embodied a form of collective representation that is counter to that of Austria's Parliament. Thus, corporatism is an orthogonal—if not necessarily incompatible—form of representation in relation to the parliamentarism of liberal democracy.

As to corporatism's geographic ubiquity, institutional arrangements similar to this form of interest representation exist in countries as diverse as Portugal and Indonesia, Greece and Turkey, Spain and Israel, Argentina and Brazil, Italy and Norway. In Europe, corporatism of some kind is present in virtually every country. Philippe C. Schmitter, arguably the most renowned political scientist identified with the study of corporatism, offers the following generally accepted classification of the predominance of corporatism in European polities: leading the pack is Austria, closely followed by Sweden, Norway, Finland and the Netherlands. A second group of countries, exhibiting a much weaker form of corporatism comprises, according to Schmitter, Denmark, Ireland, Switzerland, Belgium and the Federal Republic of Germany. Britain, France and Italy are in the third group, sporting the weakest manifestation of corporatism in their interest representation. Rounding out his comparative framework with three non-European countries, Schmitter lists the United States and Canada as having an even weaker level of corporatism than the bottom three European countries. Conversely, he mentions Australia as representing "an interesting case of a non-European country where 'social contracting' between the state and peak associations has become a regular (if controversial) feature of its politics."[2] (Austria and Australia seem in fact to share this hitherto little known characteristic of interest representation.)

What has made the Austrian case of corporatism so special? And, closely related to that question, why has it been so widely admired by students of comparative politics? Beginning with the former, I shall divide my presentation into two distinct categories: first, I will briefly discuss the institutions of corporatism and the structural arrangements which in my view have made Austrian corporatism so strong. I will then turn to an analysis of the cultural and behavioral aspects of Austrian corporatism which, though much more elusive than its structural-institutional components, are of equal, if not greater, importance in maintaining this corporatism's presence.

The Special Characteristics of Austrian Corporatism: Institutions and Structures

Concerning the institutions of corporatism and its structural arrangements, it is important to note that not one of the items subsequently discussed is unique to Austria. Nor are they in and of themselves sufficient to creating a corporatism of any strength, let alone one of Austrian dimensions. These items have to be viewed as a package in which the whole is clearly more than the sum of its parts.

The Aforementioned Chambers

These legally sanctioned parastatist institutions "incorporate" virtually every Austrian citizen who is gainfully employed in industry and manufacturing (Chamber of Labor), is a managerial member and/or owner of some business establishment ranging from the corner drug store to huge multinational companies (Chamber of Business), or is engaged in agricultural pursuits of any kind (Chamber of Agriculture). Membership in these three institutions is compulsory, thus furnishing one of the most important factors of any successful corporatism: a high concentration, perhaps even monopolization, of interest representation in a few "peak associations." These chambers serve as self-contained ministates. They feature regularized elections which are contested by the country's parties and/or its proxies, similar to regular parliamentary campaigns. One of the telling signs that the strength even of Austria's corporatism has been waning in the past few years is the precipitous decline in the level of participation in the recent chamber elections.

The Role of Austrian Labor

It is interesting to note that all countries of Schmitter's first group (Austria, Sweden, Norway, Finland and the Netherlands) have a strong social democratic tradition of labor politics. Indeed, these are precisely the countries that another seminal student of comparative politics, Walter Korpi, classifies as particularly democratic by virtue of the power of their labor movements which, over the years, displaced the most pernicious aspects of the class struggle from the highly undemocratic (because private) market to the much more democratic (because public) state.[3] Thus, one could almost transpose Barrington Moore, Jr.'s famous dictum of "no bourgeoisie, no democracy" onto the topic at hand: "no social democracy, no corporatism."

There can be little doubt that social democracy as an institution and organized labor as a political actor have played a crucial role in the construction and maintenance of Austrian corporatism during the postwar era. That this has been very much a phenomenon of the Second Republic is best demonstrated by its virtual absence during Austria's previous regimes, most notably the ill-fated First Republic. This is a clear case where culture supersedes structure since structurally speaking, the organized working class institutions—essential in Austria's corporatist arrangement of interest representation during the Second Republic—were already largely in place during the First. Concretely, the "red" subculture, the cradle-to-grave social democratic *Lager* with its dense network of ancillary organizations, had been in place by the beginning of the twentieth century. It most certainly monopolized social democratic interest representation by the beginning of the First Republic. Thus, one of the key ingredients of *any* successful corporatist arrangement—namely a highly organized working class with institutionalized interests—was already present in Austria's First Republic.

Yet, far from being a source of reliability, stability and systemic support, this red *Lager* remained deeply suspicious of the state and capital, the two other players in any corporatist arrangement. Imbued with the culture of Austro-Marxism instead of Austro-corporatism, the First Republic's social democrats still paid sufficient lip service to a revolutionary brand of socialism. This verbal radicalism made them far from actual revolutionaries, but it was genuine enough to relegate them to passive resistance to, deep suspicion of, and reluctant participation in the affairs of the First Republic. Above all, the dilemma posed by ideological radicalism and cultural exclusivity on the one hand and structural institutionalization and organizational integration on the other led the interwar social democrats into defensiveness and negativity which, in a pernicious combination, contributed to their violent defeat in 1934. The only benefit which this combination offered the Austrian social democrats—in major contrast to their German cousins—was the crucial fact that they, singular among central Europe's working classes, succumbed to fascism only after an armed struggle. This moral victory could not have happened without the combination of revolutionary ideology and organizational tenacity. As such, it was the positive flip side of an otherwise negative arrangement. Austrian social democracy's ideological radicalism rendered the red *Lager* much less *staatstragend*, in spite of its institutional anchoring, than was the much weaker and also meeker German social democracy. The Austrian First Republic was a state that no one wanted.[4]

The Weimar Republic, in contrast, was a state that the SPD did in fact desire. The problem was that German social democracy lacked the institutional strength to exert its will in defense of a republic which the much mightier forces of the bourgeoisie and the aristocratic Junker class sought to destroy. German social democracy's relative weakness compared to Austria's also informed the postwar arrangement of the two countries' respective corporatisms. Examples abound. Austrian social democracy held governmental power from the very beginning of the Republic until 1966 and then again from 1970 until the present. Add to this the fact that between 1970 and 1983 the SPÖ governed Austria all by itself, unencumbered by any coalitional constraints. In contrast, the SPD remained excluded from governmental power in Bonn until 1966 and even then was only able to govern with the help of a coalition, first as the junior partner in an Austrian-style Grand Coalition until 1969 and then as the senior member of a so-called social-liberal coalition with the FDP until September 1982. Excepting the brief hiatus between 1966 and 1970, Austrian social democracy has—at a minimum—shared governmental power throughout the Second Republic's existence. This feat has remained unmatched by any other European social democracy, even the venerable Swedish which had to relinquish governmental power for six years during the same time span. Being in power for nearly half a century offers all kinds of possibilities to articulate, represent and defend the interests of one's constituents. Not surprisingly, the record of Austrian social democracy is better on this account than the German's. If one merely looks at the implementation of Keynesian policies of demand management—as the article by Hans Seidel does with eloquence in this volume—then it is clear that what became commonplace in Austria to the point of being dubbed "Austro-Keynesianism" remained simply beyond the SPD's capacities (though not its wishes) for most of the years in which the SPD shared governmental power, let alone the much larger amount of time when it did not.[5]

Labor's power, as Korpi teaches us, is easier brought to bear in the arena of the state than in the market. Here, too, the Austrian social democrats enjoyed a decided advantage vis-a-vis their German cousins since—in notable contrast to the undisputed market domination of the German economy—the state's role in the Austrian economy is among the most prevalent of all capitalist countries in the world. Virtually all of Austria's large industrial plants, as well as its major financial institutions and leading manufacturing firms, are in some fashion (directly or indirectly) state owned. This has meant that the political parties, in this case the SPÖ, have spent nearly fifty years entrenching their position in the country's economy. While on the one hand, this created a lot of protection for the parties' respective clients, it also caused much waste and corruption on the other. Whatever the case, it represented an ideal setting for the flourishing of corporatism.

The strength of the two social democratic parties relative to the size of their respective membership reinforces my argument. The SPD has approximately 900,000 members (almost all in the western part of Germany) in a country of nearly 80 million inhabitants while the SPÖ has 700,000 members in a country of 7.5 million people.

In other institutional aspects, too, Austrian social democracy has consistently found itself more powerful vis-a-vis Austrian politics than German social democracy in the context of German politics. For one thing, Germany has nothing even vaguely comparable to the Chamber of Labor in which all wage earners are involuntary members. While the Austrian Chamber of Labor is nominally independent of the SPÖ, there has existed an almost perfect overlap between this chamber and the Social Democratic party in terms of ideology, interest articulation, personnel and every conceivable item that matters in politics. Similarly, the Austrian Trade Union Federation (*Öesterreichischer Gewerkschaftsbund*—ÖGB), while also nominally independent of the Social Democratic Party as well as of the Chamber of Labor, embodies yet another major organization in which social democratic interests prevail. The ÖGB, just like its German counterpart the German Trade Union Federation (*Deutscher Gewerkschaftsbund*—DGB), is a unitary labor organization (*Einheitsgewerkschaft*), meaning that officially the union federation does not fall in the purview of any political party. But whereas in Germany parties cannot run candidates for union offices and are banned from any intra-union affairs, in Austria parties can participate in intra-union elections and other matters internal to unions. For these reasons, as well as many others, relations between the ÖGB and the SPÖ are much closer on all accounts (organizational, ideological, personnel-related) than they are between the DGB and the SPD. Yet another strengthening ingredient in Austrian labor's corporatist role has been the ÖGB's direct involvement in collective bargaining. Unlike in Germany where collective bargaining—arguably the most essential aspect of all union activities—falls in the purview of the individual unions and excludes the DGB, collective bargaining in Austria remains the prerogative of the ÖGB, the all-encompassing umbrella organization. This means that collective bargaining in Austria has a much more centralizing character than in Germany, lending Austrian corporatism yet another element of institutional superiority over its much weaker and more diffuse German counterpart.[6]

The Grand Coalition

In most liberal democracies, coalitions between the two largest parties are usually the result of some exceptional circumstance or emergency. Thus, for example, the Marach-Likud Grand Coalition in Israel in 1986/7 was an explicit arrangement to deal with the country's runaway inflation. It was an uneasy and unwieldy alliance between two rivals who coalesced as a last resort to prevent the country from entering into a crisis of perhaps irreparable damage. Once the immediate crisis was banned, the coalition broke up, as expected. In Germany, too, the only experience with a Grand Coalition between the Christian democrats (CDU/CSU) and the social democrats (SPD) occurred between 1966 and 1969 in the wake of the country's first economic recession since the founding of the Federal Republic and, concomitantly, the nascent development of extremist politics on the far right in the form of a neo-Nazi party. This coalition also dissolved within three years. Only emergencies of the magnitude of World War II compelled Britain to have a wartime coalition between the Conservative party and Labour. Coalitions of some sort are the governmental norm in most liberal democracies, especially among those whose electoral system is based on some variant of proportional representation. Most West European democracies have routinely been governed by coalitions. But Grand Coalitions—i.e. coalitions between the two largest and strongest parties whose alleged role is to compete with one another—are very rare. Only in Switzerland are Grand Coalitions more commonplace than in Austria. But in Switzerland, parties are—by virtue of the country's all-inclusive form of government—instruments of political collusion rather than of competition, as they are, at least nominally and in part, in Austria. Switzerland's all-party government cannot be compared to Austria's Grand Coalition since in the Swiss case the coalition has attained constitutional status, whereas in Austria the Grand Coalition is a completely voluntary arrangement with no legal or constitutional standing at all.[7]

The origins of Austria's Grand Coalition also hail from crisis situations: the legacy of the Austrian Civil War in 1934; Austria's role as part of the Third Reich between 1938 and 1945; the liberation/occupation by the Western Allies and the Soviet Union between 1945 and 1955; the difficulties of economic and political reconstruction in the immediate postwar period; and the attainment of independence and full sovereignty in 1955. What is interesting—and unique in the Austrian case—is that a governmental arrangement designed to deal with exceptional situations demanding the coalescence of society's major institutions became the norm of government. After all, for thirty of the Second Republic's fifty years, Austria has been governed by a Grand Coalition of some kind with the ÖVP furnishing the senior partnership in the coalition's first installment until 1966 and the SPÖ's assuming this role since 1986. To be sure, there have been many reasons for this arrangement. Not least among them has been that the third Austrian party, the Freedom Party (FPÖ), has been unacceptable as a coalition partner by virtue of its close ties in ideology and personnel to National Socialism. Thus, the governmental arrangements most common to the rest of Europe, so-called small coalitions, remained beyond the acceptability and legitimacy of Austrian political culture for much of the postwar period until the social democrats formed a small coalition with the FPÖ in 1983 which lasted until 1988.[8] Whatever the reasons for its existence, the Grand Coalition's durability and institutional stability created a structural framework—as well as a cultural atmosphere—which proved conducive to the continued flourishing of corporatism as an arrangement of interest representation and conflict mediation.

"Social Partnership" and the Joint Commission
on Prices and Wages

Much of corporatism is driven by economic policy. The "economization" of politics constitutes one of corporatism's defining identities. This has been the case with one of Austrian corporatism's major ingredients, the institutionalization of "social partnership." It began in the immediate postwar period when rebuilding the damaged Austrian economy was of paramount importance. Starting in 1947, the first of a series of wage and price agreements was institutionalized by the three Chambers and the ÖGB. The agreement was implemented by a newly formed body called the Economic Commission. The initial success of this overt income policy led to its regularized repetition into the early 1950s (see the Kindley essay in this volume). This informal arrangement became such an essential ingredient for Austrian capital, labor and the state in their guiding of the Austrian economy, as well as their own interests within it, that by 1957 an institution was established to formalize in a systematic manner a "concerted action" among the three "players" pertaining to all essential decisions of the Austrian economy. Thus began the Joint Commission on Prices and Wages (*Paritätische Kommission*) which has successfully pursued its unofficial (but highly corporatist) mandate of concerted action to this day, an amazing feat of Austrian corporatism considering how similar arrangements of institutionalized income policy have proven over the long run to be abysmal failures in most countries.[9] To use the German structural equivalent as yet another basis of comparison, the "*Konzertierte Aktion*," which did not exist until early 1967, was officially dissolved exactly one decade later when the trade unions withdrew their participation over a dispute with the employers about extending a labor-supported codetermination model (*Mitbestimmung*) to large and medium-sized companies beyond the coal and steel industries.[10] But even during the decade of its existence, the German "*Konzertierte Aktion*" was little more than a welcome media event for the leaders of the three groups. The "*Konzertierte Aktions*" actual decisions, let alone its policy implementations, amounted to very little beyond ceremonial gatherings.[11]

The Special Characteristics of Austrian Corporatism: Culture and Behavior

Whereas I could have easily extended the list in the previous section, the discussion here will perforce be much briefer. The reason for this is simple: culture and behavior, though of equal importance to political outcome as structures and institutions, are much more amorphous and intangible, thus more difficult to concretize.

For reasons beyond the scope of this paper, Austrian elites made it their task to forge an accommodationist atmosphere as the very foundation of the Second Republic. The cleavages which tore the First Republic apart and which led to two fascist regimes in the wake of its demise—"black," clerical Austrofascism from 1934 until 1938 followed by "brown," *völkisch* German-dominated National Socialism from 1938 until 1945—had not disappeared by the end of World War II. The three *Lager* which had defined Austrian political culture since the 1880s were still present. Yet, each one of these *Lager* emerged defanged. The social democrats became a good deal less "red"; the Christian socials

underwent a deradicalization process which even led them to change
their name to the much more inclusive and innocuous People's Party
(*Oesterreichische Volkspartei*—ÖVP); and the *völkisch* German
nationalists had pretty much lost all their legitimacy in the wake of
Auschwitz and the total destruction of their Third Reich.

The experiences of the decade between 1934 and 1945 had been so
devastating (though often for very different reasons) that—possibly for
a lack of another alternative—accommodation had become the only
venue for future political action. Add to this self-reflective elite
realization a completely altered international and European context
wherein Austria had become an occupied (and potentially divided)
country at the front line between the capitalist West and the communist
East, and the politics of pragmatism and accommodation assumed pride
of place. Suddenly, the formerly maligned Austrian behavior of
"*durchwurschteln*" (muddling through) attained the valor of a pragmatic
method of conflict resolution and crisis management. Back-room deals
in parapublic institutions which presented the public with *faits accomplis*
came to be regarded as acts of statesmanship safeguarding stability and
tranquility in a very dangerous and inhospitable outside world. Stability,
prosperity and predictability rather than participation, debate and choice
became the operative concepts of this new political order.

And the regime delivered on all three counts. Austrians, like most
West Europeans, enjoyed an unprecedented increase in their economic
prosperity in the course of the 1950s and 1960s. Their polity, buttressed
by neutrality in relation to their immediate neighbors and the world, was
ably guided by a consensus between the two large parties. And as long
as no unforeseen events or unexpected sources caused any crises for this
finely-tuned structure, its precarious but safe existence was to benefit
virtually all in Austria. Thus developed what later became known as
"the island of the blessed" in an otherwise turbulent sea, an entity that
constructed its identity vis-a-vis the outside world as well as itself on the
basis of two essential pillars: neutrality in foreign politics and
corporatism in domestic affairs.

Conclusion

By now it should be obvious why the model of Austrian corporatism
had become so attractive to students of comparative politics and
international political economy in the 1970s and 1980s. Starting with an
explanation based on the sociology of knowledge, most of these

comparativists became interested in the study of political economy in the wake of the New Left's fundamental influence on the social sciences in the late 1960s. While not explicitly Marxist in their scholarship, these young comparativists had studied enough of Marx's writings (in the numerous *Grundrisse* study groups for example, which proliferated in university environments from Berlin to Berkeley) to introduce concepts of Marxian economics into the study of comparative politics. Combined with a Weberian interest in bureaucracy and the state, and a Millsian (as in C. Wright rather than John Stuart) critique of existent elites and their power, these younger representatives of comparative politics developed the new subfield of international and comparative political economy. The fact that this new approach synthesized politics and economics, and that it revived the name of a discipline which boasted Marx as one of its most eminent representatives bespoke the intellectual debt which these new comparativists owed to Marx as a scholar and Marxism as a framework of analyzing capitalism. Out of this neo-Marxist, neo-Gramscian and neo-Weberian fusion emerged major studies on topics such as the state in capitalist society as distinct from the capitalist state; the interaction of market and state under conditions of advanced capitalism; and the analysis of interest representation (the class vs. groups debate) among which the study of corporatism developed into a veritable growth industry by the late 1970s and early 1980s. In addition to its intellectual genealogy, the preoccupation with corporatism also had a normative side among this group of comparativists.

Most of these political economists were advocating some sort of progressive reforms which, if not socialist in nature, were at least to transform capitalism into a more humane, egalitarian as well as efficient mode of production. At the very least, these scholars viewed social democracy as the most attainable, if also compromised, of capitalism's possible reforms. There existed a great interest in virtually all aspects of the working class, be they its relations with the state and the employers or the politics of its institutions such as trade unions and social democratic parties. Tellingly, many studied unions and workers; few looked at employers' associations and managers. With true socialism not a genuine option as an empirical reality, social democracy was the next best thing. While many of these comparativists and political economists made a career of criticizing social democracy's shortcomings, at the same time they upheld it as the best form of governing advanced capitalism in terms of efficiency as well as collective justice. Enter

Sweden, everybody's model of capitalism with a human face, followed by Austria, the island of the blessed: small countries with an extensive social net, large social democratic parties, powerful trade unions, neutral in their foreign policy, and—as a consequence of their smallness and relative powerlessness—completely harmless in the brutal arena of international power politics. Loyal to their intellectual origins as descendants of the New Left, these scholars remained basically distrustful of any exercise of power, particularly by the state. However, since states were empirically unavoidable, the more innocuous their presence the better. Sweden and Austria fit the bill perfectly. The normative attractiveness of Sweden and Austria, as opposed to, say, Switzerland, Norway or Denmark in the eyes of these political economists and new comparativists hailed from a combination of three crucial attributes which only Sweden and Austria possessed: those of smallness, neutrality and the strength of social democracy in all aspects of political life. After all, it was in corporatist countries such as Sweden and Austria that the institutional power of the working class managed to render the economic crisis of the 1980s the most bearable among advanced capitalist societies.

Corporatism also had its critics among this group of new comparativists. As is obvious to many who advocated reforms of radical democracy and genuine working-class power corporatism represented a hijacking of the rank and file's autonomy by institutional bureaucrats of party and union. Above all, it entailed a clear preference for stability and discipline to the direct detriment of democratic change and participation. Corporatism, to its radical critics, was nothing less than a structural arrangement to stymie working-class power on behalf of capitalist interests.

Corporatism, like so much in Europe, changed on the night of 9 November 1989. While there already appeared discernable cracks in its previously impenetrable armor in the course of the crisis-ridden 1980s, its whole context changed as a consequence of the monumental shifts in Europe since the fall of the Berlin wall. With the end of the Yalta world, one of the two major pillars of postwar Austrian politics has lost its previous meaning: neutrality, though still existent on paper, means something fundamentally different today than it did in the era of the Cold War. Whereas the shifts for corporatism may not be quite so dramatic, they are fundamental, to be sure. For one, the Austrian party system has experienced a small revolution. The once mighty "Big Two" have emerged with serious wounds, which might in fact be fatal. In the parliamentary election of October 1994 the SPÖ slipped to 35.2 percent from the previously mediocre 42.6 percent. The ÖVP dropped to a frightening 27.7 percent from the previously abysmal 32.0 percent. The Grand Coalition that once again rules Austria has the air of a desperate defensive maneuver instead of the usual optimism of corporatist problem solving. Austria now sports five parties in its parliament instead of the usual three. And due to Jörg Haider's meteoric rise, the FPÖ has now become one of the three players. The topography of Austria's party landscape as well as the tenor of its political discourse have drastically changed in the course of the 1990s. On the one hand, these developments are alarming since they are spearheaded by a right wing populist movement and party which is among the most prolific in Europe. On the other hand, these changes might merely attest to a belated Westernization of Austrian politics. Simply put, Austria may have finally become like everybody else in western Europe. It seems to have caught up with the good as well as the bad of pluralist politics. As to the fate of corporatism in this new environment it would be premature to announce its imminent demise. However, as the students of corporatism teach us, one of its major—and decisively superior adversaries—is the true pluralism of a developed liberal democracy. Whether this will bode well for Austria or not is beyond anybody's predictive powers at this time.

NOTES

1. That this competition between the identity of *"Stand"* and "class" remained one of the major conflict areas for the Austrian working class well into the twentieth century is best demonstrated by Anton Pelinka's study *Stand oder Klasse: Die Christliche Arbeiterbewegung Österreich 1933-1938* (Vienna: Europaverlag, 1972).

2. See Phillipe C. Schmitter, "Corporatism" in Joel Krieger, ed., *The Oxford Companion to Politics of the World* (New York: Oxford University Press, 1993), 197.

3. Walter Korpi, *The Democratic Class Struggle* (London: Routledge and Kegan Paul, 1983).

4. Hellmut Andics, *Der Staat, den keiner wollte: Österreich 1918-1938* (Vienna: Herder, 1962).

5. For the best comparative account of the respective capacities of the two social democracies (Austrian and German) in terms of economic policies implemented during the crisis of the 1980s, see Fritz W. Scharpf, *Sozialdemokratische Krisenpolitik in Europa* (Frankfurt am Main: Campus Verlag, 1987).

6. For a fine comparison of the DGB and the ÖGB, see Anton Pelinka, *Gewerkschaften im Parteienstaat: DGB und ÖGB in Vergleich* (Berlin: Duncker und Humbolt, 1980).

7. For a perceptive analysis of coalitional governments in Europe, see Anton Pelinka, *Die kleine Koalition: SPÖ-FPÖ, 1983-1986* (Vienna: Böhlau, 1993).

8. Ibid.

9. For the most complete study of the Joint Commission on Wages and Prices, see Bernd T. Marin, *Die Paritätische Kommission. Aufgeklärter Technokorporatismus in Oesterreich* (Vienna: Internationale Publikationen, 1982).

10. See Andrei S. Markovits, *The Politics of the West German Trade Unions: Strategies of Class and Interest Representation in Growth and Crisis* (New York: Cambridge University Press, 1986).

11. Rolf Seitenzahl, *Einkommenspolitik durch Konzertierte Aktion und Orientierungsdaten* (Cologne: Bund Verlag, 1974).

Roots of Austro-Corporatism: Institutional Preconditions and Cooperation Before and After 1945

Emmerich Tálos and Bernhard Kittel

Introduction

Austrian social partnership is a specific mode of interest intermediation and interest politics. Characteristic of this mode is the cooperation and concertation of interests among a few large interest associations, which—due to their organizational structure and state-sponsored privilege after 1945—have a quasi-monopolized position[1] with the state. Cooperative-concerted interest politics takes place in a network of interactions among the above-mentioned actors and is based on consent about national economic targets (see Tálos, Leichsenring, Zeiner 1993, Pelinka 1981). This pattern was institutionalized during the first half of the 1960s and is regarded as a special, though not singular, manifestation of neocorporatism in international comparisons (Schmitter 1981; Schmidt 1982; Cameron 1984; Bruno, Sachs 1985; Calmfors, Driffill 1988; Ferner, Hyman 1992).

In political science, neocorporatism is defined in terms of structure and process (Williamson 1989). The structural perspective, as introduced by Schmitter (1979, 1982), implies that the coordination of economic policy can only be realized under specific institutional conditions. The coordination of the interests of various groups is facilitated by the concentration of their representative bodies in encompassing peak associations (see Schmitter 1981). The process dimension (Lehmbruch 1979, 1984), however, emphasizes that structural conditions do not necessarily imply the actual concertation of economic policy. A basic consent among the actors is also required: because of the interdependence of capital and labor, opposing interests have to be handled in a cooperative way.

The structural dimension of interest associations encompasses the potential for representing interests to the outside as well as enforcing accords between associations in case of internal resistance. Schmitter calls this concept "interest *intermediation.*" The notions of monopolization and centralization respectively operate these two dimensions of interest intermediation (see Schmitter 1981; Cameron 1984; Golden, 1993). A major element of the process dimension of neocorporatism is the concertation of decisions in the realm of economic policy on the grounds of the fundamental readiness of all involved actors to cooperate, presuming that particular and general interests can be combined. Therefore, it is important that all the actors participate in the decision-making process.

The main thrust of this contribution is the proposition that the institutional structures, as preconditions for social partnership, have been shaped in the immediate postwar years as a result of explicit political decisions. The creation of institutions such as the *Paritätische Kommission*, a commission with equal rights, would not have been possible without the specific structural characteristics of the Austrian interest organizations. This structural dimension has been prominent since 1945-46 with the re-installation of the chambers, installation of the *Bundeswirtschaftskammer*, and the law of collective agreements. But from a process point of view, concerted policy-making can only be noted between 1947 and 1951, and lost its importance during the 1950s. With the establishment of the *Paritätische Kommission* in 1957, an essential institutional condition was shaped that provided a frame for a systematically concerted pattern of policy-making in the first half of the 1960s. Therefore, only since then can one speak of a neocorporatist system if both institutional and process factors are considered.

To find the roots of Austrian social partnership, we must go back to the period before 1945. In fact, we will trace the roots of social partnership back to the nineteenth century when political-institutional and *realpolitische* configurations arose that have continued to exist to the present and have been an integral part of the political pattern of social partnership.

The first part of the paper deals with these roots and with the factors that prevented the development of neocorporatist patterns before 1945.

In the second part, we will concentrate on the roots of Austro-Corporatism in the postwar years, until the end of the 1950s.

Developments Before 1945

Preconditions—Traces of Social Partnership Before 1945

The Position of Government and Administration

This can be regarded as one of the most notable aspects of the political structure and development of Austrian social partnership. The state's participation in political coordination, decision-making and interest intermediation stands in close connection with the tradition of centralized government (during the monarchy, particularly after 1861 and during the First Republic; in each case on a constitutional level) and professional administration (see Lehmbruch 1991). The government constituted an important target of associative lobbying, both at the time of the monarchy and the First Republic (see Hanisch 1994; Tálos 1995). The strong position of the government in the political process of interest coordination is underlined by its legislative activities in the form of government bills in the First Republic. So, for example, not only during the first years of the First Republic (see Pribram 1920-21) but also during the following period, all important bills in the field of social policy were based on government initiative. That the role of the government has been upgraded substantially as a result of the transformation of the political structure during Austrofascism and National Socialism (see Tálos; Manoschek 1988a, 1988b; Wohnout 1993; Broszat 1983; Frei 1987) is noteworthy.

Legally Institutionalized Interest Associations: The Chambers

Equally important was the establishment of a specific form of interest organization, the legally-constituted chambers. The beginnings of this organization date back to the mid-nineteenth century. In the states (*Länder*) of the monarchy, Chambers of Commerce were installed as representative bodies of trade, industry and business. After 1918, the system of chambers was expanded by the establishment of the Chambers of Labor and Agriculture.

The system of chambers can be regarded as an integral part of the infrastructure of social partnership in more than one respect: the chambers represent an instrument of concentration of societal interests. The concentration of the workers' and the entrepreneurs' interests is ensured by the legally institutionalized compulsory membership of workers and employees on the one side and of the self-employed on the other. This is connected with the task of intermediating thoroughly heterogeneous interests within each chamber. However, both aspects made possible the first traces of a uniform observation of interests vis-a-vis the government, the parties, and other organizations. The integration of societal interest organizations into the process of implementing state policies is manifest in the chambers' character as public corporations entrusted with state authority.

The chambers open institutionalized channels to societal interests in influencing the formulation of policies and the decision-making process: they are entitled to make opinion statements and proposals. In the case of government bills, the chambers are entitled by charter to render an opinion on those bills that touch their clientele.

At the beginning of the First Republic, even the installation of joint committees (as a form of horizontal cooperation) was laid down by identical formulations incorporated into the laws constituting the Chambers of Commerce and Labor. However, these legal provisions seem never to have been realized (see Tálos 1995), due to reasons that will be discussed later.

Institutionalized Cooperation Between State, Government and Societal Interest Associations

Closely connected to the political weight of government administration are administrative strategies, which intermediate societal interests and institutionalized forms of cooperation between the administration and interest associations. This is manifest in the foundation of advisory boards, commissions etc., which—following the enlargement of the radius of state activities—have existed since the second half of the nineteenth century (Layer 1905; Hofmeister 1986; Pellar 1986). Although the situation has occurred in other countries as well, the intentions occasionally associated with this pattern are closely related to neocorporatist options. A statement by the Minister of Trade in the cabinet of Chancellor Körner, Freiherr von Call (1900-05) illustrates this: "The negotiations will be of particular practical value, if they are led in the spirit from which has arisen the Joint Labor Board and if they succeed, far off the playgrounds of party slogans, in considering evenly and—with that—in uniting the legitimate interests of all factors in domestic production. Propositions and desires for the improvement of social conditions that are agreed upon by representatives of the entrepreneurs and the workers, assisted by impartial experts, will, by their own weight, influence efficiently the legislative and administrative apparatus" (cited in Pellar 1986).[2]

Furthermore, one can note that the interactions between the state and the societal interest organizations have intensified in the twentieth century. This is shown in the considerable extension of the forms of involvement of the societal interest organizations in the formation of political will. During the First Republic, many joint boards and commissions were installed by law or by decree: the "Board on the Eight-Hours-Working-Day," the "Board on Unemployment Insurance," the "Board on Traffic," the "Board on Tariffs," the "Central Commission on Homework," and the "Industrial District Commissions." It is noteworthy that, with respect to the composition of such institutions, by the time of the First Republic many of these boards and commissions privileged the large societal interest organizations such as the chambers and the peak associations of the free interest associations. Consider also that, just as after 1945, (see Bulda et al. 1990) entrepreneurs and workers were equally represented in a considerable number of these institutions (see Tálos 1995).

Vertical Networks of Interactions Among Societal and Political Actors

Distinct outlets for the establishment of vertical networks were already in place in both political camps during the First Republic. This net of relations within each political camp[3] came to play an important role in the development and support of social partnership in the Second Republic. The special relationship between the Social Democratic Party and the free trade unions is signalled by the slogan of the "Siamese twins."[4] The social democratic network was extended by the formation of a social democratic group in the Chamber of Labor that dominated this institution during the First Republic. This domination manifested itself in the 1921 Chamber elections, which resulted in a share of 341

mandates for the social democrats out of 421. The network between the
party and the interest associations becomes apparent on institutional-
organizational level: representatives of the free trade unions are
integrated in the executive committee of the Social Democratic Party. It
is also expressed in the cumulation of functions: not less than 32 out of
the 71 social democrats elected for Parliament in 1927 occupied a
confidential post in the trade unions or in the Chamber of Labor at the
same time (see Tálos 1995).

The network on the bourgeois side (between the bourgeois parties
and the entrepreneurs' associations) was comparatively looser (but
nevertheless existent). This existence was confirmed by a projected
bourgeois single list in elections for the National Assembly that was
pushed by the entrepreneurs' representations and by considerable
financial support of bourgeois parties and the *Heimwehrverbände* (see
Haas 1979). Other strands of the bourgeois network consist of regular
contacts between the entrepreneurs' representatives and the bourgeois
parties, clubs and the bourgeois delegates in Parliament. The element of
personal cumulation of functions was also present (see Tálos 1995).

Options of Social Balance and Cooperation

Ideological elements such as social balance, cooperation and
consensus building in spite of conflicting interests that mark social
partnership as well, have a long-standing tradition in Austria.
Representatives of the *"christliche Soziallehre,"* the Christian social and
the Deutsch-national camp have propagated ideologies of consent and
balance since the second half of the nineteenth century with a
pronounced thrust against the notion of class conflict advocated by the
social democratic workers' movement. The 1907 manifesto of the
Christian Social *Reichspartei* expresses this clearly: "The Christian
Social Party rejects the poisoning fight between the classes with its
disastrous consequences particularly for the weak and poor. Instead, it
strives for a just balance of the legitimate interests so that by the
prospering of all working estates the common best is furthered" (cited
by Berchtold 1967). Similar ideas (rejection of class conflict, a sense of
community, an ideology of social balance) are formulated by the
Großdeutsche Volkspartei in its programmatic statement of 1920 (see
Berchtold 1967, p. 446). This ideology of social balance and societal
consent was specified in a concept that is relevant to the relationship

between societal interests and the intermediation of societal interests in the political realm: the concept of a *berufsständische Ordnung* (a system of societal organization by estates). This has been advocated in different variants in Austria—as in other countries (see Mayer-Tasch 1971)—since the late nineteenth century. The important points of such notions of the Christian workers' movement lay in the ideas of cooperation, solidarity and the organizational integration of entrepreneurs and workers. A realization of this concept was the *Verein für berufsgenossenschaftliche Handwerker und Arbeiter*, which failed in the 1890s. The Christian workers' movement carried their notions on and embedded them in their manifesto of 1923. Societal organization by estates means that the common occupation is the ground for the common organization of entrepreneurs and workers. The estates have to observe self-governing functions and simultaneously represent and intermediate occupational interests complementary to the parliamentary-democratic representative institutions. However, in the course of the political transformations of 1933-34 and during the Austrofascist period, this concept has undergone considerable modifications (see Tálos, Manoschek 1988a; Pelinka 1972).

Options of Immediate Representation of Societal Interests in the Decision-Making Process

In the Second Republic, a main channel for the inclusion of associations into the political process of consensus-building and decision-making consists of neocorporatist cooperation and interest concertation. This fact has been represented in the 1960s and 1970s by the critical catchword *Nebenregierung* ("side-government"). The argument whether societal interests could be observed outside the channel of Parliament and party representation has a long tradition in Austria. At the turn of the nineteenth century the idea of occupational corporations was advanced by the Christian social movement (see Streitenberger 1975), and a committee on national economic problems (*Volkswirtschaftsrat*) was ventilated in Schönerer's call for the foundation of a national German party 1881 (see Berchtold 1967). For the First Republic, this question was regularly on the political agenda. Political and societal actors contributed practical proposals (see Tálos 1995). Obviously, this was mainly intended to secure a stronger political position of the entrepreneurs' representations in the decision-making process.

Repeatedly, representatives of the Greater German Party (*Großdeutsche Volkspartei*) advocated the institutionalization of an autonomous participation of the economic interest representations in the legislative process. This reached from the introduction of a consultative *Reichswirtschaftskammer* to the replacement of the *Bundesrat* by an economic chamber as a second legislative institution. Even the best-known representative of the Christian Social Party of the First Republic, its long-standing chairman and repeated Chancellor Seipel pleaded for an economic chamber as a representative body of the estates (see Streitenberger 1975). Similar considerations were pursued by the *Landbund* in its demand for a Chamber of Estates (*Ständekammer*) with equal entitlements. In the 1929 amendment to the constitution, however, neither these nor the much more radical demands of the *Heimwehren* for a *Ständestaat* were considered explicitly. However, the amendment simultaneously upgraded the position of the state, especially of the president, and restricted the power of Parliament and, as a consequence, of the parties. The immediate participation of interest organizations was only intended under the common roof of a *Länder-* and *Ständerat*. The constitutional provision did not take effect before the elimination of the constitutional democracy in 1933-34, because the likewise intended constitutional law, which had to lay down the rules for the composition of the *Ständerat,* had not yet been issued. The debate on the incorporation of the interest representations into the legislative apparatus continued until 1933—though without practical results. Unlike the definitely negative position of the social democratic workers' movement, the entrepreneurs' representations picked up the subject of an economic parliament (*Wirtschaftsparlament*) at several occasions. It is noteworthy that they participated in the debate with little initiative[5] and discernibly little engagement. In addition, they repeatedly referred to the fuzziness of the project of incorporating the occupational estates, a fuzziness that extended into the process of removing democracy in 1933-34.

Traces of Practical Cooperation

Cooperation and interest concertation of associations and the government became a stable pattern in the Second Republic, and despite current tendencies of erosion (see Tálos 1993) its end is not foreseeable. In contrast to this stability, cooperation during the First Republic was restricted to crisis management. The reasons for this will be discussed in the following section.

By the end of World War I, economic and social matters were coordinated by interest organizations and the government in "Appeals Committees" and in the "Working Board of the Central Committee on the Economy of War and Transition." Despite the background of the end of the war and the collapse of the monarchy and the mounting problems of disarmament, rearrangements of production, unemployment, raw material and food shortage, relief payments and pensions to war victims, these early efforts at cooperation were continued. Important institutions nurturing these efforts were the Industrial Board and the Industrial Conferences (see, Fischer 1986). The Industrial Board was relevant for the legislative process in so far as it was consulted before pertinent drafts and decrees were issued and as executive directives concerning social matters were decided. Industrial Conferences—convoked at the suggestion of State Chancellor Renner in 1919—dealt with current economic problems. Especially after the stabilization of the exchange rate and the state budget in 1922 (see Haas 1994) the relations between the interest organizations dampened discernibly. In spite of singular impulses, an economic conference, convened by Chancellor Schober and held in February 1930, would be the next and last platform on which an attempt was made to develop common crisis management strategies by including representatives of the government and large interest associations (see Grandner, Traxler 1984).

According to Schober, the idea was that: "Everyone has to maintain his interests and therefore we have convened the economic conference in order to balance our interests and to do justice to each other as far as the interests of the whole state tolerate it."[6] In view of the diametrically opposed positions of the interest organizations this option did not unfold; the "last encompassing initiative for the institutionalization of a commonly supported economic crisis management of the state and the interest associations" was not successful (Grandner, Traxler 1984).

Following the elimination of constitutional democracy by the Austrofascist dictatorship (see Tálos, Manoschek 1988b), very different conditions came to prevail for cooperation between the interest organizations and their incorporation into the political consensus-building. The dictatorship's basic claim was the re-ordering of societal interest representation by the criterion of occupational estates. Despite the fact that those ideas not only differed from the Church's concepts of societal order (as in the encyclical *Quadragesimo Anno*), their contents remained vague and the realization of their claims never succeeded. The transformation took place in 1934 and the traditionally existing interest organizations were finally eliminated. The new organizations called *Bünde* were legally established as public corporations. At the same time, they reflected the process of concentration on the level of the interest organizations. These *Bünde* participated directly in the political consensus-building within the so-called *Bundeswirtschaftsrat*. This institution was one of the four consultative bodies (not entitled to make decisions) that were designed for the legislative process. These bodies provided legal opinions to government bills. Their position in the system of Austrofascism has been characterized aptly by März: "The bodies participating in the federal legislative are constructed in such a way as to provide the government with absolutely reliable helpers, loyal to their fatherland and government, in the authoritarian guidance of the state in the fatherland's sense."

The re-ordering of interest intermediation consisted also in the authoritarian regulation of interaction between the interest organizations. Its main aspects were the elimination of disruptive potential in the associations (by defending strikes and lockouts and by the introduction of compulsory settlement) and the institutionalization of cooperation between the interest organizations of the workers and employees and the entrepreneurs on the sectoral and plant levels. Examples were the introduction of plant communities, cooperation in the Federal Economic Board (*Bundeswirtschaftsrat*) and so-called *berufsständische Ausschüsse* (see Tálos / Manoschek 1988a).

Unlike in the First Republic, these authoritarian institutional conditions officially facilitated a basic consent in important questions of economic and social policy. Altogether, this setting did not result in a societal realization of the proclaimed intention of social balance. The imbalance of power that was reinforced by the Austrofascist dictatorship had such negative effects on the labor market that even powers loyal to the system such as the Church, repeatedly uttered critiques (see Tálos 1988).

Obstacles to the Development of a
Neocorporatist Pattern in Austria

Notwithstanding the above-mentioned preconditions for social partnership as well as the beginnings of cooperation in Austrian political development before 1945 (not taking account of 1938-1945), there existed several institutional and political configurations that constrained or prevented the development of social partnership. Unlike in the Second Republic, the workers' and entrepreneurs' interest organizations reveal considerable organizational differentiation and ideological fragmentation. For example, in the trading sector in 1926, 316 interest organizations existed in addition to the chambers (Stiefel 1978). The same is true for centralization. The group of entrepreneurs revealed several centers, and a lever for entrepreneurial policy, comparable to the development after 1945, was lacking.

The ideological fragmentation of the entrepreneurs' organizations was exhibited by the affinity of various associations to the bourgeois parties or, in the trade union sector, by the existence of different fragmented groupings. This situation resulted in conflicts and strains in the field of entrepreneurs' organizations and trade unions. Accordingly, processes of concertation between the interest associations were difficult. This is closely connected to the fact that in the First Republic particular interests, conflicting strategies and pressure politics as a pattern of interest representation and intermediation were basic characteristics of interest politics. The consequence was that cooperation remained "collaboration on recall," and the first steps of cooperation were unstable.

One of the most important obstacles to the development of a neocorporatist pattern was the lack of basic consent about the targets of economic and social policy among all involved actors. Another obstacle was the increasing political polarization in the First Republic. The ideas of social harmony and societal balance propagated by the Christian Social and to some extent also by the *Deutschnationales Lager* correlated negatively not only with the contrasting interests and conflicts on the level of associations but also with a political configuration characterized by increasingly polarized political camps since the 1920s. Even more blatant political claims and social reality diverged in the period of Austrofascism.

Roots in the Second Republic

Structural Conditions After 1945
The above-mentioned obstacles have been removed in the Second
Republic as the associational system is now characterized by
encompassing, monopolized, and centralized peak associations.

Centralization of the Interest Organizations

The trade union federation ÖGB, conceived as an impartial
representative organization of workers and employees, combines a
sectoral differentiation into initially sixteen (today fourteen) trade unions
united under a common peak association with a favorable decision-
making structure. The single trade unions do not have a legal status and
are dependent on funds raised by the peak association. This structure
privileges the peak association, which also defines the basic political
positions of the trade unions. Associational decision-making occurs
formally in the bodies of the ÖGB, though it usually rests on previous
informal agreement among the trade unions and among the political
groups inside the ÖGB. The latter are particularly important for the
definition of the political orientation of the ÖGB (see Traxler 1982,
1991).

The Chambers of Labor are—as public corporations—organized
along the territorial boundaries of the *Bundesländer*. All dependent
employees, with the exception of civil servants, are compulsory
members of a Chamber of Labor. On the federal level, the chambers are
united in the peak organization *Österreichischer Arbeiterkammertag*
(respectively—since 1992— *Bundeskammer für Arbeiter und
Angestellte*) where the concertation of the positions of the
Länderkammern concerning federal issues is facilitated (see Weissel
1993).[7]

The Federal Chamber of Business (BWK) is the peak association of
the legally installed entrepreneurs' organizations, which also have
compulsory membership for all entrepreneurs. The structure of the
entrepreneurs' representations is less hierarchically organized than those
of the ÖGB. The Chambers on the level of the *Länder* and sectors have
legal status (Traxler 1986). However, in the system of the entrepreneurs'
representation, the competence for an issue is given to that
organizational unit that represents all interested members. In cases of

disagreement, the more encompassing unit takes over the competence. Thus, though the territorially and sectorally differentiated units can bargain over tariffs, they are coordinated by the BWK to prevent nationally unwanted precedences of singular agreements. In the delivery of legal opinions the aggregation of opinions proceeds gradually. In the end, the BWK presents the final position (see Traxler 1991).

The Chambers of Agriculture are, like the other chambers, organized within territorial boundaries. They have no central organization with the status of a public corporation. The presidents of the Chambers of Agriculture are united in the *Präsidentenkonferenz der Landwirtschaftskammern Österreichs* and participate in the process of decision-making on the federal level. As a result, the *Länder* units were in a more dominant position than in the other large interest organizations (see Krammer 1991).

As a whole, the Austrian system of interest representation is determined by the delegation of decisions to the top. This results in a tendency to suppress minority positions in the process of aggregation (see Marko 1992). This structure enables the leadership to select their goals and strategies relatively independent of the rank and file and to introduce them as the organizations' single opinion into the political process of decision-making.

Monopolization of the Interest Organizations

The Austrian interest organizations are not only strongly centralized; the system of interest representation operates via representational monopolies. Apart from the public Chambers of Labor, the ÖGB is the only occupational association on the workers' side. Within the organization, a division of labor has been established because the trade unions' peak association determines the parameters for tariff bargaining and the general political direction of the workers' representation. The chambers add expertise and supply a range of services to workers and employees as, for example, legal advice.

On the entrepreneurial side, the Federal Chamber of Business integrates both functions. Although a wide range of interest associations exists among employers, only one of them, the industrial association *Vereinigung Österreichischer Industrieller* (VÖI), has enough clout to exert influence on the federal level. All other associations are in fact confined to the status of talebearers of the BWK (Traxler 1991).

This constellation is singular in its international comparison. On the one hand, it is a result of the organization of interests within public corporations with compulsory membership (the chambers), and on the other hand, a result of a deliberate policy of discrimination against small associations since the first days of the Second Republic. The chambers have been incorporated in the Austrian political process since the mid-nineteenth century; the roots of the trade union movement reach that far back as well.[8] Nevertheless, the centralization of the business chambers did not occur until the time of Austrofascism. Likewise, the foundation of a monolithic trade unions' association was facilitated by the dissolution of the fragmented trade unions in the wake of the civil war of 1934 and by their successive concentration through governmental decree (Tálos 1986; Ucakar 1982).

After World War II trade union leadership could act in an "institution-free space" and implement its concept of a unitary trade union by the foundation of the ÖGB on 15 April 1945, even before the constitution of the provisional government of Austria. Thus, the monopolization of the trade unions' movement was a *fait accompli* that has not been seriously questioned since.[9]

The fragmentation of the associational representation on the side of capital in the first years after World War II is still reflected by the asymmetric bargaining structure of the tariff system. The federal concentration of the entrepreneurs' interest representation could not be accomplished on the associational level. During the process of legislating the structures of the tariff system and the incorporation of interest representations into the legislative process, the BWK became the only institution on the entrepreneurs' side that has constituted a balance for the ÖGB.[10] Therefore, tariff bargaining is done by sectoral units of the BWK—thus by a public corporation—on the entrepreneurs' side and by the sectoral trade unions on the workers' side. Likewise, the ÖGB has been incorporated into the decision-making process since the beginning of the Second Republic.[11]

The stability of this structure was institutionalized in the drafting of the law on collective bargaining on 26 February 1947. While expert opinions were being gathered, the question of what organizations should get the power to conclude collective agreements became a central point of dissent. It was discussed whether, on the workers' side, all occupational associations or only the ÖGB and its sectoral associations should be conceded the right of bargaining and whether, on the entrepreneurs' side, (in view of the lack of central sectoral associations) the chambers should be granted that right.

The Ministry of Social Affairs described the construction it aimed at in the following way: "The draft creates a monopoly for the ÖGB to conclude collective agreements on the employees' side, while on the employers' side—besides public corporations—only the recognized occupational associations should gain this right."[12] While the Chamber of Labor and the ÖGB accepted the proposal without further comment, the Viennese Chamber of Commerce repeatedly uttered its preference for the dominance of encompassing chambers: "We can only say that business has expressed its preference for a monopoly of the Chambers, that is, the divisions of the Chamber should be conceded the right to conclude collective agreements while they should be able to transfer this right onto their units. In addition, the industry sector wished to have the possibility of delegating this right to a free association of industrial employers and its sectoral and territorial units."[13]

The Ministry of Agriculture and Forestry was the only institution involved that objected to the monopoly of the ÖGB on the workers' side because the final structure of the trade unions' federation was not yet clear.[14] Furthermore, it demanded together with the Presidential Conference of the Chambers for Agriculture the admission of more occupational associations than the ÖGB, at least for the agricultural sector.[15] Also the British occupying power did not approve of the monopoly of the ÖGB.[16]

The final formulation of the draft conceded the right of collective bargaining to the free occupational associations. However, at the same time, it was formulated in such a way as to prevent any competition for the ÖGB on the workers' side. Only those associations whose sphere of activity extended on a wide occupational and territorial range and who could claim substantial economic impact according to their membership were conceded the right.[17]

That this formulation was intended to secure the monopoly position of the ÖGB was openly stated by the Minister of Social Affairs Maisel: "By the provisions for adjudicating the right to conclude collective agreements . . . it is adequately secured that unimportant occupational or politically intolerable associations should be restrained from the right to conclude collective agreements . . . . Furthermore, . . . only the ÖGB will for quite a long time appear as a party in collective agreements, because—in view of the almost closed organization of the employed in the trade unions' federation—among employed persons there is no need for the installation of new occupational associations outside the federation."[18]

On the entrepreneurial side, a temporary arrangement was set up given the lack of an encompassing associational representation. This arrangement has ensured that in those sectors in which no encompassing entrepreneurs' associations existed the chambers took over the right of concluding collective agreements until free associations could be formed.[19] Since to this day no entrepreneurs' associations have met all requirements, this temporary provision is still in force.[20]

The ÖGB also attempted to control as much of the policy of the workers' representation as possible during a debate on the amendment to the law on the Chambers of Labor soon after it had taken effect. The state government of Upper Austria demanded to restrict eligibility in the Chamber of Labor to members of the ÖGB.[21] The Ministry for Social Affairs picked up the question and presented it as a government bill. Maisel substantiated the draft in his presentation before the Council of Ministers by referring to the close connection between the two organizations. He argued that someone who had become a member of the trade unions' federation by free will would also fulfill his agenda as a member of the Chamber with adequate insight and diligence.[22] Only the Ministry of Agriculture and Forestry disagreed and argued that "the question of the required membership in the ÖGB for members of the Chamber of Labor is a fundamental one and touches upon the principle of equality of all citizens before the law; it therefore has to be left to the elected representation of the people to decide."[23] Subsequently, the bill was postponed and finally withdrawn.[24] In fact, all functionaries of the Chamber of Labor are members of the ÖGB (Traxler 1982).

The establishment of centralized and monopolized structures of interest representation at the beginning of the Second Republic was an institutional precondition of the close cooperation between the government and the interest organizations as well as between the interest associations. The small number of actors and the relative independence of leadership decisions from rank and file positions of all involved organizations facilitated the intimate, consent-oriented political style characteristic of the subsequent "Economic and Social Partnership."[25]

Involvement of Interest Organizations in Political and Administrative
Decision-Making Structures

Interest organizations and government institutions are connected by a dense network of interdependencies. A political precondition of this vertical network was the clear division of the Austrian political system and society into a socialist and a bourgeois camp. These groups were (and are) dominated by the Social Democratic Party and the People's Party. Another precondition was the cooperation of the leadership of these parties in a Great Coalition between 1945 and 1966, in which the functions of government and of the complete administrative apparatus are distributed according to the principle of proportional representation.

Both in the leadership of the SPÖ and the ÖVP the interest organizations are strongly represented by a cumulation of functions. Top functionaries in the ÖGB and the Chamber of Labor who represent the socialist group are members of executive boards in the SPÖ; functionaries of the BWK and the Chambers of Agriculture occupy important functions in the ÖVP. The reproduction of the political divisions inside the chambers clearly demonstrates the influence of the parties in a chamber.

The interlacing of interest organizations and the state is manifest both in government and Parliament. The interest organizations delegate representatives via the parties to both bodies in which they claim certain positions "by custom." Since 1945, the political careers of ministers of social affairs have started in the ÖGB. Most of the ministers of finance and commerce have held important positions in the BWK. Many top politicians are top functionaries of interest organizations at the same time. Some of the already-mentioned politicians are good examples: the first president of the Viennese Chamber of Labor, Mantler, also occupied the function of undersecretary in the Ministry of Property and Economic Planning. After his retreat from the Chamber of Labor, he was succeeded by former Minister of Social Affairs, Maisel. Raab, who later became chairman of the ÖVP and chancellor, was president of the BWK earlier in his political career and also a member of Parliament. During the Second Republic, representatives of the chambers and economic associations occupied for a long time up to two-thirds of the seats of a party, which were distributed by a differentiated and complex system of proportionate placement on party lists (see Pelinka 1981; Traxler 1982).

In many government bodies, as in the territorial authorities of the *Länder* or in the National Insurance and labor offices, the interest organizations are involved in the decision-making process via joint boards.

The involvement of the large interest organizations in political decisions is thus regarded as a matter of course. The interest organizations are involved early in the process of draft formulation. The state frequently takes the role of mediator of interests.[26] It is not always clear whether the close cooperation between the government and the interest organizations results from a government strategy of involving the organizations in the decision-making process or from the loyalty of the government representatives to their sending organizations and their interest in cooperating on an associational level.[27]

On the economic level, the nationalization of big industries and banks was a factor that facilitated the development of the social partnership. On the one hand, it weakened private industrial capital and its interest association (the VÖI); on the other hand, it strengthened the influence of social democracy and the trade unions on economic policy. This enabled the trade unions to participate directly in economic decisions, which facilitated the establishment of a position favorable to the whole economy. Therefore, the problems of the postwar economy did not result in increased distributional conflict, as after World War I, but in cooperative advancement of economic growth.

The Development of a Cooperative-Concerted Policy Style in Austria[28]

A first attempt at the subsequent institutionalization of social partnership is represented by five agreements on wages and prices between 1947 and 1951, agreements that were concluded by the three large Chambers and the ÖGB in the Economic Commission in 1947 and officially announced by the government (see also the Kindley essay in this volume). The agreements aimed at slowing down increases in prices and wages. This double strategy was initiated by the ÖGB and the Chamber of Labor, which tried to contribute to the fast rebuilding of the economy by restrained wage demands, and, at the same time, tried to avoid the impoverishment of the population. As the president of the Chamber of Labor put it: "I want to note explicitly that the task the trade unions' federation and the Chamber of Labor had to accomplish in the agreement on wages consisted only of averting a further decrease in the real wage of the workers and employees . . . It would have been possible, as such, for the separate unions to demand wages in order to balance inflation. We have discussed this question and concluded that this path is not practicable, because the workers could not have compensated for the increases in prices for a long time, and some trade unions would not even have been able to hold pace."[29] In other programmatic statements, the Chamber of Labor pointed out that the subsistence of workers could not be defended just by wage increases, because these would only induce further price-hikes.[30] Instead, the strategy had to be to push modernization of the economic structure: "Economic policy in Austria is a task that asks for toughness, patience and continuous containment of claims of individual groups that are only concerned with their own interests. Such demands may appear legitimate if considered separately, but they may disturb the general concept. The trade unions and the Chambers of Labor, which seem to be the only Austrian factors that have the country's economic fate at heart, will not yield but do everything within their power to accelerate the rebuilding of the economy . . . not individual or group interests, but only the determined attitude of our whole population toward this aim and its consequent pursuit will enable us to reach our destination."[31]

This policy was criticized in particular by the communist group in the trade union federation and the Chamber of Labor, who pleaded for a strategy of confrontation. They saw their chance in increasing worker discontent with the policy of the trade unions. Since the agreements were conceived to compensate for past increases in prices and since it turned out to be impossible to forestall subsequent increases, the workers had to accept a real wage cut during the late 1940s and early 1950s.[32] After the third agreement on wages and prices in May 1949, unrest arose in many big industrial plants. Finally, the discontent of the workers spilled over into spontaneous strikes and strong controversies between the trade unions' rank and file and the leadership after the fourth agreement in September and October 1950, which ended with a victory of the leadership (see Mulley 1991; Gruber, Hörzinger 1975). This last revolt of the workers against their representatives' strategy of national economic growth set down two signposts for the further development of the concerted and cooperative pattern of politics. On the one hand, the communist activists were expelled from the trade union after the strikes, and the position of the central leadership was strengthened extensively. On the other hand, by suppressing the revolts, the trade union federation demonstrated both their authority and their growth-oriented economic concept to their economic partners.

Despite this cooperative position of the trade union federation, the entrepreneurs' associations were not prepared to carry on with the agreements on wages and prices.[33] Their distance from the workers' organizations was still apparent in the fact of addressing them as "the side inimical to the employers"[34] and in the critical analysis of the agreements, accentuating only their inflation-accelerating effect.[35] Their continuous postponement of legislative initiatives in the field of industrial law also indicated the unwillingness to compromise.[36]

As a further instrument of cooperation one can regard the economic directorate that was installed in 1951 together with a packet of laws on economic regulation (laws on external trade, traffic, raw materials, food and price regulation) for a limited period. It was entrusted with the "coordination of the activities of the ministries involved with regard to the provisions to be taken according to the respective regulations."[37] Members of the directorate, who had a seat and a vote, were the chancellor, the vice chancellor and the ministers of internal affairs, social affairs, agriculture and forestry, finance, traffic, nationalized industries and external affairs. Without vote, the president of the central bank, the presidents of the ÖGB and the BWK as well as one representative of the Chamber of Labor and the Chambers of Agriculture participated in the directorate.

The incorporation of the interest organizations into economic policy-making was not yet self-evident at the time, as was demonstrated by a press statement of the Chamber of Labor: "The central part of the new economic laws is the installation of an economic directorate which was demanded by the Austrian trade union federation and the Chamber of Labor. Its task is to coordinate the economic provisions taken by various administrative and governmental agencies. After some hesitations, the government has decided to take into account the demand for involving representatives of the economic organizations *on advisory terms* in the drafting of laws on the installation of an 'economic directorate' on the federal government. During the debate on this bill in the constitutional committee of the National Assembly, this provision has been deleted. The reasons were decisive for the political parties were announced. The constitution does not prevent the satisfaction of this demand; it just concerns an advisory function without right to vote. The decision of the constitutional committee robs the representatives of the workers of the possibility of bringing their influence to bear adequately in a particularly sensible situation of economic administration. The Chamber of Labor is not willing to leave its lawful task of representing the workers and employees to other institutions."[38]

With the completion of economic stabilization, the cooperation of the interest organizations stepped into the background in favor of the parties, whose central lever became the Coalition Committee installed in 1953. Before that, the importance of the economic directorate had been turned down by a ruling of the Constitutional Court on 17 June 1952, which became a necessary precondition for the informal institutionalization of the social partnership a few years later. It stated that this is "constitutionally not provided" economic board was unconstitutional (see Tálos 1985).[39] Though this ruling eliminated a central element of its functioning, the law on the economic directorate was prolonged until June 1954, when it stopped its activity. The Economic Commission continued to exist formally but played only a marginal role. Nevertheless, attempts at inter-associational harmony were discernible, as negotiations between the Chamber of Labor and the Chamber of Business on the Austrian tariffs demonstrated.[40] The Chamber of Labor, however, deplored the "intransigent attitude of some functionaries" that prevented an agreement.[41]

For the workers' representatives the growth-oriented policy remained decisive. After a futile attempt to reactive the Economic Commission at the end of 1955, the President of the ÖGB, Böhm, proposed in the spring of 1956 to the president of the BWK, Dworak, and the Chairman of the Conference of Presidents of the Chambers of Agriculture, Strommer, to create a joint institution of the chambers and the ÖGB for the elaboration of proposals and advice of the public organizations. Dworak and Strommer basically agreed to discuss questions of economic policy jointly but refused to install a separate institution for this matter. Dworak called such an institution inappropriate, because only questions of importance for the whole economy could be objects of consultation (Meixner 1976; *Institut für angewandte Sozialforschung* 1966). Nor was Chancellor Raab fond of the idea since he regarded such a commission as a possible "side government" (*Institut für angewandte Sozialforschung* 1966).

Due to the increasing conflict about wages and the threat of strike in some sectors of industry as well as the increase in prices after the boom of 1956, the Economic Commission was finally convoked again at the demand of the ÖGB in the fall of 1956.[42] One of the results of these negotiations was the establishment of a sub-committee in which representatives of the Ministries of Finance and of Internal Affairs as well as the three Chambers and the ÖGB each had a seat.[43] This subcommittee had to ascertain price increases and recommend measures to lower excessive prices. In the beginning of 1957, the ÖGB and the Chamber of Labor attempted to institutionalize the cooperation between the interest organizations again. They proposed to constitute a joint commission that should assist the government's stabilizing policy by controlling the development of prices and wages. They also proposed to "exert a strongly moderating influence" on demands for wage increases that had already been deposited and to examine new demands for wage-regulation within a joint commission both in respect to their level and their urgency before negotiations between the bargaining parties start."[44]

This offer was discussed in the Economic Commission and led to the constitution of the Joint Commission on Prices and Wages (*Paritätische Kommission*) on 27 March 1957. Its mandate was limited until the end of 1957; and the representatives of the entrepreneurs resisted both its transformation into a permanent—though informal—institution and the enlargement of its powers until the first half of the 1960s.[45] It has constituted the institutional framework for the social partnership ever since. The foundation of the Subcommission on Wages in 1962 and of the Advisory Board on Economic and Social Questions was a mere extension (Pelinka 1986; Marin 1982). As with the trade unions, which impressively demonstrated their orientation toward general economic targets at the beginning of the 1960s, the entrepreneurs also changed their position. Due to increasing conflicts in the coalition, economic decisions were blocked in the Coalition Committee. Both the government and the ÖVP lost their importance to the entrepreneurs in pursuing their interests. Furthermore, the consent among the entrepreneurs' and the workers' representations about the priority of economic growth to questions of the distribution of income, seems to have contributed to the acceptance of the Joint Commission by the entrepreneurs' associations.[46] This transformation is reflected in the definition of duties of the Advisory Board on Economic and Social Questions: "Its duties will be to study questions of economic and social policy from the point of view of general economic targets and to work out recommendations that contribute to the stabilization of purchasing power, to steady economic growth and to full employment" (*Institut für angewandte Sozialfragen* 1966).

The further development of the social partnership is marked by institutional consolidation—*Präsidentenvorbesprechung* (preliminary meeting of the presidents of the associations involved), *Verbändekomitee* (associations' committee)—and, compared to Germany by considerable continuity and stability (see the Karlhofer essay in this volume).

NOTES

1. These are the four non-competing central peak organizations: the Austrian Central Chamber of Labor (*Österreichischer Arbeiterkammertag - ÖAKT / Bundeskammer für Arbeiter und Angestellte - BAK*), the Austrian Trade Union Federation (*Österreichischer Gewerkschaftsbund - ÖGB*), the Federal Chamber of Business (*Bundeskammer der gewerblichen Wirtschaft - BWK*) and the Presidential Conference of the Chambers of Agriculture (*Präsidentenkonferenz der Landwirtschaftskammern - PräKo*).

2. All citations have been translated from German into English by the authors.

3. Political camps (*Lager*) in our meaning are a type of network encompassing ideological, social, and in particular political configurations.

4. See for example V. Stein, in: *Arbeit und Wirtschaft* 1932, column 705-708.

5. Apart from an advance of the *Hauptverband der Industrie*, which in 1922, charged the well-known scholar constitutional law Professor Kelsen with working out a draft for an autonomous participation of the interest organizations in the legislative process, the basic idea of this commission was to amend the constitution by an economic parliament. Kelsen's draft turned out to be quite moderate: it proposed to install an advisory board for the government in which entrepreneurs' and workers' representatives should participate on equal terms (see Tálos 1995). However, the *Hauptverband* did not pursue the matter further.

6. Proceedings of the Economic Conference of 28 February 1930, *Staatskorrespondenz*, 6. Bogen, in: Christlichsozialer Parlamentsklub, Box 103, AdR, ÖStZA.

7. With "Chamber of Labor" we mean the peak organization.

8. The Viennese Chamber of Commerce as the first Austrian chamber was founded in 1848, the first trade unions' congress that covered all of Austria convened in 1893, and the Chamber of Labor was installed in 1920.

9. Until the strikes of October 1950 Communist work councils had some influence and the Communist representatives in the ÖGB attempted to pursue their own policy. The strikes finally were a welcome occasion for the trade unions' leadership to throw out the leading Communists (Mulley 1991).

10. As the VÖI just represents industrial entrepreneurs, it cannot claim inclusiveness in view of the predominance of small business in the Austrian economic structure.

11. For example, the Ministry of Social Affairs asked the Chamber of Labor as well as the ÖGB for its opinion on the drafts of the law on works councils of 1946 and the law on collective bargaining 1947 (GZ III/30591/9/46, SA 5, 1946, Box 28, BMfsV, Soz. Pol., AdR, ÖStZA; GZ III/6751/9/46, SA 1, 1946, Box 27, BMfsV, Soz. Pol., AdR, ÖStZA). It is noteworthy that both the chamber and the ÖGB received the draft, but they delivered a joint opinion. In its statement of 19 April 1946 the ÖGB just referred to the chamber's comment, indicating that it was formulated in a joint consultation (Enclosure to GZ III/6751/9/46).

12. Covering letter to the draft of the law on collective agreements sent out by the Ministry on 28 February 1946, GZ III/6751/9/1946, SA 1, 1946, Box 27, BMfsV, Soz. Pol, AdR, ÖStZA.

13. Expert opinion of the Chamber of Commerce for Vienna and Niederösterreich, 28 January 1946, enclosure to GZ III/6751/9/1946, SA 1, 1946, Box 27, BMfsV, Soz. Pol., AdR, ÖStZA; see also ibid., GZ AV2098/II/6/46, AV III/75474-9/1946.

14. Expert opinion of the Ministry of Agriculture and Forestry, 27 March 1946, enclosure to GZ III/6751/9/1946, SA 1, 1946, Box 27, BMfsV, Soz. Pol., AdR, ÖStZA.

15. See Presidential Conference of the Chambers for Agriculture, ibid.

16. Memorandum of conversation with "Mr. Greenhouse," ibid.

17. This formulation was proposed on the occasion of a joint consultation of ministers and representatives of the Chambers and the ÖGB on 23 November 1946 by former divisional head Wlcek, who participated as a representative of the Viennese Chamber of Commerce, see GZ III/78346-9/1946, SA 1, 1946, Box 27, BMfsV, Soz. Pol., AdR, ÖStZA.

18. Presentation in the council of ministers, 2 December 1946, AV III/82719-9/1946, SA 1, 1946, Box 27, BMfsV, Soz. Pol., AdR, ÖStZA.

19. Minutes of the Council of Ministers, 11 December 1946, No. 49, item 28, GZ III/86893-9/1946, SA 1, 1946, Box 27, BMfsV, Soz. Pol., AdR, ÖStZA. This provision must be the reason why both the chambers and free associations conceded the right to conclude collective agreements in the final formulation of the law.

20. The formulation of this provision implies, that in fact it is a discretionary decision of the legislator whether the requirements are met by an association. The VÖI can indeed be regarded as doubtful case. The reason why no encompassing entrepreneurs' organizations have been formed may be that the existence of the BWK has severed the problem of collective goods of such associations (see Traxler 1986, 1995).

21. GZ AV.51126/II/6/1945, SA 4, 1945, Box 2, BMfsV, Soz. Pol., AdR, ÖStA. It is apparent that such a rule had to prevent conflicts of opinion between the trade unions' federation and the Chamber of Labor that could be used to fragment the workers' representation.

22. Ibid.

23. Opinion of the Ministry of Agriculture and Forestry, 29 October 1945, ibid.

24. Minutes of the Council of Ministers on 23 November and 28 November 1945, No. 39 and 40, respectively, enclosure to GZ AV.51126/II/6/1945, SA 4, 1945, Box 2, BMfsV, Soz. Pol., AdR, ÖStA.

25. The small number-argument is also central to explanations of neocorporatist patterns of politics by the size of the country. In small states both the network of political and economic actors is more dense (Katzenstein 1985) and the organization of mass movements less costly (Wallerstein 1989).

26. Often the ministry prepares a list of dissenting opinions of the interest organizations after these have provided their statements on a draft. Subsequently, this list is discussed by the representatives of the interest organizations under mediation of the minister or his representative. This procedure is for example followed in formulating the draft of the law on works councils and documented in a very clear way in the files of the Ministry of Social Affairs (GZ III/23907/9/46, ÖStA, SA 5, 1946, Box 28, BMfsV, Soz. Pol., AdR).

27. For example, the Minister of Social Affairs, Maisel, asked the presidents of the ÖGB and the Chamber of Labor, Böhm and Mantler, to discuss the draft of the law on works councils before it was officially sent out for expert opinions. He informed both that they were the only persons involved at that early time (see GZ III/23907/9/46, SA 5, 1946, Box 28, BMfsV, Soz. Pol., AdR, ÖStA). One should note that this draft was an example of a law on which no agreement could be found at the associational level. Finally a compromise was elaborated in parliament (see Tálos 1991b).

28. See the following discussion: Tálos 1985; Müller 1985; Lachs 1976; Meixner 1976.

29. From a speech before the full assembly of the Viennese Chamber of Labor. *Pressedienst der Arbeiterkammer,* No. 65, 30 September 1947. It is noteworthy that, at that time, the Austrian representatives of Labor already argued in favor of a centralized bargaining system that are discussed in the current economic discussion (see Calmfors 1993; Moene, Wallerstein 1993).

30. *Pressedienst der Arbeiterkammer* No. 83, 25 October 1947. See for a similar position: Circular Letter No. 40 of the ÖGB, 1 August 1947.

31. *Pressedienst der Arbeiterkammer* No. 127, 1948.

32. This is reflected by the fact that during the whole period of the agreements on wages and prices, almost all press statements of the Chamber of Labor addressed unjustified increases in prices and excessive prices. Only in the course of the 1950s did this subject becomes less important.

33. This took place in spite of the entrepreneurs' representatives' later recognition that "the Austrian trade unions federation has practically observed the wage freeze agreed upon in the fall of 1951 and has thus made a decisive contribution to the stabilization of the price system during the period of stabilization." *Jahresbericht der Bundeskammer der gewerblichen Wirtschaft* 1954, 16.

34. *Tätigkeitsbericht 1950 der Kammer der gewerblichen Wirtschaft für Wien*, 43.

35. *Tätigkeitsbericht 1952 der Kammer der gewerblichen Wirtschaft für Wien*, 33.

36. By the late 1940s the first initiatives for the codification of the law on working time were taken. But due to conflicting interests between the entrepreneurs' and the workers' representations an agreement could not be reached until 1969.

37. *Bundesgesetzblatt* 104, 4 April 1951.

38. *Pressedienst der Arbeiterkammer* No. 388, 2 March 1951.

39. As a matter of fact, the Constitutional Court repealed the provision that the minister was bound by the opinion of the directorate from the law on external trade. The SPÖ, however, opinion should be stated that not the fact of being unconstitutional was decisive for the attacks on the economic directorate, but "the influence of representatives of the workers on external trade had to be eliminated." (Delegate to the National Assembly Proksch, Sten. Prot. NR, 27 May 1952, 3498).

40. *Pressedienst der Arbeiterkammer* No. 741, 25 August 1956.

41. This is a common theme of statements of the Chamber of Labor, see for example: *Pressedienst der Arbeiterkammer*, No. 206, 8.11.1948; No. 239, 31.3.1949; No. 388, 2.3.1951; No. 391, 14.3.1951; 398, 6.4.1951.

42. *Pressedienst der Arbeiterkammer* No. 750, 22 September 1956.

43. See *Jahrbuch der Arbeiterkammer* 1956, 280.

44. *Jahrbuch der Arbeiterkammer* 1957, 181.

45. See *Jahresbericht der Bundeskammer der gewerblichen Wirtschaft* 1957, 12. Even in the ÖGB itself, the limitations on wage policy were criticized (see Tálos 1985).

46. See *Jahresbericht der Bundeskammer der gewerblichen Wirtschaft* 1961, 15 and *Protokoll des Bundesvorstandes des ÖGB* of 19 January 1962 and 4 December 1962.

FURTHER LITERATURE

Klaus Berchtold ed., *Österreichische Parteiprogramme 1868-1966* (Vienna, 1967).

Martin Broszat, *Der Staat Hitlers* (Munich, 1983).

Ilse Bulda et al., "Das österreichische Beiratsystem in den siebziger und achziger Jahren," *Österreichisches Jahrbuch für Politik 1989* (Vienna, 1990), 763-787.

Michael Bruno and Jeffrey D. Sachs, *Economics of Worldwide Stagflation* (Cambridge: Harvard University Press, 1985).

Lars Calmfors and John Driffill, "Bargaining Structure, Corporatism and Macroeconomic Performance," *Economic Policy* 3 (1990): 13-61.

_____, *Centralisation of Wage Bargaining and Macroeconomic Performance: A Survey* (Paris: OECD, 1993).

David Cameron, "Social Democracy, Corporatism, Labor Quiescence and the Representation of Economic Interests in Advanced Capitalist Countries," in John H. Goldthorpe, ed., *Order and Conflict in Contemporary Capitalism. Studies in the Political Economy of Western European Nations* (Oxford: Clarendon Press, 1984).

Anthony Ferner and Richard Hyman, *Industrial Relations in the New Europe* (Oxford: Blackwell, 1992).

Peter Fischer, "Ansätze zur Sozialpartnerschaft zu Beginn der Ersten Republik," in Gerald Stourzh and Margarete Grandner, eds., *Historische Wurzeln der Sozialpartnerschaft* (Vienna, 1986), 225-242.

Norbert Frei, *Der Führerstaat. Nationalsozialistische Herrschaft 1933-1945* (Munich, 1987).

Miriam Golden, "The Dynamics of Trade Unionism and National Economic Performance," *American Political Science Review* 87 (1993): 439-454.

Margarete Grandner and Franz Traxler, "Sozialpartnerschaft als Option der Zwischenkriegszeit?," in Erich Fröschl and Helge Zoitl, eds., *Februar 1934* (Vienna 1984), 75-117.

Ronald Gruber and Manfred Hörzinger, *. . . bis der Preistreiberpakt fällt. Der Massenstreik der österreichischen Arbeiter im September/Oktober 1950* (Vienna, 1975).

Karl Haas, "Industrielle Interessenpolitik in Österreich zur Zeit der Weltwirtschaftskrise," *Jahrbuch für Zeitgeschichte 1978* (Vienna, 1979), 97-126.

_____, "Aspekte der Interessenpolitik in der ersten Republik," Working Paper (Vienna, 1994).

Ernst Hanisch, *Der lange Schatten des Staates. Österreichische Gesellschaftsgeschichte im 20. Jahrhundert* (Vienna, 1994).

Herbert Hofmeister, "Die Rolle der Sozialpartnerschaft in der Entwicklung der Sozialversicherung," in Gerald Stourzh and Margarete Grandner, eds., *Historische Wurzeln der Sozialpartnerschaft* (Vienna, 1986), 278-316.

Institut für angewandte Sozialforschung, *Materialien zur Sozial- und Wirtschaftspolitik*, Heft 2, *Zur Paritätischen Kommission für Preis- und Lohnfragen* (Vienna, 1966).

Peter J. Katzenstein, *Small States in World Markets. Industrial Policy in Europe* (Ithaca: Cornell University Press, 1985).

Josef Krammer, "Interessenorganisation der Landwirtschaft: Landwirtschaftskammern, Präsidentenkonferenz und Raiffeisenverband," in Herbert Dachs et al., eds. *Handbuch des politischen Systems Österreichs* (Vienna: Manz, 1991), 365-376.

M. Layer, "Beiräte," in E. Mischler and J. Ulbrich, eds., *Österreichisches Staatswörterbuch*, Vol. 1 (Vienna, 1905) 436-466.

Gerhard Lehmbruch, "Liberal Corporatism and Party Government," in Philippe C. Schmitter and Gerhard Lehmbruch, eds., *Trends Toward Corporatist Intermediation* (London: Sage, 1979), 147-183.

_____, "Concertation and the Structure of Corporatist Networks," in John H. Goldthorpe, ed., *Order and Conflict in Contemporary Capitalism. Studies in the Political Economy of Western European Nations* (Oxford: Clarendon Press, 1984), 60-80.

_____, "The Organization of Society, Administrative Strategies and Policy Networks," in Roland M. Czada and Adrienne Windhoff-Héritiér, eds., *Political Choice* (Frankfurt: Campus, 1991), 121-158.

Bernd Marin, *Die Paritätische Kommission. Aufgeklärter Technokorporatismus in Österreich* (Vienna: Internationale Publikationen, 1982).

Joseph Marko, "Verbände und Sozialpartnerschaft," in Wolfgang Mantl, ed., *Politik in Österreich. Die Zweite Republik: Bestand und Wandel* (Vienna: Böhlau, 1992), 429-478.

Peter Cornelius Mayer-Tasch, *Korporatismus und Autoritarismus* (Frankfurt, 1971).

Hans Meixner, *Die Entwicklung der Sozialpartnerschaft in Österreich zwischen 1945 und 1966*, M.A. thesis, Economics University, Vienna, 1976.

Karl Ove Moene and Michael Wallerstein, "The Economic Performance of Different Bargaining Institutions: A Survey of the Theoretical Literature," *Wirtschaft und Gesellschaft* 19 (1993): 423-450.

Klaus Dieter Mulley, "Der ÖGB und der "Oktoberstreik" 1950," in Michael Ludwig, Klaus Dieter Mulley and Robert Streibel, eds. *Der Oktoberstreik 1950. Ein Wendepunkt der Zweiten Republik* (Vienna: Picus, 1991), 41-52.

Anton Pelinka, *Stand oder Klasse? Die christliche Arbeiterbewegung Österreichs 1933 bis 1938* (Vienna, 1972).

_____, *Modellfall Österreich? Möglichkeiten und Grenzen der Sozialpartnerschaft* (Vienna: Braumüller, 1981).

_____, *Sozialpartnerschaft und Interessenverbände* (Vienna, 1986).

Brigitte Pellar, "'Arbeitsstatistik,' soziale Verwaltung und Sozialpolitik in den letzten zwei Jahrzehnten der Habsburgermonarchie," in Gerald Stourzh and Margarete Grandner, eds., *Historische Wurzeln der Sozialpartnerschaft* (Vienna, 1986), 153-190.

Karl Pribram, "Die Sozialpolitik im neuen Österreich," *Archiv für Sozialwissenschaft und Sozialpolitik* 48 (1920-21): 615-680.

Manfred G. Schmidt, "Does Corporatism Matter? Economic Crisis, Politics and Rates of Unemployment in Capitalist Democracies in the 1970s," in Gerhard Lehmbruch and Philippe C. Schmitter, eds., *Patterns of Corporatist Policy Making* (London: Sage, 1982), 237-258.

Philippe C. Schmitter, "Still the Century of Corporatism?," in Philippe C. Schmitter and Gerhard Lehmbruch, eds., *Trends Toward Corporatist Intermediation* (London: Sage, 1979), 7-52.

_____, "Interest Intermediation and Regime Governability in Contemporary Western Europe and North America," in Suzanne D. Berger, ed., *Organizing Interests in Western Europe* (Cambridge: Cambridge University Press, 1981), 285-327.

_____, "Reflections on where the Theory of Neo-Corporatism Has Gone and Where the Praxis of Neo-Corporatism May Be Going," in Gerhard Lehmbruch and Philippe C. Schmitter, ed., *Patterns of Corporatist Policy-Making* (London: Sage, 1982), 259-279.

Dieter Stiefel, "Im Interesse des Handels," in *Zur Geschichte der Handelskammerorganisation* (Vienna, 1978), 31-59.

Wolfgang Streitenberger, *Das Leitbild "Ständische Ordnung" im politischen Denken Österreichs von der Jahrhundertwende bis 1938,* Ph.D. dissertation, University of Vienna 1975.

Emmerich Tálos, "Sozialpartnerschaft: Zur Entwicklung und Entwicklungsdynamik kooperativ-konzertierter Politik in Österreich," in Peter Gerlich, Edgar Grande and Wolfgang C. Müller, eds., *Sozialpartnerschaft in der Krise. Leistungen und Grenzen des Neokorporatismus in Österreich* (Vienna: Böhlau, 1985), 41-83.

_____, "Voraussetzungen und Traditionen kooperativer Politik in Österreich," in Gerald Stourzh and Margarete Grandner, eds., *Historische Wurzeln der Sozialpartnerschaft* (Vienna: Verlag für Geschichte und Politik, 1986), 243-264.

_____, "Sozialpolitik im Austrofaschismus," in Emmerich Tálos and Wolfgang Neugebauer, eds., *"Austrofaschismus." Beiträge über Politik, Ökonomie und Kultur 1934-1938* (Vienna: Verlag für Gesellschaftskritik, 1988), 161-178.

_____, "Sozialpolitik und Arbeiterschaft 1945 bis 1950," in Michael Ludwig, Klaus Dieter Mulley and Robert Streibel, eds., *Der Oktoberstreik 1950. Ein Wendepunkt der Zweiten Republik* (Vienna: Picus, 1991), 25-40.

_____, ed., *Sozialpartnerschaft. Kontinuität und Wandel eines Modells* (Vienna: Verlag für Gesellschaftskritik, 1993).

_____, "Interessenvermittlung und partikularistische Interessenpolitik in der Ersten Republik," in Emmerich Tálos et al., eds., *Handbuch des politischen Systems Erste Republik* (Vienna, 1995 forthcoming).

_____, Kai Leichsenring and Ernst Zeiner, "Verbände und politischer Entscheidungsprozeß - am Beispiel der Sozial- und Umweltpolitik," in Emmerich Tálos, ed., *Sozialpartnerschaft. Kontinuität und Wandel eines Modells* (Vienna: Verlag für Gesellschaftskritik, 1993), 147-185.

_____ and Walter Manoschek, "Politische Struktur des Austrofaschismus (1934-1938)," in Emmerich Tálos and Wolfgang Neugebauer, eds., *"Austrofaschismus." Beiträge über Politik, Ökonomie und Kultur 1934-1938* (Vienna: Verlag für Gesellschaftskritik, 1988a), 75-119.

_____ and Walter Manoschek, "Zum Konstitutionsprozeß des Austrofaschismus," in Emmerich Tálos and Wolfgang Neugebauer, eds., *"Austrofaschismus"* (Vienna, 1988b), 31-52.

Franz Traxler, *Evolution gewerkschaftlicher Interessenvertretung. Entwicklungslogik und Organisationsdynamik gewerkschaftlichen Handels am Beispiel Österreich* (Vienna-Frankfurt: Braumüller/Campus, 1982).

_____, *Interessenverbände der Unternehmer. Konstitutionsbedingungen und Steuerungskapazitäten, analysiert am Beispiel Österreichs* (Frankfurt: Campus, 1986).

_____, "Gewerkschaften und Unternehmerverbände in Österreichs politischem System," in Herbert Dachs et al., eds., *Handbuch des politischen Systems Österreichs* (Vienna: Manz, 1991), 335-352.

Karl Ucakar, "Die Entwicklung des Verbändewesens in Österreich," in Heinz Fischer, ed., *Das politische System Österreichs* (Vienna: Europa, 1982).

Michael Wallerstein, "Union Organization in Advanced Industrial Democracies," *American Political Science Review* 83 (1989): 481-501.

Erwin Weissel, "Die Arbeiterkammer," in Herbert Dachs et al., eds., *Handbuch des politischen Systems Österreichs* (Vienna: Manz, 1991), 353-364.

Peter J. Williamson, *Corporatism in Perspective. An Introductory Guide to Corporatist Theory* (London: Sage, 1989).

Helmut Wohnout, *Regierungsdiktatur oder Ständeparlament?* (Vienna, 1993).

The Evolution of Austria's Neo-Corporatist Institutions

Randall W. Kindley

As Andrei Markovitz's contribution has suggested, Austrian neo-corporatism is multi-faceted. It can be viewed as a set of cultural values which stress cooperation among class groups over both class conflict and individualistic competition. The label *Wirtschafts- und Sozialpartnerschaft* captures the sense of this meaning. Tracing the forces responsible for cultural norms can be difficult.[1] It is, however, possible to distinguish and explain the birth of a specific set of *institutions* by which Austria's economic and social partnership became identified.[2] These institutions are now being transformed, but understanding how they emerged can teach lessons vital to our response to today's challenges.[3] At the international level, the Cold War etched the major contours of European regional politics. Inside European nations, however, politics were shaped by the peace treaties reached between business and labor. In several small (western) European states, notably in Austria and Scandinavia, a relatively new set of institutions, later labelled neo-corporatist arrangements, evolved to manage that settlement.[4] Put in place from the mid-1950s to mid-1960s, these institutions would come to have an overriding impact on the formation of economic and social policy in their respective countries. Much has been written about the favorable effect of these arrangements on postwar economic outcomes.[5] Thus it is somewhat surprising that scholars have not inquired more systematically into the conditions for their emergence and longevity. After all, in today's era of transition, how governance institutions emerge and how they can stably replicate themselves should be *the* major question of scholars and practitioners alike.

Historical Attempts to Establish Direct Intermediation
Between Austrian Labor and Business Organizations
in Post-Imperial Parliamentary Regimes

Institutional Characteristics

Name	Institution Established	Longevity	Form	Scope
Industrial Commission (1918)	Industrial Commission and several ancillary committees	One Year	non-autonomous, single meeting	Wage Control via indexation
Industrial Conference (1919)	Industrial Conference and several ancillary committees	Two Years	non-autonomous, single meeting	Wage Control via indexation
Abbaugesetz (1921)	Parity Commission	Three Years	non-autonomous, continuous	Wage Control via indexation
Economic Conference (1930)	Program Commission	Four Months	non-autonomous, single meeting	None
Five Price-Wage Agreements (1947-1951)	None	Five Years	non-autonomous, single meetings	Wage, subsidy and price exchange with index thresholds
Parity Commission (1957 -)	Parity Commission and subordinate committees (for wages and for prices) and (in 1963) the Council for Economic and Social Questions	Thirty-five plus years	autonomous, continuous	Wage and price guidelines and bargaining unit authorization; review validation of price and wage changes. Legislative initiatives.

Since the late 1950s the premier institution of Austrian neo-corporatism has been the Parity Commission. It has antecedents in a series of less successful attempts dating from the interwar and early postwar years.[6] Within the first half decade of interwar peace (1918-1921), several attempts were made to establish cooperation between business and labor organizations. The failure of these ventures, of a belated attempt in the initial stages of the worldwide depression (1930),[7] and of Austria's parliamentary government were followed by catastrophic class violence,[8] the Austro-fascist *Ständestaat* and, eventually, Nazism.[9] In the post war period, there were two more attempts to establish a mechanism for directly intermediating the interests of capital and labor. The final one, the regime established around the Parity Commission of 1957, has lasted some three and a half decades and forms the core of Austria's well-known *Wirtschafts-und Sozialpartnerschaft*. Only this last formula proved enduring.

In this contribution I show that elite learning, producer group reorganization and the dynamics of postwar political bargaining resolved the shortcomings of earlier attempts. The key to this successful institutional construction, I show, was the establishment of a more bipartist and autonomous neo-corporatist arrangement.[10] The peculiar Austrian style of high corporatism that finally emerged contrasts both with earlier Austrian attempts and postwar Scandinavian experiments especially with regard to the role of the state and the scope and style of economic governance (Appendix 1).

Austrian Neo-Corporatism

Pluralism and Neo-corporatism are terms scholars have used to describe two very different forms of interest group relations.[11] Pluralist interest group systems are populated by a large number of relatively small, narrow interests. Their lobbying attention is focused on a variety of parliamentary and other state agencies. Coalitions among groups are temporary and shift issue by issue. Winning a policy victory may depend as much on focusing public opinion as on having a better policy alternative. Observation of countries like Austria during the postwar period suggested an opposite style of mediating interests. Neo-corporatist relations have been highly ordered around a few major interest groups. These *Verbände* represent economic sector (e.g., industry, agriculture) and class (e.g., business and labor), are centrally organized and count as members most economically active citizens in their respective spheres of influence, have been explicitly recognized by government officials and work closely with each other and with government to formulate and implement policies. These relations were "neo" because close cooperation between state and producer groups in the postwar period incorporated labor organizations.[12]

These relations facilitated a distinctive form of national economic management.[13] Workers agreed to restrict wage demands and militancy, while business re-invested profits and held a lid on prices. The state role was to ensure long term cooperation.[14] In Austria these relations were institutionalized in the Parity Commission for Wages and Prices, its subcommittees, and the Advisory Council for Economic and Social Questions, all of which were put in place in the golden years of postwar institutional formation of 1957-1963 (Appendix 2).[15] The latest addition to the Parity Commission is the Subcommittee for International Affairs (November 1992). Cooperation has been predicated on the intense coordination of elites in labor, business and government and highly centralized and encompassing organizations of labor and business: respectively, the ÖGB and Chamber of Labor, on the one hand, and the Chamber of Economics and the Austrian Industrialists' Association on the other. The President's Conference of the Chambers of Agriculture has also participated. A host of ancillary units have provided informational and personnel support for this cooperative apparatus (e.g., WIFO, IHS). Bargaining between labor and business in Austria has, in contrast to corporatist arrangements in Scandinavia, been more autonomous (from the state), of more comprehensive scope and of greater contact density among elites.[16]

This partnership of functionaries has been complemented by, but at times found itself in competition with, a political partnership between the SPÖ and ÖVP.[17] Throughout most of the postwar period single party and majority coalition governments have been the exception in Austria.[18] For the first twenty years of the Second Republic, Austrian governments were some form of Grand Coalition (either three-party: SPÖ, ÖVP and KPÖ from 1945-46 or the standard two-party - SPÖ, ÖVP from 1947-66). In the second two decades, single party and majority coalition rule were observed (ÖVP, 1966-1970; SPÖ, 1970-1983; SPÖ-FPÖ, 1983-1986). Austria returned to a Grand Coalition in 1986 (SPÖ-ÖVP) and, to the extent it is still 'grand,' SPÖ and ÖVP cooperation continues.[19] To the overriding organizational and political loyalties can be added sectoral and regional interests and well developed basis-level corporatism.[20] Though changing in scope and character, traditional economic governance has been through a system of factor cost control by continuous price-wage management and policy coordination. Austrian unemployment, inflation and economic growth indicators have consistently been among Europe's best.[21]

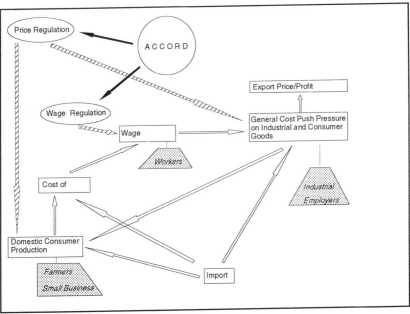

The Low Factor Cost Economy

Corporatist Institutional Formation:
A Theoretical Perspective

Two contending explanations claim to account for the creation and endurance of Austrian neo-corporatism. A *tripartite* version suggests that successful concertation, the joint formulation of policy by opposing interests, emerges because of the asymmetrical power and collective action problems of labor and capital organizations.[22] Each organization's particular internal problems and their common need for economic survival in a competitive world market can only be solved if the state recognizes each as monopoly organizations, provides external resources for achieving internal cohesion and leads the way in fashioning a three-way arrangement (state-capital-labor). Thus only tripartite (or state-based) institutional arrangements can spring up and endure. Similarly, rational choice approaches stress the crucial role of the state in decreasing the longer term risks of cooperation for workers and firms (or increasing their discount parameter).[23] Despite agreements made today, tomorrow's situation may make bargained obligations impossible to keep. Without state assurances to workers that wage sacrifices made today will be compensated for tomorrow (for example, through social

Select Small European States	Growth		Unemployment		Inflation	
	1973-1980	1989-1994	1973-1980	1989-1994	1973-1980	1989-1994
Austria	3.0	2.2	5.9	3.3	1.8	3.7
Denmark	1.6	1.3	9.9	2.6	6.4	10.7
Norway	4.7	2.0	9.1	3.1	1.8	5.6
Sweden	1.8	-0.1	10.6	5.9	1.9	4.7
Select Large States						
US	2.3	2.0	7.7	3.9	6.7	6.4
Japan	3.7	2.5	7.1	2.0	1.9	2.4
Germany	2.3	2.5	4.7	3.4	3.2	7.7
Italy	2.8	1.5	17.6	5.5	6.7	11.1
UK	0.9	0.8	16.4	5.3	5.7	8.5

Source: OECD, figures for 1994 are OECD estimates

welfare spending) or that a business's prices will be sustained in the face of a cyclic downturn (e.g., through subsidies), parties to the class bargain could scarcely depend on the value of future cooperation.

The *bipartite* logic, in contrast, is less sanguine about the role of state elites in the emergence of such regimes. Rather, the strategic perceptions and capabilities of the two main protagonists are decisive. The utility of cooperation derives from a consideration of each class's (class organization's) strategic alternatives. Those utilities depend on elite historical learning and reputation effects and assessments of the bargaining partner's (opponent's) capacity to pursue its preferred option.[24] The principle difference between the approaches concerns the role of the state. In the latter theory, state guarantees may actually stymie peak-level cooperation and reduce the possibility of successful institutional emergence and endurance. In the real bargaining world, the state role may be a liability. Even if the state had no class bias, state elites are captives of transitory business cycles and varying expressions of public opinion.[25] The behavior of state elites hardly engenders confidence sufficient to generate a sense of lower risk about the future benefits of cooperation. Parliamentary regimes are not well noted for time consistent economic policy.[26] Finally, strategic calculations are significantly more complex in three rather than two actor peak bargaining.[27] With the state as the third actor, it becomes more likely that bargainers will delay settlements in hopes of bidding greater rewards from the state for settling. In short, the bipartite logic of institutional emergence suggests success in more autonomous but organizationally balanced (bipartite) arrangements.[28] My contention is that the earlier failures were more tripartist, non-autonomous and narrow in scope and that the success of the 1957 regime was due to its more bipartist, autonomous and encompassing orientation.

Lessons from the Interwar Cases: The Industry Commission, Industry Conference and *Abbaugesetz* Attempts

An executive order of 4 November 1918 created a parity Industrial Control Commission 'from above' that built on wartime labor, business and state cooperation.[29] The loss of food and energy resources made economic conditions extreme.[30] Austria was burdened by dependence on external loans as remaining domestic capital fled.[31] These crises fostered a sense among most Austrians of mutual dependence and political uncertainty.[32]

Much of the commission's work took the form of recommendations forwarded to the Provisional Assembly's Executive Committee.[33] Primarily, the commission addressed labor market problems.[34] Later, similar parity-structured sub-committees were established such as those for the demobilization and liquidation of the defense economy, central commission for returning workers, agricultural councils and a State Commission for Socialization.[35] But their efforts were meant to *feed the decision-making apparatus of the Provisional Assembly rather than to contribute to the construction of autonomous agreements between capital and labor.*

Only a year later, a more comprehensive arrangement emerged under the direction of Renner's third government of national concentration (November 1919). Given a new name, the parity-staffed Industry Conference was to consider a wider scope of economic problems. By all accounts, only the sub-committee concerned with wages and prices achieved any effective results.[36] With the chancellor playing a leading role, the conference adopted a 'sliding scale' wage indexation mechanism.[37] Under this regime, the living standard of the SDAP's (Austrian Social Democratic Worker's Party) constituency was protected by a state-sponsored incomes policy.

The two Renner-led attempts at business-labor concertation foundered at the end of the Grand Coalition. Backed by the *Arbeiterkammer*, a new attempt began during the 'Civil Servant Government' of Schober.[38] The renewed attempt was triggered by the inflation takeoff of 1920-21, looming capital scarcity, state budget deficits, the end of the illusory *Inflationskonjunktur,* and the policy standoff between the SDAP and the CSP (Christian Social Party). A market disadvantaged labor movement meant initial stalemate. Business was willing only to supplement rising food costs, while the state demanded subsidy rollbacks to address its budget deficit.[39]

The Schober government *unilaterally* imposed a settlement after the December (1921) riots: the *Abbaugesetz.* Food subsidies were abolished and a Parity Commission established. Employers partially took up the food subsidy.[40] Growing crisis, budget deficit, and policy stalemate had forced the state's hand. Business felt it could do best by waiting for conditions to be imposed. Labor, on the other hand, had been incapable either of winning the policy debate (the SDAP Financial Plan) or of channelling member militancy.

On the other hand, concertation enjoyed some marginal success. Besides explicit wage bargains, wage restraint by labor and price restraint by business can be achieved in a less obvious fashion. It is sometimes easier to *manipulate the premises* on which member demands and economic decisions will be predicated. A 'benchmark' can be established which will knowingly be breached, but will nevertheless dampen bargaining expectations. In the context of the index-driven bargaining arrangement in Austria of the early 1920s, a negotiated index bias was the key, however weak, to some successful concertation. As mentioned before, several cost-of-living indices were prevalent during the period. One highly respected index was that published by the *Österreichischer Volkswirt.* A comparison of the food cost components of this index to that established by the Parity Commission suggests *implicit* cooperation over the premises on which wage bargaining was to based.[41] By subtracting the Parity Commission's index (FPI$_{pk}$) from that of the öV's (FPI$_{öv}$), we get an idea of the extent of 'benchmarking' by the Parity Commission. According to this indicator, cooperation existed under the interwar Parity Commission at least until the time of the *Genfer Sanierung*.[42]

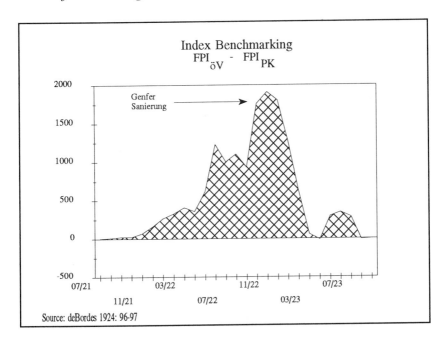

Source: deBordes 1924: 96-97

Put simply, there were twin Achilles heels in the interwar attempts at enduring concertation: a state assured wage-price indexation and food subsidy program for income maintenance and lack of adequate labor organization. Indexation was problematic, as it caused conflict constantly to shift from the issue of wage management to a continuous debate over the construction and importance of the index.[43] A wide variety of ambiguous indices sprang up by which to determine the wage scale.[44] Both business and labor were hesitant to include automatic escalator clauses in agreements.[45] Wages quickly suffered from price increases and this caused frequent renegotiation. In a system where there were multiple regional negotiations and relatively little centralized control over producer group affiliates, this simply ratcheted the wage-price spiral.

Comparison of Interwar and Postwar Austrian Labor Movement			
	Interwar Period[a]		Immediate Postwar Period[b]
Organization			
Number of Sub-Confederals	43 (BFG)		16
Type	Craft and Sector		Industrial Sector
Organizational Density			
Bund Freir Gewerkschaften	32%		
all Unionists	44%		51%
Political Orientation[c]			
	Distinct Political Unions (Richtungsgewerkschaften)		Electoral Fractions
	Membership Distribution[d] (1932)	Workers Chamber Elections[e] (1926)	Works Council Mandates[f] (1947)	Workers Chamber Elections[g] (1949)
Socialist	77.2 %	78.8 %	62.0 %	64.4 %
Catholic	14.9 %	10.4 %	3.6 %	14.2 %
German National	7.9 %	7.8 %		
Communist		2.8 %	6.8 %	9.7 %
Independent		0.2 %	27.6 %	11.6 %

a: Circa 1932, Traxler 1982:150, 168.
b: The number of sub-confederals established in 1945 was 16. Today there are 15 (Klenner 1953:1608). Density figures calculated from US Allied Commission for the year 1946 (1948:225-230). Organizational density has averaged between 60 an 65 percent through the remaining post-war years.
c: Prior to 1934 Socialist unionists belonged to the Bund Freier Gewerkschaften, Catholic unionists to the Christlicher Gewerkschafter and nationlists to the Deutscher Gewerkschaftsbund. Independents consist, in these figures, of those not claiming political affiliation as well as those later affiliated with the right-wing Free Party of Austria (FPÖ).
d: Bundesamt für Statistik, 1933, XIV Jg., 172.
e: Klenner, 1951: 714.
f: Klenner, 1953: 1714.
g: Klenner, 1953: 1720.

Percentage of Workers Covered by Collective Agreements Involving More than One Firm			
Era of Institutionalized Cooperation		Withdrawal and Afterwards	
1918	95.3	1925	88.1
1919	91.5	1926	83.7
1920	91.3	1927	83.7
1921	-	1928	83.0
1922	93.4	1929	78.3
1923	96.7	1930	71.8
1924	95.2	1931	68.2
Mean	93.9		79.5
Source:	*Statistische Handbuch für die Republik Österreich*, various issues		

Food subsidies were also an integral component of the overall scheme. Here the state bore the cost of most food staples by issuing them at below market prices.[46] While concertation is usually a means to restrain labor and business demands, this early system led to restraint only among relatively weaker unions. In fact, wage gains and the strength of union groups are closely correlated from 1919 to 1921.[47]

Institutionalized cooperation of the sort described above terminated in all but name after the *Sanierung*. It was formally ended in April 1925 by the *Bund Freier Gewerkschaften* executive committee.[48] The stabilization of prices meant real wages had been pushed downward. To the extent cooperation had occurred, it had not been rewarded. The labor leadership lost legitimacy. Afterward, collective bargaining became less encompassing.[49] On the other hand, civil violence rose in intensity.[50] The course toward civil war was set.

Evaluating the Lost Opportunity

The experiences of the immediate interwar years augured well for the *outbreak* of attempts at institutionalized cooperation but not for their continuation. On the positive side of the ledger, both political and economic conditions made early cooperation between labor and capital desirable. There was a rough political balance as a result of fin-de-siecle industrialization, war and the dissolution of the old regime. Labor-capital relations during the war had been cooperative. The labor movement's constituency had grown significantly and the SDAP demonstrated a willingness to control the left extremes. Business was weakened by war. The state was used to bolster both the political balance and the terms of concertation. Secondly, the transition to interwar democracy came with economic uncertainty. The immediate interwar years were hand-to-mouth; the future was bleak and uncertain as evidenced by the debate over the survivability of the Austro-German rump state. Anything but a truce in class conflict seemed impossible.

Other conditions dampened chances for the *maintenance* of cooperation. Uncertainty made rational elites, especially business, avoid any long term commitment (i.e., institutionalization of bargaining) because something better would likely turn up.[51] Only the state, and to some extent labor, saw no better morrow by late 1921. Electoral gains also emboldened the CSP as did a growing international consensus over Austria's need for an injection of funds under the right (pun intended) conditions. Critical historical encounters had not induced elites to pursue uncertainty reduction by institutionalizing a balanced and better constructed compromise. *Labor was unable*, for reasons of cyclic economic change, internal politics, and lack of organizational centralization, *to mount a counter-balancing strategy.* Cooperative endeavors—always with the state as lead partner—emerged and continued only so long as an indecisive electoral-governmental balance held. That indecision dissolved and a new course was chartered with Seipel's (CSP) accession to the Chancellor's office and the pursuit of a classical and austere economic policy.

The Emergence of Postwar Economic Governance: From the five *PLA*s to the Parity Commission

The earliest postwar labor-business relationship was characterized by nominal state authority over a disjoint wage and price determination process. Initially, in 1945, prices were frozen by government decree and criteria were established for granting increases.[52] Price change authority fell to the Department of Price Information and Supervision in the Ministry of Interior. In addition, provincial authorities had pricing responsibilities.[53] Lack of centralized control invited special interest bargaining. Oversight was also weak as the price department of the Ministry of Interior had few staffers for enforcement.[54]

Wage changes were managed by an unconnected process. Like the stop on prices, German-era wage scales were retained and a wage freeze ordered. In the spring of 1946, authority over wage issues was transferred from the old Labor Trustee to the Central Wage Commission in the Ministry of Social Administration. Wage demands were lodged at local employment offices (*Landarbeitsamt*), where they were taken to the parity-constituted Central Wage Commission for decision.[55] The Inter-Allied Wage Board could then review and approve/veto these findings.[56]

These decentralized and uncoordinated processes soon became associated with wage and price waves and the specter of inflation like that which had set in motion the catastrophic political failure of the interwar years. That earlier experience is key to understanding how inflation triggered renewed attempts at coordinated management.[57] Indeed, one can flatly state that inflationary spikes were the principle economic signal associated with the five *Preis-Lohn Abkommen* from 1947 to 1951.[58] The coming stimulus from Marshall Plan assistance and the inflationary upswing it occasioned, coupled with the weakness of a state sponsored management apparatus triggered interwar memories and account for the timing and style of renewed postwar labor-capital concertation.[59] It was these conditions that spurred Böhm to his famous *Astgemeinschaft* statement.[60]

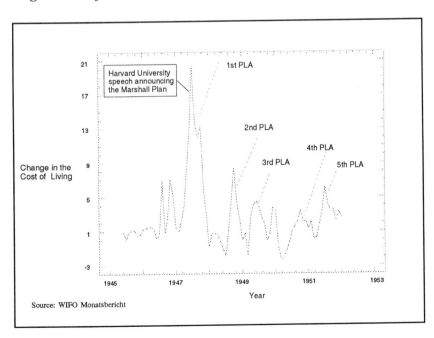

Source: WIFO Monatsbericht

Militancy also triggered old fears. The wage pushing strikes in the summer of 1946 were, in all likelihood not supported by the new ÖGB.[61] Clearly, choices were to be made. Either the state had to acquire more power or cooperation among the re-established interest representatives would have to succeed. The former course was precluded for a host of reasons including the government's pre-occupation with Allied oversight, a democratic appearance and its intrinsic fiscal and political weakness.

Fortunately, necessity combined with organizational and political capacity. Following Renner's admonition of *"Nicht Kampf, sondern Organisation ist die Zeitparole"* (Not struggle, rather organization is the watchword),[62] the ÖGB adopted the industry group principle, internalized political fractions, centralized finance and made sure that administrative workers stayed within the single federation.[63] This occurred simultaneously with *Bundeswirtschaftskammer* centralization. Rather, early cooperation over the Currency Act of 1947 demonstrated the ability of both to control dissenters and forge a new cooperative coalition.[64] Similarly, in party competition, cooperative capacity was enhanced. Though neither the SPÖ nor the ÖVP could claim a majority, neither were there effective small party extremes to pull them away from the center.[65] The Grand Coalition embodied the emerging elite consensus over economic and social policy. The five PLAs were couched in this new organizational and political climate (Appendix 3).[66]

The purpose of the first of the *Preis-Lohn Abkommen* was to balance agriculture's demands for European price parity with worker's demands for real wage stability .[67] The state was a partner insofar as fees for public services were increased, but these were still under cost.[68] Wages were to increase by about 50 percent and the price of necessities by 25 percent. Inflation over 10 percent was to abrogate the bargain. Manufacturing and industrial prices were not specifically regulated as, it was presumed, the international market would determine these. Marshall Plan assistance was to provide the bulk of investment funds.[69] Also, considerable ERP funds were used to subsidize the bargained adjustments of the first and remaining PLAs.[70]

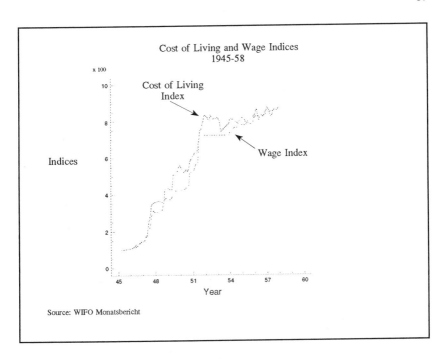

Cost of Living and Wage Indices
1945-58

Source: WIFO Monatsbericht

While inflation pushed beyond the 10 percent level and thus broke the first accord, the trade union held rigorously to wage and militancy restraint. Real growth, investment and productivity advanced sharply. Price control, typically the business side responsibility, was more problematic, however. The strongest rise occurred in consumer products, while services and rents rose less. The state meanwhile compensated farmers' price restraint.[71]

The second PLA was again triggered by agricultural demands and the state's *weakness* as its became ever more obvious that ERP funds had to be siphoned to service the accords. The second agreement was to allow agricultural prices to rise, compensate workers with higher wages and shift the formula's burden to business.[72] Even so, the threat of an expanding state deficit was cause for the third PLA. After this accord, the burden shifted to workers as real wages plunged to their lowest level since war's end. The culprit was not just the terms of the negotiation, but the fall in the British pound's value and accompanying inflation.

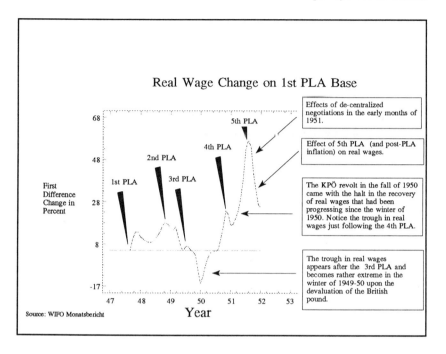

The continuing problem of state subsidies, the slowing of Marshall Fund aid, and poor real wages brought on the fourth PLA. But an additional problem surfaced at the fourth: inflationary expectations on pricing behavior. A close look at the movement of the cost-of-living index compared to the wage index clearly reveals sharp adherence of wages to accords. But after the first few *Abkommen* the cost-of-living index looses its sharp step-like appearance. Another lesson was in the making here.[73] Sellers were advancing prices in anticipation of a settlement of grievances at the next round which, everyone knew, would take place in summer or early fall.[74]

The continued loss in real wages following the forth PLA touched off the KPÖ militancy of late September 1950. Ironically, given the institutional chain of events it elicited (the Economic Directorate and short-lived decentralized wage bargaining), few other incidents contributed as much to the evolving *Wirtschafts- und Sozialpartnerschaft*. The creation of the directorate was to have allowed labor to lay claim to part of the state apparatus and enhance ÖGB legitimacy, while shifting responsibility for tough decisions away from the federation. It was to be the cornerstone of the 'planned economy' approach to Austrian economic management in the 1950s.[75] Correspondingly, wage bargaining would be decentralized. In this way, workers in each sector would get their share (of international market-induced) advantages, while macro-economic levers would be pulled by a government dominated tripartite committee (e.g., the statist or French model).

This institutional trajectory was derailed because of a *weakening state capacity* in economic management. Economic conditions merely enhanced the effect: ERP fund managers were decrying the back channel use of aid in bargaining. Assistance was, in any case, scheduled to terminate soon. Generalized price adjustment in a continually integrating European economy was also becoming more than the small state could bear.[76] The planning system's policy structures were part of a general reaction to the KPÖ uprising of 1950. They were also short-lived, based, as they were, on a weakened state apparatus and purse. New price developments (e.g., the coal shock of 1951), the SPÖ presidential victory and rapid real wage gains following decentralized bargaining triggered the fifth PLA. That experience illuminates clearly the tripartite dilemma. Negotiations foundered over state compensation as issues constantly rolled back into the parliamentary (prices discussions) and ministerial arena (e.g., public employee wage negotiations), there to become politicized and founder on the shrinking margins for compensation that the Marshall Plan had once provided.[77]

The Kamitz course, an interregnum between the five PLAs and the Parity Commission Regime, must be seen in light of the institutional experiments at concertation, both interwar and postwar. It was essentially a search for a new formula in the evolving system of cooperation, and whether by design or not, was an essential prerequisite for the Parity Commission regime. Its hallmark was the movement away from institutionalized bargaining of the PLA variety and toward a standard combination of monetary and fiscal policy. Labor acquiesced to this social market approach because the PLA regime was not much more than a disguised (and unsuccessful) wage indexation scheme, where, because of mark up behavior, labor always lost.[78] The failure was on the capital side. Now the classic 'low factor cost' economy is very vulnerable to this effect. Each cost arena is associated with particular producer groups; successful competition requires cost absorption by some or all of them. Distributional battles ensue as one group perceives inequality or the possibility of revision *and* has the capacity to act politically. Coalitions emerge over the distribution issue based on perceptions of strength, reputation and interest. In the early 1950s, labor could absorb its cost share *and* demonstrate coalitional capacity. The 'price-making' side could not, divided as it was between large state-affiliated industries and smaller downstream firms.[79] In this light, the Kamitz course, a turn to market discipline, was actually a collusive choice by the ÖGB and the Chamber of Business to restore order to prices and, though they may not have foreseen it, to take a necessary corrective before building the Parity Commission regime.

Initially, conditions in the international economy backed the hand of this ambitious monetary and fiscal policy. Meanwhile, the *Koalitionsausschuß* continued to evolve economic policy as labor adhered to the last wage accord. The proof is in the pudding: the price index plummeted from a 20 percent yearly increase to about a 3 percent yearly increase by the mid-1950s. What a different outcome than that of the *Genfer Sanierung*! Success had required significant advances in ÖGB organization, a weakened and disciplined business sector, and a cross-class producer group coalition. One more step remained.

Genossenschaft Österreich: The Emergence of the Parity Commission Regime

While the change in policy regime (to the Kamitz course) may have been thought permanent by employers, the labor federation elite viewed it only as a necessary purgative that would allow capital time to restore discipline in its ranks. Soon, however, inflation set off renewed debate. The Kamitz course had been (fortuitously?) credited with price control in the recession of 1953-54. But, unfortunately, structural inflation was emerging as the GDP price index began rising faster than the cost of living. To promote exports, the low factor cost economy can only dampen the former by cost absorption. This was not happening in the 1955-57 period. It was also time to pay labor's piper. With nominal price control, ÖGB organizational capacity was now used to renew wage negotiations. Simultaneously, at the federation's third Federal Congress, President Böhm called again for *institutionalized* concertation.[80] The strategic timing was ripe. Unemployment had eased and chances were good in the future for another European growth spurt.

Finally, employers were confronting a dilemma at the end of a business cycle. As an economic boom shows signs of softening, uncertainty is increased and two principle interests come to the fore for employers. First, they would prefer to consolidate their power positions vis-a-vis labor. The threat of unemployment invariably leads to significant renegotiation in the power distribution between worker and boss. A second employer preference is to continue the upswing as long as possible. This was an especially acute interest for capital in Austria at the time. Elites had staked their reputations on the economic policies of the mid-fifties, an international boom was in sight, and domestic policy problems could easily damage the international standing and position earlier gained (not to mention the reputations of those that urged the Kamitz course).

Where trade unionists are relatively weak these preferences may be quite complimentary. Employers can *pas de bourrée* across a short cyclical downswing by rolling back worker gains. But rollback was foreclosed in the Austria of the mid-1950s given the ÖGB's preoccupation with organizational discipline. This fact presented an unambiguous tradeoff between the employers' two preferences. Odds were that a domestic policy impasse would damage Austria's competitiveness and cause it to miss a coming boom if the labor organization were not re-integrated. Success had brought with it a significant constraint on business's future institutional options.

Of course, the actors at the time did not possess our clear hindsight. Establishing the Parity Commission regime required several rounds of blunt exchanges between labor and capital in which the ÖGB made explicit its ability not only to deliver but to threaten capital interests. The first round, in the fall of 1955, was an offer by Trade Union Federation President Böhm to establish a broadly conceived Commission for Economic and Social Questions under which more than wage-price issues could be considered. The initiative was rejected by business and agricultural chambers on grounds that informal council was fine, institutionalization was not. The next, more fully elaborated offer by Böhm, contained more than institutional plans:

> I bid you to consider, that in the event, contrary to expectations, my proposal should be dismissed, workers will be forced to the opinion that their chamber is not inclined to try to reach agreement on questions of the collective welfare. The perspective would then prevail that a reckless showdown between interests with all its economically damaging consequences will follow, behavior which in no way could serve the welfare of the fatherland.[81]

The hermeneutics here are not difficult. Organizational strength meant the federation either could direct or would allow disruption of the regulated economy absent an exchange over an institutionalized means of policy concertation. There was another rejection (March 1956), this time from the Federal Chancellor, Raab (former Business Chamber President), who saw labor's proposal not just in light of business dread of institutionalized class cooperation but as a threat to the state's prerogatives.[82] A fig leaf of sorts was finally designed in which cooperation was pursued under a reactivated Economic Commission. In the Commission plans were then drawn up for the Parity Commission, which became operational in March 1957.[83]

Two plainly political factors crucially affected business's acceptance of the specific price-wage regulating institution (later to be considerably broadened to include a Council for Economic and Social Questions in 1963). First Böhm's implied threat was activated. The year 1956 brought the largest wave of strikes in Austria's postwar history. This wave of militancy rode on a new international economic upturn, one that could prove highly beneficial to Austria, begun in the previous year. Large (and federation approved) strike waves preceded the creation of the Parity Commission (1957) and later its Council for Economic and Social Questions (1963).

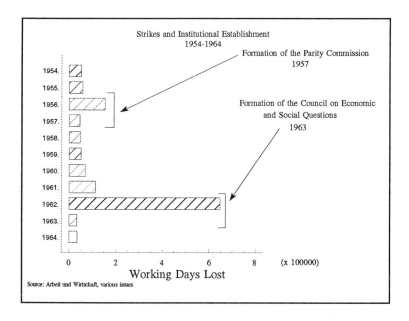

Strikes and Institutional Establishment
1954-1964

Formation of the Parity Commission
1957

Formation of the Council on Economic
and Social Questions
1963

Working Days Lost

(x 100000)

Source: Arbeit und Wirtschaft, various issues

Secondly, sectoral politics figured strongly in the outcome. The necessity to compete in the international economy intensified the two principal cleavages in a small state's political economy: the sectoral and producer (class) cleavages.[84] While the business chamber and federation occupied opposite poles on the key *class* axis of interest conflict over the Parity Commission, they, in the guise of export oriented industry and labor, had always been potential allies along the sectoral cleavage dividing exposed and protected economic sectors.[85]

		Sectoral Exposure Cleavage	
		Closed	Open
Party/Class Cleavage	ÖVP	Agricultural Interests Peasants Small Commerce	Industrialists Employers Association
	SPÖ	Protected Labor Parliamentarians	Labor Functionaries

In fact, we could interpret labor's role in the PLAs as that of exposed industry's coalition partner. From that perspective, both business and labor were concerned with lowering the feed-through effect that high consumer prices had on wages and hence industrial prices. But again, with weak labor, a one-class coalition of exposed and protected business sectors can have its cake and eat it too. That, as we have demonstrated, was not possible. With growth in the promise of European integration, a class truce became ever more enticing. *Neigung* became necessity when further integration was threatened by the opposing sectoral coalition of agriculture, small commercial interests and protected labor in the debate over EFTA or EC.[86] Logic dictated an easing of the reluctance to pay Böhm's institutional price. Raab, as chancellor, was really not in a position to block this development.[87] With gradual agriculture and state elite acquiescence to the commission, only parliamentarians remained opposed since they stood to lose authority in either direction (integration and/or institutionalization of the *WSP*).[88]

Implications

What key factors accounted for the successful emergence of this final concertative institution? The economic cycle argument, that during an upswing labor's bargaining position is better and hence capital is more willing to establish concertative institutions, helps but does not fully account for the emergence of a lasting regime. Most predictive of cooperative *outbreaks* was a high level of inflation: the five PLAs track almost in lock-step with jumps in the cost of living. But all these 'inflationary crisis' attempts foundered. In fact, when the Parity Commission was established (1957), inflation was at an all-time low and 1950s economic growth had already peaked. On the other hand, the fear of renewed inflation pushed along the establishment of the Council for Economic and Social Questions. The evidence is suggestive. Economic cycles were important but not sufficient.

Poor institutional instruments may be explanatory. Wage indexation schemes never really worked. In fact, they may actually have helped bring about the downfall of concertation regimes in both interwar and postwar periods. Surely the technical experts had learned this lesson. But new methods, while helping to account for the *Sozialpartnerschaft*'s longevity, do not necessarily explain its initial establishment.

From this analysis of concertation's institutional evolution in Austria, the following seem most crucial. Foremost, without labor's capacity to constrain the strategic options of capital by demonstrating both an ability to deliver wage restraint, to mobilize and control militancy, and to threaten the precarious sectoral coalition, no neo-corporatist regime would exist today in Austria. This capacity was born from the hard experiences of the 1930s and 1940s in which those who had once pushed sectional and particular interests perished. The same lesson was not lost on the leaders of the business *Lager*. Politically and socially, the threats and militancy of 1956 and 1962 meant much more than they would have in a land that had not experienced authoritarianism, civil war and Nazism.

Finally what made this political/social threat all the more potent in the postwar period was the dynamics of high politics and high economics. The export promotion path on which Austria was forced in the postwar period made the low factor cost economy unavoidable and put labor, if well enough organized, in the driver's seat in the flow of factor costs across the economy. A weak state, unable to pay the bill of compensation often referred to in theoretical treatments of neo-corporatist class compromise, sharpened hard interest adjustment between the protagonists. Significant problems in government formation also regularly impinged on the state's ability to fashion policy. *At practically every crucial juncture in the further development of concertative institutions, state capacity, either in financial or political terms, was low.* Other paths of class compromise were cut with the decline in the state's ability to pay or decide. There were certainly memories of 1922 operating here. But state withdrawal also served a crucial but often overlooked function in the establishment of concertation in the 1950s. Without a retreat to macro-economic policy levers (the Kamitz course), its initial success in the international economy, and then discrediting of broad macro-economic policy unflanked by producer group cooperation, price discipline would probably never have been achieved, and labor would have had little on which to spend its bargaining chips. These conditions, in contrast to those around earlier attempts, made possible the emergence of an Austrian economic governance institution that is only now in transition.

These lessons should not be lost either on the new regimes of the east or on the changing small states of the west. The Scandinavian experiences in the 1970s, and Austria's pre-1950s experiments, suggest that tripartism was only a "second-best" alternative.[89] Reliance on the state to shore up organizational weaknesses among producer groups soon runs awry. It burdens the state with more extensive expenditures, and relatedly, it fashions an incentive for bargainers not to settle in hopes of bidding more from the state. Thus a resurrection of traditional Scandinavian neo-corporatism and corporatist emergence in the east are not likely.[90] The former is burdened with an inappropriate policy legacy; the latter with weak producer groups organizations. Besides, the state is considerably weaker in Scandinavia today. It is a prejudiced social force in countries like Hungary.

This evaluation implies neither the absence of a modern role for concertation nor the abrogation of an active state role in institution building and economic governance. Indeed, in Austria, we might expect a *greater* state role, albeit modified to conform to the lessons learned here, as labor and business peak organizations loose their former power. But it will certainly be a new and more strategic corporatism.

Appendix 1

Institutional Indicators of Neo-Corporatism

	Indices						Characteristics of Concertative Institutions (Kindley 1992) *			Corporatism and the State (Pahre 1994)		
	Neo-Corporatist Potential:			Labor Organization:			Bargaining Density	Autonomy	Scope	State Role in Corporatism	Monetary Intervention	State-led Restructuring
	Kindley	Pahre (1994)	Kindley (1992)	Schmitter (1977)	Korpi/ Shalev (1979)	Lange/ Garrett (1985)						
	(a)	(b)	(c)	(d)	(e)	(f)	(g)	(h)	(i)	(j)	(k)	(l)
Austria	1.00		1.00	1	2	3.06	hi	hi	hi			
Norway	0.84	Strong	0.92	5	2	3.33	hi	low	med.	occasional	occasional	medium
Sweden	0.82	Strong	0.46	5	2	3.52	med.	low-med.	low	rare	rare	weak
Netherlands	0.77		0.39	2	2	1.90						
Denmark	0.54	Medium	0.52	8	0.5	2.77	low-med.	low	low	regular	occasional	medium
Finland	0.52	Medium	0.40	5	1	2.76		low	low	regular	frequent	medium (strong 48-53)
BRD	0.41		0.54	9	0	1.80						
Italy	0.26		0.13	13	0.5	1.47						
France	0.00		.010	10	0	0.68						

* The institutions considered are, in the Austrian case, the Parity Commission; Sweden, the post Rehn-Meidner system of collective bargaining; Denmark, the post 1960 Basic Agreements; Norway, the system of regularized 'frame agreements' and the Contact Committee.

a. Standardized (to one) factor scores determined by factor analysis of number of federations, number of unions in 2nd largest federation, % union members in largest federation, % of unions in largest confederal, systems orientation, federation bargaining power and scope estimates and % votes for left parties in the late forties and fifties. See Kindley 1992 for elaboration of most variables.

b. Pahre's estimates of comparisons in Scandinavian states. See Pahre 1994.

c. Additive index from data sources in "a" above with the exception that Lange and Garrett's (1985) left cabinet assignment was used instead of %votes for left parties in the early postwar period. See Kindley 1992: 315-325.

d. Index of organizational centralization of producer groups (labor and business). See Schmitter 1977

e. Index of centralization of wage bargaining. Korpi and Shalev, 1979.

f. An additive index of the % total work force unionized and the centralization of unions into peak organizations. See Lange and Garrett 1985.

g. Bargaining density is the frequency of contact between principle bargaining elites. High means daily, ongoing contact between representatives of the labor and capital peak organizations. Medium denotes contact during regular centralized wage negotiations. Low indicates that representatives are in irregular contact during decentralized negotiations.

h. Autonomy is the extent to which the negotiating process is free from influence by cabinet and parliamentary elites. High means officials neither participate in nor ratify decisions reached by the bargaining partners. No case is fully autonomous, but in relative terms the Austrian is more autonomous than its Scandinavian cohort. Medium indicates that influence is limited, participation may be only pro forma. Low means that elites influence by state elites is substantial and that agreements, in large part, must be supplemented by parliamentary legislation.

i. Scope is the breadth of policy-related issues bargained in the institutional setting. High scope consists of most related issues, not only wages but prices, investment and social issues. Medium includes prices in addition to wages. Low includes wages only.

j-l. See Pahre 1994 for explanations.

Appendix 2

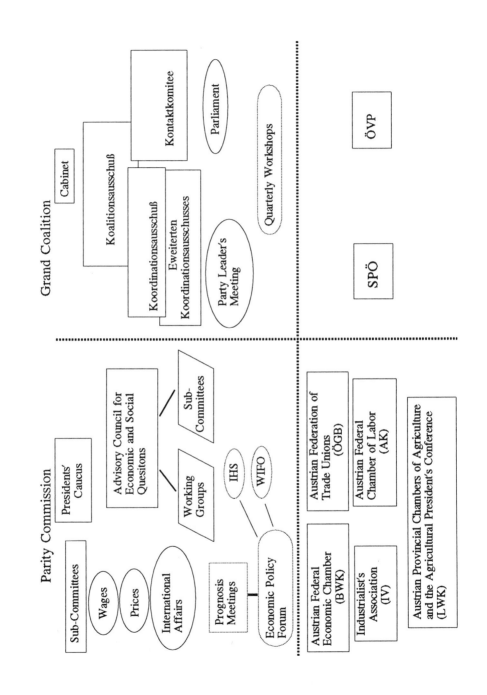

Appendix 3

	1st PLA August 1947	2nd PLA October 1948	3rd PLA June 1949	4th PLA October 1950	5th P._A June 1951
Prices	Agriculture: 27.3% increase / Necessities: Maximum 25% increase / Public Services Increases / Rail: 45% / Trolley: 57% / Post: 135% / Tobacco: 50% / Gas and Elec. 75%	Agricultural prices allowed to rise and price supports on most foods abandoned. / Supports for grain and potatoes remain since industry not willing to absorb even greater increases in expected labor costs without rise in industrial prices.	Occupation tax of 20% of existing income tax. Increase in agricultural taxes, excise, utilities and transportation. Subsidy cut on imports and agricultural products.	State expenditure for subsidies cut by 50% (implying rise in prices) on most necessities (e.g., coal) and allowed for price increases in foodstuffs, utilities and public services.	Wholesale foodstuffs price increases (e.g., flour) of about 50% (and corresponding import subsidy reduced). Retail price increases of grocery items also increased by about 50% (e.g., bread and cheese). Increases in public service rates: public transport: 20-27% goods transport 6% Post 100% Gas 74% Elec. 35% Some additional tax shifts with employers increase in children's allowance contribution from 3 to 6% of payroll; VAT increases from .85 to 1 7%.; excises on vehicles, oil and transportation, cut in municipal trade tax.
Wages	Blue Collar: 50% / White Collar: 36% / Agriculture: 50 öS/mo. / Public and Pensioners: 36%	Base increase of 6% with supplements of 340S from employers / and 230S from state or about 21.7% increase	Employer's Food Supplement cut (formerly 340S). / Children's allowance (from state) rose by 140S to 370S. / Wage increase of 30 öG. plus 4.5% (aggregate gross increase of about 9% or net of about 3.3% for unmarried and 10.2% for unmarried).	An increase of 10% (minimum 100 öS/mo.). / State subsidy for children increased 23 öS from 370S to 600öS/mo. Or an estimated 13% wage increase.	Blue Collar: 10% / White Collar: 12% / Public Servants: 12%
Conditions and Notes:	Conditions: No extra tax applied to wage income increment/ Three month freeze after adjustment to accord. Wage agreement valid so long as cost of living index does not exceed 10% increase.		Note: based on conservative estimate of 13.7% rise in cost of living	Note: Business experienced an estimated 8 to 10% increase in total production costs.	Note: Children's assistance increased by 75%. General supplement increased 10% to public servants and pensioners for rental increases.
Sources:	Edelman 1954, Klenner 1953, Ausch 1965, WIFO *Monatsberichte*, various issues				

NOTES

1. But see Ullman-Margalit, 1977. The emergence of the partnership's cultural norms may be connected to such experiences as mutual concentration camp experiences and to aspects of Catholic social doctrine. Pribyl, 1991, has produced a good guide to many of these sources. Eleanor Ostrom, 1990, provides considerable theoretical guidance on unravelling the processes by which certain interactions can produce norms oriented to collective action.

2. By institutions I mean here not the little "i's" of Douglass North, 1990, such as property rights, customs, etc., but rather the big "I's" that characterize repetitive patterns of social interaction having an organizational embodiment such as the Parity Commission.

3. Just how and why the current *Wirtschafts- und Sozialpartnerschaft* is changing is beyond the scope of this essay.

4. Schmitter and Lembruch, 1979, are credited with the label.

5. On the relationship between structure and national economic adjustment and performance see Schmidt, 1982a, 1982b, 1983, Hicks and Swank 1984a, 1984b, Hicks, et. al., 1986, Crouch 1985, Bruno and Sachs, 1985, Lange and Garrett, 1985, Katzenstein, 1983, 1985, Castles,1987, Scharpf, 1989. On corporatist arrangements and political stability see Schmitter, 1981. Cameron, 1982, 1984, and Castles, 1987, speak to the linkage to social spending. Freeman, 1989, addresses the linkage to inter and intra-generational welfare outcomes. Traxler, 1991, and Traxler and Unger, 1991, address the potential for neo-corporatist systems actually better to restructure in the face of world market pressure than loose market regimes.

6. One could of course reach much further back in time for the antecedents of Austria's *Sozialpartnerschaft*. Herbert Pribyl, 1991, has prepared a compendium that traces its philosophical underpinnings back to the mid-eighteenth century and, in general terms, lists some of the principle events in its history. Of course Karl Ucakar, 1977, among others, finds actual institutional antecedents in the long history of guilds and *Verbände* in Austria. As well the *Kriegshilfsgesetze* and Social Democratic support for the war effort in WWI certainly paved the way for early interwar cooperation. But I am concerned really with 'politically modern' attempts, or those in post-Imperial parliamentary regimes.

7. Since nothing really came of the 1930 talks about establishing cooperation, I do not include it as a case. See Traxler and Grandner, 1984, for an examination of the 1930 talks. That particular episode does however deserve attention in comparison with the successful Scandinavian labor-business cooperation of the period (e.g., Saltsjöbaden). Also see Gourevitch, 1986.

8. See for instance, Botz, 1987.

9. The latter experience, leading as it did to the Nazi's *Deutsche Arbeitsfront*, demonstrated at least the technical advantages of highly organized producer groups and mutual, if forced, cooperation, Talos, 1985.

10. Autonomous here refers to a lack of imposition by government elites of policies about and for the economic partners (e.g., incomes policy, etc.). The economic and social partnership has been characterized as having both autonomous and non-autonomous arenas, Pelinka, 1981. The term can also be used in a cross-national comparative sense to designate the aggregate extent of government elite involvement in the institutions and processes. Parliamentary wage indexation (e.g., Denmark) would be an example of non-autonomous relations between business and labor. See also Kindley, 1992 and Pahre, 1994 and further elaboration in this article.

11. An easily understandable introduction to these terms can be found in Ball and Millard, 1987.

12. In contrast to earlier periods of more traditional corporatism which excluded worker representatives. For an overview of the uses of the concept and associated labels and prefixes see Schmitter and Lembruch, 1979.

13. Katzenstein, 1985, is the best known explicator of neo-corporatist economic management.

14. For a rational choice explanation of the interaction between business, labor and the state see Przeworski and Wallerstein, 1982.

15. See also Marin, 1982.

16. For a comparison of Scandinavian and Austrian forms of neo-corporatism see Kindley, 1995.

17. From an economic standpoint, these parties have traditionally represented these class interests. This neither means that other interests are excluded nor that each exclusively represents these respective class interests. For example, there is a business party section in the SPÖ and the ÖAAB is a significant influence in the ÖVP.

18. Müller, 1992, 193.

19. After the elections of October 1994 a less robust Grand Coalition has emerged in which the share of parliamentary seats controlled by the two major parties gives the coalition a voting majority but not enough votes freely to pass constitutional issues (i.e., less than a two-thirds majority).

20. On the interplay between region and center in Austrian neo-corporatism see Andrlik, 1983. Considerable overlapping of positions in works council, local government and party also reinforces and reflects the national system. See for instance Kindley, 1992, 403-404.

21. For empirical comparisons, see references in earlier footnote. There are a variety of possible strategies for country-level economic performance enhancement. Some may be advantaged by market leader strategies in which an accentuation on research and technology allow early market capture and the benefits of such leadership, others by concerted efforts to find niche markets or strong pressure on individual productivity enhancement (e.g., active labor market policy in the Sweden of the early seventies), and still others by consistent pressure to keep export prices low. Austria's has been principally, though not exclusively, a factor cost reduction economy. See also Leamer, 1984, Ostleitner, 1992.

22. Traxler, 1991, Streeck, 1981.

23. Przeworski and Wallerstein, 1982. Przeworski further argues the necessity of a more intrusive *enforcer* state role, Przeworski 1988: 36, fn. 39 and 1988, 38, to reduce the risk of compromise. Castles, 1987, and Lange, 1987, 48, have suggested a *compensator* state role to moderate bargained demands and meet future claims (e.g., social services spending). The state may act as *guardian* to prevent one-sided exploitation. Lange, 1987, 50, also hints at a more latent *facilitating* state behavior to reduce transaction costs. Functionalist exchange explanations also rely heavily on a strong *resource interlocutor* state role (see Traxler, 1991).

24. On reputation effects in the rational choice literature see Kreps, et. al., 1982.

25. On the view of the state's class bias from a Marxist perspective see Miliband, 1969, 22. Gold, 1975, 36, presents a concise review.

26. This is the argument of many writers about the political-business cycle and the political economy of parliamentarism. See for instance Tufte, 1978 and Buchanan, 1989.

27. Shepsle, 1986, rather clearly explains this logic.

28. I should, of course, add that parallel to these explanations, contextual conditions can alter the calculus of institutional emergence. Economic cycles (e.g., unemployment) raise or lower the bargaining power of labor or business, Kalecki, 1939. Greater integration in the world economy may impress both workers and commercial interests of the need for competitiveness through cooperation (Lange, 1987, 24, Przeworski, 1988, 39). Economic chaos and structural change may even spur short run cooperative attitudes (Lange, 1984, 112-117). But all these should complement the basic bargaining logic spelled out above.

29. See for instance, Klenner, 1951, 468 for an account.

30. Descriptions can be found in Meihsl, 1961 and Hertz, 1921.

31. See for instance de Bordes, 1924, 7, 19, and Gulick 1948, 145.

32. This was, for instance, one of Bauer's points. See Bauer, 1970, 183-250.

33. Talos, 1985, 50

34. Klenner, 1951, 468.

35. Described in Nick and Pelinka, 1984, 76.

36. According to Gulick, 1948, 152, Glatz and Talos, 1974, 318, Nick and Pelinka, 1976, 76.

37. See Klenner, 1987, 239 on the sliding scale. Workers' pay was to be determined in two conceptually distinct parts. A basic wage was to vary with movements in prices (wage indexation); another was to be made up of the additional earnings of skilled workers (the 'political wage concept'). See also Glatz and Talos, 1974, 318 and Gulick, 1948, 152.

38. I call this the neutral state period and label it a Civil Servant Government because nearly three-fourths of Schober's ministers were officially non-partisan (data from Kleindl, 1976).

39. Butschek, 1985, 33, Rothschild, 1947, 30, Gulick, 1948, 157.

40. Klenner 1951, 539.

41. See de Bordes 1924, 96-97.

42. Similar differences can be seen in comparison of the PK index with the Index of the Federal Statistical Office and the Viennese Working Family Necessities Index. See for instance, Klezel, 1925, 147. Hence, my impression that it is not just a statistical artifact.

43. See de Bordes, 1924, 65-66, 70-77.

44. See for instance Kautsky, 1925, 113-14.The Reparations Commission Index, the Federal Statistical Office's Wholesale Price Index, Retail Price Index and Necessary Foodstuffs Index, the Parity Commission's (1922) Cost of Living Index and the *Österreichischer Volkswirt*'s Cost of Living Index (de Bordes, 1924, 70).

45. Gulick 1948, 152.

46. The issue of Austrian state food subsidies just after the close of World War I and the impact of readjustment in the early twenties is rather complex and beyond the scope of this article. There are several good starting points for exploring this issue like deBordes, 1924, Hertz, 1920, Gulick, 1948, Kautsky, 1925, Klenner, 1951, Rothschild 1947, Wieser, 1925, Kernbauer, März and Weber 1983, Klezl, 1925. For a modern critique of indexing schemes in the incomes policy context see Braun, 1986, 36-39.

47. See Kindley 1992, 120.

48. Klenner, 1951, 687.

49. Kindley 1992, 140.

50. See Botz 1987, 17, Kindley 1992, 141.

51. Much of this uncertainty was attributable to international economic conditions. There was not only the *Überlebensfähigkeit* issue, but low international demand. One purpose of the postwar Marshall Plan was to remedy this problem.

52. Kravis, 1948, 24. Rothschild, 1950, suggests that the government was both unable and unwilling to stem the rise of the black market.

53. Bauer, 1981, 43.

54. Kravis 1948, 26.

55. Hietler, 1967.

56. This arrangement was very early on protested by the newly formed ÖGB as the freeze did not allow for re-structuring of the wartime wage scale nor much real voice for labor. See Bauer 1981, 34-37, and Executive Committee, Allied Council in Austria, "Proceedings of the Executive Committee", 24 October 1945, EXCO/M (45) 10.

57. Rothschild, 1950, 40, Edelmann, 1954, 21 and Ausch, 1965, 51.

58. It is unclear whether the price change peak of late 1946 was responsible for the wage spike of early 1947 or whether the wage change of early 1947 fueled the even greater and major inflation threat of early and mid-1947. Observe for instance the Austrian Institute for Economic Research's series, found partially in Edelman (1954, 70-73), consisting of an index of the cost of living and an hourly earnings index (WIFO, *Monatsberichte*). The initial sequence (1946) of wage increase then price rise that I observed is opposite that suggested by Maisel's 1946 article ("Vom Stopp zur Lenkung," *Der österreichische Arbeiter und Angestellte*, 19/1946) as reported in Bauer 1981, 41-42. Maisel was then Minister for Social Administration and head of the *Arbeiterkammer*. His claim was that prices had already significantly outpaced wages in the previous year by some 40 percent. This line of reasoning suggests that prices were driving wages hence the culprit was the former. In hindsight the relationship simply is not that clear.

59. Signs of a classic wage-price spiral appear immediately after the Second Allied Control Agreement in the summer of 1946 which 'normalized' commerce (Butschek 1985, 84).

60. Böhm 1948, 3.

61. After the beginning of the PLAs, strikes were contained, Klenner 1953, 1586.

62. See for instance Renner's address to the First Federal Congress of the ÖGB about the evolution of the working-class struggle under capitalism (Klenner 1953, 1641-1644). Unfortunately, scholars of Austro-Marxism seem not to have picked up on the development of this brand of thought after the second world war. Hence Renner's speech and similar theoretical developments within the SPÖ and ÖGB have really never been adequately addressed. Compare for instance Bottomore and Goode, 1978.

63. Klenner 1953, 1611-1629, Traxler 1982, 177-184, Proksch 1945.

64. According to Ausch, 1965.

65. The 'major party share,' the percentage of the vote going to the two major parties, climbed over 10 percent in the early postwar period as opposed to the interwar years.

66. Notwithstanding, of course, the fact of allied occupation until 1955. Indeed, the fact of Soviet occupation *without* the isolationary approach used in Germany likely contributed to the sense of urgent cooperation between business and labor.

67. Nemschak 1955, 87.

68. This according to Ausch 1965, 59.

69. Seidel 1951, 342 in Butschek 1985, 91. Seidel recently mentioned to the author that perhaps claims about the impact of the Marshall Plan have been inflated (Interview June 1994).

70. Elsewhere I have assessed the impact of Marshall Plan Funds on the PLAs (Kindley, 1994)

71. The Marshall Plan had a considerable impact on the political calculus here. First, most early UN and ERP assistance was in food. This weakened agricultural prices (and farmers' bargaining position) considerably and brought demands for an accord from agriculture. But aid certainly eased the way for the wage price agreements by regularizing those prices, cutting their bite into the accords and by bringing agriculture to the table. See Kindley 1994.

72. There was not much protest over this development. In fact it is intimated by Edelman, 1954, and Ausch, 1965, that employers actually came out on the good side of the deal as prices gradually came under control and the disparity between official and black market prices narrowed. Earlier, side payments had been made to employees in the form of food and necessities that could be sold on the black market and thus represented one form of wage compensation. The value of these products fell as the economy stabilized. The above-the-board supplement was an attempt to make up for this.

73. What I refer to here is that wage movements through to the fourth PLA and after the fifth explicitly exhibit the effect of the accords. Price movements are not as controlled as wages after the 2nd PLA. (see Klenner 1987, 405 and Bachinger and Matis 1974, 219).

74. See for instance Nemschak, 1955, 85.

75. See Seidel's 1992 recent discussion of this period.

76. Edelman 1954, 49-50.

77. Note, for instance, the volume of discussion in Viennese newspapers and Edelman's, 1954, remarks about these reports.

78. On the other hand, the essential outcome of the PLAs was that the labor organization had demonstrated rather consistent discipline.

79. There were also other battles on this side of the class fence. One of the most obvious was the 1947 Currency Act struggle between Raab, leader of the industrial and manufacturing interests and Kienbock, former Finance Minister under Seipel, leader of the financiers. The coalition cleavage showed most clearly when the KPÖ sided with the latter. See Ausch, 1965.

80. Butschek 1985, 138.

81. Attributed to Böhm in Materialien 1966, 144 in Talos 1985, 69, author's translation.

82. Again see Materialien 1966, 147 in Talos, 1985, 69.

83. Klenner, 1977.

84. See for instance Frieden, 1991, 438.

85. For a more general treatment of the effect of trade exposure on political coalitions, see Rogowski, 1987.

86. I would like to thank Oliver Rathkolb for making me aware of this facet of the debate. Only I am to blame, however, for any errors in interpretation.

87. In fact, according to Klenner's, 1977, account, Raab seems to have given his blessing to the Parity Commission. But I suspect that his acquiescence was meant to lend an impression of state legitimacy to the arrangement and too assuage offended honor in the controversy over integration.

88. See Marin, 1982.

89. See for instance Schwerin, 1981

90. Compare for instance Traxler 1993. See also Vartiainen 1993.

FURTHER LITERATURE

Karl Ausch, *Erlebte Wirtschaftsgeschichte: Österreichs Wirtschaft seit 1945* (Vienna: Europa Verlag, 1963).

Eva Bauer, "Entwicklungsbedingungen für eine kooperative Gewerkschaftskonzeption unter Besatzungskontrolle: Am Beispiel des ÖGB, 1945-48," M.A. Thesis, University of Vienna, 1982

Otto Bauer, *The Austrian Revolution* (New York: Burt Franklin, 1970).

_____, *Bolschevismus oder Sozialdemokratie* (Vienna, 1920).

_____, "Kautsky und der Bolschewismus" *Der Kampf*, October 1919.

J. Böhm, "Das Verhältnis zwischen Arbeitgeber und Arbeitnehmer einst und jetzt." *Arbeit und Wirtschaft*, 1948/49, Nr. 8.

Gerhard Botz, *Krisenzonen einer Demokratie: Gewalt, Streik und Konfliktunterdrückung in Österreich seit 1918* (Frankfurt: Campus Verlag, 1987).

Michael Bruno and Jeffrey Sachs, *Economics of Worldwide Stagflation* (Cambridge: Harvard University Press, 1985).

James Buchanan, *Essays on the Political Economy* (Honolulu: University of Hawaii Press, 1989).

Felix Butschek, *Die österreichische Wirtschaft im 20 Jahrhundert* (Stuttgart: Gustav Fischer Verlag, 1985).

David Cameron, "Social Democracy, Corporatism, Labour Quiescence: The Representation of Economic Interest in Advanced Capitalist States" Conference on Representation and the State, Stanford University, October 1982.

Francis Castles, "Neo-Corporatism and the 'Happiness Index,' or What the Trade Unions Get for Their Cooperation" *European Journal of Political Research* 15/4 (1987): 381-393.

Colin Crouch, "Conditions for Trade Union Wage Restraint" in *The Politics of Inflation and Economic Stagnation*, ed. L. N. Lindberg and Charles Maier (Washington, D.C.: The Brookings Institution, 1985).

J. de Bordes van Walre, *The Austrian Crown: Its Depreciation and Stabilization* (London: P.S. King, 1924).

Murray Edelman, *National Economic Planning by Collective Bargaining* (Illinois: University of Illinois, 1954).

Robert Flanagan, David Soskice and Lloyd Ulman, *Unionism, Economic Stabilization and Incomes Policies: European Experiences* (Washington, D.C.: The Brookings Institution, 1983).

John Freeman, *Democracy and Markets: The Politics of Mixed Economies* (Ithaca: Cornell University Press, 1989).

Jeffrey Frieden, "Invested Interests: The Politics of National Economic Policies in a World of Global Finance," *International Organization* 45/4 (1991).

Harald Glatz and Emmerich Talos, "Sozialpartnerschaft: Ein pluralistisches Modell der Gesellschaft Am Beispiel Österreich," *Österreichische Zeitschrift für Politikwissenschaft* 3 (1974).

David Gold, Clarence Lo, and Erik Wright. "Recent Developments in Marxist Theories of the Capitalist State" *Monthly Review* 27 (1975): 29-43.

Peter Gourevitch, *Politics in Hard Times: Comparative Responses to International Economic Crises* (Ithaca: Cornell University Press, 1986).

Charles Gulick, *Austria from Habsburg to Hitler*, 2 vols. (Berkeley: University of California Press, 1948).

Karl-Heinz Hietler, "Die Entwicklungsphasen der österreichischen Lohnpolitik seit 1945," Dissertation, University of Vienna, 1967.

Friedrich Hertz, "Die Kohlenfrage in Österreich," *Der österreichische Volkswirt* 13 (20 November 1920).

F. Hertz, *Ist Österreich wirtschaftlisch lebensfähig?* (Vienna, 1921).

Alexander Hicks and Duane Swank, "Governmental Redistribution in Rich Capitalist Democracies," *Policy Studies Journal* 13 (1984): 265-286.

_____, et al. "Welfare Expansion Revisited: Policy Routines and their Mediation by Party, Class and Crisis," Paper prepared for the 82nd Annual Meeting of the American Political Science Association, 1986.

_____, and Duane Swank. 1984a. "On the Political Economy of Welfare Expansion: A Comparative Analysis of 18 Advanced Capitalist Democracies. *Comparative Political Studies* 17 (1984): 81-119.

Michal Kalecki, *Essays in the Theory of Economic Fluctuations* (London: G. Allen & Unwin, Ltd, 1939).

Peter Katzenstein, *Small States in World Markets: Industrial Policy in Europe* (Ithaca: Cornell University Press, 1985).

_____, "The Small European States in the International Economy: Economic Dependence and Corporatist Politics," in *The Antimonies of Interdependence*, ed., J.G. Ruggie (New York: Columbia University Press, 1983).

Benedikt Kautsky, "Löhne und Gehälter," in *Geldentwertung und Stablisierung in ihren Einflüssen auf die soziale Entwicklung in Österreich.* Schriften des Vereins für Sozialpolitik, vol 169, ed. Julius Bunzel (Munich: Verlag von Dunder & Humblot, 1925).

Randall Kindley, "International Trade, Domestic Bargaining and the Structure of Corporatist Arrangements: The Marshall Plan and Institution-Building in Postwar Austria," America and the Making of the Second Republic, Center for Austrian Studies Symposium 1994, November 1994.

_____, "Rational Organization: Labor's Role in the Emergence and Endurance of Austrian Neo-Corporatism," Dissertation, Duke University, 1992.

_____, "Reassessing the Legacy of the State in Economic Governance Institutions", forthcoming in J. Rogers Hollingsworth, ed., *Social Actors and the Embeddedness of Institutions* (London: M. E. Sharp, Co., 1995).

Fritz Klenner, *Die Österreichischen Gewerkschaften,* 2 vols. (Vienna: Verlag des Österreichischen Gewerkschaftsbundes, 1951-53).

_____, *Die Österreichische Gewerkschaftsbewegung* (Vienna: Verlag des Österreichischen Gewerkschaftsbundes, 1987).

_____, *Hundert Jahre österreichische Gewerkschaftsbewegung* (Vienna: Verlag des Österreichischen Gewerkschaftsbundes, 1981).

Felix Klezl, "Die Lebenstofen" in *Geldentwertung und Stablisierung in ihren Einflüssen auf die soziale Entwicklung in Österreich*. Schriften des Vereins für Sozialpolitik, vol. 169, ed., Julius Bunzel (Munich: Verlag von Dunder & Humblot, 1925).

Walter Korpi, "Labor Movements and Industrial Relations" in *Nordic Democracy*, ed. Erik Allardt. (Copenhagen: Det Danske Selskab, 1981).

_____, *The Democratic Class Struggle* (London: Routledge, 1983).

Irving Kravis, "Prices and Wages in the Austrian Economy," in *Monthly Labor Review* (January 1948): 20-27.

David Kreps, Paul Milgrom, John Roberts and Robert Wilson. "Reputation and Imperfect Information", "Predation, Reputation and Entry Deterrence", "Rational Cooperation in the Finitely Repeated Prisoners' Dilemma," *Journal of Economic Theory* 27.

Peter Lange and Geoffrey Garrett. "The Politics of Growth: Strategic Interaction and Economic Performance in the Advanced Industrial Democracies," *Journal of Politics* 47 (1985): 792-827.

_____, "The Institutionalization of Concertation", Paper prepared for American Political Science Association, Annual Meeting, 3-6 September 1987.

_____, "Unions, Workers and Wage Regulation: The Rational Bases of Consent" in *Order and Conflict in Contemporary Capitalism*, ed. John H. Goldthorpe (Oxford: Clarendon Press, 1984).

Bernd Marin, *Die Paritätische Kommission: Aufgeklärter Technokorporatismus in Österreich* (Vienna: Internationale Publikationen, 1982).

P. Meihsl, "Die Landwirtschaft im Wandel der politischen und ökonomischen Faktoren, in W. Weber, ed., *Österreichs Wirtschaftsstruktur gestern-heute-morgen* (Berlin, 1961).

Ralph Miliband, *The State in Capitalist Society* (New York: Basic Books, 1969).

Franz Nemschak, *Ten Years of Austrian Economic Development: 1945-1955* (Vienna: Association of Austrian Industrialists, 1955).

Douglass North, "A Transaction Cost Theory of Politics," *Journal of Theoretical Politics* 2/4 (1990): 355-67.

Elinor Ostrom, *Governing the Commons: The Evolution of Institutions for Collective Action* (Cambridge: Cambridge University Press, 1990).

Robert Pahre, "Risky Business: External Uncertainty and Nordic Economic Policies, 1929-1969" Working Paper, Institute of Public Policy Studies, University of Michigan - Ann Arbor. 31 May 1994.

Anton Pelinka, *Modelfall Österreich?: Möglichkeiten und Grenzen der Sozialpartnerschaft* (Vienna: Braumüller, 1981).

Anton Proksch, "Der Aufbau des Österreichischen Gewerkschaftsbundes" *Der österreichische Arbeiter und Angestellte* (28 July 1945).

Adam Przeworski, "Material Bases of Consent: Economics and Politics in a Hegemonic System" *Political Power and Social Theory* 1 (1980).

_____, *Capitalism and Social Democracy* (Cambridge: Cambridge University Press, 1985).

_____, "Capitalism, Pacts: Revisited" Conference on the Micro-Foundations of Democracy, University of Chicago, 29 April - 1 May 1988.

_____, "Class and Politics: A Reply to Buraway" *Socialist Review* (1989): 87-111.

_____ and Michael Wallerstein. "Democratic Capitalism at the Crossroads" *Democracy* 2 (1982): 52-68.

_____ and Michael Wallerstein, "The Structure of Class Conflict in Democratic Capitalist Societies," *American Political Science Review* 76/2. (1982): 215-238.

Rainer Nick, and Anton Pelinka, *Bürgerkrieg - Sozialpartnerschaft* (Vienna: Jugend und Volk, 1984).

Kurt W. Rothschild, *Austria's Economic Development Between the Two Wars* (London: Frederick Muller, Ltd., 1947).

_____, *The Austrian Economy Since 1945* (London: Royal Institute of International Affairs, 1950).

Philippe Schmitter and Gerhard Lembruch, eds., *Trends Toward Corporatist Intermediation* (Berverly Hills: Sage Publications, 1979).

Don Schwerin, "Incomes Policy in Norway: Second-Best Corporate Institutions," *Polity* 14 (1982): 465-480.

Hans Seidel, "Der Beirat für Wirtschafts- und Sozialfragen," WIFO, Vienna, 1992.

Kenneth Shepsle, "Cooperation and Institutional Arrangements." Harvard Conference on International Regimes and Cooperation, 13-15 February 1986.

Wolfgang Streeck, *Gewerkschaftliche Organisationsprobleme in der sozialstaatlichen Demokratie* (Knigstein/Ts: Athenäum, 1981).

Emmerich Talos, "Sozialpartnerschaft: Zur Entwicklung und Entwicklungsdynamik kooperativer-konzertierter Politik in Österreich" in *Sozialpartnerschaft in der Krise*, eds., Peter Gerlich, Edgar Grande and Wolfgang Müller (Vienna: Herman Böhlau Nachf., 1985).

Franz Traxler and Brigitte Unger. "Governance, Restructuring and International Competitiveness" Paper prepared for the 87th Annual Meeting of the American Political Science Association, 29 August - 1 September 1991.

_____, "Political Exchange, Action and Interest Governance. Towards a Theory of the Genesis of Industrial Relations and Corporatism" in *Governance and Generalized Exchange: Self-Organizing Policy Networks in Action* (Frankfurt: Campus/Westview, 1991).

_____, "European Transformation and Institution Building in East and West." Paper presented at a symposium on "The End of the Cold War and Small European States: European Reintegration and Institution-Building in Austria, Denmark, Estonia, Finland, and Hungary," Center for Austrian Studies Symposium 1993, October 1993.

_____, *Evolution gewerkschaftlicher Interessenvertretung: Entwicklungslogik und Organisationsdynamik gewerkschaftlichen Handelns am Beispiel Österreich* (Vienna: Wilhelm Braumller Verlag, 1982).

Edward Tufte, *The Political Control of the Economy* (Princeton, N.J.: Princeton University Press, 1978).

Karl Ucakar, "Die Entwicklung des Verbändeswesens in Österreich" in *Das politische System Österreichs,* ed. Heinz Fischer (2nd ed. Vienna: Europa Verlag, 1977).

Edna Ullman-Margalit, *The Emergence of Norms* (Oxford: Oxford University Press, 1977).

J. Vartiainen, "Challenges to Nordic Corporatism." Paper presented at a symposium on "The End of the Cold War and Small European States: European Reintegration and Institution-Building in Austria, Denmark, Estonia, Finland, and Hungary," Center for Austrian Studies Symposium 1993, October 1993.

Social Partnership and Austro-Keynesianism

Hans Seidel

Economic and social policy in Austria since World War II has been based on two pillars:

* the democratic institutions (government, Parliament) as defined by the constitution, and
* the social partners (the cooperation of the big social groups).

The interaction between the two systems has determined to a substantial degree the process of political decision-making and its outcome. Loosely speaking, the social partners were strong when the government was weak and vice versa. This was a cyclical phenomenon, however; after removing the cyclical component, a clear trend from a neo-corporative system toward a pluralistic society becomes visible. This trend already existed during the Kreisky government from 1970 to 1983 and has intensified since then.

Social Partnership

Preconditions for Cooperation

Economists who use the market system with perfect competition as their reference model have been predominantly skeptical about the welfare implications of special-interest organizations. These organizations restrict competition, prevent social and economic change, facilitate rent-seeking and contribute to stagflation. Mancur Olson's (1982) influential book on *The Rise and Decline of Nations* is one prominent example of this critical attitude.[1]

There is, however, one notable exception: if special-interest groups develop encompassing and highly centralized organizations, they have to consider the impact of their actions on society and the economy as a whole.[2] They may discover that cooperation between labor and capital or between employees and self-employed persons will result in higher payoffs than class war. Cooperative solutions do not come about automatically. Historical experience, the capacity for strategic behavior and the gradual build-up of confidence between the partners in "repeated games" might be necessary to realize potential gains from cooperation.

These preconditions were met in Austria. Four peak associations form the core of social partnership: the Economic Chamber, the Chamber of Agriculture, the Chamber of Labor and the Trade Union Federations. The first two represent capital and the last two labor, although this distinction is somewhat misleading, since capital mainly is represented by small businesspeople and small farmers. Membership in the chambers is compulsory and in the trade unions voluntary. History (the civil war and the Nazi period) has taught the social groups that ruthless class war may lead to disaster. In the ten years of occupation after World War II the two leading political parties as well as organized capital and labor were forced to cooperate to secure the survival of the Republic of Austria (see the Kindley essay in this volume).

The relation between the government (or Parliament) and the social partners may take different forms: dominance, leadership, cooperation, complementarity, resistance or even outright opposition. Social partnership can only dominate economic policy under three conditions:

* The social partners must be ready to include important economic and social matters on their agenda. This is not self-evident. In recent years, the social partners complained that the government shifted delicate problems to the peak associations.
* The social partners must be able to agree unanimously on important matters. The primary task of special-interest organizations is to represent the common interest of their members. An ability to solve problems by compromise and consensus, however, is necessary for a durable partnership.

* The social partners must be so strong politically that the government or the Parliament cannot easily disregard their recommendations (K. Korinek, 1980).

These conditions were never met fully, not even in the 1960s when the power of the social partners peaked. Nevertheless, these criteria are useful to measure the degree of social partnership. The most ambitious concept developed by the Trade Union Federation in the late 1950s, proposed that all important new legislative initiatives should be presented to an economic commission (*Wirtschaftskomission*) consisting of members of the government and members of the social partners. These proposals (which very likely were unconstitutional) were never realized. Nevertheless, they remained on the agenda of the representatives of labor until 1970 when the socialists formed a one-party government.[3]

This paper focuses on the period from 1970 to 1983, which will be labeled the Kreisky era. With respect to social partnership, it was a transition period. The Kreisky government cooperated with the representatives of labor, business and farmers, and relied heavily on the support of these groups in policy matters. Nevertheless, the government strengthened its position gradually and dominated, especially in the field of macroeconomic policy.

The Institutions

In Austria, the organizations of labor, business and farmers use different channels to promote the interest of their members:

Evaluation of Bills

The chambers are entitled to evaluate bills before they are passed to Parliament. Since they have to be asked anyway, the ministries in charge of preparing new legislation often consult experts from the chambers in the drafting process.

Advisory Councils

For more than 100 years, the Austrian bureaucracy has set up advisory councils to get information and opinions from independent experts and representatives of special-interest groups. In many cases, no decision is taken before an agreement is reached in the advisory councils.

Personal Interlocking with Political Parties

Representatives of the social partners, both high-level executives and functionaries, play an important role in the two large political parties. During the Kreisky government, many experts of the Chamber of Labor and the trade unions became ministers, state secretaries or high-level executives. These channels of influence exist whether the organizations of labor, business and farmers cooperate or not. To foster cooperation among the social partners, special institutions and procedures were set up. In 1957 the social partners established the Parity Commission for Prices and Wages.

Parity Commission for Prices and Wages

The Commission was established to foster a social contract. The representatives of labor felt strong enough to enforce any wage claims, but they were prepared to moderate their claims if they got something in return. Specifically, they wanted to control price-setting in oligopolistic markets and to gain competence in general economic policy matters.

The price-wage controls introduced by the Commission were flexible and with some exceptions voluntary. The trade unions promised to contact the Commission before they started a new wage round. Firms had to ask the Commission for approval if they wanted to raise prices. In discussions of this procedure two questions usually came up. Why were firms prepared to comply with voluntary price constraints? And if they did follow the rules, would not the administered prices distort the allocation of resources?

The second question[4] is easier to answer. Prices in oligopolistic markets exceed marginal costs. Lowering these artificially high prices might have improved the allocation of resources. Moreover, firms under the rules of the Commission might have changed their strategic pricing behavior. A fixed-price regime might have helped promote a high level of employment with a minimum of inflation.

The first question is more complicated. It appears that firms were willing to cooperate because they depended in many ways on the good will of different policy agencies and because the constraints posed by the Commission were not very severe. Very likely, all that the price surveillance of the social partners could have achieved was to postpone and moderate price increases. Unfortunately, not much empirical evidence is available. The social partners only hesitantly opened their files for scientific research. They feared that unfavorable results might upset the delicate balance of power.

Advisory Council for Social and Economic Affairs

The second point of the social contract, the participation of the social partners in general economic policy, is facilitated by a council. The Advisory Council for Social and Economic Affairs was set up in 1963 as the third subcommittee of the Commission. For the representatives of labor, the Council was the second choice: as noted above, they wanted a *Wirtschaftskomission*, a top-level forum, consisting of the relevant ministers and the presidents of the four peak associations. Since the *Wirtschaftskomission* could not be realized, the Advisory Council was expected to fulfill part of its functions.

The Council was based on the technocratic idea of an economic policy guided by scientific research and advanced economic models. Members of the Council were experts from among the four social partners. The Council has worked to identify important economic questions, to analyze them with the assistance of external experts and make policy recommendations. If the presidents of the chambers and the Trade Union Federation accept the Council's proposals, the government can hardly refuse the unanimous will of the social partners.

Economic Policy Forum and High-Level Contact Group

At the end of the 1960s, the conservative party then in office established two forums for discussion between the government and the social partners on economic policy matters: the Economic Policy Forum (*Wirtschaftspolitische Aussprache*) and a High-Level Contact Group (*Verbändekomitee*). The Economic Forum was established by the chancellor as a special meeting of the Parity Commission for regular discussion of current economic prospects and their policy implications. The High-Level Contact Group was initiated by the minister of finance for an exchange of views among experts from the social partners.

Economic Policy of the Kreisky Era

The term "Austro-Keynesianism" was coined in 1979 to characterize the economic policy of the Kreisky era after the first oil price shock. In the present context the term will be used in a pragmatic way. From the very beginning, the Kreisky government was heavily, even stubbornly, committed to full employment. The administration was convinced that this dominant economic goal could not be maintained by market forces alone. Kreisky himself was skeptical about the prospects of capitalism and professed deep concern long before the 1975 recession. His government represented an outstanding example of what political scientists call the Keynesian welfare state (Lehmbruch, 1984) both in the prosperous years up to 1974 and in the adjustment period in the wake of two oil price shocks.

The relationship between the Kreisky government and the social partners can be summarized as follows:

* The policy of the socialist government encouraged social partnership to continue.
* The specific macroeconomic strategy of the Kreisky government called for an effective income policy and therefore needed the support of the social partners.
* The Kreisky government took the initiative if new problems arose. It aimed at consensus solutions but did not hesitate to act if the social partners disagreed on specific questions.

Socialist or Pragmatic Policy?

Social partnership is based on consensus on key economic and social parameters, such as the economic order (market economy or planned economy), the ownership of productive capital (private and public property) and the distribution of income (factor payments, personal incomes). Roughly speaking, social partnership favors the status quo. Since all decisions have to be taken unanimously revolutionary changes are unlikely to occur.

When in 1970, for the first time in the Second Republic, a socialist government came into office, the crucial question was whether the economic and social reforms of the new government would impair the fundamentals of social partnership. Actually, such fears were unwarranted; the main thrust of economic and social policy did not change much. Socialist governments are expected to emphasize economic planning, nationalization of core industries and a fair income distribution. Judged by these criteria the Kreisky government was only weakly socialist. It exhibited a high degree of continuity with its conservative predecessor (H. Knapp, 1986). The pragmatic stance of economic policy is illustrated by the gap between the 1968 economic program of the Socialist Party and the policy decisions by the Kreisky government.

Indicative Planning

One of the most controversial issues in the second half of the 1960s had been indicative planning according to the French model (planification). The representatives of labor had urged the representatives of capital and the conservative government to introduce this technique. In the economic program of the Socialist Party of 1968, indicative planning played a prominent role. Nevertheless, the whole idea was dropped at the very moment when the socialists had the political power to implement it. Left-wing experts criticized this decision even at a time when government planning was discredited on a worldwide scale (J. Uher, 1993). On the other hand, Ferdinand Lacina (1993), the minister of finance in office since 1985, declared that Austrian economic policy benefited from the refusal to introduce a technique that disregarded the complexity of modern industry.

Control of Public Ownership

When Kreisky formed his cabinet, Austria had the largest share of public ownership among the market economies in the West. There were no further plans for nationalization. However, the monitoring of the sector under public ownership appeared to be inefficient. The nationalization act of 1946 had established two groups of nationalized firms in manufacturing: those firms nationalized by the act and those firms belonging to the nationalized banks. In the whole postwar period, the property rights of direct and indirect nationalized industries were exercised by different ministries. The minister of finance—who until the Kreisky era came from the conservative side—was responsible for the banks, and another ministry—that traditionally was headed by a socialist—was responsible for the nationalized industries.

The Kreisky government took various steps to improve the structure of the direct nationalized firms and to reduce the political influence in this industry group. The split of ownership control, however, was not abolished. In this case, the Kreisky government deviated from the 1968 economic program of the Socialist Party. This program had proposed to reduce the power of the ministry of finance and to create a large economic ministry which would also control the indirect nationalized industries. The tension that had developed between the minister of finance and the chancellor since the middle of the 1970s was intensified by the fact that both members of the cabinet had to represent different groups of the business community (for instance, in the race for subsidies that started at the end of the 1970s).

Income Redistribution

The Kreisky government made some attempts to increase the progressivity of the system of taxes and transfer payments. The first tax reforms reduced the tax burden, especially in the lower income brackets. Furthermore, fiscal policy substituted transfer payments for tax exemptions. Yet on balance, the net redistribution was small, primarily because the government aimed at a high investment rate. To achieve this goal, investment promotion by taxes and subsidies was extended. Moreover, self-employed persons benefited from a systemic change in personal income tax in 1972 (the tax was based on individuals rather than on families). It is also worth mentioning that the Kreisky government protected farmers more than the European Community did. In 1970 farm prices in Austria were below the EC level. During the 1970s the gap was reversed. Finally, tax changes were limited by the willingness of capital to cooperate. When in 1977, the taxes on profits were increased to reduce the budget deficit, the system of social partnership was about to crash.

Credibility

In 1970 when Kreisky formed a government without a majority in Parliament he had to rely on the support of non-socialist members. In the government declaration of 1970, Kreisky did not use the word "socialism." He spoke of a modern Austria, a development towards an industrialized society. Competition was mentioned as an instrument to promote efficiency. Actually, this declaration was prepared for a coalition with the conservatives. Kreisky did not change it when he formed a minority government. Even in late 1971 when the socialists got the majority in Parliament, he maintained his stance on economic policy. J. Uher (1993) criticized the government for becoming too bureaucratic and the chancellor for leaving economic policy to his minister of finance. However, another explanation is more plausible: Kreisky believed that his government could achieve in a foreseeable future the "modernization" of the Austrian economy and society. To attain this goal he needed the votes of social groups that traditionally did not vote for the socialists: the middle classes, especially the white collar workers, parts of the rural population and the Catholics. And he needed the cooperation, or at least the tacit acceptance, of organized capital. This view is confirmed by many facts, such as his contacts to the association of manufacturing, or the selection of non-socialist ministers and state secretaries.[5]

The Kreisky government could only partly buy acceptance of its economic policy by making concessions to special-interest groups. In the whole postwar period, ministries responsible for economic issues were led by conservative ministers. What the new government badly needed was competence and credibility in economic matters. The economic program of 1968 was a first attempt to demonstrate the ability of the Socialist Party to address economic problems (F. Lacina, 1993). The real test, however, came when the socialist government had to demonstrate that it could carry out a sustainable economic policy.

One aspect of the credibility problem was that the new ministers had to come to terms with the non-socialist bureaucracy of their ministries. Hannes Androsch, the minister of finance, won the support of the civil servants in his ministry by declaring that he was looking for competence and not for party membership. Josef

Staribacher, the minister of trade and industry, declared that he would execute what the social partners had agreed upon.

"Activist" Macroeconomic Policy

The Kreisky government practiced macroeconomic fine-tuning. Economic policy had the task of steering the economy on an even path using such instruments as fiscal policy, monetary policy, exchange rate policy and—what seemed most important in the Austrian case—income policy. Fine tuning, of course, was not a special feature of economic policy in Austria. In the first half of the 1970s, most industrialized nations practiced an activist or discretionary economic policy to achieve macroeconomic goals such as full employment, internal and external financial stability and economic growth.[6]

This type of policy was largely based on what is called mainstream Keynesianism (although an interpretation from the point of fundamental Keynesianism is not excluded). This specific branch of Keynesian policy was discredited later on[7] and given up. Creating a stable framework (rules rather than discretion) became the new guideline for policy makers. In 1988 the OECD published a booklet, *Why Economic Policies Change Course* demonstrating the change of the policy stance in eleven industrialized countries between the mid-1970s and the mid-1980s.

Austria adhered to an activist economic policy longer than most other countries. The interventionist policy of the Kreisky government began in 1970 with a package of measures to contain inflation, and it ended 1982/83 with a series of public work programs designed to stimulate employment.

Coordination between different agents was a prerequisite for the success of this activist policy. Discontent could easily jeopardize the success of specific policy measures. To implement this type of policy, social partnership and the institutional framework that had been set up since 1957 was vital. This was especially true with regard to income policy. In the 1960s and 1970s a few industrialized countries had introduced wage guidelines and other techniques designed to moderate wage claims more or less voluntarily. The experience with income policy, however, was at best mixed; but in Austria income policy was reasonably successful because in was embedded in the long-standing relationship of the social partners.

The government found it easy to come to terms with the social partners because both refused to fight inflation with purely monetary measures. Monetary restrictions create unemployment, except perhaps in situations where excess demand pulls up the level of prices. Obviously, neither labor nor capital wanted demand constraints. The Advisory Council on various occasions recommended productivity enhancing measures rather than tight money to cope with inflation.[8]

The aversion to monetary restraints was probably one reason why the international recession in 1973 did not affect Austria. When the recession 1975 started, a pent-up demand in many sectors dampened the fall of output and employment.[9] On the other hand, the accommodating monetary policy fueled inflation. Although the appreciation of the currency curtailed imported inflation, in 1974 prices rose by 9.5 percent and wages by 13.6 percent.

Kreisky and Social Partnership

Kreisky was not very enthusiastic about social partnership, but his economic policy required consensus among the large social groups. This dilemma was solved pragmatically. The Kreisky government accepted and used the already-existing institutional setup designed to facilitate cooperation. The relative importance of the players, however, changed considerably. The Economic Policy Forum became more important and the scope of the Advisory Council was reduced considerably.

Concerted Actions at Top Levels

The Economic Policy Forum was convened once a quarter to implement macro-economic fine-tuning. In the morning, the Austrian Institute of Economic Research (WIFO) discussed short-term economic prospects in a working group with experts of the social partners, the central bank and ministries of economic affairs. The external experts had a chance to get familiar with the forecast and supplied the WIFO with insider information (administrative details, plans). In the afternoon, the Economic Policy Forum was convened. The meeting was introduced by short statements by the director of the Institute of Economic Research, the governor of the National Bank and the Minister of Finance. Afterwards the floor was open for discussion. Although no final decision was taken at the meeting, it had many advantages. To begin with, the top politicians had a chance to become familiar with the latest economic perspectives. If one could agree what problems had to be solved, a procedure for future actions could be set up without delay. The government had the opportunity to explain what type of action it considered appropriate. The representatives of labor, business and farmers could indicate to what degree they were prepared to follow the lead of the government.

During the 1970s, the forum was convened fairly regularly four times per year. When problems needed immediate action, special meetings were arranged. The coordinating power of the forum was confined to the 1970s. It was less influential in the last years of the conservative government because the representatives of labor used the meetings to push their ideas on medium-term strategies. And it became obsolete when economic policy refrained from fine-tuning. Since the beginning of the 1980s, the forum was convened irregularly at large intervals without any visible results.[10] In the forum, the presidents of the special-interest organizations acted as representatives of their members. They did not present themselves as social partners who had coordinated their view before the meeting and therefore were able to speak with one voice.

Actually, the social partners did not make many unanimous decisions on key issues except in their own domain of price and wages policy. The labor representatives—formerly the active part of the social partners—did not want to embarrass the socialist government. Although the trade unions always stressed that they were neutral, there obviously was a lot of coordination within the Socialist Party between the members of the trade unions and the members of the government, much more at any rate that at present. On the other hand, the conservative opposition did not use the representatives of business and of farmers to bully the socialist government as the representatives of labor did when the conservatives were in office.

The political decision-making process can be best described as a tripartite system in which the government took the lead and tried to find a consensus solution with the social partners.

Reduced Role of Experts

The gradual development of a tripartite system in which the government took the lead necessarily reduced the scope of the

Advisory Council. Originally, the social partners considered the council an important instrument for codetermination or even dominance in economic policy beyond their narrow competence (price wage policy). The fate of this council in the Kreisky area, therefore, to some degree indicates the shift in power from the social partners to the government.

The idealistic picture of a technocracy determining economic policy via the strength of the social partners was never a very accurate one.[11] The limits of the Advisory Council were already visible during its first study in 1963. To contain inflation, the council designed a stabilization program with a package of measures. The recommendations were endorsed by the presidents and presented to the government. When the government reacted slowly, the social partners urged the implementation of their program. At this stage a conflict developed, not so much between the government and the social partners but rather among the latter. The members of the Economic Chamber moaned that their internal decision-making process was unduly prejudged by the recommendations of the council. As a consequence, the maneuvering room of the council was constrained considerably, long before the Kreisky era.

The experts of the Advisory Council sought to avoid undue political pressure by emphasizing medium-term problems. A sub-group for medium-term forecasts was set up to develop a model for economic growth that could inform policy makers about the rate of economic growth to expect under specific constraints. The council obviously underestimated, however, the technical difficulties of an accurate medium-term model. The working group was dissolved in 1970. Given their preferences for medium-term planning, the representatives of labor probably would have opposed such a step under a different government.

The Advisory Council did not get a mandate to develop business-cycle strategies. In 1973, the rate of inflation was much higher than in 1963 when the first stabilization program was launched. Nevertheless, the council remained silent, which created a lot of criticism. The journal of the Economic Chamber (*Wirtschaftspolitische Blätter*, 1973) debated whether the Advisory Council was at a turning point. Actually, in 1973, the presidents of the social partners even briefly considered dissolving the council. The Advisory Council from there on produced many useful reports and helped their organizations to find solutions to problems of common interest. However, it could not fulfill its original aim: to lead the social partners in shaping economic policy in principle and in details. The word "Austro-Keynesianism" was not even mentioned by the council. Macroeconomic policy over most of the Kreisky era was shaped by the minister of finance in coordination with the national bank.

A minor point may help to complete the picture. Experts were not in great esteem with Kreisky. He mocked forecasts and was certainly not willing to accept a "dictatorship" of technocrats. He liked to confer with economists but hesitated to accept their recommendations. He was most pleased when experts declared that they could not, at least not unanimously, recommend solutions for pending problems.

Gradual Decline of Consensus

The tripartite consensus system gradually degenerated. The government became more determined to realize its plans, even if one social partner did not agree. There were some attempts to gain the support of the government when the social partners could not reach consensus in negotiations. Finally the social partners had to learn that the political parties did not automatically accept any unanimous recommendation of labor and capital.

In the first years of the Kreisky government when its position was not yet settled, the government seemed willing to accept proposals from the social partners. But when the social partners could not agree what had to be done, the government had to act. And although the government avoided overruling any one social partner, the representatives of the Economic Chamber complained that the government made up its mind before consulting the social partners (Farnleitner, 1991). In 1977, the minister of finance increased the tax burden on profits to consolidate the budget. This tax law (2. *Abgabenänderungsgesetz*) was heavily opposed by the representatives of capital.

Two further events illustrate the gradual loss of vigor in the system of social partnership. In the mid-1970s the labor representatives wanted a new law regulating working conditions. Since no agreement could be reached between the social partners, the labor representatives negotiated unilaterally with the government. The corresponding bill, however, was not presented to Parliament because the government accepted a veto by organized capital in a vital question.

The second case came up when Austria had finished the construction of an atomic power plant. Before putting the plant into operation, the chancellor wanted the approval of the opposition in Parliament, which was refused. Since the social partners favored the use of atomic energy, the president of the Trade Union Federation expected that the president of the Economic Chamber would induce the conservatives to change their minds. This attempt failed.

Strategies after OPEC I

Until the mid-1970s, Austria's economic policy was not unusual. Of course, this country had specific institutions, notably the cooperation of the big social groups and income policy based on the consensus of these groups. But neo-corporatist arrangements existed also in other European countries, especially in the Scandinavian countries. But in the second half of the 1970s, Austria attracted the attention of the international community by the temporary success of a specific macroeconomic policy. I present the main ideas in the simplified way economic policy makers face alternative strategies. The model used was textbook Keynesianism (see, for instance, Sachs/Larrain, 1993).

To minimize the adverse macroeconomic effects of the first oil price shock, Austria used a mixture of exchange rate policy, budgetary policy and income policy. The basic idea was straightforward. Higher oil prices push up costs and prices (cost-push inflation) and at the same time absorb domestic demand (demand deflation). Containing inflation by pulling the monetary brakes could dampen price increases but very likely would lead to unemployment and to a fall in output. The monetarist assumption that a credible nonaccommodating monetary policy could influence expectations in the short run was not regarded realistic. In this respect, Austria's policy-makers shared the pessimistic view of mainstream Keynesianism (Tobin, 1980).

In order to deal with both problems, cost-push inflation and demand deflation, two different sets of instruments had to be applied. Austrian economic policy solved the assignment problem in the following way: income policy and foreign exchange rate policy were used to contain cost pressures; budgetary and monetary policy were used to keep domestic demand at a full employment level.

The fact that the oil price surge was a supply shock was not overlooked. Economic policy makers understood that the adverse shift in the terms of trade and adjustment costs would call for real wage moderation. Furthermore, it was clear that the higher oil bill would threaten the trade balance. Supply side measures to reduce energy inputs and to stimulate exports to the OPEC countries were launched. Structural adjustment, however, takes time. The Austrian macro-economic policy mix was designed to buy time for an orderly adjustment process.

The Austro-Keynesian Policy Mix

The basic assumption behind the macroeconomic policy mix was that prices are sticky: firms set prices with a mark-up on prime costs, and changes in demand do not change the mark-ups, at least not in the short run. The Parity Commission supported the fixed-price regime by accepting only cost increases as a reason for higher prices. Under these conditions, aggregate demand influences output and employment in the short run.[12] It also makes sense to distinguish between cost stabilization and demand stimulation. However, policy makers probably overestimated the fixed-price property of the Austrian system of price-wage-determination.

Lead of Hard Currency Policy

The different components of the policy mix could not be used simultaneously. As far as cost stabilization is concerned, exchange rate policy took the lead. From the beginning of the 1970s the Austrian schilling was increasingly pegged to the deutschmark. As a result, the effective exchange rate rose considerably. In the first half of the 1970s, the exchange rate moved in the right direction because the AS was somewhat undervalued (Austria had not followed the appreciation of the DM in 1969). In the second half of the 1970s, however, sticking to the DM meant "leaning against the wind." The hard-currency option of Austrian economic policy seemed to be at variance with the fundamentals (the external balance and domestic inflation). For that reason, international organizations advised Austria to devalue the schilling. The monetary authorities disregarded this advice because they relied on the Austrian system of income policy. The trade unions were expected to adjust their wage claims to the hard currency option rather than the other way round.

Wage Moderation

In the first half of the 1970s, nominal wages were increasing at an accelerating rate. In 1975, during the first serious recession since World War II, effective earnings rose by more than 14 percent. Also, the trade unions felt that the wage round of 1975 was excessive. There was a general willingness to correct collective mistakes by collective actions (Scharpf, 1986). This "error correction mechanism" was one of the most important properties of the Austrian system of social partnership.

The wage moderation that started in 1977 can be illustrated by the following comparison. From the beginning of the 1970s to the beginning of the 1980s, the annual increases in nominal wages dropped from 11 percent to 5 percent, and those of real wages from 5 percent to 0.5 percent. This wage flexibility was achieved without additional unemployment. Econometric studies on an international scale showed that Austria belonged to the countries with a high wage flexibility both in nominal and in real terms.

It is an open question whether wage flexibility was a salient feature of wage negotiations in Austria. I rather guess that in 1977/78 when the foreign balance of the Austrian economy deteriorated at an alarming pace, the Austrian trade unions under president Benya made a great one-time effort to assist the socialist government. This view is to a certain degree confirmed by a working paper from Winkler and Hochreiter (1993). They found that in this (and only in this) critical period, the real appreciation of the Austrian currency was followed by a real wage moderation of the trade unions. According to K. Pichelmann's econometric studies (1990), the NAIRU (the rate of unemployment "required" to prevent inflation from accelerating) has risen sharply since the beginning of the 1980s.

Budget Deficits

The role of supporting aggregate demand was mainly assigned to budgetary policy. In 1975, a big budget deficit was incurred. This deficit was regarded as a sign of advanced macroeconomic management. No attempts were made to reduce it in 1976. Prior experience had taught that it was easy to incur a deficit, but extremely difficult to consolidate the budget afterwards. Therefore, after a year of budget deficits, strong efforts were necessary to get the budget back on track. In 1976, on the contrary, additional expansionary measures were taken. The continued budgetary stimulus was announced in January 1976 at a big economic conference in one of the main concert halls in Vienna. To this conference, the elite of policy makers and high-level executives were invited: the ministers, the bureaucracy, the social partners, the banking sector, economists and other policy relevant groups. After speeches from an expert of the OECD and the director of the Institute of Economic Research, the chancellor announced the plans of his cabinet to fight the recession.

In the first half of the 1970s, the chancellor by and large left economic policy to his minister of finance. This point is stressed by some critics who were not satisfied with the policy stance of the Kreisky cabinet.[13] In the case of fiscal policy, he defended vigorously the decision of his government. "One billion more of national debt is cheaper than 1 percent more unemployment," was one of his well-known slogans. Undoubtedly, he overestimated the possibilities of stabilizing employment in the medium-term by running budget deficits (H. Ostleitner, 1993).

Shifts in Emphasis

The policy mix of the mid-1970s for obvious reasons did not offer a sustainable solution. A small country that expands aggregate demand faster than its main trading partners is liable to run into balance of payment difficulties. That is exactly what happened. In 1977 the balance of payments on current account deteriorated rapidly. E. Streißler (1982) noted ironically: Austrian economic policy had demonstrated that budget deficits could stimulate effective demand. Unfortunately, mainly foreign suppliers benefited from the demand pull.

A shift in policy was unavoidable. In the course of 1977, a package of corrective measures (especially a sales tax on luxury goods which reduced the demand for imported cars) were taken to reduce the balance of payments deficit. At the same time, fiscal policy began to consolidate the budget. This package was coordinated between the government and the trade unions. There was a good chance that these corrective actions would suffice to consolidate the external account without a permanent loss of output and employment. The rate of inflation was brought down to 3½ percent on the average before the oil price shock. To cope with the high oil prices, programs to save energy and to stimulate exports to the OPEC were launched. Many experts believe that the Austrian policy stance could have been a lasting success if the world economy had returned to its previous growth path.

When the second oil price shock came, there was no maneuvering room left. The group of industrialized countries under the leadership of the International Monetary Fund (IMF) opted for "structural adjustment" rather than financing. The Austrian economy had become more open, and domestic economic policy had to be credible on an international scale.[14] Economic policy shifted from Austro-Keynesianism to Austria-Pragmatism (an expression first used by Herbert Salcher, the minister of finance in the last years of the Kreisky cabinet). The difference between the economic policy after OPEC-I and OPEC-II can be best illustrated with reference to aggregate demand. Between 1974 and 1977, domestic demand rose by 11 percent in real terms; between 1980 and 1983, only by 0.2 percent.

Nevertheless, until the end of 1981, the rate of unemployment could be kept below 2 percent. This was achieved by non-Keynesian measures aiming at influencing supply and demand in the labor market directly rather than indirectly via the goods markets (F. Butschek, 1985). The supply of labor was reduced by canceling permissions of foreign guest workers and by providing elderly people who had lost their jobs with early retirement pensions. The demand for labor was enhanced by shortening working hours and by keeping surplus labor on the payroll. The nationalized industries especially hoarded labor. Lowering productivity, of course, was an additional burden for wages policy. Chancellor Kreisky fought personally to secure jobs. He organized conferences for ailing firms, he talked to the workers in the factories, and he tried to attract foreign capital.

Epilogue

The Austrian policy mix, although broadly in line with mainstream Keynesianism, violated in various respects what was regarded as "conventional wisdom" at that time. According to standard policy recommendations, exchange rate policy should equilibrate the foreign balance rather than serving as a nominal anchor to contain inflation. Furthermore, structural deficiencies should be tackled at an early stage. Later, both the adjustment costs and the resistance of pressure groups will be much higher. The OECD complained of the delay of corrective actions (1986). Austria's economic policy chose longer adjustment periods to spread the social costs over a longer period and preserve consensus.

Nevertheless, the Austrian system seemed to work, at least temporarily. The fact that a small country could combine a low rate of inflation with a low rate of unemployment attracted the attention of the international community both at an academic level and on an economic policy level.

Curiously enough, the discussion and acknowledgment of Austrian economic policy started at a time when its possibilities were almost exhausted. As noted, the term "Austro-Keynesianism" was coined rather late. The main contributions of Austrian economists on a theoretical level were made between 1979 and 1985. At the same time, the international "neo-corporatism" discussion reached a peak. F. Scharpfs' book (1987) on sociodemocratic therapy against economic crisis in Europe was based on preliminary studies in the years before. Later works on Austro-Keynesianism were classified as "economic history."

The main justification for using the word "Austro-Keynesianism" is that Kreisky himself liked it. He once remarked that Austro-Keynesianism had as much to do with Keynes as Austro-Marxism had to do with Marx, namely nothing.[15] That invites questions about what Kreisky really meant: was Austro-Keynesianism just Keynesianism in Austria or something special?

According to the Keynesian paradigm, a high level of aggregate demand can be attained either by demand management or by built-in stability of the economic system. I have stressed the macroeconomic policy mix because I am more familiar with that line of reasoning and because it corresponds to the understanding of the policy makers of that time (Ostleitner, 1993). This view does not exclude additional structural components stressed by other authors. According to Gunther Tichy[16] (1990), the Austrian economy has shown a high degree of cyclical stability over the whole postwar period. The observed resistance against shocks can be explained by systemic properties that tend to stabilize expectations in a world characterized by fundamental uncertainty.

Herbert Ostleitner (1993) offers a interesting bridge between "mechanistic" and "structural" views. He argues that structural features made the macro policy of the Austrian government "dynamically consistent." The system of social partnership implied an ex-ante coordination of economic policy with the representatives of the big social groups. The high degree of centralization of the trade unions enhanced their capacity to act strategically. Last but not least, the representatives of labor learned to look at microeconomic problems from the viewpoint of the management.

These explanations evaluate events in a specific time span. Egon Matzner (1993), on the other hand, uses a normative interpretation. He regards Austro-Keynesianism as an unfinished program to change the decision-making structure of the economic network.

In the field of economic policy, the Austrian strategy gained international reputation between 1980 and 1983. In spring 1981, for example, a representative of the Austrian government was invited to the Joint Economic Committee of the U.S. Congress to testify on "Austria's Income Policy: Lesson for the United States."

In Austria's economic policy, the separation from Austro-Keynesianism was accelerated by the end of the Kreisky era in 1983. Succeeding governments found that Austro-Keynesianism was a short-term device to bridge a recession partly by delaying adjustments. They complained that they had to solve the structural adjustment problems on a macro-level (budget deficits) and on a micro-level (restructuring the nationalized industries) that they had inherited from Austro-Keynesianism.

NOTES

1. M. Olson (p. 53): "Encompassing organizations have some incentive to make the society in which they operate more prosperous, and an incentive to redistribute income to their members with as little excess burden as possible . . . ."

2. The market paradigm of economists probably explains that "neo-corporatism" was mainly analyzed by political scientists and economists outside the mainstream.

3. According to F. Klenner (*Arbeit und Wirtschaft*, April 1970), the Trade Union Federation's claims to a new government consisted of active labor market policy, nationalization of the basic industries, a long-term economic concept, social partnership, the enlargement of the Parity Commission for Prices and Wages to an Economic Commission.

4. This point was especially raised when I had the opportunity to present the Austrian stabilization policy before the economic policy committee of the German economic association. (H. Seidel, 1983).

5. One of his "bonmot" was: "In Austria we do not have big capitalists. We just have small ones, and with the small ones we socialists can live."

6. The term "activist" is used in conformity with standard macroeconomics. See for instance: Sachs/Larrain, 1993, Chapter 19.

7. That is probably one of the reasons why in defining Austro-Keynesianism some authors stressed fundamental or structural features.

8. For that reason the term "Austro-monetarism" favored by K. Socher (1982) seems to me misplaced. On the other hand, one has to agree that it was never discussed why an exchange rate constraint is less "restrictive" than a monetary constraint.

9. According to F. Scharpf (1986), this was one of the main differences between German and Austrian economic policy. The Germans had pulled on the monetary brakes when the recession started.

10. Between 1968 and 1981 I had the opportunity to participate in more than fifty meetings. In the same time span afterwards my successor in the Institute of Economic Research attended less than a dozen meetings.

11. B. Marin (1982) in sociological analysis spoke of revolution of the technocratic elite against the traditional way of policy making. This characteristic was flavored by interviews with leading personalities of the Advisory Council. See H. Seidel (1993).

12. The "new Keynesian approach" tries to explain nominal and real rigidities with imperfections in the markets for goods, labor and credit. See especially: O. J. Blanchard, S. Fischer (1989).

13. In many cases, economic policy makers rightly stress that their decisions were based on inaccurate forecasts by the Institute for Economic Research. In that case, the forecasters cannot be blamed. The mid-December forecast for 1976 indicated that an upswing was already under way.

14. At the beginning of the 1980s I had the opportunity to represent Austria on various occasions. The first question I was confronted with was, "How big is the Austrian exposure to Eastern Europe?"

15. H. Ostleitner (1993) mentioned that Kreisky was not aware of the term "Austro-Keynesianism" until very late. However, Kreisky was familiar from 1975 on with the above-given interpretation of the oil price shocks and approved it. In 1977 I was asked to support him preparing a speech in Parliament. In my short note I explained the Austrian policy mix. He liked the basic idea and asked me if he could quote me in his speech in Parliament. In the debate, one member of the opposition sneered: "Policy mix - policy nix."

16. Convenient summaries and surveys of the literature on Austro-Keynesianism can be found in *Wirtschaftspolitische Blätter* 1982, in Mitter/Wörgötter 1990, and in Weber/Venus, 1992.

FURTHER LITERATURE

Sven Arndt, ed., *The Political Economy of Austria* (Washington & London: American Enterprise Institute, 1982).

O. J. Blanchard and S. Fischer, *Lectures on Macroeconomics* (Cambridge, Massachusetts, London, England: The MIT Press, 1989).

Felix Butschek, *Die österreichische Wirtschaft im 20. Jahrhundert* (Vienna: Österreichisches Institut für Wirtschaftsforschung, 1985).

Josef Farnleitner, "Die Zukunft der Sozialpartnerschaft," *Wirtschaftspolitische Blätter* 38/1 (1991): 96-105.

P. Gerlich, E. Grande, and W. C. Müller, *Sozialpartnerschaft in der Krise?* (Vienna: Hermann Böhlaus Nachf., 1985).

Randall W. Kindley, "Rational Organization: Labor's Role in the Emergence and Reproduction of Austrian Neo-Coporatism," Ph.D. Dissertation, Duke University, 1992.

Karl Korinek, "Das System der österreichischen Sozialpartnerschaft. Skizze der Bedingungen, der Prinzipien und der Grenzen des Systems," in *Phänomen Sozialpartnerschaft*, ed. Georg Schöpfer (Vienna: Hermann Böhlaus Nachf., 1980) 9-21.

Ferdinand Lacina, "Austro-Keynesianismus," in F. Weber/T. Venus, eds., *Austro-Keynesianismus in Theorie und Praxis*, 15-20.

Gerhard Lehmbruch, "Österreichs sozialpartnerschaftliche System im internationalen Vergleich," in *Methoden der Politikberatung im wirtschaftspolitischen Bereich*, Nr. 44 der Studien des Beirats für Wirtschafts - und Sozialfragen (Vienna, 1984): 41-62.

Berndt Marin, *Die Paritätische Kommission* (Vienna: Internationale Publikationen, 1982).

Egon Matzner, "Was bleibt von 78-er Programm? Der radikale Keynesianismus und das Konzepte der Entscheidungsverhältnisse," in F. Weber/T. Venus, eds., *Austro-Keynesianismus in Theorie und Praxis*, 150-54.

P. Mitter and A. Wörgötter, eds., *Austro-Keynesianismus. Festschrift für Hans Seidel zum 65. Geburtstag* (Heidelberg: Physica-Verlag, 1990).

OECD, *Why Economic Policies Change Course* (Paris, 1988).

Mancur Olson, *The Rise and Decline of Nations* (New Haven and London: Yale University Press, 1982).

Herbert Ostleitner, "Die Budgetpolitik des Austro-Keynesianismus," in F. Weber/T. Venus, eds., *Austro-Keynesianismus in Theorie und Praxis*, 105-12.

Anton Pelinka, "Gegenwind - Die Änderungen des politischen Umfeldes und die Arbeit der Handelskammerorganisation in den neunziger Jahren," *Wirtschaftspolitische Blätter*, 38/1 (1991): 67-73.

Karl Pichelmann, "Unemployment Dynamics; Wage Flexibility and the NAIRU in Austria," *Empirica. Austrian Economic Papers* 17/2 (1990): 171-86.

Fritz W. Scharpf, *Sozialdemokratische Krisenpolitik in Europa* (Frankfurt: Campus Verlag, 1987).

Hans Seidel, *Der Beirat für Wirtschafts- und Sozialfragen* (Vienna: Österreichisches Institut für Wirtschaftsforschung, 1993).

_____, *Austrian Incomes Policy: Lesson for the United States*, Prepared Statement before the Joint Economic Committee, Washington D.C., 1981.

J. D. Sachs and B. F. Larrain, *Macroeconomics In The Global Economy* (Englewood Cliffs, New Jersey: Prentice Hall, 1993).

Sozialistische Partei Österreichs, *Reform der österreichischen Wirtschaft: Leistung, Aufstieg, Sicherheit* (Vienna: Vorwärts Verlag, 1968).

Erich Streißler, "Das Ende des Austro-Keynesianismus," *Wirtschaftspolitiche Blätter*, 29/3 (1982): 65-77.

Gunther Tichy, "Vom Glanz und Elend des Austro-Keynesianismus," in *Wirtschaftspolitiche Blätter*, 29/3 (1982): 65-77.

James Tobin, "Stabilization Policy Ten Years After," *Brookings Papers on Economic Acitivity*, 1/1980: 19-71.

Julian Uher, "Entstehung und politische Durchsetzung des Wirtschaftsprogramms 1968," in F. Weber/T. Venus, eds., *Austro-Keynesianismus in Theorie und Praxis*, 37-59.

F. Weber and T. Venus, eds., *Austro-Keynesianismus in Theorie und Praxis in* Stiftung Bruno Kreisky Archiv vol. 1, (Vienna 1993).

Hannes Wimmer, ed., *Wirtschafts-und Sozialpartnerschaft in Österreich* (Vienna, 1984).

"Der Beirat für Wirtschafts-und Sozialfragen vor einer Wende?" *Wirtschaftspolitische Blätter*, 20/6 (1973): 378-401.

The Present and Future State of Social Partnership

Ferdinand Karlhofer

Introduction

The past one and a half decades have not been the heyday of
European corporatism. Essential constituents of macro-economic
steering, above all centralism, were severely challenged by the
international neoliberal drive of the 1980s. Virtually all national
economies have become deregulated and more flexible. Yet
corporatism has not been simply replaced by pluralist modes of
governance. Some scholars' diagnoses about the future of organized
capitalism have been, possibly, premature: Scott Lash and John Urry,
for example, predicted an irreversible trend toward disorganized
capitalism.[1]

While countries with long corporatist traditions have reflected no
definite decline, other countries with weak corporatism[2], such as the
Mediterranean countries, France, and Ireland, have intensified their
efforts for social concertation. Tripartism, (that is, formal or informal
relations among labor, capital, and the state) has been limited in
scope, but has not been terminated where it had existed before.[3] All
in all, it is surprising how little the structure of industrial relations
systems has changed. As Oliver Clarke pointed out in a recent essay,
"What happened was that the forces at work changed the output of
the system without necessitating systemic change."[4]

What can be observed, however, is a general shift of the "center
of gravity" of economic and industrial-relations systems from the
level of macro-economic management to the micro-level of firms.[5]
As a result, the sectoral level has gained importance at the expense
of centralized national governance.[6] Corporatist regimes have,
perforce, been affected by this development, with the result that the
1980s witnessed "the decomposition of many national corporatisms

within Europe, not into pluralism, but into varieties of meso-level corporatism."[7]

This pattern does not strictly apply to Austrian *Sozialpartnerschaft* (social partnership). Austro-Corporatism is still characterized by giving higher priority to the macro-level. Yet the winds of change are also blowing in Austria. The following essay will examine the extent of change in Austro-Corporatism as well as its present problems and future prospects.

Defining Austro-Corporatism

Like the Scandinavian countries, Austria has a highly corporatist economy. Experts consider these countries to be neocorporatist models,[8] in contrast to Switzerland and Japan, which—despite their low degree of centralization—feature peculiar consociational systems.[9] In terms of organization, Austrian corporatism indeed has much in common with Scandinavia, particularly Sweden:

* small number of labor and employer organizations (monopoly or oligopoly);
* high degree of concentration and organizational centralization;
* a certain degree of autonomy of the elites from the rank-and-file (upward delegation, downward control);
* existence of inter-organizational networks of interest representation ensuring stable and calculable political exchange;
* coordination and synchronization of sectoral collective bargaining by the national peak associations;
* collaboration of worker and employer organizations with the government in macro-economic steering (in particular concerning income policy);
* labor-dominated corporatism, in which the unions play the leading role (not possible without the existence of a strong Social Democratic party).

What is exceptional about Austro-Corporatism? It is the interplay of at least three features that has kept the Austrian version of corporatism stable—the legal framework, the chamber system, and the interlacing of associations and political parties.

The Legal Framework

The legal provisions regulating the relations between employers and employees (both individually and collectively) took shape in the First Republic and were slightly modified after 1945.[10] Most important is the Works Constitution Act (*Arbeitsverfassungsgesetz*) which provides that in plants with at least five employees a works council (*Betriebsrat*) is to be elected by the staff. Acting as the shop-floor representation of workers, the *Betriebsrat* holds a key position for union power. The relationship between works councils and unions is one of interdependence. The enterprise is the domain of the works council, whereas the union is dominant at the supra-plant level. The works council relies upon information, legal advice, and various support provided by the union. The union, in return, depends on the organizing activities of the works council, which undertakes the recruitment of, and service to, union members. A huge majority of works council members are union members (100 percent of blue-collar, and about 85 percent of white-collar representatives); disposing of revenues of their own, the *Betriebsräte* provide relief to the union financially.

Since the works council is urged by law to cooperate with management, it decisively contributes to the low level of strike activities in Austria.

The Chamber System

All relevant status groups are organized in self-governed chambers with compulsory membership: employers, peasants, physicians, lawyers, etc. And, arguably the most remarkable feature, there is also as institution covering all employees except public servants: the Chambers of Labor (*Kammern für Arbeiter und Angestellte*). From the very beginning, the Chambers of Labor have been an instrument of the unions: the latter taking care of "political" questions, the former providing expertise and services. The membership fee of the Chamber of Labor amounts 0.5 percent of the employee's gross income; hence, the chamber system represents a most helpful "external" support for union power, both organizationally and financially.

The chambers, as statutory corporations, are entitled to represent their members' interests extensively. Their sphere of influence includes the self-governance of the social security system, formal involvement in social and economic legislation, representation in an immense number of tripartite advisory boards.

Interlacing of Associations and Political Parties

Both the chambers and the ÖGB (*Österreichischer Gewerkschaftsbund*, Austrian Trade Union Federation) are governed by political factions deriving their strength from elections. Throughout the Second Republic, the predominant groups have been supported by the *Lager* (camp) parties ÖVP (*Österreichische Volkspartei*, Austrian People's Party) and SPÖ (*Sozialistische Partei Österreichs*, Austrian Socialist Party), the former holding the majority in employers organizations (Chambers of Business, Chambers of Agriculture), the latter controlling the associations of employees (Chambers of Labor[11], ÖGB). The close ties between associations and political parties have been conducive to the efficiency of the social partnership, the more so as the *Lager* parties until recently controlled the overwhelming majority of seats in the Austrian parliament (see below).

To emphasize the striking peculiarities of Austria's political system, scholars coined the terms *Kammerstaat* (also: *Verbändestaat*, chamber-state) and *Parteienstaat* (party-state)[12]: a political system distinguished by stability of structures, mutual calculability for the actors, and continuity in the formulation and implementation of policies.

Social and Economic Performance

Industrial Disputes

Austria has one of the lowest strike rates of the OECD, ranking second behind Switzerland. It is noteworthy that the other countries with strong corporatism described above have considerably higher rates of industrial disputes. Sweden's rate, for instance, is about 20 times higher record than Austria (see appendix 1). From this we can conclude that corporatist arrangements do not necessarily result in labor quiescence.[13]

Recent research on neocoporatism suggests plausibly taking different cultures and mentalities into consideration. As Pekkarinen et al. pointed out, there is a big difference between Austrian and Nordic corporatism.[14] The latter rests on the institutionalization of conflict, the former is based on the institutionalization of consensus. Institutionalization of conflict refers to a model where "labour and capital are organized from below according to the principles of democracy and are regarded as labour market parties whose autonomy and conflict rights are respected and not violated . . . . The institutionalization of partnership or consensus is different in the sense that industrial peace may be achieved at the expense of groups which are either economically or politically too weak to have any considerable bargaining power, that is by excluding them from the bargaining table."[15] In other words, compared to the Scandinavian system which is more solidaristic, egalitarian, inclusive, Austrian corporatism is more selective, non-egalitarian, exclusive.

In Austria, a strike is often regarded as an alarming event that should be overcome immediately (obviously a reminiscence of Austria's authoritarian heritage); it is the responsibility of the ÖGB to decide whether a strike is legitimate. In the 1970s, when the share of spontaneous stoppages increased, many strikes were refused the official authorization by the union.[16] Today, particularly in the private sector, the total of working days lost due to strikes is infinitely small. As appendix 2 shows, 80 percent of the days lost are caused by disputes in the public service sector which has become substantially more militant in the past decade.

Income Policy

With regard to income policy we have once more to distinguish between inclusive corporatism of the Scandinavian type, and Austria's exclusive corporatism. From a union perspective, income policy has to focus on redistribution from capital to labor and on solidaristic wage policy, that is promotion of wage equality and avoidance of wage drift.[17] As for income distribution, the "wage ratio (adjusted for changes in employment structures) of national income oscillated about 65 percent since the sixties—with a tendency to decline last year [i.e. 1990]." However, there are "no explicit targets concerning income distribution. Implicitly, by tying wage increases to productivity growth, the trade unions accept a constant functional distribution of income."[18] Wage drift in the Austrian economy is considerably higher than in other corporatist economies. Union activities have not contributed to a reduction of wage inequality. Frequently, in large enterprises with strong Works councils, a low national wage agreement is followed by plant-level wage rounds by which the wage drift is increased. "However, at least for Austrian workers this lack of wage solidarity is to some extent compensated by a generous welfare state. State expenditure was particularly strong in the 1970s, rising from 42.2 percent of GDP in 1970 to 49.7 percent in 1975 and then again to 56.3 percent in 1987."[19]

With respect to inter-industry wage differentials (dispersion), Austria ranks highest in Europe, closely behind the United States and Canada within the OECD (see appendix 3). The differences in Austria are expected to increase due to "wage dumping" by the neighboring East European economies.[20]

Another indicator for wage inequality is the differential in men's and women's earnings (see appendix 4). The gender gap is considerably higher in Austria than in other countries. Evidently, social partnership does not pursue an active policy of overcoming wage discrimination against women.

Economic Performance[21]

About a decade and a half ago, the *New York Times* called the Austrian economy "a Strauss waltz," and praised the then-union president as "probably the only European union leader who regularly lectures visitors about the need for profits" (22 March 1981). Today's observers agree that there is a close correlation between social partnership and economic performance.[22]

According to the most common indicators of economic performance, Austria passed through the recession of the turn of the decade comparably well (see appendix 5). In terms of economic growth, inflation, and unemployment, Austria is above the average of the European OECD-countries and shows better results than the Scandinavian countries as well. With an unemployment rate of 3.6 percent in the period 1990-3, Austria ranked third, behind Switzerland and Japan; in growth rate it ranked fourth and in inflation rate, eighth.

The Institutional Reform of 1992

In the early 1990s, the increasing frictions between the social partners, in particular between business and labor, could hardly be ignored. It is tempting to explain this friction in terms of the change of power that had occurred in the late 1980s. Both the

Bundeswirtschaftskammer (Federal Chamber of Economics) and the ÖGB had been headed by the same persons about twenty-five years. It was an open secret that these men, both strong personalities undisputed within their respective organizations, maintained friendly relations free of resentment and distrust. Of course, economic interests have always determined the relations between labor and capital. The advantage of friendly relations became obvious when the succeeding generation took over the presidency; suddenly, the atmosphere became icy. In default of intra-organizational unanimity, internal weakness was externally compensated by changing the tune.[23]

In November 1992, the presidents of the "big four" (Chamber of Business, Chamber of Agriculture, ÖGB and Chamber of Labor) came together to reconsider the corporatist framework. The meeting was concluded with an agreement concerning the reform of the basic institutions of social partnership.[24] Beyond the institutional need for reform, this document expressed the good will to continue the well-tried pattern of conflict resolution: "Social partnership is characterized by a special culture of exchange of ideas and negotiation, and by the willingness of the associations involved to stand for a compromise internally and externally, and to represent diverging interests under consideration of medium-term objects and societal interests. This requires a permanent dialogue and a continuing exchange of ideas."[25]

The institutions of social partnership were modified as follows (see appendix 6).

Parity Commission

The Parity Commission, the core of the Austrian model of corporatism, was founded in 1957 and is composed of the four big associations, which send an equal number of representatives (in total 54). On the whole, this core has remained unchanged up to this day. The members of this board come together at least four times every year, while the presidents of the "big four" meet every month. Any majority rule would violate the principle of voluntary cooperation.[26] Since 1966, the representatives of the government, including the federal chancellor, have been non-voting members of the Commission. In 1992, the minister of finance became a permanent (non-voting) member of the Parity Commission.

Sub-Committee for Prices

Joint price setting for certain products (e.g. flour, bread, gas, etc.) became anachronistic in the course of time. To abolish this sub-committee, however, would have affected the symmetry of labor and business representation. Instead, the field of activities was altered: the sub-committee for prices primarily has focused on questions of competitive trade and on the observation of developments in the economic sectors.

Sub-Committee for Wages

Now as before, the Sub-committee for Wages controls the timing of collective bargaining at the national or sectoral levels. The initiative for applications lies with the ÖGB.

Advisory Board for Economic and Social Questions

Established in 1963, the Advisory Board consists of several teams which prepare recommendations for the Parity Commission. Its growing importance in recent years has been demonstrated by the increasing number of working groups (to which each association sends four members). In 1992, for example, a permanent working group for environmental questions was established.

Sub-Committee for International Issues

Internationalization has increasingly become a challenge for national economic policy as well as for the national industrial-relations systems. Thus, the establishment of the Sub-committee for International Issues, agreed upon in the 1992 paper, is the most essential innovation since 1963. It grew out of Austria's entry into the EU on the one hand and the opening of the Eastern market on the other. Its primary task is to evaluate the current international process and to submit expertise and proposals to the Parity Commission.

The Crisis of the Structural Preconditions

Apart from some urgent modifications as mentioned above, the past decade was a period of unbroken institutional stability; in particular, the Parity Commission has remained unchanged. Below the surface, however, major changes in the environment began to undermine the *structural* preconditions of corporatist interest mediation. The transformation of Austria's political system is reflected in the rapid decomposition of the ideological camps (*Lager*), the hesitant withdrawal of the associational representatives from Parliament, and, most recently, a serious decline of the legitimacy of the chambers. These changes were accompanied by a series of political scandals attributed to the *Lager* parties' "clientilistic" practices which contributed to the decomposition of the political *Lager*.

Decomposition of the Political Lager

The dominant political parties, SPÖ and ÖVP, formed ideological camps according to class cleavages and other structural features: the SPÖ, the party of the working class, was oriented toward the urban and secular part of society; the ÖVP, the party of peasants and self-employed, was directed towards the rural and Roman Catholic sector of the population. There was little scope for additional actors beyond this configuration of homogeneous social milieus characterized by conflict in the rank-and-file and consensual relations among the elites.[27]

Though lagging behind developments in Western European countries, the social structure in Austria became increasingly heterogeneous. With the decay of the social milieus, the foundations of the *Lager* started to crumble as well. The party concentration, that is the shares of votes of the two largest parties, gradually declined from 93.3 percent in 1975 to 84.4 percent in 1986 (see appendix 7). With every following election, SPÖ and ÖVP lost a total of some 10 percent. Since 1994, they have depended on the support of a third party to enact laws that require a two-thirds majority.

Thirty-three percent of skilled workers (the former core group of the social democratic labor movement) and 30 percent of entrepreneurs (until the turn of the decade a clear ÖVP domain) voted for the right-wing populist FPÖ.[28] Given the strong drive against the chamber system by this party, the landslide election hit the *Lager* parties to an extent that induced a commentator to coin the metaphor "tectonic dislocations." As a matter of fact, the Austrian political landscape has changed thoroughly; no longer can it be classified as a "two-and-a-half-party system" as had been the case since the 1950s.

Retreat of Associations from Parliamentary Representation

The interlacing of associational and political functions is a specific feature of Austro-Corporatism, dating back to the year 1945. Ever since then, political parties have controlled the associations' political composition. This is expressed best in the internal structure of the ÖVP which consists of three sub-groups representing business, labor and peasants, while the SPÖ has primarily a formal group of social democratic unionists. In 1978, more than half of the members of Parliament (55.7 percent) were high-ranking leaders of labor or business organizations (see appendix 8). The ratio decreased significantly until 1987 (43.7 percent) and then again to 33.9 percent in 1991. Although the most recent biographical data of representatives are not yet available, there are good reasons to estimate the share of high-ranking leaders of labor or business organizations at lower than 25 percent. In 1994, for instance, the newly elected president of the Federal Chamber of Labor gave up her seat in Parliament.

The most plausible explanation for the declining influence of the associations is that they no longer furnish the social core groups for the political parties. Manual workers are no longer a reliable core group of the SPÖ, and entrepreneurs or farmers have ceased to be a natural reservoir of voters for the ÖVP. Due to the emergence of new societal cleavages—gender, ecology, or simply the dichotomy libertarian vs. authoritarian—electoral behavior has become volatile and therefore less calculable for the political parties. Their link with certain social groups might prove to be counterproductive in the end.

The Chambers' Legitimacy Challenged

The organizational density of both labor and employer associations has decreased worldwide since the 1980s. On the labor side, albeit less dramatically than in most other countries, this could be noticed in Austria, too: the union density rate fell from 48.1 percent in 1986 to 42.3 percent in 1993 (see appendix 9). Given the ÖGB's monopoly in workers' interest representation, union power is still high. This might change abruptly, however, once the density rate falls below 40 percent, and there is no indication for a reversal of the trend.

The chambers, as organizations with compulsory membership, are not faced with density problems since there is no exit option for discontented members. Thus, it is not associability but the turnout in elections (as a measure for legitimacy) that must serve as an indicator for organizational stability.

Austria is a country with an extraordinary high level of participation in elections, amounting to more than 90 percent in national elections.[29] For decades, the chambers enjoyed a satisfying turnout, too: about 70 percent with peasants and entrepreneurs, more than 60 percent with workers.

Since the late 1980s all the big chambers have registered turnout declines of 10 percent and more. The Chamber of Labor elections of 1989, with the background of irregularities of high-ranking functionaries, hit a new low of only 48 percent. This was regarded with alarm and led to a reform of the chamber structures passed in 1991. The chambers, traditionally instruments of the unions, have begun to emphasize their autonomy, which has triggered friction between chamber and union officials.[30]

The elections of 1994, overshadowed by new scandals (exorbitant incomes of chamber officials), ended in a disastrous participation rate of only 31 percent. This decline has caused many to question the very existence of the chamber system. As a consequence, the coalition parties and the social partners made an agreement concerning ballots about compulsory membership to be held in all chambers not later than 1996.

According to opinion polls, an overwhelming majority of Austrians is against compulsory membership. Should the chambers fail to regain the confidence of their members, the ballots will definitely result in the dissolution of the chambers since voluntary membership is incompatible with the chambers' legal basis.[31] Moreover, indirectly this would shake the social partnership to its very foundations.

Coping with the European Challenge

Significantly more successful were the social partners with respect to Austria's integration into the European Union. Since January 1995, Austria has been a member of the EU. In a referendum, the population voted 2 to 1 to join the Union. Many observers forecast a drastic decline of corporatist macro-economic steering after the entry. Various areas of responsibilities, for example income policy and social policy, are partially removed from national control and will henceforth be substantially determined by Union regulations.[32] Why, then, did the social partners, both labor and employers, unanimously support the government's efforts? The prospects for social partnership in the EU are without doubt ambiguous. The actors themselves, however, have regarded it as more attractive to join the EU than to remain outside.

Integration effects were to be expected even in case Austria had not joined the EU. Hence, organized labor and business decided to play a proactive role—and it paid. On 22 April 1994, two months before the referendum, the coalition parties SPÖ and ÖVP entered into an agreement concerning the formal incorporation of the social partners into Austria's representation in Brussels:

> The Austrian Chamber of Business (including the Federation of Austrian Industrialists), the Federal Chamber of Labor, the Austrian Trade Union Federation and the Presidential Conference of the Austrian Chambers of Agriculture, having been involved in the preparation and execution of the talks with the EU and the respective committees of the EES, are assured full equality in participating in Austrian decision-making in all important subject matters concerning them. For this purpose representatives of these interest organizations are given a share both in domestic opinion making and in the relevant EU bodies (e.g. committees, Council groups, funds, endowments). The integration of the social partners into the Austrian mission has proven beneficial in concrete terms since Austria's application for membership and shall be continued with the object of optimal representation and coordination of Austrian interests in future EU activities. In order to assure this, financial support for international and EU activities of the social partners will be provided, and the social partners will be permanently integrated into the Austrian mission in Brussels.

As a result, the Austrian mission in Brussels is the only representation of a member state harboring both government officials and interest organizations in one house. From the very beginning, social partners and officials have cooperated closely. The principle of continuous streamlining of interests is expressed in a weekly *jour fixe* involving all representations. So far, the creation of the Austrian mission has extended the domestic corporatist pattern to the supranational level.[33]

Prospects

Some scholars expect a slow fading out of corporatism due to the European integration process that involves a shift of numerous responsibilities from the nation-state to the supranational level and so erodes the national properties.[34] Others point out that it is not only European integration that undermines the national systems but also the internationalization of the economy. Even before Austria's entry to the EU, "large privately-owned companies have continuously increased their economic weight over the last decade." This development "will make Austrian firms as independent as those in other countries of labour's support in advancing their interests."[35]

We have to take into consideration, however, that just as the nation state is not simply withering away the national arrangements cannot be abolished so easily, as Philippe C. Schmitter has noted:

It will take more than the removal of barriers of trade, the liberalisation of finance, the globalisation of production and the standardisation of consumer tastes to extirpate capitalism's national orientation. Firms (not to mention, individual capitalists) will still identify themselves with a particular society and seek the special protection of a particular state for the foreseeable future. They may adventitiously create new supra and subnational ways of doing business at the sectoral level, but they will continue to depend on the considerable variety of national governance mechanisms that they have so painstakingly (if often surreptitiously) constructed over the years.[36]

As mentioned above, the social partners were fully aware of the changes to be expected after Austria joined the EU. This and the active role they played in the negotiations between Austrian and EU authorities allowed them to secure "seat and vote" in the Austrian Mission in Brussels. It remains to be seen whether Austro-Corporatism stands the test in the supranational arena.

As for domestic development, Austrian corporatism in the mid-1990s finds itself in an apparently paradoxical situation. Now as before the social partnership enjoys a high reputation right across all social groups. Some two-thirds of the population regard this system to be beneficial for Austria's economy (see appendix 10). On the other hand, in striking contrast with the former, the actors of the system, i.e. the big chambers, suffer from a severe crisis of legitimacy.

The puzzle can be solved when one recalls that only a small minority of the Austrians have an idea what social partnership really is and how it works. It is mainly the connotations of the term *Sozialpartnerschaft*, suggesting harmony and absence of conflict, that make the people support the system. This does not apply, however, for the actors of the system. As pointed out above, the criticism of compulsory membership is increasing—mainly because of material reasons and not just as a reflex to patronizing.

Certain groups of employers, such as wholesalers, and the tourist industry, emphasize their regional or sectoral particularism of interest and oppose the traditional practices of interest mediation. In recent years, several branches at the province level have repeatedly refused to approve the collective agreements concluded between the chambers of commerce and the ÖGB at the national level.

In October 1993, when the annual wage negotiations in the metal industry were opened, the ÖGB made an offer concerning a so-called "opening clause" in wage agreements: managers and works councils at individual firms could decide jointly whether to spend some of a planned pay increase on investment instead.[37] Due to numerous cases of improper use, the opening clause was not renewed in the following year.

This incident indicates the need to loosen the traditional centralism in wage negotiations. It cannot be ignored that the social partnership, established in the aftermath of World War II for steering the economic recovery process, is now troubled with "oversteering"[38] and major difficulties in regaining the balance. A certain decentralization of the structures, as has already been occurring in other corporatist countries, is absolutely necessary for the system to survive.[39]

APPENDIX 1: Strikes in OECD European Countries
(Workers involved in strikes per thousand employees)

	1988	1989	1990	1991	1992	1988-92	Rank Order
Switzerland	0.26	0.08	1.20	0.15	...	0.34	1
Austria	3.04	1.04	3.03	19.59	2.48	5.84	2
Netherlands	1.70	4.44	37.33	16.84	14.93	15.05	3
Germany	1.76	4.14	14.56	6.03	60.24	17.35	4
Denmark	40.80	22.83	41.89	30.07	26.98	32.51	5
France	60.98	43.84	28.48	26.61	18.64	35.71	6
Norway	45.44	9.50	78.74	1.46	207.45	68.52	7
UK	166.32	182.16	83.10	34.23	24.17	98.00	8
Sweden	199.11	100.94	187.66	5.38	7.32	100.08	9
Finland	87.63	97.52	445.73	230.32	41.38	180.52	10
Italy	197.38	262.88	299.59	170.74	...	186.12	11

Source: ILO, *Yearbook of Labour Statistics*; OECD, *Quarterly Labour Force Statistics*.

APPENDIX 2:   **Strikes in Austria 1984–93**
Most Affected Economic Sectors

Year	Number of Strikers	Number of Working Days Lost	Most Affected Economic Sectors	
			Sector	Days lost (share of total)
1984	289	544	Construction industry	52%
1985	35,531	22,752	Public service	96%
1986	3,222	3,253	Public service	92%
1987	7,203	4,822	Public service	69%
1988	24,252	8,542	Public service	88%
1989	3,715	2,986	Public service	97%
1990	5,274	8,870	Food industry	53%
1991	92,707	58,341	Public service	98%
1992	18,039	7,562	Public service	99%
1993	7,512	16,420	Transport, storage	83%
Ø	19,774	13,409	Public service	80%

Source: Official strike reports.

APPENDIX 3: **Dispersion of Industry Earnings Within OECD Countries, 1975/86**
(Variance of Logarithm of Earnings by Industry, Multiplied by 100)*

	Earnings Dispersion	
	1975	**1986**
High and Increasing		
USA	25	28
Japan	26	29
Canada	22	26
Austria	**21**	**25**
Increasing		
New Zealand	14	20
UK	19	19
Australia	21	24
Norway	10	12
Moderate and Stable		
Belgium	19	20
Ireland	19	20
Germany	17	19
Netherlands	15	16
Switzerland	19	17
Decreasing		
Italy	22	13
France	15	14
Low		
Denmark	10	10
Sweden	9	10
Finland	14	14

* BLS data, except New Zealand, Norway, Finland (ILO data, 1975/84); Australia (UN data, 1973/83).

Source: Dell'Aringa/ Lodovici, *Industrial Relations*, 51.

APPENDIX 4:   Wage Differentials by Sex

**Women's Earnings as Percentage
of Men's (1987)**

Austria	67
Switzerland	68
USA	69
Canada	69
Germany	71
France	78
Norway	83
Sweden	90

Source: Appelt, "Sozialpartnerschaft und Fraueninteressen," in Tálos, ed., *Sozialpartnerschaft*, 260.

APPENDIX 5: Growth, Unemployment and Inflation 1986-93
(Percentage Change from Previous Year-Average
Over Period)

	Real GNP			Standardized Unemployment Rates			Consumer Prices		
	a 1986-89	b 1991-93	b-a	a 1986-89	b	b-a 1990-93	a 1986-89	b	b-a 1990-93
Austria	2.7	2.2	-0.6	3.4	3.6	0.2	1.9	3.6	1.7
Belgium	3.2	1.3	-1.9	10.6	10.1	-0.5	1.8	3.2	1.4
Denmark	1.4	1.1	-0.3	8.4	10.8	2.4	4.3	2.1	-2.2
Finland	4.2	-3.3	-7.5	4.6	10.5	5.9	4.7	4.3	-0.4
France	3.4	0.9	-2.5	10.1	10.1	0.1	3.0	2.8	-0.3
Germany	2.8	2.7	-0.1	7.5	7.2	-0.3	1.1	3.6	2.5
Ireland	3.7	4.8	1.1	16.8	15.9	-0.9	3.3	2.8	-0.5
Italy	3.3	1.1	-2.2	11.9	10.8	-1.1	5.6	5.6	0.0
Netherlands	2.6	1.9	-0.7	9.2	7.4	-1.8	0.3	3.1	2.8
Norway	1.6	2.1	0.5	3.1	5.7	2.6	6.8	3.0	-3.9
Portugal	4.6	1.9	-2.7	6.7	4.5	-2.2	10.9	10.1	-0.8
Spain	4.7	1.4	-3.3	19.6	18.4	-1.2	6.4	5.8	-0.7
Sweden	2.5	-1.2	-3.7	1.9	4.5	2.6	5.2	6.4	1.3
Switzerland	2.9	0.4	-2.6	0.7	2.2	1.5	1.8	4.6	2.8
UK	3.9	-0.1	-3.9	9.1	8.6	-0.5	5.1	5.2	0.1
USA	3.1	1.5	-1.6	6.0	6.6	0.6	3.6	3.9	0.3
Japan	4.4	2.4	-2.0	2.6	2.2	-0.4	0.9	2.3	1.4
OECD	3.5	1.5	-2.0	7.2	7.4	0.2	4.5	4.6	0.2
OECD Europe	3.4	1.4	-2.0	9.5	9.3	-0.2	3.5	4.5	0.9

Source: OECD, "Main Economic Indicators"; OECD, "Economic Outlook."

APPENDIX 6: Structure of the Parity Commission

formal decision	Assembly of the Parity Commission

informal decision	"Preliminary talks" of the four presidents

preliminary decision	Sub-committee for wages (1957)	Sub-committee for prices (1957)	Advisory Council for Economic and Social Issues (1963)	Sub-committee for International Issues (1992)

Chambers of Labor	Chambers of Agriculture
Austrian Trade Union Federation	Chambers of Business
Employees' Associations	*Employers' Associations*

Source: Pelinka, *Modellfall Österreich*, 1981 (updated by Ferdinand Karlhofer).

APPENDIX 7: Party Concentration 1975-94

Shares of Votes of the Two Largest Parties (Percentage)

	SPÖ	ÖVP	Total
1975	50.4	42.9	93.3
1979	51.0	41.9	92.9
1983	47.6	43.2	90.8
1986	43.1	41.3	84.4
1990	42.8	32.1	74.9
1994	35.2	27.7	62.9

Source: Anton Pelinka, "Parteien und Verbände," in Tálos, ed., *Sozialpartnerschaft*, 71 (updated).

APPENDIX 8:   Members of Parliament in Major Associations

	1973		1978		1987		1991	
	n	%	n	%	n	%	n	%
Labor Associations								
SPÖ	45	48	42	45	33	41	30	38
ÖVP	11	14	13	16	13	16	7	12
FPÖ	-	-	1	10	0	-	1	3
Plenum	56	31	56	31	46	25	38	21
Employer Associations								
SPÖ	1	1	2	2	1	1	2	3
ÖVP	14	18	19	24	15	20	9	15
FPÖ	2	20	2	20	2	11	2	6
Plenum	17	9	23	13	18	10	13	7
Agrarian Associations								
SPÖ	3	3	2	2	1	1	0	0.0
ÖVP	18	23	21	26	14	18	10	17
FPÖ	-	-	-	-	1	6	1	-
Plenum	21	12	23	13	16	9	11	6
Total								
SPÖ	49	53	46	50	35	44	32	40
ÖVP	43	54	53	66	42	55	26	33
FPÖ	2	20	3	30	3	17	4	12
Plenum	94	51	102	56	80	44	62	34

Source: Pelinka, *Modellfall Österreich*, 1981 (updated by Ferdinand Karlhofer).

APPENDIX 9:   Union Membership 1985–93

	Dependent Labor Force	Union Members	Union Density*
1985	2.833	1.671	47.2
1986	2.780	1.671	48.1
1987	2.785	1.653	47.5
1988	2.810	1.644	46.8
1989	2.862	1.644	46.0
1990	2.929	1.645	44.9
1991	2.997	1.638	43.7
1992	3.055	1.633	42.8
1993	3.055	1.616	42.3

* Union members as percentage of labor force (less 20 percent retired union members).

Source: Union reports

APPENDIX 10: Public Opinion on Social Partnership 1983 - 93

"For Austria's economy, social partnership is . . . " percentage

	" . . . favorable"	" . . . unfavorable"	(indifferent)	n =
1983	69	6	25	2214
1985	58	4	38	1000
1988	61	9	30	1872
1990	63	6	31	1778
1993	66	6	28	4000

Source: Karlhofer, *Geschwächte Verbände*, 117.

NOTES

1. See Scott Lash and John Urry, *The End of Organized Capitalism* (Oxford: Polity Press, 1987).

2. Weak corporatism "is distinguished by the institutionalized participation of organized labor in the formation and implementation of policies only within limited sectors of policy or by its participation only in specific stages of the policy process—for example, consultation or implementation." Gerhard Lehmbruch, "Concertation and the Structure of Corporatist Networks," in *Order and Conflict in Contemporary Capitalism*, ed. John H. Goldthorpe (Oxford: Clarendon Press, 1984), 65.

3. See Hans Slomp, "European Labor Relations and the Prospects of Tripartism," in *Participation and Public Policy-Making. The Role of Trade Unions and Employers' Associations*, ed. Tiziano Treu, (Berlin-New York: De Gruyter, 1992), 159-73.

4. Oliver Clarke, "Towards a Synthesis of International and Comparative Experiences of Nine Countries," in *International and Comparative Industrial Relations*, eds. Greg J. Bamber and Russell D. Lansbury (London: Routledge, 1993), 273.

5. Marino Regini, ed., *The Future of Labor Movements* (London: Sage, 1992), 7.

6. Philippe C. Schmitter, "Sectors in Modern Capitalism: Modes of Governance and Variations in Performance," in *Labor Relations and Economic Performance*, eds. Renato Brunetta and Carlo Dell'Aringa, (London: Macmillan, 1990), 14.

7. Alan Cawson, "Interests, Groups and Public Policy-Making: The Case of the European Consumer Electronics Industry," in *Organized Interests and the European Community*, eds. Justin Greenwood, Jürgen R. Grote and Karsten Ronit (London: Sage, 1992), 100.

8. Carlo Dell'Aringa and Manuela Lodovici, "Industrial Relations and Labor Policies in European Countries," in John R. Niland, Russell D. Lansbury and Chrissie Verevis, eds., *The Future of Industrial Relations* (London: Sage 1994), 394.

9. An overview of the various scales is given by Carlo Dell'Aringa and Samek Lodovici, "Industrial Relations and Economic Performance," in *Participation and Public Policy-Making. The Role of Trade Unions and Employers' Associations*, ed. Tiziano Treu (Berlin-New York: de Gruyter, 1992), 26-58.

10. See Tálos and Kittel in this volume; see also Ferdinand Karlhofer and Anton Pelinka, "Austria," in, *European Labor Unions*, ed. Joan Campbell (Westport-London: Greenwood Press, 1992), 13-25; Franz Traxler, "Austria: Still the Country of Corporatism," in *Industrial Relations in the New Europe*, eds. Anthony Ferner and Richard Hyman (Oxford: Blackwell, 1992), 270-97.

11. In two of the nine provinces (*Länder*), Tyrol and Vorarlberg, the respective sub-group of the ÖVP holds the majority of votes and provides the president.

12. Anton Pelinka, "Österreich: Was bleibt von den Besonderheiten?" in *Aus Politik und Zeitgeschichte*, B 47-48/92, (13 November 1992): 12-19.

13. See Michael Shalev, "The Resurgence of Labour Quiescence," in Regini, ed., *Labour Movements*, 102-32.

14. Jukka Pekkarinen, Matti Pohjola and Bob Rowthorn, "Social Corporatism and Economic Performance: Introduction and Conclusions," in *Social Corporatism: A Superior Economic System?*, eds. Jukka Pekkarinen, Matti Pohjola and Bob Rowthorn (Oxford: Clarendon Press, 1992), 1-23.

15. Pekkarinen et al., *Social Corporatism*, 3.

16. See Ferdinand Karlhofer, "Die österreichische Sozialpartnerschaft—vom Modellfall zum Normalfall?" in *Westliche Demokratien und Interessenvermittlung*, eds. Ralf Kleinfeld and Wolfgang Ludthardt (Marburg: Schüren, 1993), 180-92.

17. "Wage drift refers to wage increases which are agreed at a plant or firm level in addition to the centrally negotiated rate." Andrew Henley and Euclid Tsakalotos, *Corporatism and Economic Performance* (Aldershot: Edward Elgar, 1993), 61.

18. Ewald Nowotny, *The Austrian Social Partnership and Democracy*, Working Paper No. 10, Vienna University of Economics and Business Administration, 1991, 6.

19. Henley and Tsakalotos, Performance, 143. The authors refer to Alois Guger, "Corporatism: Success or Failure? Austrian Experiences," in Pekkarinen et al., *Social Corporatism*.

20. Alois Guger, "Lohnpolitik und Sozialpartnerschaft," in Tálos, *ed., Sozialpartnerschaft*, 235-7.

21. A detailed analysis is given by Seidel in this volume.

22. For instance, *World Trade*, June 1994, pp. 104-5; *Global Investor*, No. 7, 1994, 5-14.

23. Ferdinand Karlhofer, "Geschwächte Verbände—stabile Partnerschaft? Zur Externalisierung innerverbandlicher Loyalitätsprobleme," in Tálos, *Sozialpartnerschaft*, 117-130.

24. "Sozialpartnerschaft. Vereinbarung zwischen der Bundeskammer der gewerblichen Wirtschaft, der Bundeskammer für Arbeiter und Angestellte, dem Österreichischen Gewerkschaftsbund und der Präsidentenkonferenz der Landwirtschaftskammern Österreich" (23 October 1992). The document is reprinted in *Kammern und Pflichtmitgliedschaft in Österreich*, ed. Peter Pernthaler, Anton Pelinka, Ferdinand Karlhofer et al. (Vienna: Schriftenreihe Arbeit, Recht, Gesellschaft 1993), 264-266.

25. Ibid., 266.

26. This is, admittedly, a very academic consideration since both partners—the Chambers of Commerce and the Chambers of Agriculture on the one side, and the ÖGB and the Chambers of Labor on the other—are represented with an equal number of delegates.

27. Anton Pelinka, *Modellfall Österreich? Möglichkeiten und Grenzen der Sozialpartnerschaft* (Vienna: Braumüller, 1981), 20.

28. Exit poll figures. See Fritz Plasser, Peter Ulram, Erich Neuwirth and Franz Sommer, *Analyse der Nationalratswahl vom 9. Oktober 1994* (Vienna: Zentrum für angewandte Politikforschung, 1994), 30.

29. See Jan-Erik Lane and Svante O. Ersson, *Politics and Society in Western Europe*, 3rd ed. (London: Sage, 1994), 181-2.

30. See Ständiger Organisationsausschuß des ÖGB, *Strategiekonzept zur Weiterentwicklung der ÖGB-Organisation*, 1 March 1994 (unpublished).

31. See Peter Pernthaler, "Kammern und Pflichtmitgliedschaft in Österreich aus der Sicht des öffentlichen Rechts," in Pernthaler et al., *Kammern und Pflichtmitgliedschaft*, 19-91.

32. Gerda Falkner, "Sozialpartnerschaftliche Politikmuster und europäische Integration," in *Sozialpartnerschaft. Kontinuität und Wandel eines Modells*, ed. Emmerich Tálos (Vienna: Verlag für Gesellschaftskritik, 1993), 79-102.

33. Ferdinand Karlhofer, "Sozialpartnerschaft und EU," in *Das EU-Referendum. Zur Praxis direkter Demokratie in Österreich*, ed. Anton Pelinka (Vienna: Signum 1994).

34. See e.g. Peter Gerlich, "A Farewell to Corporatism," in *Politics in Austria: Still a Case of Consociationalism?* ed. Kurt Richard Luther and Wolfgang C. Müller (London: Cass, 1992), 144.

35. Traxler, *Still the Century*, 296.

36. Philippe C. Schmitter, *Sectors in Modern Capitalism*, 32.

37. See *The Economist*, 2 October 1993.

38. See Fritz Plasser and Peter A. Ulram, "Überdehnung, Erosion und rechtspopulistische Erosion," in *Österreichische Zeitschrift für Politikwissenschaft* 21 (1992), 147-64.

39. See, e.g., Franz Traxler, "Vom Angebots—zum Nachfragekorporatismus," in Tálos, ed., *Sozialpartnerschaft*, 113.

FORUM

Austrian Social Partnership—A Model for Central and Eastern Europe?

Introduction

Birgitt Haller

The situation in the new democracies of Eastern Europe resembles that of Austria after World War II. Both Austria after 1945 and the former communist countries after 1989 were confronted with the need to develop democracy, to set up competitive economies, to establish new state and market institutions.

The model of social partnership has been the basis of the Austrian economy since 1945 and of its successful performance (in most economic data Austria ranks above the OEEC average). Nevertheless, social partnership has been increasingly criticized since the 1980s. The erosion of the party system, the calling into question of the compulsory membership in the chambers, the changing economic conditions within the European Union—these are factors that jeopardize the stability of social partnership or at least demand an adaption of the classic model. Yet, owing to the undisputed role of social partnership in the postwar era, its advocates have tried to export it to the new democracies: the Austrian Social Democratic Party (SPÖ) and the Austrian People's Party (ÖVP) as well as the Austrian Federation of Labor (ÖGB) and the Federal Chamber of Commerce (BWK) are engaged in this task.

Since 1989, the educational institutions of the parties, Renner-Institut (SPÖ) and Politische Akademie (ÖVP) have been organizing seminars for politicians, members of Parliament, journalists and scientists from the new democracies. In these courses, which take place both in Austria and in the countries of Eastern and Central Europe, the participants are confronted with the concept of and the experiences with Austrian social partnership, and they are assisted in their efforts to transform the Austrian model.[1] In addition to the activities of the educational institutions, politicians of SPÖ and ÖVP are in direct contact with their party colleagues in the Eastern democracies.

The ÖGB cooperates closely with the trade unions in Eastern Europe, on a national and regional level, as well as directly with enterprises. It organizes specific training courses in Austria and in the countries concerned, courses that deal with union structures, labor law and similar topics and offer the opportunity to discuss the implementation of social partnership.[2] Also, the BWK advances the concept of social partnership via organizing training courses for managers in the new democracies and meetings between East European delegations and representatives of Austrian enterprises. The BWK's training courses for public servants seem even more interesting under the aspect of "exporting" social partnership. They bring participants to Austria after a two-week instruction in their countries to acquaint them first-hand with the Austrian practice. These courses have been taking place since spring 1993 in cooperation with the Austrian Federal Ministry of Economic Affairs.[3]

The efforts to spread the Austrian model of social partnership have been rather successful. None of the four countries presented in this Forum adopted the Austrian model, but in all of them, especially in Slovenia and in Hungary, the concept and the practice of "tripartism" is—at least to some extent—influenced by the Austrian social partnership. It would not be realistic, in fact, to presume that the Austrian postwar model could be copied by the new democracies in Eastern Europe. Although economic and social parallels exist, the political systems differ significantly.

The most striking economic parallel is that both in Austria after World War II and in the former communist states, capitalism had to be built up without capital and without capitalists. During and even before the Nazi regime, Austria's economy depended on economic centers in Germany and on German capital. After 1945, economic independence was achieved by the nationalization of the most important industries and banks. Here the similarities end: in the former socialist economies, industries and banks were nationalized; this form of property is discredited, but there are no private owners. The political elite therefore encourages the investment of foreign capital by foreign capitalists.

As to the social parallels, both Austria and the former communist states aim at guaranteeing social peace and at keeping unemployment and inflation low. But at this point, it is necessary to make reference to the change in external economic factors. Capitalism in the 1990s does not much resemble that of the 1940s and 1950s. Capitalism in the 1990s means post-industrialism; it means a "two-thirds" society that can no longer assure everyone full employment. Therefore, keeping social peace has become more difficult.

The most important differences exist in the political systems. The centralization of the Austrian party system, with the two main actors SPÖ and ÖVP and of the basic economic interests in form of ÖGB and BWK, was a vital condition of the functioning of social partnership. And although the organizations of business and labor are independent of political parties, there are close connections between SPÖ and ÖGB on one hand and between ÖVP and BWK on the other. The political parties as well as the economic pressure groups accept the same values, such as a balance between pure capitalistic and pure socialist concepts. This means that the trade unions do not demand an income redistribution, nor do the employers try to lower wage levels. Economic growth guarantees profits for employers and employees alike, but both groups renounce a fundamental political innovation. Another important structural difference is the balance of powers between parliament and social partnership, expressed by the relative autonomy of Austrian social partnership with regard to parliamentarism. It depends neither on party competition nor competes with parliamentarism.

The political systems of the Central and Eastern European states differ markedly from the Austrian one. Their party systems are highly fragmented, they have weak organizational structures, and the parties are heterogeneous. As a result of the fragmentation of the party system, the parliaments are highly fragmented. Distinct party camps representing basic economic interests do not exist.

Employers' organizations have been founded within the last years, but they are still rather unstable and, as privatization is not completed, they have to compete with the governments representing the nationalized economy. Also the trade unions have no representative monopoly; they are not centralized and in most countries there exist different unions in opposition to one another. A further reason for the weakness of the employers' and employees' organizations is the absence of chambers (except in Slovenia and for some little time in Hungary) and therefore of compulsory membership which would increase their power of representation—but compulsory membership is discredited owing to the communist past.

As a result of the economic and social challenges during the transition to democracy, the political elites were interested in the cooperation of government and the representatives of employers as well as employees. So in most of the former communist states tripartite institutions were established to guarantee a smooth transition. But the competence of the tripartite institutions never was settled; therefore, they only act as moral institutions. As there are no institutionalized linkages between the political parties/the parliaments and the representatives of the basic economic interests, they do not complement one another but compete. Tripartism is not able to influence the parliamentary decision-making process as it is not politically accepted by the Parliament—the tripartite institutions are no "social partnership."

NOTES

1. Information by Dr. Nowotny (SPÖ) and Mag. Steppan (former employee of the Politische Akademie, ÖVP), December 1994.

2. Information by Dr. Sauer (ÖGB), December 1994. Between 1990 and the end of 1993, 350 seminars for trade unionists from Eastern Europe took place.

3. Information by Dr. Pötscher and Dr. Kowa (both BWK), December 1994.

Social Partnership in the Czech Republic

Lubomir Brokl and Zdenka Mansfeldova

Several months after the Czechoslovakian "velvet revolution" in November 1989 a way was sought to support and regulate the transformation not only of the political system but also of the economy from a planned to a liberal market one. A form of cooperation was looked for in the area of social policy as well to prevent instability brought about by social conflicts. Collective bargaining and agreement at the firm level, at the branch level and at the national level were also mentioned in the scenario of economic reform, approved in the federal Parliament in September 1990.

Using examples of the renewal of economic systems after the Second World War and after the fall of totalitarian regimes in different countries, the new government explored the role of social partnership in subsequent economic development. New forms of political dialogue and consensus were sought and an attempt was made to create a model of cooperation, and to regulate and manage economic problems and processes of the cooperation of the government (the state), management (employers, capital) and labor (employees).

The necessary prerequisites for the creation of such an institution were in place:

a) the legal conditions
b) an infrastructure (centralized trade unions and employers' associations)
c) the will to negotiate and reach a consensus; the tripartite institution was conceived in such a way as to ensure that all the main sectors of the economy and all forms of ownership should be represented in it.

In the autumn of 1990, the government, the trade unions and representatives of employers decided on a tripartite-corporate form of intermediating of interests. The agreement on the creation of a tripartite organ—the *Council for Economic and Social Agreement* (*Rada hospodářské a sociální dohody—RHSD*)—was signed at the federal level on 3 October 1990 and at the level of the republics (Czech and Slovak Republics) a few weeks later.

The social partnership was created "from above," supported from government and not as a consequence of existing problems and the articulation of interests from below. It was at the time when the government's concept of economic reform was beginning to be realized, but at that time there had not yet occurred any liberalization of prices, privatization, significant unemployment or a decline in the standard of living.

Three partners (which represent three seven-member delegations) work together in the Council for Economic and Social Agreement: the government, the trade unions[1] and the employers. All the delegations have to have substitutes, advisors and experts; their number and participation at negotiations is set by the Statutes of the Council for Economic and Social Agreement and their Procedural Rules. Besides the monthly plenary sessions of the Council, work groups represent auxiliary expert bodies and are ensuring an expert assessment of materials with the aim of preparing the proposals of standpoints for the ordinary members. The chairperson of the Council is the representative of government; at the present time, the chair is the deputy prime minister, who is also the minister of finance.

According to the statute, the Council for Economic and Social Agreement deals with proposals of law principles, law proposals, proposals of public notices, and proposals of the general agreement. Questions about economic and social policy, which are substantially connected with the standard of living and employment, are also discussed.

All the laws that deal with employees should be discussed in the tripartite institution, where each member has one vote. When the motion is carried, it is accepted by all parties represented in the Council. If members of the Council are not all able to reach an agreement during the negotiations, the government is obliged before making its decision to take into account the viewpoint of the social partners and to present these viewpoints during the introduction of bills in Parliament. The Council cannot initiate a law or present a bill in Parliament. The initiative function is applied during the preparatory period by submitting standpoints to legal proposals.

The most important agreement in the tripartite body is the general agreement (general social pact on the national level),[2] which defines for every year economic and social tasks, falling into the government's and Parliament's jurisdiction, and creating a starting point for collective bargaining for the social partners. It establishes the conditions and relations in this area in a regular pre-agreed period and is the result of political consensus between the participating partners. The general agreement, unlike collective agreements, which are results of bargaining on branch and enterprise levels, is a political document, the observance of which cannot be enforced by legal but only by political means. The social partnership is not a part of the constitutional system; no formalized relationship exists between social partners and Parliament.

Problems of legitimacy belong to the chief issues of social partnership. On the tripartite level this concerns especially the legitimacy of elections (of or by the organization leadership) and the review of union representatives' activities (the absence of control mechanisms and reciprocal ties between the leadership and the rank and file).

The possibility of the represented to get their needs put on the agenda and of keeping the representatives accountable is limited and not even precisely established. In view of the fact that membership in trade unions and in employers' and business organizations is voluntary, the legitimacy of the representatives is moot from the point of view of non-members. The representatives' separation from the base is the subject of criticism by trade unionists and employers. Similarly, a decision is binding downwards only in a moral sense, and the possibility of asserting it is problematic. The top does not have much possibility of asserting a decision simply because of the non-obligatory nature of membership.

Employers' and business organizations are trying to be thoroughly unpolitical (apart from individual membership in political parties) and are concentrating on their own particular economic and socio-political goals. This unpolitical nature from an institutional point of view means that there is no link with political parties and no interlinking of elites or political factions with associations and organizations. Lack of interest in the connection of employers' organizations with one or more political parties is also expressed by the actual parties.[3] Thus, there remains only the usual way to assert interests: lobbying.[4] Members of Parliament prefer informal contacts, since at least half of them (judging by official tax returns) are involved in business.

The trade unions' relationship to political parties is burdened by the legacy of the past when trade unions were "transmission belts" for the policies of the Communist Party. There are, therefore, no official links to political parties; the use of political means to assert trade union interests is firmly rejected. Unofficial contacts with political parties are sought after across the entire political spectrum, as is a different political orientation of trade unions and all trade union associations.

The existence of the Council and its activity is evaluated positively by its participants. The represented base, however, has a rather reserved relationship to this institution and sees it as somewhat superfluous and meaningless. The conviction about possible benefits of tripartism is not high. The significance of the tripartite institution is emphasized as dialogue and knowledge of the viewpoints of the participating parties.

Tripartite partnership has not been understood as the adequate institution to solve all problems; it was intended more as an advising and suggesting institution, complementary to other possibilities such as direct negotiation of social partners with government or particular ministers in Parliament.

The currently functioning tripartite model can be understood as *temporary*, because the government itself stakes its existence on the successful completion of basic reform and even now, in 1994-95, is thinking in terms of a bipartite system involving the employers and unions, with the state in a merely consultative role. Therefore, it would be premature to extrapolate these processes into a model of neoliberal corporatism, replacing the earlier socialist corporatism.

A balance of power does not yet exist among the social partners. The state is still a great owner and employer. The employers' associations are still the weakest party in the tripartite body. They are less experienced and less representative because many business enterprises are not members of any employers' association.

In general, the influence of the Council is clear but should not be overestimated. It is functioning as an instrument of internal policy rather than as a philosophy. The main task of tripartism has been and is to prevent social conflicts and to promote consensus in the areas of social and economic development. The employers respect the preserving of the social conciliation as "the most valuable goods."[5] The trade unions evaluated the tripartite Council positively. Along with the other partners, they appreciate its contribution for the preserving of social consensus in society and for the development of democratic structures.

The Czech republic has not created chambers that discharge similar functions as the Austrian chambers do. Czech chambers, the Chamber of Business and the Agrarian Chamber, with voluntary membership fulfill advisory and service tasks and do not have any relation to tripartism.

Before the tripartite body was created, the social partners, especially the trade unions, were intensively interested in different models of tripartism, including those in Portugal, Scandinavia, and Austria.[6] The Austrian model of social partnership was a subject of study for all three partners in the tripartite council. In view of the specific conditions (obligatory membership in the Chambers, political linkage) this model would not be followed. Taking into account that the pure market economy was set as a common goal, the Austrian model of social partnership was not found by government and employers as attractive in the 1990s.

NOTES

1. The supreme central trade union body in the Czech Republic is the Bohemian-Moravian Chamber of Trade Unions, which, by March 1994, brought together thirty-eight trade unions and has 3.5 million members. For example, the members' base of trade unions is made by about forty percent of people in productive age, mostly social servants and employees in the state and administrative sector. The private sector is generally not covered by trade unions at the present time.

2. Pure tripartite agreement (our General Agreement) has been signed only in Portugal. The partners mostly adhere to "gentlemen's agreements." (In *Téze přístupu vlády k Radě hospodářské a sociální dohody České republiky*, background study, October, 1993.)

3. This standpoint is based on interviews made in 1992-1993 with representatives of Parliament parties. (Research report "Möglichkeiten der sozialpartnerschaftlichen Konfliktregelung in der Tschechischen und Slowakischen Republik," Projekt 4177 des Jubiläumsfonds der Österreichischen Nationalbank, Innsbruck, December 1993.)

4. Lobbying is still understood as something inappropriate, even illegal to formalize democratic mechanisms.

5. Press conference with the chairman of the Association of Employers of the Czech republic in České Budějovice, April 1994.

6. Interview with the executive secretary of the Council for Economic and Social Agreement, Petr Pavlík, 24 May 1993.

Social Partnership in Slovakia

Monika Čambáliková

The institution of social partnership and collective bargaining was created in Slovakia in 1990, before its chief components—the original associations of capital and labor—existed. It was created *from the outside* (the inspiration of international documents and praxis in democratic countries) and *from the top* (by the initiative of government). Although the institution predated its foundations, so to speak, it was at the same time possible to foresee economic and social changes that would result from the realization of economic transformation. Simultaneously, it was a signal for foreign countries that emerging economic and social transformation would occur in a democratic way and that great importance would be given to the social dialogue and to the keeping of social peace.

The important pre-condition for social partnership and collective bargaining requires, first, the creation of appropriate institutional and legal conditions. The second necessary precondition seems to be the social *acceptance of these institutions* by social and political corporations as well as by the citizens themselves.

Legal Conditions

Act no. 83/1990 on the association of citizens, renewed Act no. 300/1490 introducing the principle of evidence of trade union and employers' subjects, thus forming a liberal regime of plurality and association. Important for the development of tripartism in Slovakia was the determination of competence of the republics in the federation, concerning especially the sphere of labor, wages and social policy by the Act no. 556/1990. The renewal of the Act no. 3/1991 abolished the monopoly of the single trade union, and under the freedom of association there were developed terms to build up the

system of the social partnership, Labor Code and the Collective
Bargaining Act (Act no. 2/1991).

Institutional Conditions

The Council of Economic and Social Agreement (RHSD) defined
institutional conditions at the federal level on 3 October 1990 and at
the level of the Slovak Republic on 30 October 1990. In judging the
effect of the tripartism in the Slovak Republic on the efficiency of
collective bargaining and on the formation of public policy as a tool
for tempering the social tensions resulting from economic and social
transformation, we have to consider at least the *"de iure"* and *"de
facto"* levels. On the *"de iure"* level the RHSD is ". . . a common,
voluntary bargaining and initiative organ of the government . . . of
the trade union . . . of the employers in the Slovak Republic with the
aim of achieving agreement in both the economic and social sphere."
In the statute, the bargaining conclusions shall be ". . . agreements,
standpoints and recommendations . . ." forming part of the proposals
of legal regulations by the government. But on the *"de facto"* level,
the model of tripartite behavior does not always function. The
relationship between the partners comprises the range from the
authoritative behavior of executive power through consultations and
bargaining up to common and coordinate operations.

The government of the Slovak Republic as the locus of executive
power often declares in the tripartite bargaining process to be
responsible for the state as well as the process of social
transformation. As the government is now the largest employer
(organs of the state administration, budget paid organizations in the
branches, state-owned enterprises and joint stock companies), it has
to play simultaneously the dual role of both the government and the
employer. In the present social circumstances the government copes
well with this role although this position is a temptation in the
direction of authoritative behavior towards the social partners. For
example, the opinion of the tripartite social partners was not asked in
the preparation for proposals of some important legal acts, such as

*   the proposed Act of Bankruptcy and Settlement
*   the proposed renewal of the State-Owned Enterprise Act
*   the proposed renewal of the Privatization Act

* the proposal of the 1994 State Budget of the Slovak Republic (containing also other proposals for act alterations)

* the proposal for the second rise of retirement benefits in 1993.

In Slovak tripartism, the prime role is played by the government, while the adversaries are the trade unions. The employers alternately join either of these partners according to their own needs. The problems of existing jurisdiction and the concrete form of the realization of social partnership, in particular in the first year of making tripartism work, were reflected in the trade union documents in the following manner:

The common problem of the RHSD ČSFR, RHSD Czech Republic and RHSD Slovak Republic is the realization of the principle of the equivalent partnership of the tripartite subjects. The dominating position of the government in the tripartism is manifested by the fact that the government and the ministries have their position and competence anchored directly in legal regulations, which do not know the institution of tripartism . . . . Even if the party in power would develop legislative initiatives with the intention of the agreed standpoint of the RHSD, the system of the other government and legislation bodies can approve regulations (acts) being in contradiction to the standpoint of the RHSD. The mutual relations of competence between the organs of the party in power on one side and the legislative corporations on the other side, do not provide an objective security of keeping the agreements of the RHSD and their projection into legal regulations in the form of legal acts. The opinion of the party in power that the government has no obligation to respect standpoints of the tripartite partners differing from those of the government, finds support in the legislation, but it could deny the proper institution of tripartism.[1]

The main problems in the activity of the RHSD were summarized in the statement of the confederation of trade unions KOZ Slovak Republic of 30 January 1993. On the basis of this statement, we can

record the following general shortcomings in the activities of the
RHSD:

* delayed submission of the materials for collective bargaining;
* to some questions no RHSD materials are submitted at all,
   meaning that the RHSD was omitted in the judgment of some
   important proposals of the government;
* no control of the RHSD conclusions, weakening the effect of
   the RHSD on the management and legislative processes;
* the frequent absence of government representatives (at least
   four ministers should be present) hinders collective
   bargaining.

The members of Parliament voiced positive response to the social
partnership idea in the name of their political parties. The analysis of
the critical comments made by some members of parliament shows
elements or, at least, indications of criticism of the social partnership
from traditional, liberal, legislative, "democratic" and reformist
positions. With the exception of the Marxist criticism of social
partnership, all other types of criticism were analyzed by Anton
Pelinka.[2]

Tripartism is represented in the parliament by the members of the
party in power. The standpoint of the tripartite partners to legislation
passed is announced to the members of Parliament by the submitting
agency. The stances of the agencies in the tripartite arrangement
become part of the bills proposed to Parliament or are contained in
the report attached to it. In the tripartite proposals to bills under
consideration in Parliament the spheres of social, economic and labor
legislation are discussed. Neither of the participants has shown
interest in extending those spheres.

Economic and social development are the manifest preference of
the associations of employers' and employees' representatives in the
RHSD. The tripartite partners consider economic revival and
prosperity to be the fundamental prerequisite for the social
development. The majority of the top representatives of both the
employers' and employees' associations (active members of
tripartism) and of almost all members of Parliament presently
consider the institution of tripartism as a consulting body of both the
government and the Parliament. The (common) decision-making

function of tripartism is in fact considered more a possibility than a reality. The strengthening of the decision-making function of tripartism by legislative measures is neither demanded nor refused by the tripartite members.

The government's philosophical approach to tripartism is a combined political and economic one. The weight of both aspects varies depending on the questions discussed and on the specific political, social and economic situation. It is further extended by questions of economic and social policies, and it is remarkably connected with the living standard, labor and general contentment of the citizens.

The problems of representation and the criteria of legitimacy belong to the most important theoretical and practical problems of collective bargaining and social partnership. The success of the non-corporate policy of interest depends on the internal structure of the association, what is called the Achilles' heel of corporatism. In the Slovak situation there exist problems of internal integration and agreement in the associations of employers and employees. The following problems crop up:

1. The legitimacy of the choice of employers' and employees' associations to represent the members in the processes of agreement and common decision-making on the platform of collective bargaining and tripartite negotiations.
2. The legitimacy of choice of the representatives into those institutions inside the associations.
3. The missing feedback between the bargainers and those they are bargaining for (that means a possible actual participation in the content and outcome of the bargaining process or in the control of the bargainers).

On the macro-level (bargaining in the RHSD), neither of the associations has yet established institutional presumptions to reach internal consensus and agreement in this matter. This fact along with voluntary choice and a certain loss of trade union members, forms certain limits for the realization of a corporation policy on the social macro-level. (These factors are also obstacles to the copying of the Austrian model of social partnership in Slovakia.)

On the macro-level of tripartism, the institutional legitimacy of choice (by delegation or election "of the associations' top staff and by the top members of them") and particularly the control of the bargainers and the feedback to the members is not secured sufficiently by "democratic" criticism. This holds also for the parties of the employers and employees. The fact that tripartism affects—or could affect to a certain extent—the process of decision-making (i.e., it has some power functions and competence, although not precisely defined and controlled by acts), makes it a target of criticism from the state-legislative position. In practice, during bargaining everything is legitimate that is considered by all participants to have legitimacy. In the present conditions neither of the participating parties denies each other legitimacy.

The "official" trade union was several times and in various connections criticized by government representatives, but its position in tripartism as the monopoly representative of the employees was never questioned. The employers' party has the same position vis-a-vis the trade union (and vice-versa). At present, the government prefers an organized dialogue to a possible "diffused menace of violence." Such a situation was analyzed by Middlemas in *Policy in the Industrial Society*: "The governments were interested in reality in a strong trade union—unlike the strategy of Bismarck, the leaders of the British Tories were aware of the advantages of organization, compared with the diffused menace of violence—and they also supported the establishment of employers' associations."[3]

The Austrian model of social partnership is attractive for the Slovak Republic mainly because of the positive impact it had on Austria's postwar reconstruction and on the later stability of the Austrian economy. The idea and the functioning of the Austrian model are admired in Slovakia. They have grown out of common (central) European tradition, deeply anchored in social-democratic and Christian social thinking.

The present way of applying the ideas of social partnership and dialog in Slovakia have more similarities with the Portuguese model. In both countries the tripartite organs were built after the fall of the totalitarian regimes. Compared to most European countries with a market economy where organs of social partnership were created either between 1947 and 1952 (reconstruction of national economies destroyed in the war), or between 1953 and 1970 (reaction to the

163

waves of strikes), the tripartite organs were created late in Portugal. Slovakia and Portugal have similar systems of concluding tripartite agreements and pre-negotiated laws concerning the social and labor-legal domains in the tripartite organs.

NOTES

1. KOZ (Confederation of the Slovak Trade Unions) materials, 1991.

2. Anton Pelinka, *Modellfall Österreich? Möglichkeiten und Grenzen der Sozialpartnerschaft.* (Vienna, 1981).

3. Ralf Dahrendorf, *Moderný sociálny konflikt* [Modern Social Conflict], trans. Ferdinand Pál (Bratislava: Archa, 1991).

Social Partnership in Slovenia

Igor Lukšič

Corporatism and social partnership have always been one of the most powerful political doctrines in Slovenia. After the encyclical, *Rerum Novarum* of Leo XIII, a powerful peasant movement emerged, which was called *"Krekovstvo,"*[1] after its leader, Janez E. Krek. Its main goal was to protect the Slovene language and the Slovene people, who were mostly poor peasants. The movement organized peasants in cooperatives, which instructed people on farming and helped them in natural disasters. The cooperatives promoted the corporatist ideas of the Christian community, unity and nationalism. The movement was anti-liberal and anti-capitalist. In the 1930s, after the encyclical *Quadrogesimo Anno* of Pius XI, Christian intellectuals promoted the idea of the corporatist state with a main role for corporations.[2]

After World War II, the idea of corporatism came under the hegemony of the socialist ideology. Yugoslavia practiced self-management, which was a kind of social partnership based on "social ownership," especially after the Constitution of 1974. The Parliament of the Republic comprised three chambers: a Chamber of Communes, a Chamber of Associated Labor—where questions concerning economic and social policy were discussed—and the Sociopolitical Chamber. For every vital social interest, a special so-called "self-management interest community" was organized, with an equal number of representatives of "producers" and "consumers." Each could participate in a session of the Parliament as a fourth chamber on a matter within competence.

In the Chamber of the Associated Labor, representatives of workers and managers were elected for every vital branch of the economy and social services. In addition to articulating their economic interest, they could also speak in the Sociopolitical

Chamber through a delegation of the trade union. The delegations of the League of Communists and the Youth Organization also had a tight grip on economic questions. The Chamber of Economy (*Gospodarska zbornica*) had a special status when a matter of the economy was on the parliamentary agenda. It also had a direct relationship with the government.

There existed a developed system of self-managing agreements and societal compacts as a model of cooperation between sociopolitical communities (commune, republic), interest and economic organizations, which was to replace the anarchy of market forces and state interventionism. This type of social partnership has survived in the new Constitution of 1991 embodied in the State Council. The Constitution in Article 96 defines the State Council as "the representative of bearers of social, economic, professional and local interests."[3] It represents the main, vital interest organizations of labor (trade unions), business (Chamber of Economy), agriculture, trade and free professions, social services (medicine, university, social policy, education, science and culture and sport) as well as twenty-two representatives of local interests. The Council has forty representatives, all elected indirectly through electorates, which are formed by representatives of the relevant interest organizations.

In Slovenia, the chamber system has been developing from the beginning of the democratic transformation. Under socialism only the Chamber of Lawyers and the Chamber of Economy existed. However, at the beginning of the 1990s a major system of chambers began to emerge and the number of chambers increased immediately to include a Medical Chamber, a Chamber of Economy (with new competence), a Chamber of Tradesmen, a Chamber of Social Security, a Chamber of Advertising, a Chamber of Nurses, a Chamber of Agriculture and Forestry, and a Chamber for Personal Security. They all have specific competence in creating and implementing public policy. A judgment of the Constitutional Court, stating that compulsory membership in the Medical Chamber is not in contradiction with constitutional freedom of association has been very important for strengthening the chamber system. Compulsory membership is now "constitutionally" allowed and has constructed the base for membership in the chambers. Chambers are the basis for election into the State Council, which represent the crown of the chamber system.

After the elections in 1990, a tripartite body was established in the Ministry of Labor, at the request of trade unions and the Ministry of Labor to oversee employment policy. It was not until the creation of an Association of Employers of Slovenia (AES) in the beginning of 1994 that the idea of a tripartite organ acquired strong support on the nonlabor side as well. In April 1994 a tripartite agreement on wage policy for 1994 was adopted and signed by representatives of six trade unions, AES, the Chamber of Economy of Slovenia (CES) and the Chamber of Tradesman of Slovenia (CTS) and by the president of the government. The subtitle of this agreement is "Part of the Social Pact." The Economic-Social Council (ESC) (*Ekonomsko-socialni svet*) was established by that agreement, counting fifteen members, five from each partner. The governmental delegation[4] involves the Minister of Economic Relations and Development, the Minister of Labor, Family, and Social Questions, the Director of the Institution for Macroeconomic Analysis and Development, the State Secretary of the Ministry of Finance and a member of the office of the head of the government. The delegation of employees[5] consists of the President of the Association of Free Trade Unions of Slovenia (AFTUS), a member of the presidency of the AFTUS, the President of the trade union PERGAM, the President of the Independence (Confederation of New Trade Unions of Slovenia) and the President of the Confederation of Trade Unions 90' of Slovenia. The delegation of employers[6] is constituted of the President and Vice-president (for small scale industry) of AES, a member of the Executive Committee of AES (for large industry), the President of the Chamber of Economy, and the President of the Chamber of Tradesmen. Each of them has his own alternate member to ensure a full quorum at sessions. Up to now, representatives of the trade unions and employers have participated, but the government side, especially the Minister of Economic Relations and Development, has ignored the meetings.

The main purpose of the ESC is to deal with questions and measures concerning economic and social policy. The Council also prepares the other elements of the social pact[7] and supervises its implementation. The Council has adopted standing rules that determine fundamental fields:

* social pact
* social rights
* employment and working relations
* system of collective agreements
* taxes and prices
* economic policy
* juridical security
* cooperation with the International Labor Organization and the Council of Europe.

The Council creates statements, initiatives, proposals and recommendations and sends them to the organs and organizations in charge: the government, the State Chamber, the State Council and the mass media. Unanimous conclusions of the ESC are obligatory for all organs and working bodies of all three social partners. ESC is financed by the state budget. By the end of July 1994 ESC had had five meetings discussing the standing rules and nature of the ESC.

There are two major problems of Slovene social partnership relations:

1. pluralization of the trade union movement, which was created by the fragmentation of the former communist trade union, and
2. tepidity of government.

To create relevant partners on the side of labor for collective agreements, a law on representation of trade unions was adopted. But because of the sacredness of the idea of pluralism, criteria were adopted giving eighteen trade unions (almost all of them) that status. At present, there exist

* the biggest Association of Free Trade Unions of Slovenia (435,716 members), which is recognized as left and has some relations with the Associated List of Social Democrats;
* Independence-Confederation of New Trade Unions of Slovenia (162,000 members), which is identified with the right and has some connections with the Social Democratic Party of Slovenia; and
* sixteen other representative trade unions (with under 50,000 members each), recognized as more or less in the center or without clear political option.

In the name of pluralism, ideological conflict has very often emerged that has threatened to weaken the labor side or even to complicate the work of the whole ESC.

In Slovenia, a consensus among experts exists that the government follows a liberal policy that does not favor social partnership. According to the main actors, the ESC was squeezed out of the government by the trade unions, AES and the Ministry of Labor. The Minister for Economic Relations and Development, which is a member of the ESC, has not taken part in any of the five meetings. That should be an important indicator of the governmental position toward the ESC. Until now, it is clear that the government is not a generator of social partnership and only observes what is going on among other partners. According to the statement of the AFTUS, the government tries to generate conflict, because it made procedural corrections to the law on labor participation in July without previous consultation with trade unions or discussion on the ESC.

All of the parliamentary parties are in favor of social partnership relations and the creation of a social pact, but they are in fact not familiar with the topic. The only exceptions are the Associated List of Social Democrats and Slovene Christian Democracy that also have a labor faction in the party and a person responsible for labor policy and social partnership.

All partners, especially the biggest two trade unions have an exact knowledge of the functioning of social partnership in Austria. Some of them have knowledge about the models of Cyprus, Scandinavia, Italy and Germany, and they have mentioned them as possible patterns for creating structures of social partnership in Slovenia. In practice, clearly the most important influence is coming from Austria. On the one hand, that is because of similarities of social structures between Slovenia and Austria, and on the other hand, because Austria perfectly incorporates the concept of social partnership.

NOTES

1. For a more detailed analysis of this phenomenon, see Slavoj Žižek, *Jezik, Ideologija, Slovenci*. [Language, Ideology, Slovenes] (Ljubljana: Delavska enotnost, 1987), 9-60.

2. For a more detailed analysis, see Milan Zver, "Korporativizem v slovenski politišni misli v 20. in 30. letih" [Corporatism in Slovene Political Thought in the 20s and 30s], *Casopis za kritiko znanosti* 20 (November 1992): 37-47.

3. *Ustava Republike Slovenije* [Constitution of the Republic of Slovenia] (Ljubljana: Mladinska knjiga, 1992), 37.

4. The idea of the employers' and employees' side was that the Prime Minister should be a member of ESC, but he refused. The Minister of Labor suggested that a delegation should include three ministers to show the other two partners that the government was serious about social partnership and the ESC. Even that proposal did not pass.

5. Trade unions made an agreement that a criterion for the number of members in the delegation had to be based on the number of union members. According to this criterion, the trade union with two-thirds of the members of all trade unions has the right on two mandates in the delegation.

6. All members were appointed by AES.

7. To create a social pact is the main task of the ESC. Actors also put this task at the top in interviews. They stress the consensus according to minimize the budget for 1995 that should be seen as a kind of social pact for a year.

Social Partnership in Hungary

Sándor Kurtán

Tripartitism in Hungary is six years old. The formal establishment occurred in October 1988 when—during the economic recession, the political leadership of the country was forced into a social dialogue—the Council of Ministers ordered the most important trade unions[1] to establish an institutional system of economic interest reconciliation, namely the *National Reconciliation Council* (*Országos Érdekegyeztető Tanács*). This motion had unequivocal support on the part of the (unified) trade union of that time.[2] Austrian and the German labor relations were the models for the Hungarian reformers, and the basic task of the new tripartite organization was the development of important wage policy decisions.

Following the 1990 elections the political system changed according to the suggestion of the newly established Ministry of Labor. With new players this newly created *Interest Reconciliation Council* (*Érdekegyeztető Tanács*)—(*IRC*) had only one session. Its operational principles, structure and tasks were included in the bylaws approved a year later. Accordingly, the task of the IRC is to deal with general and basic economic, income, social and labor matters. The aim of the IRC is to assess, reconcile the efforts of the employees, employers and the government to prevent possible conflicts, as well as to develop agreements based on the exchange of information and the examination of proposals and alternatives.

The participating members of the IRC are the government, the unions of the employees and the employers. Their activity occurs at plenary sessions and in ten standing committees, as well as in subcommittees and in special ad hoc ones. The preparation and coordination of the work of the IRC is done by the Secretariat in which all parties are represented by their respective secretaries. The bylaws stipulate the following:

* The authorities of the IRC must inform the Parliament about the opinions of the employees' and employers' organizations regarding basic acts related to the workplace;
* The social partners are entitled to consult about the important issues raised by the partners (for example, economic policy or related measures of the government), as well as to discuss legislation so that the IRC can give recommendations to Parliament, to the government and to the ministries;
* Decisions about important aspects of the wage system (minimum wage, general wage tariff system, wage allowances by law and the elements of the wage regulation), the official working time, as well as general rules relating to working conditions can be made only if the social partners agree.

The IRC is based on the informal agreement and cooperation of the social partners; its operation and structure are not stipulated in an act, but a part of its authorizations are included in legislation. The Employment Act of February 1991 assigns certain competencies to the Labor Market Committee that was formed to deal with employment interest reconciliation. Their task is to make decisions from the "Solidarity Fund for the Unemployed"—following the fulfillment of allowances entitled as subjects—about the utilization of funds remaining. It considers draft legislation having a direct impact upon employment by the government or on its members.

The Labor Code passed in March 1992 says: "On matters on national significance involving labor relations and employment, the government shall cooperate with the organizations that represent the employees' and the employers' interests in the Interest Reconciliation Council," (Article 16); "with the Interest Reconciliation Council's agreement the government shall determine the regulations that depart from this Law in relation to the termination of employment on economic grounds affecting a larger group of employees, in the interest of employment"; and "the government shall initiate national wage negotiations in the Interest Reconciliation Council."

Finally, the Act on the Chamber of Commerce of March 1994 touches upon the authority of the social partners. This legislation, along with the practically mandatory membership for the economic organizations stipulates the establishment of regional chambers having public association rights. These regional chambers should establish the national chambers: the Hungarian Chamber of Commerce, the Hungarian Chamber of Agriculture and the Hungarian Chamber of City and Guild.[3] The Act on the Chambers clearly separates the activity of the chambers from the activities of the representatives of interests. The act empowers the chambers to present motions to the government. The law distinguishes those employers' interest-representing organizations from the national representatives of interests which are members of the IRC. The opinion of the national Chamber of Commerce is required only if a draft will go to the government that is related to the tasks of the chambers. The Act on the Chamber of Commerce stipulates an implementation of these bodies by January 1995 . These are the structures then on for the macro level of labor reconciliation and economic consultations in Hungary. The realization of this opportunity, however, means the efficiency of the IRC is influenced by many factors, among them the fragmenting of the unions and the attitude of the government.

During 1988, parallel to the development of the multi-party system, a more radical situation developed in the world of unions. In May following the establishment of the first Democratic Trade Union, a real foundation fever started. The 2,000-2,500 trade unions joined into several national confederations, and today six trade union federations are taking part in the IRC.[4] The general weakness of the trade unions within the developing market economy can be deduced not only from their low membership and internal fragmentation but also from the conflicts among them. These conflicts focused on the legitimacy of these trade unions as well as on the equity of the old party state and for a long time effectively inhibited representation of the employees' interest.[5] The question of legitimacy was decided by the "Trade Union"[6] elections and Factory Committee elections in May 1993; today, the equity problems have also been solved.

The employers' side is also rather fragmented: there are nine organizations sitting on their side of the IRC.[7] Although their internal conflicts are less obvious, problems exist. Their attitude to the reconciliation of interests by the first democratic government after 1990 is, at best, ambivalent, combining negligence with intentions to negotiate, and persuasion with arrogant refusal. Throughout the four years in power, it maintained the institution of IRC. However, the employers' approval of the tripartite interest reconciliation is problematic and contradictory (It is characteristic that József Antall during his time as prime minister never received union leaders.) The approval was made even more difficult by the lack of the necessary economic policy and the heavy division of the governing powers in respect to the trade unions and interest reconciliation. Among such conditions, the coalition could not push through in Parliament many of the deals made with the social partners because these were changed by motions coming from their own section.

In the Hungarian transition, the role of the parties loomed large from the very beginning. The parties seized all initiatives and tried to make Parliament into a single center of decision making. They did not seek to develop relationships with the unions, and because of sharp political confrontations, there was no political aim or unity of the ideological values behind the Hungarian tripartite structure.

What could be achieved by the tripartite reconciliation in Hungary among the given institutional and political conditions? It can be considered a positive result that during the past four years the IRC has worked without any major disturbance. The outcome so far points to the following conclusions:

* Agreement has always been possible on the issue of minimum wages (however, its implementation means the success of the reconciliation is doubtful in this context);
* In difficult social conflict situations, (such as the taxi driver strike in autumn 1990) the IRC has served as a ground for working out compromises and has proved that economic problems can be solved by negotiations and reconciliation;
* It has been possible, at least partly, to involve the opinion of the unions in certain acts (for example: in case of the Labor Code);
* The "First Social Pact," forged in November 1992, has resolved a wide range of controversial issues.

One of the encouraging results of the election campaign of 1994 was that most of the leading parties had a positive view about a possible social pact. The unions, based on earlier experiences, were understandably upbeat about this idea. There was an argument about the institutional structure and about the field of preliminary negotiations before the deal. There were also questions about who the participants should be, and it was suggested that a "fourth side," representing civil organizations, be added to the three-part social partnership. The direction of the expected negotiations was determined by the coalition agreement, namely the program of the government formed by the victorious Hungarian Socialist Party and its coalition partner, the Association of Free Democrats. These documents, however, suggested the IRC as the institutional framework for the socio-economic agreement. They decided to go for tripartite interest reconciliation.

The aim of this agreement, according to the governing parties is "with the employees' and employers' interest representations, their main direction must make an impact on the economy and social policy." The government needs—for the next four years—such an agreement because their economic policy will put heavy burdens in the upcoming years on wide segments of the population but even more on the entrepreneurs. Both the employees' and the employers' sides in the IRC have started to develop concepts for the new pact. Again, we can see what was already known from the past four years of the IRC, namely that the trade unions consider employment, wage and social policy important, while the employers are interested in economic legislation.

In the first meeting of the IRC after the forming of the new government, even the new prime minister was present. This inevitably implies a change of style and might indicate a renewed interest of the new government in tripartite reconciliation. The coming weeks and months will decide how the government and the social partners can best utilize the new opportunity.

NOTES

1. In this case we have to mention the National Association of Hungarian Unions and the Hungarian Chamber of Commerce.

2. The National Association of Hungarian Trade Unions (MSZOSZ) has already developed its connections with the DGB and the ÖGB. An intensive exchange of experiences was going on with the latter about the methods of macro level wage negotiations. The International relations of the MGK were characterized more by the Chamber's than the employer's aspects.

3. The Act—among others—stipulates the tasks of the chambers as promoting infrastructural development of economic activities, support of technical development beyond the interest of direct entrepreneurship, and contribution to vocational training and in-trade development.

4. The federations are as follows: MSZOSZ, Democratic League of Independent Trade Unions, National Association of Workers Councils, Solidarity Trade Union Workers Association, Trade Union League of Intellectuals, The Cooperation Forum of Trade Unions, Autonomous Trade Unions. Solidarity was excluded in the spring of 1994 by the employees' side.

5. Walter Sauer, "Um Legitimität und Vermögen. Zur Geschichte der ungarischen Gewerkschaftsbewegung 1988 bis 1993," *Jahrbuch des Vereins für Geschichte und Arbeiterbewegung* 9 (1993), 114-160.

6. This means the election of the Social Security Local Governments in which all citizens have voting rights.

7. These are the following organizations: National Association of Employers, National Association of Entrepreneurs, National Association of Hungarian Industrialists, National Association of City and Guild, National Association of Merchants, National Association of Industrial Cooperatives, National Association of General Consumer Cooperatives, National Association of Agricultural Cooperatives and Producers, Hungarian Chamber of Agriculture.

FURTHER LITERATURE

Erzsébet Berki, ed., *A munkaügyi kapcsolatok kérdése.* Az ILO támogatásval létejött Szakértöi Testület vitaanyagainak gyüjteménye [Questions Concerning Industrial Relations. A Collection of Discussion Papers from the ILO-Supported Experts Committee] (Munkügyi Intézet (Institute of Labor Studies), Budapest: 1993).

László Bruszt, "The Antall Government and the Economic Interest Groups," in *Balance. The Hungarian Government 1990-1994*, ed. Csaba Gombár, Elemér Hankiss, László Lengyel, Györgyi Várnai (Budapest: Korridor, 1994), 212-233.

Lajos Héthy, *Tripartizmus és politikaformálás Magyarországon.* Az 1992. novemberi ÉT megállapodás és összefüggései, "Tripartizmus Közép és Keleteurópában" címû konferencián prezentált anyag, [Tripartism and the Formation of Policies. The Council of Reconciliation Agreement of November 1992 and its Relevance]. Paper presented at the conference "Tripartism in Central and Eastern Europe," Budapest, 1994.

Sándor Kurtán, "Sozialpartnerschaft in Ungarn?," in *Sozialpartnerschaft. Kontinuität und Wandel eines Modells*, ed. Emmerich Tálos (Vienna: Verlag für Gesellschaftskritik, 1993), 267-284.

The Importance of the Second Rank: The Case of the Art Plunderer Kajetan Mühlmann*

Jonathan Petropoulos

Although many academic historians are reluctant to admit it, biography lies at the core of most scholarly projects. While often eschewed as "popular" or theoretically unsophisticated, the history of individuals nonetheless remains an important tool in the construction of narratives and the interpretation of events. Biography is actually a vast and diverse genre of history, and this article concerns one of the specific variants: the history of second-rank figures. This subfield is especially important for the National Socialist epoch in that so much has been written about the top leaders. Hitler, Göring, Himmler, and the like have been studied exhaustively. And indeed, many scholars have reacted to this historiographic tradition by directing their energies toward the opposite end of the spectrum, as evidenced by the many fine works on "the history of everyday life" during the Third Reich. Yet the experiences of middle-level functionaries have remained inadequately explored.[1] As the case of Kajetan Mühlmann illustrates, the history of these operatives tells us much about how the Nazi regime functioned and how individuals responded to the unique circumstances of the time. Ultimately, National Socialist rule would have been very different, if not impossible, without their complicity.

* The author would like to express appreciation for the assistance provided by Oliver Rathkolb in Vienna, Christopher Jackson in Berkeley, S. Lane Faison in Williamstown, Steven Rogers in Washington, D.C., and Geoffrey Giles in Gainesville.

Mühlmann's story is highly instructive for more specific reasons as well. With a Ph.D. in art history, Mühlmann was a successful member of the Austrian intelligentsia. His biography reinforces the often forgotten fact that National Socialism was not an exclusively lower-class phenomenon, but relied upon the cooperation and skills of the *Bildungsbürgertum*. This erudite individual made a Faustian bargain with his masters and became the most prodigious art plunderer of the twentieth century. Beyond his personal devolution, Mühlmann's case underscores the crucial role played by Austrians in bolstering the Nazi regime. Recent studies have drawn attention to the Austrians' involvement in the deportation measures and the extermination camps.[2] Yet similar developments occurred in other branches of the government, including the cultural bureaucracy. Finally, Mühlmann's story sheds light on the denouement and aftermath of the war and the ethically problematic environment caused by a devastated continent and a burgeoning Cold War. After cooperating with the United States' Counter Intelligence Corps and Office of Strategic Services/Art Looting Investigation Unit by testifying against his superiors and helping locate missing art works, Mühlmann procured documents attesting to his supposed activities as a resistance fighter. This deception, as well as a number of useful contacts, enabled him to escape from a prison hospital and quietly live out his life in a lakeside resort near Munich, Mühlmann, like many of the second-rank figures, avoided postwar justice. It is therefore especially important that he not escape the scrutiny of historians.

Early Life

Mühlmann was born in Uttendorf near Zell am See, Austria, on 26 June 1898. Emblematic of the shadows that darken his biography, it is unclear whether he spelled his first name, Kajetan, with a "K" or a "C" (most documents use the spelling Kajetan, but others, such as his folder in the SS Hauptamt, now in the Berlin Document Center, feature the alternative). While little is known about his childhood, it was evidently tumultuous. Because he had a half-brother, Josef, an art critic and restorer who, as a member of the SS and Gestapo teamed up with Kajetan as a plunderer in the occupied lands, one presumes that there was some sort of disturbance in his parents' lives.[3] He grew up on a farm—or as he claimed in his official biography in the late 1930s, he stemmed from a "peasant lineage."[4] This might have been mere personal publicity—peasant stock being much valued among the "blood and soil" Nazis. His childhood milieu was not entirely rural, however, as he attended school in nearby Salzburg. It is difficult to ascertain much about his personality or views at this point in time, but given that he volunteered for the *Salzburger Infanterie Regiment Nummer 59* as soon as he had reached the legal age of 17 in 1915, his sense of nationalism cannot be doubted. It was typical of many ethnic Germans living in border regions to feel an exaggerated attachment to *Deutschtum*—or all things German (Hitler, who grew up nearby, and Alfred Rosenberg from Estonia in the Baltic offer two better studied cases).[5] Later, in a 1919 vote, Salzburgers "voted overwhelmingly" (158,058 to 463) for a union with the Reich.[6]

Mühlmann served with distinction in World War I and received multiple decorations. He was seriously wounded in 1918, and he suffered considerable pain while recuperating in the years directly after the war. In feeling that he had sacrificed a great deal during his service, Mühlmann viewed the ensuing Treaty of St. Germain as an unjust and unnatural fate for the Habsburg Empire: the third largest nation in Europe prior to the war with a population of 52 million was reduced to a country of seven million, dominated by an oversized, cosmopolitan capital of three million. The provision that Austria could never unite with Germany added to the sense of grievance felt by Mühlmann, as well as many other Austrians of a variety of political persuasions.[7] Feeling injured and betrayed, Mühlmann gravitated to the *Sozialistische Partei* in Salzburg, of which he was a member for several years.[8] The Austrian Social Democrats could not replace the comradeship that soldiers had known at the front, and Mühlmann gradually seemed to become more apolitical in the years after his demobilization.

Mühlmann finally pursued university studies in 1922, and he spent the next four years in Vienna and Innsbruck. He concentrated upon art history, and he himself evidently had an interest in painting (when he disappeared after the war a Viennese newspaper actually described him as a "*Kunstmaler*").[9] He received his doctorate in 1926 from the University of Innsbruck, with his dissertation entitled *Barocke Brunnen und Wasserkunst in Salzburg*. Moving back to Salzburg in 1926, Mühlmann professed an interest in the city and its monuments: he wrote for many of the local newspapers, most notably, the *Salzburger Chronik* and the *Salzburger Volksblatt*, and penned articles such as *"Neugestaltung der Salzburger Gärten," "Wo ist das Denkmalamt?"* and *"Der St. Peters Friedhof gefährdet."*[10] He established a name for himself as a concerned civic activist: his public lecture *"Die Ziele einer modernen Stadtverschönerung in Salzburg"* received coverage in the local press; and in 1932, he published a lavish book entitled *Stadterhaltung und Stadterneuerung in Salzburg an Beispielen der Restaurierungen Franz Wagners*, which not only lauded the accomplishments of a leading refurbisher of old buildings, but included an advertisement section at the end promoting numerous local construction and design firms.[11]

Mühlmann established a name for himself in Salzburg through articles on the city's historic structures, as well as numerous reviews of local art exhibitions, but his primary avocation was the Salzburg festival. In 1926, he became the *Propagandaleiter* of the *Festspiele*, or its chief publicity agent. This position proved a suitable match for his talents and views: the scholar Michael Steinberg has argued recently that the festival, despite its associations with the liberal and worldly Max Reinhardt and Hugo von Hofmannsthal, served to promote Austrian culture—that is, both the high tradition, as represented by Mozart, and the folk variety, as featured in the many choral and dance groups that performed there.[12] Mühlmann's publicity celebrated this tradition, and also reflected his strong sense of civic pride: in one article in the *Münchener Illustrierte Fremden-Zeitung*, he quoted Hofmannsthal, "Central Europe has no place more beautiful—Mozart must have been born here!"[13] Mühlmann's position afforded him considerable visibility in the community and helped him make contacts with important individuals. As an art critic, he was strikingly gentle and his reviews were almost invariably positive.[14] His early career, then, indicates an aptitude for what we would today call networking.

1934-1938

Even prior to working at the Salzburg Festival, Mühlmann displayed the ability to cultivate relationships with important individuals. For example, he was friends with Hermann Göring's sisters, who both lived near Salzburg. An apocryphal story has also appeared in accounts of his life, whereby he supposedly helped the future Reichsmarschall flee Germany after the latter took a bullet near the groin in the failed Beer Hall putsch of 1923.[15] Mühlmann denied the story when on the witness stand in 1947 in the trial of Guido Schmidt, but he noted that he was invited to Göring's home on the Obersalzberg in the mid-1930s to discuss art and politics.[16] This alliance would later prove crucial to the course of Mühlmann's career, but it would be secondary to that which he formed with Arthur Seyss-Inquart, an attorney from Moravia who practiced law in Austria. Mühlmann and Seyss-Inquart began working together in the service of the Nazi party in Austria in 1934, when they both played roles in the "*Aktion Reinthaller*," which was a project undertaken by members of the recently banned NSDAP to strengthen the position of the party in Austria.[17] Although this enterprise ended in failure, it marked the start of a relationship that would endure throughout the Third Reich, as Mühlmann and Seyss-Inquart teamed up in Vienna, Cracow and the Hague.

The reasons and circumstances behind Mühlmann's gravitation to the Austrian Nazi party remain unclear.[18] In his postwar interrogations, he himself denied ever being an "*Illegaler*": he stated under oath in 1945 that "I was never an illegal Nazi" and testified in 1947 that he was "neither before the ban or during the ban a member of the NSDAP."[19] Mühlmann admitted only to social relationships with Nazis, such as Seyss-Inquart. Yet he testified to this while knowing that party membership prior to 1938 was grounds for conviction.[20] Many sources, however, including the American Counter Intelligence Corps, identified him as a NSDAP member and part of the "fifth column."[21] A more problematic issue about his relationship to the National Socialists was raised by Wilhelm Höttl, a high-ranking member of the *Sicherheitsdienst* (SD), who declared in a 1967 protocol that Mühlmann was one of Reinhard Heydrich's agents from 1934 to 1938. This assertion was supported by the historian Wolfgang Rosar, who wrote a serious and well-documented study published in 1971.[22] Still other scholars have chosen to tread carefully when discussing Mühlmann's links to the SD, such as Radomir Luza, who offered the careful formulation that "Mühlmann was probably an SD collaborator."[23] Indisputable is the fact that Mühlmann was arrested in 1935 after the infiltration of an SD group in Salzburg (an operation that resulted in so-called trial of Dr. Jennewein).[24] Mühlmann himself claimed after the war that he was unjustly charged—that the record of his donation to help the wife of the county judge (*Bezirksrichter*) Dr. Jennewein was falsely construed as evidence of his membership in this group.[25] He also noted here that the charge of high treason was changed to participation in a secret society by the Salzburg *Landesgericht*, and that he was let off with a light sentence of time already served. As he had induced high-ranking members of the regime to intercede on his behalf—most notably, the Secretary of the *Vaterländische Front* Guido Zernatto—the objectivity of the judge's verdict remains in doubt.[26]

Despite this experience, Mühlmann's association with the Austrian Nazi Party remained sufficiently concealed so as to enable him to work as a seemingly independent front-man, or liaison during the *Verbotzeit*. The Nazi Party in Austria had been banned by Chancellor Kurt Schuschnigg in July 1934 after an SS battalion murdered Chancellor Engelbert Dollfuss. Even before this point in time, selected Austrian Nazi leaders had been arrested because of terrorist activities (the Viennese *Gauleiter* Alfred Frauenfeld, for example, was sent to the concentration camp at Wöllersdorf in June 1933). These brushes with government forces compelled the Nazis to move much of their organization, and many of their paramilitary forces to Bavaria: the Austrian Legion had its headquarters in Dachau, where they shared training facilities with the German SA, SS, Army, and police.[27] Mühlmann was particularly valuable as a messenger, as he ferried shipments of illegal propaganda and weapons that were used to destabilize the *Vaterländische Front* government.[28] Mühlmann nonetheless played both sides of the fence, as he possessed contacts within the Austrian government: he was used, for example, as a conduit of information and ideas between the Austrian Nazis and Guido Schmidt in the *Bundeskanzleramt*.[29]

Even with his efforts to avoid the appearance of any firm commitments, Mühlmann was repeatedly embroiled in conflicts and controversy. He was arrested at least four times in the mid-1930s for offenses ranging from reckless driving to the "defamation [*Beleidigung*] of a public official."[30] Many of his greatest imbroglios came from within the Nazi party: *Landesleiter* (Head of the Austrian Nazi party) Josef Leopold wrote in 1937 that Mühlmann "was rejected by the Salzburg Party members and accordingly not taken into the Party"; and five years later, the Salzburg *Gauleiter* Dr. Gustav Scheel wrote to Martin Bormann, the head of the party chancellery, "With respect to politics and character, the subject does not enjoy a good reputation among the Salzburg National Socialists . . . . According to the views of the Salzburg Party members, Mühlmann should be kept away from all political activity."[31] These attacks were entirely consistent with the nature of the Austrian National Socialists in the 1930s: what one historian described as a party " . . . rent with factions and . . . constant disagreements . . . that sometimes led to violent confrontations. The *Gauleiter* would not cooperate with one another and behaved in an irresponsibly egotistical manner."[32] Still, while Mühlmann provoked criticism among his comrades, he also, as mentioned above, cultivated influential and loyal benefactors.

Mühlmann allied himself principally with Seyss-Inquart and other Austrian National Socialists who were viewed prior to the Anschluß as the "moderates" in the party. This designation arose by way of contrast with two other principal factions: one, led by Hauptmann (Captain) Josef Leopold frequently turned to terrorist acts and other radical tactics as a means of destabilizing the government. The other notable faction was headed by Carinthians Odilo Globocnik and Friedrich Rainer. They were also not known for their willingness to compromise with the existing government, although those in this second faction did work with Seyss-Inquart, Mühlmann and the moderates to the extent that some observers view them as intra-party allies (Mühlmann and Globocnik even appear to have been friends).[33] Both Seyss-Inquart and Mühlmann, however, had contacts with members in Schuschnigg's regime that surpassed those of the other Austrian Nazis. Most notably, they counted as a friend the folk poet (*Heimatdichter*) and General Secretary of the *Vaterländische Front* Guido Zernatto (Mühlmann was on a *"Du"* basis with him).[34] Zernatto's efforts in 1935 to extricate Mühlmann from prison in Salzburg helped solidify their friendship, and led to subsequent attempts to repay the debt.[35] Mühlmann also established ties with the very influential *Staatssekretär* (State Secretary) Guido Schmidt, visiting him at the Federal Chancellery once or twice a month to discuss the political situation in Austria.[36] Schmidt was the confidant of Schuschnigg, and their decision in June 1937 to place Seyss-Inquart on the *Staatsrat*——the most influential organ in terms of the initiation of legislation——reflected not only the progress that the moderate faction had made in terms of respectability, but also Mühlmann's rise in influence.[37]

Because the moderate faction of the Austrian NSDAP eventually prevailed as the victors in this internecine conflict, their views warrant reconstruction. Significantly, the leading figures began their political careers outside the Nazi party. Both Seyss-Inquart and Mühlmann underwent a process of gradually warming to the Nazi cause. In Seyss's case, he first joined organizations affiliated with the party, such as the *Deutsch-Österreich Volksbund*.[38] Mühlmann, as was his nature, tried to avoid any overt political commitments. Later, both developed loyalties to Hitler and sought closer relations between Austria and Germany, but neither ever imagined the complete evaporation of their country (a not uncommon position among Austrian Nazis).[39] They hoped that closer ties with the Reich would bring greater economic prosperity, as well as end the sense of being diplomatically isolated (a sentiment that became even stronger after the September 1936 agreement between Mussolini and Hitler). The aspirations of these two men are reflected by Guido Zernatto in his assessment of Seyss-Inquart, written while in America: "From his speeches one gathers that he thought of a federal configuration . . . . He rejected any policy of cooptation (*Gleichschaltungspolitik*) for Austria. The idea of an independent Austria was self-evident to him and in his actions."[40] Instead of merely serving as Hitler's agents, they hoped to combine a pride in things local or Austrian with the notion of being a part of a larger German and fascist block. Wilhelm Keppler, an SD official (and SS *Gruppenführer* or Major General) who served as one of the "point men" in Austria for the Berlin government, also put their views in perspective when he noted that they "favor[ed] the path of evolution . . . [versus] the other faction which was bent on continuing strictly revolutionary and illegal activities."[41] Mühlmann testified that a main topic of conversation in his discussions with Schmidt was: "Is it possible to obtain a pacification of the Nationalists, National Socialists, and the Fatherland Front with respect to the government?"[42]

Mühlmann and Seyss-Inquart were naturally also careerists, and this in part explains why they assisted Hitler and his German associates in the annexation of Austria. The famous Berchtesgaden meeting between Hitler and Schuschnigg in February 1938 was prefaced by talks between Seyss-Inquart and the chancellor. The essence of their agreement was that the Austrian Nazi party would become less extremist in exchange for participation in the government and the easing of anti-Nazi sanctions. The specifics of their negotiations included the provision that Seyss-Inquart would be appointed Minister of the Interior and Public Security if the extremist Josef Leopold was removed as *Landesleiter*.[43] Mühlmann played a critical role in the discussions, as he briefed Hitler personally about the negotiations between Seyss-Inquart and Schuschnigg, and by doing so, betrayed the promises of confidentiality to the *Bundeskanzler*.[44] Mühlmann revealed what Schuschnigg's maximum concessions would be, and Hitler exploited this advantage by using them as a starting point in the Berchtesgaden negotiations.[45] Despite his infamous hard-line stand in this meeting, Hitler still decided to push the more acceptable faction to the fore. Historian Bruce Pauley summarized, "In a final effort to eliminate his rival, Seyss-Inquart sent the moderate Nazi and art historian Kajetan Mühlmann to Berchtesgaden ahead of Schuschnigg. Mühlmann was instructed to insist to Hitler and Keppler . . . that Leopold and the Landesleitung be removed from Austria. Seyss-Inquart got his way."[46] Hitler sacrificed Leopold in return for official toleration of the Austrian NSDAP. Seyss advanced his careerist ambitions by receiving the post of Minister of the Interior on 16 February.[47] The following month, he even acted as chancellor for forty-eight hours of the critical phase of the Anschluß. Still, Seyss-Inquart was duped by Hitler in that he never received the autonomy that he desired (either individually or for the government in Austria in which he served). Forced to settle for the position of *Reichsstatthalter* (Reich Governor), he was hemmed in when Josef Bürckel was sent from the Reich and placed in direct competition, wielding the title the Reichskommissar for the Reincorporation of Austria. For good measure, Odilo Globocnik from the more radical faction received the powerful post of *Gauleiter* of Vienna.

Mühlmann also benefitted from his efforts in helping prepare the Anschluß when Seyss-Inquart appointed him *Staatssekretär*, first in the *Bundeskanzleramt*, and then the following month after changes in the governmental structure, in the Ministry for Interior and Cultural Affairs.[48] Mühlmann also had a position directly subordinate to Seyss-Inquart as the Representative for State Art Policy and Foreign Tourism and Leader of Department III of the Office of the

Reichsstatthalter. These positions offered great promise, as
Mühlmann administered the budgets for all state cultural
organizations and played an important role in the personnel changes
that were then taking place, as the Nazis awarded adherents the plum
positions. For example, Dr. Friedrich Dworschak, a former
"*Illegaler*," was made the Director of the *Kunsthistorisches Museum*
in Vienna on 15 March 1938. In another illuminating case, Rector
Ernst Späth of the *Wiener Universität* sent Hitler a congratulatory
telegram on the day of the *Einmarsch*, and then quit three days later,
recognizing the university could be led only by a party member.[49]
With his connections and an influential post, Mühlmann initially
appeared to have been one of the fortunate ones. But like many other
Austrian officials, he quickly became frustrated with the arrogant and
assertive *Reichsdeutsche*. To start with, the Reich Minister of the
Interior Wilhelm Frick and his associates in Berlin refused to
recognize Mühlmann's appointment as *Staatssekretär* in the
Bundeskanzleramt because Seyss had made the appointment after he
had legally ceased to be Chancellor.[50] This dispute eventually proved
more a matter of semantics, with Mühlmann continuing in the full
authority of his title. However it did prefigure the subsequent
bureaucratic battles.

Seyss-Inquart and Mühlmann tried in their own ways to combat
the growing influence of the "Prussians," as the Austrians often
referred to those from the *Altreich*. Most notably, they attempted
certain bureaucratic innovations of their own, as Seyss-Inquart
proposed the creation of a Viennese (or alternatively *Ostmärkisches*)
Kulturinstitut, which would oversee all cultural activities in the
Ostmark. Seyss-Inquart planned to make Mühlmann the director.[51]
The *Reichsstatthalter* drafted long and detailed memoranda and
submitted them to Hitler seeking approval, and then even sent
Mühlmann to Berlin to present them in person.[52] This idea was
energetically opposed by *Reichskommissar* Bürckel, and thus went no
further. Hitler issued a "Standstill Order" and directed that the
structure of the cultural administration was to remain unchanged.
Mühlmann nonetheless tried to pursue a cultural program that was
more open and less heavy-handed than that which prevailed in the
Altreich. He permitted performances by a cabaret called the "*Wiener
Werkel*," which produced satirical pieces that were sometimes

directed at the authorities in Berlin. Mühlmann also evidently tolerated certain types of modern art, or so claimed his bitter critic, Reich Student Leader and *Gauleiter* Gustav Scheel, who complained that he "earlier expressly supported expressionistic art."[53] Indeed, going back as far as 1926, Mühlmann wrote reviews praising the modernist artist Anton Faistauer, whose famous mural for the *Salzburger Festspielhaus* was removed by zealots after the Anschluß.[54] In late 1938, Mühlmann provided the funds for the fresco's preservation in his capacity as the state administrator for art (and then reportedly kept a painting by the artist in his private residence).[55] Mühlmann, like many other Austrians, believed in a type of National Socialist rule for Austria which differed in part from that which stemmed from Berlin. While he pledged obeisance to the National Socialists—he and his brother Josef played a role in the city of Salzburg giving Hitler a Spitzweg painting from the Carolino Augusteum Museum and Göring a picture by C. List from the Kloster St. Peter[56]—he also subscribed to the notion of a distinct Austrian culture, and accordingly interceded on behalf of artists under attack, including the former director of the Mozarteum in Salzburg, Bernhard Paumgartner, and the Salzburg painter Eduard Bäumer.[57] Besides attempting to protect a few associates from the pre-Anschluß period, Mühlmann also sought to procure government funding for Salzburg and other cities in the provinces.[58] Although he did not remain in office long enough to ensure the continuation of these policies, his legacy was unmistakable. Baldur von Schirach, the successor to Seyss-Inquart and Bürckel as *Reichstatthalter* and *Gauleiter*, continued to advocate this relatively liberal *Kulturpolitik*.[59]

Despite Mühlmann's more liberal views about culture, he felt no inclination to soften the regime's anti-Semitic program. This attitude is indicative of the Austrian variant of National Socialism (assuming there was such a thing), as anti-Semitism was as equally severe in the Ostmark as it was in the *Altreich*. The "*Wiener Modell*" entailed pioneering measures in terms of both "Aryanization" and anti-Semitic legislation. Regarding the former, the Austrians carried out both organized and "wild Aryanizations" from the outset, with 8,000 Jewish residences being taken over legally prior to 1939, and an estimated 25,000 "wild Aryanizations" also taking place before the process was effectively bureaucratized.[60] Mühlmann and his brother Josef, who hired on with the Gestapo, availed themselves of the opportunities presented by the new regime: Kajetan lived in an apartment in Schloß Belvedere, and his office was in a confiscated building on the Prinz Eugenstraße, while Josef also received an "Aryanized" residence.[61] A branch of the Gestapo was established in Vienna with the acronym *"Vugestapo"* (*Vermögensumzugsgut Gestapo*), which liquidated the property of Jews who had left the country or who were incarcerated. As an employee of the Vienna *Gauleitung* noted to the NSDAP Treasurer in Munich, "The sale of this furniture to old party members and also offices of the NSDAP was carried out at that time by the *Vugestap* at extremely favorable prices."[62] The Mühlmanns personally benefitted from this program. Kajetan also played an important role in helping determine the anti-Semitic measures imposed by the government. He attended meetings in which the guidelines for expropriating Jewish property were formulated.[63] The protocols from these meetings represented the hands-on implementation of the series of laws that were passed in the second half of 1938: the 20 November Ordinance for the Attachment of the Property of the People's and State's Enemies and the 3 December Ordinance for the Employment of Jewish Property were the most important of these anti-Jewish measures at this time.[64] While Göring and the other top leaders in Berlin assumed chief responsibility for these laws, the on-site advice from figures like Mühlmann, Eichmann, and Dr. Hans Fischböck cannot be underestimated.[65] It seems fitting that Adolf Eichmann ran his Jewish deportation office in the Rothschild palace just across the street from Kajetan Mühlmann's new home and office.[66]

The expropriation of Jewish property in Austria that began in 1938 was not simply a case of persecution and self-enrichment, as heated battles over jurisdiction arose after the plunder began to accumulate. The scholar Hans Witek has written that with the "dispossession of the Jews, the fights between the interest groups had not only a power-political character, but also were indivisibly linked to the struggle to 'divide the booty.'"[67] With respect to the Jewish-owned artworks that were confiscated by the Gestapo, SS, and police in the course of the "Aryanizations"—and these artworks were the chief concern of Mühlmann—the primary issue centered around their custody. Upon Hitler's direct order, the artworks were stored in the *Neue Burg* palace in the heart of the city, as well as in the Rothschild's hunting lodge Waidhofen an der Ybbs, which was located a short distance from Vienna. In August 1938, Hitler issued what was called the "Reservation of the Führer" with respect to the artworks, where he reserved the prerogative to determine the fate of the works. This did not prevent the subleaders from formulating their own plans, or from lobbying vigorously to implement them. Seyss-Inquart and Mühlmann represented the opinion that the artworks must stay in Austria, and above all, in Vienna. They argued that the pieces had stemmed from Vienna's Jews and were thus a part of the city's cultural patrimony. Mühlmann, who played a central role in expropriating the Rothschild's art collection, wrote Hitler a report in mid-1939 imploring a decision that would keep the confiscated artworks—which all told were valued at sixty to seventy million Reichsmarks—in the city of Vienna.[68] Seyss-Inquart suggested selling off a third of the works, thereby raising enough money to build a new natural history museum, and thus allowing the *Kunsthistorisches Museum* to expand into the *Naturhistorisches Museum* across the plaza.[69]

Most of the other *Reichsdeutsche* viewed the works as booty that should benefit the Reich. Just as the *Reichskleinodien* (Holy Roman treasures) were shipped from Vienna to Nuremberg (an attempt on the part of the Nazis to remedy what they perceived as an historic injustice), and just as much of Austria's wealth was in the process of heading to the *Altreich*, they believed that these Jewish-owned works should have a similar fate.[70] Himmler proposed very concrete suggestions to Hitler, writing him that he was prepared to take over an operation to send the plunder to storage depots in Berlin and Munich.[71] The views of *Reichskommissar* Bürckel only served to complicate the situation: while he was a *Reichsdeutscher*, he was also concerned with maintaining control over the territory under his jurisdiction. Although he rarely agreed with the proposals of Seyss and Mühlmann, he nonetheless sought to keep the confiscated art in Austria.[72] As was frequently the case, Hitler refrained from arbitrating this dispute and ordered the SS and SD to guard the treasures while art experts prepared an inventory.[73]

The confiscation of Jewish artworks had import not only in terms of the growing friction between the native Austrians and the *Reichsdeutsche*, but in terms of the increased persecution of the Jews. These measures first carried out in Vienna, and then in the wake of Kristallnacht (November 1938) in the *Altreich*, were an important juncture in what Karl Schleunes called "the twisted road to Auschwitz."[74] There is widespread consensus among historians that material interests were part of the motivation for the persecution of Jews. As Robert Koehl has written, "While Heydrich and later Eichmann seized the initiative in organizing the resettlement and killing of the Jews, they were continually abetted and even rivalled by other government and party agencies. Not the least of the motives involved in this initiative was the seizure of Jewish wealth."[75] In short, Mühlmann and his associates in the *Reichstatthalter's* office were important players in the rivalry for the booty.

Despite Mühlmann's apparent zealousness in contributing to the Nazi take-over in Austria, he was fired from his post in June 1939 by Josef Bürckel, who, having assumed Globocnik's position as *Gauleiter* of Vienna, was now the most powerful figure in the Ostmark. The official reason for the dismissal—as stated in Bürckel's notification letter to Mühlmann of 23 June—was that the *Wiener Werkel* cabaret group had been allowed to produce "anti-Prussian scenes" and that this laxness had undermined Bürckel's authority.[76] The underlying motivation for the dismissal was two-fold: to weaken those who represented what was referred to as "Austrian tendencies," and to vanquish a rival. With respect to the former reason, Mühlmann was not alone among the Austrians in suffering discrimination at the hands of the *Reichsdeutsche*: the scholar Jan Tabor has written of the second class status to which many Austrian artists and architects were relegated, even with respect to "domestic" projects such as the remodelling of Linz.[77] Mühlmann's efforts to keep the art confiscated from Vienna's Jews, as well as his efforts to direct funding to provincial cultural institutions were the main reasons for his dismissal.[78] Even Seyss-Inquart was not in a fortuitous position to battle Bürckel and save his protegé: his appointment as *Reichsstatthalter* expired on 30 April 1939, and Hitler subsequently shuffled him off as Ambassador to Slovakia.[79] Seyss still held a cabinet position in Austria, and by way of this position, he made an attempt to have Mühlmann reinstated. He contacted Hermann Göring, who just weeks earlier, had talked about expanding Mühlmann's scope of authority by placing him in charge of the Berlin state museums.[80] Seyss-Inquart not only appealed to Göring to help Mühlmann, but also attempted to challenge Bürckel directly: lettersof 29 June 1939 and 8 August 1939 included a litany of complaints and criticism, above all, that the replacement of Austrians by functionaries from the *Altreich* was having a very negative effect.[81] Seyss also contacted Himmler on 19 August, hoping to induce yet another of the powers in Berlin to intercede.[82] Yet because none of the top leaders would intervene, and because Bürckel could not be vanquished by Seyss-Inquart on his own, the net result of this showdown left Mühlmann unemployed and the two subleaders completely alienated. As Seyss-Inquart admitted in a letter of 8 August to Bürckel, " . . . Our paths have gone their separate ways."[83]

World War II

With the Germans' success in the Polish campaign in September 1939, Göring found himself in a position to offer Mühlmann a post in the occupation administration. Göring contended at Nuremberg that Mühlmann approached him with the request to confiscate art, in which case, this represents a startling case of a policy initiative coming from a secondary leader.[84] While Göring's assertion must be treated skeptically, it is not outside the realm of possibility: in a parallel case, Wolfram Sievers, who was the Business Manager of Heinrich Himmler's purported research organization, the *Ahnenerbe*, wrote to the Reichsführer-SS on 4 September 1939, requesting permission to attach artworks and monuments relating to *"germanische und deutsche Kultur und Geschichte im Osten."*[85] Regardless of the source of the initiative, there is no doubt that the two men met in Berlin on 6 October 1939, and that Göring appointed him Special Agent of the *Reichsmarschall* for the Securing of Artistic Treasures in the Former Polish Regions.[86] Three days later, Göring arranged for his aide Erich Gritzbach to sign a written commission granting Mühlmann wide-ranging powers to secure all artworks belonging to Jews, to the "former" Polish state, and to other enemies of the National Socialists (the major unresolved question was how to treat Church property, although that was also later confiscated). Mühlmann was joined by a host of other Austrians in occupied Poland. In fact, this was a conscious tactic on the part of the leaders in Berlin—to send those officials with *"österreichische Tendenzen"* away from the Ostmark to serve the Reich in the newly incorporated territories.[87] Hermann Neubacher, for example, the former Bürgermeister of Vienna who had local allegiances became an

Portrait of Kajetan Mühlmann (1939), *Institut für Zeitgeschichte*, Vienna.

Reichsmarshall Hermann Göring with his protégé Mühlmann in tow on the Heldensplatz in Vienna (1940), *Institut für Zeitgeschichte*, Vienna.

Mühlmann (on the right), donning his SS-uniform, with *Generalgouverneur* of Poland Hans Frank in the Royal Castle in Cracow (1941), *Rijksinstituut voor Oorlogsdocumentatie*, Amsterdam.

economic manager in Rumania. Hitler appointed Seyss-Inquart Deputy to *Generalgouverneur* Hans Frank on 12 October, and other Austrian officials who played prominent roles in the East included Odilo Globocnik, who headed an *Einsatzkommando* and then led *"Operation Reinhard,"* which aimed to kill all Jews in the *Generalgouvernement*; Adolf Eichmann, who oversaw deportation measures in numerous regions; Alfred Frauenfeld, the pre-Anschluß *Gauleiter* of Vienna, who became the *Generalkommissar* for the Crimea; Franz Stangl, who became the Commandant of Treblinka; and Alois Brunner, who served as Eichmann's Deputy and then Assistant Commandant of Sobibor. The statistic cited by Bruce Pauley—that 40 percent of the staff of the extermination camps was Austrian, even though Austrians made up only eight percent of the Reich's population—is perhaps even more striking than a list of noteworthy perpetrators.[88]

Mühlmann was charged with forming a cadre of agents to locate, transport and catalogue the artworks in Poland; and the experts he turned to included many Austrians. This is to some extent explained by the fact that parts of Poland, such as Lower Silesia, had once been included in the Habsburg Empire, which gave rise to the Austrians' scholarly tradition of studying the culture of this area. Those staff members who did not stem from Austria usually came from Wroclaw (Breslau), another geographically proximate area.[89] It is striking that these professionals would engage in the wholesale depredation of a neighboring land. Granted, they tried to give their activities a scholarly veneer: Mühlmann's task was called "coordinated scientific leadership," and he and his colleagues were not stealing, but "securing" (*sicherstelle*). Their scientific endeavors extended to cataloguing the plunder according to the quality of the works, with the best pieces called "Choice I" (*Wahl I*). Based on his "research" in Poland, Kajetan Mühlmann even published two short books that had scholarly pretenses, even if they were baldly ideological.[90] His half-brother Josef Mühlmann, who led one of the two commandos—the one in charge of the northern part of Poland above the fifty-first parallel that included Warsaw—reported in 1963 that he and his colleagues had only dealt with "*staatlichen Museen*," and that they had compiled two inventories (one for the north and one for the south) of such great scientific value that they were sent to major libraries. He presumed that a copy of the catalogue was still in the

Nationalbibliothek in Vienna. Josef Mühlmann claimed furthermore that the works were sent to the Reich only upon the advance of the Soviet troops.[91] After the war, Kajetan Mühlmann provided a less embellished account of his commandos' work, "I confirm that the official policy of *Generalgouverneur* Hans Frank was to take into custody all important artworks of Polish public institutions, private collections, and churches. I confirm that the mentioned artworks were actually confiscated and I myself am clear that in the case of a German victory they would not have remained in Poland, but would have been used for the completion of German art holdings."[92] Mühlmann played a key role in the plan that Hans Frank described most succinctly: " . . . the Polish lands are to be changed into an intellectual desert."[93]

As with his interlude in Vienna, Mühlmann had to contend with the personal politics of his superiors while he carried out his plundering commission in Poland. Göring, who had been appointed *Reichsmarschall* and Hitler's official successor on 1 September 1939, and who had first engaged Mühlmann, warranted Mühlmann's primary allegiance. Göring had used a favorite tactic among the top Nazi leaders by hiring Mühlmann at a time when the latter was unemployed and had no visible career prospects (Hitler often used this tactic, for example, rehabilitating the former Director of the Dresden *Gemäldegalerie* Hans Posse to head the *Führermuseum*, after Posse had been sacked by the local *Gauleiter* Martin Mutschmann). This strategy of making subordinates beholden to superiors perhaps partly explains their willingness to engage in criminal activities. Regardless of his motivations, Mühlmann made sure to appease this benefactor, and he directed prized artworks to the Reichsmarschall as special gifts, including Antoine Watteau's *La Femme Polonaise* from the Lazienski castle and thirty-one "especially valuable and world famous drawings by Albrecht Dürer from the Lubormiski collection in Lemburg [Lvov]."[94] Mühlmann also had to contend with the other Nazi powers in Poland: Hans Frank made regular selections from the plunder, which was stored in the Jagellonian library in Crackow. Frank decorated two castles with the help of Mühlmann, earning the sobriquet König Stanislaws V.[95] Heinrich Himmler, the other notable potentate in the region, likewise made claims on Mühlmann, his SS subordinate (Mühlmann was repeatedly promoted within the SS, ultimately in 1943 to the rank of SS-*Oberführer* or Colonel). This relationship matured later when Mühlmann moved to the Netherlands, as Himmler arranged to obtain artworks for both private and official purposes. Lesser leaders, such as his old ally, the Salzburg *Gauleiter* Friedrich Rainer, tried to induce Mühlmann to forward artworks. Rainer had previously obtained pieces from the Rothschilds' collection in Vienna, and he again asked Mühlmann for art to decorate *"Salzburger Schlösser"*—above all his official quarters in the *Residenz*.[96] Mühlmann could not accommodate Rainer in this instance, though he wisely advised Rainer to raise the matter with Hitler (who also turned him down).[97] Mühlmann cultivated the good will of the Führer by sending him five volumes of photographic albums depicting the *"Wahl I"* artworks, of which there were 521. Hitler reportedly studied the catalogue carefully, with an eye towards enhancing the collection of his *Führermuseum*.[98]

Because Mühlmann and his staff had worked very expeditiously in Poland—he reported to Hitler that "within six months almost the entire artistic property of the land was seized—he had developed a reputation for efficiency, and simultaneously freed himself to become engaged in other enterprises.[99] In Poland he had become acquainted with Wolfram Sievers, who was both the Business Manager of the *Ahnenerbe* and one of the leaders of the *Haupttreuhandstelle Ost*. The former was an organization under Himmler's aegis that was concerned with "pre-historical" matters, such as excavations and folkloric studies; the latter was one of the plundering agencies in the occupied East, which again, fell under the joint leadership of Göring and Himmler. Sievers and his associates in das *Ahnenerbe* were also involved in reclaiming Germanic cultural objects from the South Tyrol region, having been commissioned to do so by Himmler in his capacity as *Reichskommissar* for the Strengthening of the German People (that post which placed him in charge of the population transfers undertaken by the Nazis). As Hitler had sacrificed the South Tyrol to Mussolini in an effort to bolster the Axis alliance in 1939 (and arguably as compensation for the acceptance of the Anschluß), the Nazis were particularly anxious that all artworks and cultural objects from the region came *"heim ins Reich."* Sievers called Mühlmann down to the *Ahnenerbe's* operation base for the South Tyrol in Bolzano in the spring of 1940 and discussed the possibility of Mühlmann lending his expertise to the project. Mühlmann accepted the offer, conditional upon his being named to head the operation (then euphemistically called the *Kulturkomission*). Sievers consulted his colleagues about this demand, and he reported in a memorandum that while he had nothing against this arrangement, there were "objections of the men of the Art Group in the *Kulturkomission*, who know Dr. Mühlmann very well."[100] Mühlmann's reputation in 1940 therefore entailed a mixture of admiration, which stemmed from this technical prowess, and apprehension, which grew out of his desire to dominate and his wish to get ahead by catering to his superiors.

Mühlmann could not have been too upset that his services were not needed in the South Tyrol because by the time the matter had been decided, he had been engaged by the *Reichskommissar* of the Occupied Netherlands, Seyss-Inquart, to ply his trade in the Low Countries.[101] A Dutch intelligence officer, Jean Vlug, noted dramatically in his postwar report on art looting, "Rotterdam was still burning when Kajetan Mühlmann in his SS-uniform arrived in Holland to take up the task of his *Dienststelle*."[102] Vlug's report is flawed in many respects (Mühlmann normally wore a brown party uniform or civilian clothes), yet his observation is accurate with respect to Mühlmann's assiduousness as a plunderer. In fact, Mühlmann was especially delighted to work with his friend in the Netherlands because he had felt uncomfortable with the brutal policies that had prevailed in Poland—he had, for example, complained to Hans Frank about the dynamiting of the "*Denkmal vor dem Wavell*."[103] Mühlmann's guidelines in the Low Countries differed significantly from those in effect during his previous operation. The Dutch were perceived by Hitler, Himmler, and other policy-makers as racially kindred to the "Aryan" Germans, and the occupation was supposed to be more benign and lawful. Hitler had chosen Seyss-Inquart because of his reputation for moderation (a misassessment in light of the findings of the International Military Tribunal that determined that Seyss had ordered hostages shot, deported five million workers to the Reich, and played a leading role in killing 117,000 of the 140,000 Jews—one of the highest fatality ratios in German-occupied Europe). Yet if one is to preserve the distinctions, the occupation of the Netherlands must be recognized as having differed from that in Poland; and Seyss-Inquart was much more in his element in the West as he tried to nurture collaboration while overseeing the economic exploitation of this occupied country.

As usual, Mühlmann adapted to his surroundings, and just as he had created brutal looting commandos in Poland, he was able with equal ease to establish a type of art dealership for processing plunder from departed Jews and other enemies. The office also sought out any other artworks that could be acquired inexpensively and re-sold for a profit. Mühlmann's operation became a relatively sophisticated operation: with headquarters in the Hague (where he could be near Seyss-Inquart, who provided him with three bank accounts and the initial capital to start the venture), he eventually opened branches in Amsterdam, Brussels, Paris, Berlin, and Vienna.[104] Because the agency received works from different branches of the Nazi bureaucracy—the SD and the *Reichskommissariat* for Enemy Property stand out as the two key sources—it in many ways resembled a clearing house.[105] Mühlmann stipulated that a commission of 15 percent would be made on all sales, save those to Hitler and his agents. He surrounded himself with a small staff, including his half-brother Josef (who kept a special watch on opportunities in Brussels and maintained an office in Paris), two Viennese art historians—Franz Kieslinger and Bernhard Degenhart—and Eduard Plietzsch, a specialist on Dutch art who continued to publish monographs while he worked for the *Dienststelle*.[106] Mühlmann's efforts to gain some hint of respectability entailed not only employing these well-regarded experts, but also cultivating relationships with members of the art establishment back in the Reich. He consigned works from the *Dienststelle* to a number of respectable auction houses, including the Dorotheum in Vienna, Adolf Weinmüller in Munich and Vienna, and Hans Lange in Berlin.[107] Records show that the *Dienststelle* Mühlmann sold at least 1,114 artworks during the war.[108]

Such apparent niceties could not conceal the essence of Mühlmann's project, which was to expropriate the artistic property of Jews and other enemies of the regime, and to ensure that the booty flowed in an orderly manner to the top Nazi leaders. During the first months of the occupation, Seyss-Inquart issued *Verordnung No.* 189/1940, which required Jews to take their valuables, including jewelry and artworks, to the "Aryanized" Bankhaus Lippmann, Rosenthal, and Co. in Amsterdam.[109] This property was then handed over to the chief of the economic division of the *Reichskommissariat*—Dr. Hans Fischböck, another Austrian with whom Mühlmann had earlier worked in Vienna. Fischböck then arranged for the artworks to be delivered to the *Dienststelle* Mühlmann, where they were assessed by the art experts, and then put up for sale at a very reasonable estimated price—with Hitler and Göring accorded the right of first refusal.[110] Yet as a result of this unusual commercial enterprise, Mühlmann was now in a position to direct works to other members of the Nazi elite (unlike in Poland, where he had less autonomy). His customers included Heinrich Himmler, Ernst Kaltenbrunner, Hans Frank, Baldur von Schirach, Erich Koch, Fritz Todt, Julius Schaub, Josef Thorak, and Heinrich Hoffmann.[111]

Despite the apparent freedom of action and the undeniable profitability, Mühlmann was in a difficult position as he tried to appease a number of leaders of superior rank. He admitted in postwar interviews with American Office of Strategic Service (OSS) officers that "the competition between Hitler and Göring caused a pressure from which one could not escape . . . . I personally was in a very difficult position."[112] In the autumn of 1944, his Austrian friend Ernst Kaltenbrunner, the successor to Heydrich as head of the SD and Gestapo, reported to Mühlmann that Bormann had threatened to place him in a concentration camp as a result of his delivering an insufficient quantity of art to Hitler.[113] This was not an entirely idle threat: another major procurer of art for Hitler, Prinz Philipp von Hessen, as well as his wife, Princess Mafalda of Italy, were sent to camps in the summer of 1943 (although in this case the reason was evidently Mussolini's fall from power, as the Prinz had been Hitler's liaison to the Duce). Mühlmann too reportedly lost his position in Poland in autumn 1943 for incurring *Generalgouverneur* Frank's displeasure for failing to deliver certain valuable pictures.[114] Mühlmann, however, had a talent for self-preservation, and as the Allies invaded the continent and displaced the Germans from western Europe, he and his colleagues pulled out of the Low Countries.

Mühlmann decided to return to the relative security of Vienna. As he had provided many artworks to the city's Nazi chieftain, Baldur von Schirach, he thought there were good prospects for a safe haven.[115] At this point, his main objective was survival. Accordingly, he reduced his business activities to a minimum. Mühlmann reported after the war that from July 1944 until June 1945, he was "without any duties—more or less on sick leave."[116] Because of the deteriorating military situation, he was especially concerned about the welfare of his wife and three children.[117] When the OSS agents arrived in Vienna in early 1945, they located Mühlmann's well-stocked home and reported, "In his cellar are stored cases with Dutch products: soap, Bols [liqueur], rugs, lamps, etc."[118] This hoarding was not unique by any means. The same agents noted the efforts of his half-brother: "Josef Mühlmann was an SS captain in Poland, but was deprived of this worthy grade for installing a lady friend with objects destined for the Reich."[119] Kajetan was more successful in his corruption, and this was in part due to his connections to those with power who could offer him some sort of protection. Mühlmann stayed in touch with powerful Nazi figures right up until the end of the Third Reich. Ernst Kaltenbrunner, for example, consulted with him in April 1945 about the formation of a transitional Austrian government—one to counter that proposed by Karl Renner—as both factions sought to create a regime that would be acceptable to the Allies.[120] After the war, Mühlmann told his captors grand stories about battling SS-commando Otto Skorzeny and his contingent of fanatics in the Tyrol. Mühlmann also claimed that he had liberated Hermann Göring from his incarceration by SS forces in Schloß Mauthendorf (where he had been imprisoned by order of Hitler on charges of treason), and then, upon Göring's request (and with the consent of Field Marshal Albert Kesserling), delivered the *Reichsmarschall* to the Americans.[121] Mühlmann never considered that this story of heroic deeds was inconsistent with his other claim that he was sick and inactive at the time. In any case, the veracity of his tales remains highly doubtful; but it is ironic that Mühlmann's last act for his one-time benefactor very well may have been to deliver him to the enemy just as the war was ending.

The Postwar Period

It is similarly extraordinary to contemplate the reasons why Mühlmann escaped prosecution after the war. His name was placed on the CROWCASS (Central Registry of War Crimes and Security Suspects) list, and the Americans captured him on 15 June 1945 and took him to Camp Markus in western Austria.[122] On 20 July, he was transferred to the camp at Payerbach in Upper Austria, where he was interrogated by the Counter Intelligence Corps unit that worked on culture (also known as Culture Intelligence).[123] They induced him to discuss the deeds of Göring, Seyss-Inquart, Frank, and Kaltenbrunner—blunt and damning testimony that was submitted to the International Military Tribunal at Nuremberg and helped in the convictions and subsequent death sentences of these leaders.[124] Regarding his own actions, Mühlmann admitted responsibility in a way similar to that of Albert Speer: he confessed to a specific and non-capital offense (viz., the expropriation of Jewish property), but claimed to know nothing about the Holocaust (a bald-faced lie considering his career), and denied that his deeds led to personal enrichment. Yet unlike Speer, he failed to make a positive impression on the victors. The assessment of one Allied interrogator read, Mühlmann "is obstinate; he has no conscience; he does not care about art; he is a liar and a vile person."[125] The CIC sent Mühlmann back to the Austrian authorities in October 1946, although they demanded a written pledge that he not be released without prior American approval.[126] Art plunderers rarely faced prosecution after the war. Nonetheless, the only other subleader to rival Mühlmann in terms of scale and net worth of the artworks, Robert Scholz (another Austrian who worked for the *Einsatzstab Reichsleiter* Rosenberg in France and on the Eastern Front), was turned over to the French and sentenced to five years imprisonment.[127] With similar intentions, the Poles sought Mühlmann's extradition and pressured the Austrians to relinquish him. Historian Robert Herzstein has described how "in the summer of 1947, Austria passed a new law that appeared designed to restrict further extradition of accused war criminals of Austrian nationality."[128] While the Allied Council vetoed this provision, the Austrian authorities proved very accomplished at foot dragging. In 1951, for example, they falsely maintained that Mühlmann was either in Switzerland or Lichtenstein and that delivering him to Poland was not feasible.[129] Mühlmann remained the subject of a domestic investigation, but the Austrian government did not want a citizen featured in a foreign showcase trial at this point, when the State Treaty, based as it was on the Moscow Declaration of 1943 providing for victim status, hung in the balance.[130]

Prior to 1948, Mühlmann remained in a camp for SS members, who were automatically supposed to serve two year prison terms. In 1947, he testified in the celebrated treason case of Guido Schmidt.[131] In this public forum, he attempted to pass himself off as an insignificant bureaucrat and he denied both his SD ties and any illegal pre-Anschluß NSDAP membership. He undoubtedly hoped to avoid attention and slip away after his release from the SS prison camp. But the Austrians' and Americans' on-going inquiries into his past made this development increasingly unlikely. Mühlmann evidently placed his hopes in the exculpatory story that he had turned resistance fighter at the end of the war. But even this story proved problematic: Karl Gruber, the leader of the resistance in the Tyrol, claimed to have met him for the first time in mid-May 1945, two weeks after the capitulation.[132] Indeed, Gruber reported that he knew nothing of Mühlmann's activities, but that Mühlmann had papers signed by an American general attesting to his anti-Nazi activities (and permitting him to carry a gun).[133] Gruber therefore had signed a certificate—a *"Persilschein"*—attesting to Mühlmann's role in the resistance. It is curious that the head of the resistance would vouch for someone that he did not actually know, but Gruber had very close ties to the Americans (and the Counter Intelligence Corps in particular). The Americans returned this trust by appointing Gruber Tyrolean *Landeshauptmann* (and later supported his elevation to the position of Foreign Minister).[134] It appears, then, that both sides collaborated in providing Mühlmann with the certificate of resistance activities. Gruber testified in a libel case against a newspaper in 1950 that he "had provided the former Undersecretary Dr. Mühlmann, on behalf of the Americans, a certificate [that he had been of great service to the resistance movement]."[135] Whether the Americans also assisted Mühlmann as a result of his postwar cooperation with the Counter Intelligence Corps—and protected him as they did Klaus Barbie and Robert Jan Verbelen—and whether Gruber intentionally helped his fellow Austrian evade justice remains difficult to determine.[136] If Mühlmann actually delivered Göring to the Americans in 1945, this deed, along with damning U.S. testimony that proved so useful to prosecutors at Nuremberg, may have earned him the generous treatment. Historian Chris Simpson noted how "the great majority of early (i.e., 1944-1947) recruitment and protection of Nazis by the United States government was the product of what many people would term 'police informer' types of relationships, " and numerous scholars have identified the CIC Detachments in Austria and Bavaria as those most inclined to engineer these controversial arrangements.[137]The Counter Intelligence Corps documents released under the Freedom of Information Act have been blacked out by censors so that it is impossible to determine what transpired. It is clear, however, that in the wake of Mühlmann's testimony at the Guido Schmidt trial, the Americans arranged for his transfer back to Munich, where on 18 August 1947, he became the responsibility of the Office of the Military Government of Bavaria.[138]

Despite Mühlmann's apparent usefulness to the Americans, they allowed him to escape and then were indolent in undertaking his recapture. In February 1948, while under guard in the Hospital Carolinum near Munich, Mühlmann disappeared and was never again apprehended.[139] The details of his escape and the reasons for the authorities' inactivity in terms of pursuing him remain a mystery. The Poles, for their part, energetically continued to seek his extradition in the late 1940s and early 1950s.[140] The Austrians also pursued Mühlmann through judicial means, and they issued an arrest warrant in absentia in August 1951.[141] Because of his fugitive status, the court appointed a Viennese attorney named Otto Tiefenbrunner to represent him. Tiefenbrunner attempted to get the charges dismissed, filing an appeal with the Austrian Bundespräsident Dr. Theodor Körner.[142] The appeal was written from Mühlmann's perspective: it discussed the charges "against me" before the *Volksgericht* in Vienna and recounted Mühlmann's prewar experiences and testimony in the Guido Schmidt trial in the first person. Yet Tiefenbrunner, who filed a number of subsequent documents on behalf of his client, conveniently claimed not to know Mühlmann's whereabouts. Josef Mühlmann later testified that his brother lived abroad in Munich, although he too denied any contact.[143] Kajetan Mühlmann's widow continued to live near Salzburg where she worked as a school teacher in the small village Seewalchen am Attersee.[144] The Austrian authorities, then, had some sense of Mühlmann's movements, but there are no indications that they solicited the Federal Republic of Germany's assistance in his extradition. While one can perhaps understand the unwillingness of Austrians to release their citizens to Soviet bloc or Yugoslav governments during the Cold War, it is remarkable that justice did not transcend Western European borders. But these borders, like the occupation zones of earlier years, often served as shields for those trying to escape justice.[145]

There were nonetheless subsequent efforts to bring Mühlmann to justice. In 1952, he was again charged in absentia by the Austrian

Volksgerichtssenat. A notice in the *Wiener Kurier* reported on the trial: "A People's Court Senate considered the high treasonous activities of the notorious Nazi painter [sic] Dr. Kajetan Mühlmann on Friday, after the state prosecutor of Vienna motioned for the forfeiture of his entire property. Mühlmann, a fugitive of unknown whereabouts, stood in closest connection to the leaders of the illegal NSDAP during the *Verbotszeit* in Austria ."[146] In 1957, the case was reopened once again. Mühlmann still resided in Munich, while his wife continued to live in Seewalchen and collect a pension from the Austrian state. The prosecutors interviewed another series of witnesses and debated whether the amnesty for former National Socialists would apply to him and provide for his exoneration. As part of the investigation, they again contacted Kajetan's half-brother Josef Mühlmann. The former Gestapo agent and plunderer had never thought it necessary to leave the country and had managed an almost complete rehabilitation of his reputation in his capacity as an art restorer in the Salzburg Residenz. One visitor to Josef Mühlmann in January 1963 (who reported back to Simon Wiesenthal) described the following: "he lives here very contentedly, and despite his advanced age (78) is still active as an art restorer."[147] In the 1960s, Josef Mühlmann published books on Christmas songs and lived a comfortable life.[148] He was apparently well-regarded within the community and both the Salzburg Museum and the Residenzgalerie still possess portraits of him.[149] Kajetan Mühlmann did not fare as well nor live as long. Mühlmann had told Allied interrogators in 1947 that he had hoped to take advantage of all that he had learned and become an art dealer.[150] Considering his decision to flee, this goal was undoubtedly left unfulfilled. While his activities during his later years remain a mystery, it is certain that he died of cancer at the age of 60 on 2 August 1958.[151]

Conclusion

Kajetan Mühlmann's life and career prove instructive to the historian in numerous ways. With his origins and early life, he represents an important aspect of National Socialism; or as Gerhard Botz has noted, "that Hitler is an export-product of Austria, that his social-intellectual origins stem from the provincial city of Linz . . . .This concerns his pan-Germanness, his continental conceptions of imperial power (*Weltmachtvorstellungen*) and his suspicion of democracy; as well as his sectarian sense of mission, his (Catholic-based) political liturgy and, above all, his racial anti-Semitism."[152] Hitler and Mühlmann indeed stemmed from similar milieux: the pan-German sentiment they felt was an important historic dynamic prior to the First World War. Likewise, their enthusiasm for war, their subsequent disillusionment, and their responses to the chaotic circumstances after World War I were paradigmatic of many men of their generation. Hitler, however, distinguished himself not only by his unusual personality and charisma, but by his fanatical devotion to the key principles in his world view. Mühlmann proved more typical, because while he was a Nazi, he was above all out for himself. Mühlmann never identified with the National Socialist movement in the manner of the leaders at the apex of the regime. He was a functionary by temperament, and he supported the Nazi policies only so long as they served his interests.

Mühlmann is also particularly valuable as a subject because he was an artist-intellectual. It is striking that he, like Hitler, viewed himself as an artistic type and yet came to devote so much time to enterprises that were destructive. With Mühlmann the process of corruption was gradual, as his personal advancement coincided with diminishing scruples. Yet he was not alone in this respect. The Third Reich depended upon the efforts of intellectuals in order to survive. As Thomas Mann noted in a letter to the newspaper publisher Joseph Pulitzer in the summer of 1945, "should one make accountable only the visible political and military figures of the regime who are now assembled in the hotel-prisons? What about that thoroughly guilty stratum of intellectuals who stood and served National Socialism?"[153] Indeed, it seems that while the political and military leaders did face some measure of justice, many of the cultural servants of the regime managed to free themselves of responsibility and enjoy comfortable postwar existences.

Beyond the cultural figures who avoided responsibility for the National Socialists' crimes, the second-rank Austrian functionaries, who, like Mühlmann can be categorized as *Schreibtischtäter* (bureaucratic perpetrators) showed a special aptitude for avoiding prosecution: Hans Fischböck and Adolf Eichmann escaped to South America (with the latter, of course, eventually being brought to justice due to the efforts of the Israeli Mossad), while Alois Brunner (who prospered for decades in the Middle East), and a number of his colleagues who oversaw the deportation of Jews used the *Organisation der ehemaligen SS-Angehörigen* (ODESSA) and other networks to flee.[154] Those below Mühlmann in rank, such as the Austrian art restorer Eduard Kneisel, who spent the war repairing plundered works in Poland and then emigrated to the United States, had an even easier time rehabilitating their careers.[155] These individuals, like Mühlmann, were opportunists who exculpated themselves by way of their subordinate positions in the Nazi state and their Austrian nationality (and hence victim status). In short, they hid behind their relative anonymity and the Austrians' long-time refusal to acknowledge their complicity in the crimes of the regime. The Nazi leaders depended upon these *"Handlanger"* (henchmen), and they recruited them from virtually all parts of the continent. While many countries subjected collaborators to a harsh and even sweeping justice, there were others, like Austria, in which pangs of guilt and the desire to rebuild led to inadequate legal measures and the suppression of knowledge. The current generation of scholars therefore faces the crucial project of ensuring that the all-important functionaries like Kajetan Mühlmann do not gain another form of acquittal by being entirely ignored by history.[156]

NOTES

1. For an example of studies with this focus, see Christopher Browning, *Ordinary Men: Reserve Police Battalion and the Final Solution* (New York: Harper Collins, 1992); and Hannah Arendt, *Eichmann in Jerusalem: A Report on the Banality of Evil* (New York: Penguin, 1963).

2. See Hans Safrian, *Die Eichmann-Männer* (Vienna: Europa Verlag, 1993), and Bruce Pauley, *From Prejudice to Persecution: Anti-Semitism in Austria* (Chapel Hill: University of North Carolina Press, 1992). See also the chapter entitled "Modell Wien," in Götz Ally and Suzanne Heim, *Vordenker der Vernichtung: Auschwitz und die deutsche Pläne für eine neue europäische Ordnung* (Hamburg: Hoffmann und Campe, 1991), 33-42.

3. For Josef Mühlmann's affiliation with the Gestapo, see Josef Mühlmann to Baldur von Schirach, 17 January 1944 (on the stationery of the Geheime Staatspolizei marked "*Geheim!*"), Sammelmappe 245, Bergungsaktion, Bundesministerium für Unterricht (BMfU) II, Staatsarchiv (ÖSA).

4. See the official biography of Mühlmann issued by the Reichsstatthalterei, Wien, on 8 December 1938, as reproduced in the Munzinger-Archiv.

5. William McGrath, *Dionysian Art and Populist Politics in Austria* (New Haven: Yale U.P., 1974).

6. Bruce Pauley, *Hitler and the Forgotten Nazis: A History of Austrian National Socialism* (Chapel Hill: University of North Carolina Press, 1981), 205.

7. See Jerry Pyle, "Austrian Patriotism: Alternative to *Anschluß*," in F. Parkinson, ed., *Conquering the Past: Austrian Nazism Yesterday and Today* (Detroit: Wayne State U.P., 1989), 72.

8. *Der Hochverratsprozess gegen Dr. Guido Schmidt vor dem Volksgericht* (Vienna: Österreichische Staatsdruckerei, 1947), 244.

9. See the *Wiener Kurier*, 28 July 1952, "Vermögensverfall für Bilderkäufer des 'Reichsmarschalls' beantragt."

10. For the two articles, see the *Salzburger Chronik*, No. 254 (5 November 1926), No. 264 (18 November 1926), and the *Mitteilung des Stadt-Verschönerungsvereines Salzburg*, No. 3 (1928), 3. The articles by Mühlmann cited here can be found in the Salzburger Landesarchiv.

11. *Mitteilung des Stadt-Verschönerungsvereines Salzburg*, No. 4 (1927), 3; and Kai Mühlmann, *Stadterhaltung und Stadterneuerung in Salzburg an Beispielen der Restaurierungen Franz Wagners* (Munich/Vienna: Industrie und Gewerbe Verlag, 1932).

12. Michael Steinberg, *The Meaning of the Salzburg Festival: Austria as Theater and Ideology, 1890-1938* (Ithaca: Cornell U.P. 1990).

13. Mühlmann, "Festspiele in Salzburg," *Münchener Illustrierte Fremden-Zeitung* (25 June 1927), 3.

14. For examples of his positive reviews, see, for example, his treatment of an exhibition of Georg Behringer in the *Salzburger Volksblatt*, No. 32 (6 February 1927) and later, his two-part review of a show in the Salzburger Künstlerhaus in the *Salzburger Chronik*, No. 255 and No. 257 (4 and 7 November 1933).

15. Radomir Luza writes, "[Mühlmann] helped Göring during Göring's exile in Austria and maintained close ties with him through Göring's married sisters in Salzburg, Olga Riegele and Paula Hueber." Radomir Luza, *Austro-German Relations in the Anschluss Era* (Princeton: Princeton U.P., 1975), 35. Also A.J. van der Leeuw, *Die Bestimmung der vom deutschen Reich entzogenen und von der Dienststelle Mühlmann übernommenen Kunstgegenstände* (Amsterdam: Rijkinstitut voor de Oorlogsdocumentatie, 1962).

16. *Der Hochverratsprozess gegen Dr. Guido Schmidt*, 246.

17. Wolfgang Rosar, *Deutsche Gemeinschaft: Seyss-Inquart und der Anschluß* (Vienna: Europa Verlag), 75-82.

18. A friend of Mühlmann's, Alfons Walde, advanced the improbable thesis that Mühlmann became Nazi after being sued for killing a woman in a car accident in 1936: the financial ruin caused by the damages he was forced to pay supposedly so embittered him that he became sympathetic to the Nazis' ideas. See Walde's testimony of 27 March 1947 in Mühlmann's file at the Dokumentationsarchiv des österreichischen Widerstandes (DÖW), Vienna.

19. See the Eidliche Erklärung des SS Oberführers Dr. Kajetan Mühlmann vom 19 November 1945, Nuremberg trial document 3042-PS, *Prozesse der Hauptkriegsverbrecher*, 31:512-13. *Der Hochverratsprozess gegen Dr. Guido Schmidt*, 244.

20. Mühlmann was given a NSDAP number of 6,106,589 in March 1938. This membership number was part of the group reserved for the "so-called illegal block," although such a number did not in all cases denote that the person had been an illegal Party member (i.e., in certain cases it was honorific). See the brief from Mühlmann's lawyer, Otto Tiefenbrunner, 21 July 1952, in Mühlmann's file, DÖW, Vienna.

21. Documents supplied by Department of the Army, Freedom of Information-Privacy Act Division (date illegible). One of Mühlmann's interrogators at Alt Aussee, S. Lane Faison recalled, "He's the only self-identified Nazi I met. In a way, you'd respect him for that!" Letter to author, 28 January 1995.

22. Wilhelm Höttl protocol from 11 December 1967 in the DÖW, Vienna. Also cited by Rosar, *Deutsche Gemeinschaft*, 142, 386.

23. Luza, *Austro-German Relations*, 35. See also Peter Black, *Ernst Kaltenbrunner: Ideological Soldier of the Third Reich* (Princeton: Princeton U.P., 1984), 81 and 83.

24. Rosar, *Deutsche Gemeinschaft*, 91 and 321.

25. *Der Hochverratprozess gegen Dr. Guido Schmidt*, 243-44.

26. Ibid., 243-44.

27. Martin Kitchen, *The Coming of Austrian Fascism* (London: Croom Helm, 1980), 71.

28. Mühlmann's Gauakten in the ÖSA includes the notation that "during the time the Nazi Party was banned, he was installed as a liaison between the group of Captain Leopold and Dr. Seyss-Inquart." A letter from Odilo Globocnik of 14 April 1938 describes Mühlmann's other work for the Party "after the time of the ban of the NSDAP."

29. Rosar, *Deutsche Gemeinschaft*, 91.

30. Kaltenbrunner to Himmler, 17 February 194? (last number missing), See Mühlmann's BDC file. His arrest in the Dr. Jennewein trial is referred to here as stemming from his participation in a "secret society." Mühlmann's Gaukakte in the ÖSA notes an arrest in Salzburg on 11 October 1937 where he was involved in a fight.

31. Scheel to Bormann, 12 November 1942, Mühlmann's BDC file. Also, Leopold to Hitler, 22 August 1937, Nuremberg Trial document NG-3578 in the IfZG, Munich.

32. Kitchen, *The Coming of Austrian Fascism*, 68-69.

33. Pauley, *Hitler and the Forgotten Nazis*, 202; Black, *Ernst Kaltenbrunner*, 89; and Guido Zernatto, *Die Wahrheit über Österreich* (New York/Toronto: Longmans, Green and Co., 1938), 312. Mühlmann's Gaukakte in the ÖSA includes Globocnik's glowing letter of support, 14 April 1938.

34. *Der Hochverratprozess gegen Dr. Guido Schmidt*, 245-46. Mühlmann was friends with the *Heimatdichter* Heinrich Waggerl, who imposed upon his friend Zernatto to help free Mühlmann. Schmidt also evidently helped gain Mühlmann's release.

35. Ibid., 246. Also Pauley, *Hitler and the Forgotten Nazis*, 197 and 204.

36. *Der Hochverratprozess gegen Dr. Guido Schmidt*, 245.

37. See Hans Haas, "Der Anschluß," in Emmerich Talos, Ernst Hanisch, Wolfgang Neugebauer, eds., *NS-Herrschaft in Österreich, 1938-1945* (Vienna: Verlag für Gesellschaftskritik, 1988), 4.

38. Erich Stockhorst, *5000 Köpfe. Wer ist Wer im 3. Reich* (Wiesbaden: VMA Verlag, 1987), 362. Luza, *Austro-German Relations*, 38.

39. Maurice Williams, "Captain Josef Leopold: Austro-Nazi and Austro-Nationalist?," in Parkinson, ed., *Conquering the Past*, 58 and 68.

40. Zernatto, *Die Wahrheit über Österreich*, 179.

41. Keppler to Bormann, 2 November 1937. Cited in Luza, *Austro-German Relations*, 36.

42. *Der Hochverratprozess gegen Dr. Guido Schmidt*, 245.

43. Pauley, *Hitler and the Forgotten Nazis*, 197.

44. The betrayal of Schuschnigg and the Austrian government by Seyss and Mühlmann is stressed in the Nuremberg Trial by Prosecutor Dodd in his examination of Seyss. See *Prozesse der Hauptkriegsverbrecher*, 16:102-5.

45. Pauley, *Hitler and the Forgotten Nazis*, 197.

46. Ibid., 197-98.

47. Note that Seyss-Inquart was something of an unknown factor for Hitler. *Prozesse der Hauptkriegsverbrecher*, 16:107. Also Papen's Interrogation by the U.S. Seventh Army, 27 October 1945, MA-1300/3, Bl. 0087, in IfZG, Munich.

48. Mühlmann headed Gruppe 4, Kunstpflege und Museen, in the Ministerium für innere und kulturelle Angelegenheiten, Abteilung IV, Erziehung, Kultus, Volksbildung. He was subordinate to Staatskommissar Professor Dr. Friedrich Plattner.

49. Brigitte Lichtenberger-Fenz, "Österreichs Hochschulen und Universitäten und das nationalsozialistische Regime," in Emmerich Talos, et. al., eds., *NS-Herrschaft in Österreich*, 269.

50. Bürckel also contested the appointment of Mühlmann as State Secretary. See Rosar, *Deutsche Gemeinschaft*, 295 and 340.

51. Felix Kreissler, *Der Österreicher und seine Nation. Ein Lernprozeß mit Hindernissen* (Vienna/Cologne/Graz: Hermann Böhlaus, 1984), 149.

52. Seyss-Inquart to Hitler, 18 January 1939; and 001435-42, Seyss-Inquart to Hitler, 4 May 1939, MA-597, Bl. 001412-17 in IfZG, Munich.

53. Scheel to Bormann, 12 November 1942, Mühlmann's BDC file.

54. *Salzburger Chronik*, No. 231 (8 October 1926). For the painting by Faistauer, see the *Zeugenvernehmung* of Josef Mühlmann from 2 September 1957, in Kajetan Mühlmann's file, DÖW, Vienna.

55. For Mühlmann's role in saving Faistauer's fresco, see the statement of 5 March 1947 by the restorer Alberto Susat in Mühlmann's file, DÖW, Vienna.

56. The city of Salzburg gave two pictures to Hitler in early April 1938 (prior to the plebiscite), Spitzweg's *Sonntagsspaziergang* and Josef Mayburger's *Panorama von Salzburg* (Hitler returned the Spitzweg when he found out that it came from a municipal gallery). Göring received a "*Jagdbild*" by C. List. See the illustrated articles by Josef Mühlmann in *Kunstchronik*, No. 2 (1938), 4-6. See also Gert Kerschbaumer, "Alltag, Feiern und Feste im Wandel: Nationalsozialistische Regie des öffentlichen Lebens und Praktierte Kulturen in Salzburg von 1938 bis 1945," doctoral dissertation, University of Salzburg,

1986, 988-91. Mühlmann also helped deliver Gobelin tapestries and other art objects from the Kunsthistorisches Museum to the Reichskanzlei in 1939. See Kunstwesen 15, 1667-1945, Allgemeines Verwaltungsarchiv, ÖSA.

57. Stephen Gallup, *A History of the Salzburg Festival* (London: Weidenfeld and Nicolson, 1987), 106; and Gert Kerschbaumer, *Faszination Drittes Reich. Kunst und Alltag der Kulturmetropole Salzburg* (Salzburg: Otto Müller Verlag, 1988), 212.

58. Oliver Rathkolb, *Führertreu und Gottbegnadet. Künstlereliten im Dritten Reich* (Vienna: OBV, 1991), 64-65.

59. Schirach's "liberal" cultural policies became most evident with his sponsorship of the art exhibition *Junge Kunst im Deutschen Reich*, which was closed down on Hitler's orders in March 1943. For more on the Viennese *Kulturpolitik*, see Oliver Rathkolb, "Nationalsozialistische (Un-) Kulturpolitik in Wien, 1938-1945," and Jan Tabor, "Die Gaben der Ostmark. Österreichische Kunst und Künstler in der NS-Zeit," both in Hans Seiger, Michael Lunardi and Peter Josef Populorum, eds., *Im Reich der Kunst. Die Wiener Akademie der bildenden Künste und die faschistische Kunstpolitik* (Vienna: Verlag für Gesellschaftskritik, 1990), 247-96.

60. The Austrian economic expert Hans Fischböck arrived at the figure of 25,000 "wild Aryanizations," which has been used by most historians. Pauley, *From Prejudice to Persecution*, 284. Gerhard Botz provides a higher figure of 45,000 to 48,000, in *Wohnungspolitik und Judendeportation in Wien 1938 bis 1945* (Vienna/Salzburg: Geyer, 1975), 61.

61. For Kajetan Mühlmann's office and residence note the documents in Bürckel Materiel, 2428/0, AdR, ÖSA. For Josef Mühlmann moving into an "Aryanized" apartment, see a memorandum dated November 1938, Bundesministerium des Inneres, Karton 7682, 201929, AdR, ÖSt. Note that Chancellor Schuschnigg had previously had one of these apartments, but he was imprisoned in the Gestapo headquarters in the Hotel Metropol and sent to Dachau and other concentration camps. See Paul Hofmann, *The Viennese: Splendor, Twilight and Exile* (New York: Anchor Press, 1988), 235-38.

62. Schulze in the Wiener Gauleitung to the Reichsleitung der NSDAP, Reichsschatzmeister, 7 April 1941, NS-Parteistellen, Karton 40, AdR, ÖSA. Note that the *Vugesta* also liquidated art works owned by Jews. For Schirach's purchases from the *Vugesta*, see OMGUS 3/347 - 3/3.

63. Bürckel Materiel, 2429/2, AdR, Inneres, ÖSA; as well as AdR, Inneres, 7680 and 7691. In the latter, there is correspondence between Mühlmann and the local Gestapo chief Ebner from May 1939.

64. See Diemut Majer, *Recht, Verwaltung und Justiz im Nationalsozialismus. Ausgewälte Schriften, Gesetze und Gerichtsentscheidungen* (Cologne: Bund-Verlag, 1984), 269.

65. For the advisory role of experts similar to Mühlmann in preparing the way for the "Final Solution," see Ally and Heim, *Vordenker der Vernichtung*. Hans Fischböck, who like Mühlmann, later played a key role in the occupied Netherlands, was initially in Seyss-Inquart's cabinet, responsible for Handel und Verkehr; by 1939, he was in charge of "Wirtschaft und Arisierung" in Austria. See MA-597, 001445, IfZG, Munich. The key laws passed in 1938 include, *Die Verordung über die Anmeldung des Vermögens von Juden*, 26 April 1938 (where Jews worth property over RM 5,000 had to register it); the *Verordnung zur Ausschaltung der Juden aus dem Deutschen Wirtschaftsleben*, 12 November 1938; and the *Verordnung über den Einsatz jüdischen Vermögens*, 3 December 1938. See Hans Witek, "Arisierungen in Wien: Aspekte nationalsozialistischer Enteignungspolitik," in Emmerich Talos, et. al., eds., *NS-Herrschaft in Österreich*, 199-216.

66. Eichmann installed his Zentralstelle für jüdische Auswanderung at Prinz Eugenstraße 22. For more on individuals and offices of the Nazi bureaucracy taking over "Aryanized" property, see Dieter Stiefel, *Entnazifizierung in Österreich* (Vienna: Europaverlag, 1981), 57.

67. Witek, "Arisierungen," 203.

68. For Mühlmann's appeal to Hitler not to remove the Viennese art, see the attachment to a letter from K. Barth to J. Bürckel, 3 June 1939, in MA-145/1, frames 10406-15, IfZG, Munich. For the value of the articles catalogued in the Neue Hofburg, see Luza, *Austro-German Relations*, 280.

69. Seyss-Inquart cites experts who estimate that selling off a third of the confiscated art would raise twelve to fifteen million Reichsmarks. He also notes the support for the plan provided by the Bürgermeister Dr. Neubacher. Seyss-Inquart to Hitler, 4 May 1939, in MA-597, Bl. 001435-42, IfZG, Munich.

70. Regarding the material impoverishment of Austria to the benefit of the *Altreich*, see Stiefel, *Entnazifizierung in Österreich*, 223.

71. Himmler to Lammers, 18 June 1938, Bl. 27, R43II/1269a, BAK.

72. Bürckel's ambiguous position is conveyed in a letter he wrote to Bormann, 25 May 1939, where he attempted to give the impression of representing Berlin's interests. Bürckel Materiel, AdR, Inneres, 2429, ÖSA. Radomir Luza has also noted Bürckel's paradoxical behavior: "Bürckel, the rigid adversary of the Austrian idea, by his own stand against Berlin centralism unintentionally allowed his opponents opportunities to stress the Austrian cultural heritage." Luza, *Austro-German Relations*, 287.

73. Lammers to Himmler, 13 August 1938, Bl. 31, R43II/1269a, BAK.

74. Karl Schleuenes, *The Twisted Road to Auschwitz: Nazi Policy towards German Jews* (Urbana/Chicago/London: University of Illinois Press, 1972).

75. Robert Koehl, *The Black Corps: the Structure and Power Struggles of the Nazi SS* (Madison: University of Wisconsin, 1983). See also Hans Mommsen, Die Realisierung des Utopischen: Die "Endlösung der Judenfrage" im "Dritten Reich," in *Geschichte und Gesellschaft* 9 (1983), 400. See also Safrian, *Die Eichmann-Männer*, 58; and Arendt, *Eichmann in Jerusalem*, 68-79.

76. Kreissler, *Der Österreicher und seine Nation*, 149 and 206. Kreissler also includes excerpts from the *Wiener Werkel's* program which illustrate their satirical edge. The letter is reproduced in Rosar, *Deutsche Gemeinschaft*, 339.

77. Tabor, "Die Gaben der Ostmark," 277-95.

78. See for example, the testimony of Heinrich Hoffmann from 28 August 1951, where he notes, "Through his intervention for the artistic interests of Vienna, Dr. Mühlmann very nearly elicited the enmity of Bormann, who now kept an eye out towards removing Mühlmann from his post in order to stem his influence." Hoffmann's testimony is in Mühlmann's file, DÖW, Vienna.

79. Mühlmann's fortunes were so closely tied to Seyss-Inquart's that his official date of termination was back-dated to 30 April 1939. See Oswald Knauer, *Österreichs Männer des öffentlichen Lebens von 1848 bis heute* (Vienna: Manzsche Verlag, 1960), 65.

80. For the nine page letter from Seyss-Inquart to Göring, 14 July 1939, see the Nuremberg Trial document 2219-PS in IfZG, Munich. As noted earlier, Mühlmann and Göring had a longstanding relationship. See the letter of K. Barth to Bürckel of 3 June 1939, where he discusses a meeting where Göring raised the possibility of Mühlmann taking over the state museums in Berlin. He then goes on to explain why this assignment must be blocked. MA-145/1, frames 10362-64, IfZG, Munich.

81. Rosar, *Deutsche Gemeinschaft*, 340-65. See also Seyss-Inquart to Bürckel, 29 June 1939, NL/180, BAK.

82. Rosar, *Deutsche Gemeinschaft*, 359-65.

83. Seyss-Inquart to Bürckel, 8 August 1939, NL/180, BAK.

84. Göring stated on 14 March 1946, "Actually Mühlmann, whom I knew, came to me and said that he should try to secure the art treasures there [in Poland]." Göring then goes on to argue that he was merely protecting the artworks from the dangers of combat. *Prozesse der Hauptkriegsverbrecher,* 11:352.

85. Sievers to Himmler, 4 September 1939 in Peter Paulsen's file, BDC.

86. For a report on the activities of Mühlmann and his agents entitled, "Die Gesamttätigkeit des Sonderbeauftragten für die Erfassung der Kunst und Kulturschätze im Generalgouvernement," R43II/1341a, BAK.

87. Pauley, *Hitler and the Forgotten Nazis*, 221.

88. Pauley, *From Prejudice to Persecution*, 297-98.

89. Of the staff members (those charged with the *Wissenschaftliche Durchführung*) and the advisers (*Wissenschaftliche Gutachten*), a total of ten came from Austria and four from Breslau. Two restoration experts also stemmed from Vienna. See Mühlmann's printed (and not typed) report on the confiscation action in Poland, *Sichergestellte Kunstwerke im Generalgouvernement*, in MA-174, IfZG, Munich. This report discusses the securing of 231 first-rank art objects.

90. See the work cited above, *Sichergestellte Kunstwerke im Generalgouvernement*, as well as Kajetan Mühlmann and Gustav Barthel, *Krakau. Hauptstadt der deutschen Generalgouvernements Polen. Gestalt und Künstlerische Leistung der deutschen Stadt im Osten* (Breslau: Korn Verlag, 1940). Barthel wrote the text for this lavishly illustrated book on the history of German culture in the city. Hans Frank wrote the introduction, and closed with "*Krakau, am Geburtstag des Führers 1940.*"

91. See the summary of a meeting between Josef Mühlmann and Hermann Einziger (a representative of the *Dokumentationszentrum der Israelischen Kulturgemeinde Wien*) on 16 January 1963. The report was provided to the author by Simon Wiesenthal.

92. Eidliche Erklärung des SS-Oberführers Dr. Kajetan Mühlmann vom 19. November 1945: Nuremberg trial document 3042-PS.

93. Richard Lukas, *The Forgotten Holocaust. The Poles Under German Occupation, 1939-1944* (Lexington: University of Kentucky, 1986), 10-11.

94. Göring placed the Watteau in his home on the Obersalzburg, See Kurz, *Kunstraub in Europa*, 100. The quotation regarding the Dürer drawings, which Mühlmann handed over to Göring in person, comes from the Nuremberg prosecutor Colonel Storey, *Prozesse der Hauptkriegsverbrecher*, 4:94 and 11:353.

95. Frank's castles were in Cracow and in Krzeszowice (Kressendorf).

96. Ernst Hanisch, "'Gau der Guten Nerven': Die nationalsozialistische Herrschaft in Salzburg 1939-1940," in *Sonderdruck der Politik und Gesellschaft im alten und neuen Österreich* (Vienna: Verlag für Geschichte und Politik, 1981), 206.

97. Ernst Hanisch, *Nationalsozialistische Herrschaft in der Provinz. Salzburg im Dritten Reich* (Salzburg: Landespressbüro, 1983), 141.

98. Kurz, *Kunstraub in Europa*, 112-13.

99. Mühlmann, *Sichergestellte Kunstwerke im Generalgouvernement*, Introduction.

100. Sievers's report of 30 July 1940 based upon a meeting with SS-Brigadierführer Greifelt, Obersturmbannführer Luig, and Stabsführer Winkler, Mühlmann's BDC file.

101. Note that while Seyss-Inquart had his jurisdiction confined to the Netherlands, the Dienststelle Mühlmann's sphere of activity extended further to include Belgium.

102. Jean Vlug, *Report on Objects Removed to Germany from Holland, Belgium, and France during the German Occupation on* [sic] *the Countries* (Amsterdam: Report of Stichting Nederlands Kunstbesit, 25 December 1945), 5.

103. See an interview with Mühlmann conducted by August Prossinger, 20 August 1947. See file No. 200, 252, Oberfinanzdirektion (OFD), Munich.

104. Ibid., 7. See also A.J. van der Leeuw, *Von der Dienststelle Mühlmann übernommenen Kunstgegenstände*, 9.

105. Mühlmann's cooperation with the SD in the Netherlands was so close that he lived for some time in the Hague with Peter Gern, the SD chief for Holland. See Vlug, *Report on Objects Removed to Germany*, 21.

106. Plietzsch, who had been trained by the great museum director Wilhlem Bode and earlier written books on Vermeer and other Dutch Masters, published a book on Gerard ter Borch in Vienna in 1944. See Günther Haase, *Kunstraub und Kunstschutz: eine Dokumentation* (Hildesheim: Georg Olms Verlag, 1991), 184-88.

107. S.L. Faison, *Consolidated Interrogation Report No. 4. Linz: Hitler's Museum and Library*, (OSS Report: 15 December 1945), 45.

108. Although nearly all of the Dienststelle Mühlmann's records were burned in the Haag toward the end of the war, certain documents and a "*Geschäftsbuch*" survived. van der Leeuw, *Von der Dienststelle Mühlmann übernommenen Kunstgegenstände*, 5.

109. Kurz, *Kunstraub in Europa*, 256.

110. Note that Lammers explicitly claimed the "Reservation of the Führer" in a November 1940 decree, while Göring used his influence for a less official kind of preferential treatment. Faison, *Consolidated Interrogation Report No. 4*, 7.

111. Vlug, *Report on Objects Removed to Germany*, 49-148.

112. Ibid., 52.

113. See the 20 August 1947 interview with August Prossinger in file No. 200, 244, OFD, Munich.

114. Ibid., 249; and Haase, *Kunstraub und Kunstschutz*, 94-95 and 184.

115. Henrietta von Schirach wrote in her memoirs that Mühlmann gave her and her husband gift-wrapped packages as they boarded a train home after a visit to the Netherlands: the packages contained an Italian Renaissance painting of Tobias and an angel as well as blue fabric (the same that Göring used to make his uniforms). This story should be treated with some skepticism. Henrietta von Schirach, *Der Preis der Herrlichkeit* (Wiesbaden: Limes Verlag, 1956), 220.

116. Ibid., 253.

117. Mühlmann had married Helda Ziegler in mid-1942 after gaining Himmler's approval. Himmler to Mühlmann, 19 September 1942, Mühlmann's BDC file.

118. Vlug, *Report on Objects Removed to Germany*, 12.

119. Ibid., 63.

120. See the 30 April 1945 report of OSS chief William Donovan, in Oliver Rathkolb, ed., *Gesellschaft und Politik am Beginn der Zweiten Republik: Vertrauliche Berichte der US-Militäradministration aus Österreich 1945 in englischer Originalfassung* (Vienna: Böhlau, 1985), 217.

121. See the testimony of Alfons Walde in a Kitzbühel court on 27 March 1947. He tells of Skorzeny and 3,000 SS men in a *Sprengkommando* whom Mühlmann supposedly helped thwart in the Tyrol. He also claims that Mühlmann freed Göring from SS guards by invoking the authority of Field Marshal Kesserling. Walde's testimony is in Mühlmann's file, DÖW, Vienna.

122. See *The Central Registry of War Criminals and Security Suspects, Wanted List*, 65, National Archives, Suitland, Maryland. For more on how the Americans used "CROWCASS to locate promising Nazi intelligence recruits," see Christopher Simpson, *Blowback: America's Recruitment of Nazis and Its Effects on the Cold War* (London: Weidenfeld and Nicholson, 1988), 66-76.

123. See the testimony by Mühlmann of 30 October 1946 in his file, DÖW, Vienna.

124. See, for example, Mühlmann's Eidliche Erklärung, 3042-PS.

125. Vlug, *Report on Objects Removed to Germany*, 12.

126. See the Counter Intelligence Corps agreement with the Austrian Government of 26 October 1946 in Mühlmann's file, DÖW, Vienna.

127. Haase, *Kunstraub und Kunstschutz*, 59.

128. Robert Edwin Herzstein, *Waldheim: The Missing Years* (New York: Arbor House, 1988), 190.

129. Drechsler to Borutik of the Landesgericht für Strafsachen Wien, 14 August 1951, in Mühlmann's file, DÖW, Vienna.

130. For the importance of the Moscow Declaration of November 1943, whereby the Allies claimed that the Austrians were "victims" of Nazi aggression, see Günter Bischof, "Die Instrumentalisierung der Moskauer Erklärung nach dem 2. Weltkrieg," in *Zeitgeschichte* 20 (November/December 1993), 345-66.

131. Schmidt testified, "Mühlmann schein ein völlig kleiner, harmloser Mann zu sein . . . . Herr Mühlmann war in meinen Augen ein Unterläufel. Ich habe nie die Information bekommen, daß Mühlmann von politischer Bedeutung sei." The contempt which Guido Schmidt showed for him in his testimony might actually have helped Mühlmann, as the authorities evidently underestimated him. Mühlmann, however, claimed that he interceded on Schimdt's behalf with Kaltenbrunner on several occasions and prevented his arrest. *Der Hochverratprozess gegen Dr. Guido Schmidt*, 58-59.

132. Zeugenvernehmung of Karl Gruber, 15 November 1947 in Mühlmann's file, DÖW, Vienna.

133. There are reports that during the last week of the war, the American General Harry Collins provided Mühlmann with a letter permitting him to carry a weapon and drive an auto so that he could contribute to the resistance. Whether the Americans continued to support Mühlmann after learning about his war-time activities is unclear. But in a recent study, General Collins is portrayed not only as corrupt, but as interested in acquiring artworks and other luxury objects for personal use. See the testimony of Alfons Walde in Mühlmann's file, DÖW, Vienna. Also, Kenneth Alford, *The Spoils of World War II. The American Military's Role in Stealing Europe's Treasures* (New York: Birch Lane, 1994), 69-73, 259-261.

134. Herzstein, *Waldheim*, 167.

135. For an account of Gruber's *Ehrenbeleidigungsprozeß* against the *Tagblatt am Montag*, see the *Salzburger Nachrichten*, 21 March 1950, 4.

136. For an account of how Verbelen, a convicted war criminal sentenced to death in absentia by a Belgian court worked for the 430th CIC Detachment in Vienna from 1947 to 1956, see Neal Sher, Aron Goldberg, and Elizabeth White, "Robert Jan Verbelen and the United States Government. A Report to the Assistant Attorney General, Criminal Division, U.S. Department of Justice" (Washington, D.C., 1984). See also Allan Ryan, "Klaus Barbie and the United

States Government: A Report to the Attorney General of the United States" (Washington, D.C. 1983).

137. Simpson, *Blowback*, 70. For more on the 430th CIC Detachment in Austria and the 66th in Bavaria, see Ryan, "Klaus Barbie," 46; Sher, Goldberg, and White, "Verbelen," 1, 15-20, 28-35; and Rena Giefer and Thomas Giefer, *Die Rattenlinie. Fluchtwege der Nazis. Eine Dokumentation* (Frankfurt A.M.: Hain, 1991), 38, 168, 226.

138. Document entitled "Rogues Gallery #35": Mühlmann papers delivered through the Freedom of Information-Privacy Act.

139. Ibid.

140. Maximilian Machalski in Warsaw, appeal of 18 February 1949, in Mühlmann's file, DÖW, Vienna.

141. Drechsler for the Bundesminister für Justiz to Landesgericht für Strafsachen Wien, 14 August 1951 in Mühlmann's file, DÖW, Vienna.

142. Tiefenbrunner to Körner, 17 August 1951, in Mühlmann's file, DÖW, Vienna.

143. Zeugenvernehmung of Josef Mühlmann, 2 September 1957, in Kajetan Mühlmann's file, DÖW, Vienna.

144. Hilde Mühlmann to the Landesgericht in Vienna, 12 March 1960, in Mühlmann's file, DÖW, Vienna.

145. Stiefel, *Entnazifizierung in Österreich*, 89.

146. *Wiener Kurier*, 28 July 1952, "Vermögensverfall für Bilderkäufer des 'Reichsmarschalls' beantragt." Note that Mühlmann's own art collection is described as consisting of a "few unimportant pictures."

147. See the report of Hermann Einziger of 17 January 1963. Josef Mühlmann died in June 1972. There was no mention of his wartime activities in any of the published obituaries.

148. Josef Mühlmann, *Franz Xaever Gruber. Sein Leben* (Salzburg: Residenz Verlag, 1966). Gruber wrote *Weihnachtslieder*. For the research for this and other projects, see Josef Mühlmann's Nachlaß in the Salzburg Landesarchiv.

149. The portraits are by Felix Harta and Sergius Pauser (the latter was a leading painter during the Third Reich). Information provided to the author by the Salzburg painter and restorer Annemarie Fiebich-Ripke, letter of 20 November 1993.

150. Interview conducted by August Prossinger, 20 August 1947, file No. 200, 253, OFD, Munich.

151. Hanisch, *Nationalsozialistische Herrschaft in der Provinz*, 338. Letter to author from Annemarie Fiebichk-Ripke, Salzburg, 6 December 1993.

152. Gerhard Botz, "Eine Deutsche Geschichte 1938 bis 1945? Österreichische Geschichte zwischen Exil, Widerstand und Verstrickung," in *Zeitgeschichte* 16/1 (October 1986), 24-25.

153. Thomas Mann to Joseph Pulitzer quoted from Norbert Frei and Johannes Schmitz, *Journalismus im Dritten Reich* (Munich: C.H. Beck, 1989), 7.

154. Safrian, *Die Eichmann Männer*, 321-25.

155. Zeugenvernehmung of Josef Mühlmann, 2 September 1957, in Kajetan Mühlmann's file, DÖW, Vienna.

156. Note that Mühlmann is largely ignored by most sources on Austria in the Third Reich: see for example the following studies that fail to mention him: Walter Kleindel, ed., *Das Große Buch der Österreicher. 4500 Personendarstellungen in Wort und Bild* (Vienna: Kremayr & Scheriau, 1987); Isabella Ackerl, Friedrich Weissensteiner, *Österreichisches Personen Lexikon der Ersten und Zweiten Republik* (Vienna: Ueberreuter, 1992), which includes approximately 1,600 entries; or Erich Stockhorst, *5000 Köpfe*. The same is true for most studies of the German occupation of Poland and the Netherlands.

In the Shadow of Giants: U.S. Policy Toward Small Nations: The Cases of Lebanon, Costa Rica, and Austria in the Eisenhower Years[1]

*David McIntosh**

Throughout his presidency (1953-1961), Dwight D. Eisenhower readily committed American resources and prestige to promote the economic health, military security, and Western alignment of countries (like the Federal Republic of Germany) whose geostrategic positions and industrial capability endowed them with immediate importance to the West. Similarly, the Eisenhower administration extended support to pro-Western governments in countries (like Iran) whose natural resources were deemed vital to the NATO allies. Yet, top American policy makers believed that U.S. commitment could not end with such inherently important states. Such was the precariousness of world opinion that, even in countries deemed relatively inconsequential to U.S. security, the mere appearance of a communist gain could shake the confidence of friends in vital areas and embolden the Soviet Union to intensify its expansionist drive. Moreover, any suggestion of lacking resolve could expose the White House and the State Department to attack from Senator Joseph McCarthy (R-Wisconsin) and his allies in Congress.[2]

* The following article is a shortened version of the thesis I submitted to Harvard College's Department of History in March 1994. I would like to renew my thanks to Robert Johnson, who distilled my interests into a viable research topic and provided two years of invaluable advice. I would also like to thank Günter Bischof, who kindly encouraged me to prepare a submission for *CAS*.

Hence, even in peripheral countries where U.S. interests were not directly threatened, the Eisenhower administration felt compelled to make dramatic commitments to forestall a deadly psychological chain reaction.[3] When civil unrest erupted in Lebanon in 1958, for example, the administration fashioned a response designed to preserve America's image as a stalwart defender of pro-Western, anti-communist governments. Resolve may have been the most crucial image Washington sought to project to the world, but policy makers realized that America's moral image in defense of democracy in the hemisphere was also an important asset in the propaganda war against international communism. So, when Central American dictators launched an invasion of democratic Costa Rica in 1955, the Eisenhower administration intervened to protect America's tarnished reputation as an exponent of democracy and an opponent of aggression.

Regional objectives of a psychological nature also influenced U.S. policy in the 1950s. In responding to developments in a secondary state, the Eisenhower administration often took actions designed to send a specific message to the state's more important and more troubling neighbors. For example, the administration's response to the Lebanese crisis of 1958 was intended to caution Egypt's Gamel Abdel Nasser against expanding his influence at the cost of pro-U.S. regimes in the Middle East, and U.S. actions in Austria were intended to stymie the public appeal of demilitarization and nonalignment in West Germany.

The governments of Lebanon, Costa Rica, and Austria each sought substantial U.S. economic and military support in the 1950s. But the Eisenhower administration focused its concern on more vital or more troubling states in the Middle East, Latin America, and Central Europe. Major regional crises, often centering on countries that held primary concern for the administration, provided tests of the extent to which the three governments in this study would support U.S. regional objectives. The official responses in Beirut, San José, and Vienna to these crises satisfied policy makers in Washington and resulted in heightened American support for the three pro-U.S. governments. The Arab-Israeli conflict and the Suez crisis of 1956 provided Lebanese President Camille Chamoun with opportunities to align his government staunchly and conspicuously with U.S. policies in the Middle East. The U.S. showdown with

President Arbenz of Guatemala created an atmosphere in which Costa Rican President José Figueres demonstrated, through his moderate approach to the United Fruit Company and his acquiescence in the U.S.-led efforts to oust Arbenz, that his policies did not threaten U.S. interests in Central America. The unambiguous reaction of the Austrians to the Hungarian crisis of 1956 reassured the Eisenhower administration that Austria would not follow the dangerous and potentially contagious policies of neutralism and nonalignment. Ideology and domestic politics motivated these three governments to take positions that favored the United States. But to varying degrees, they shaped their reactions to regional crises in ways designed to attract Washington's approval.

In Lebanon, Costa Rica, and Austria, the governments that sought support from the United States succeeded, to varying degrees, in harnessing their interests to the regional and global objectives of the Eisenhower administration. The United States ostensibly held the ultimate power in these relationships, but the smaller governments took advantage of U.S. fears and objectives, gleaning significant, and often dramatic, benefits from their dealings with Washington. Degrees of manipulation and accommodation occurred on both sides, and the balance of benefits varied among the cases. The mass of U.S. power, together with the single-mindedness and intensity of U.S. Cold War objectives, created definite lines across which the governments knew they could not step and still retain U.S. support. But by placating the United States on crucial regional questions, these governments accumulated idiosyncrasy credits which they used to follow agendas that were independent of, and at times even mildly contrary to, U.S. objectives. Each of the governments under discussion probed the boundaries of its relationship with the U.S., found that they afforded considerable latitude, and pursued its independent interests. But in different ways, all three governments encountered the limits of U.S. tolerance.

The three cases in this study reveal that, though top U.S. policy makers could be pragmatic in their outlook, the psychological tactics of the world-wide Soviet offensive compelled them to pander to global perceptions which frequently failed to distinguish nationalism from communism and neutrality from nonalignment.

Even if an action taken by a foreign government did not significantly threaten U.S. strategic interests, the administration was often compelled to oppose that action if it resembled a gain for the Soviets. Similarly, the administration was sometimes compelled to jeopardize interests on the ground in secondary states in order to prevent broader, more damaging defeats in the theater of world opinion. But the Austrian case reveals that on-the-ground U.S. interests and mutual understanding, if strong enough, could free a country from the shadow of Washington's preoccupation with world-wide perceptions.

Demonstrating Resolve in Lebanon

In the late 1950s, the Eisenhower administration formulated policy toward Lebanon in the shadow of troubling developments concerning Egypt, Syria, and the Middle East as a whole. The U.S. government believed that an advancing tide of radical Arab nationalism under the leadership of Egypt's Gamel Abdel Nasser threatened to block Western access to vital oil resources and strategic transit routes in the Middle East. U.S. officials perceived the Soviet Union lurking in the background, encouraging Nasser's expansionist drive and gaining influence with the new *Ba'athist* regime in Syria. Policy makers on the National Security Council (NSC) feared that once Nasser cleared the Arab Middle East of Western influence, the USSR would fill the power vacuum, brushing Nasser aside and taking hold of the oil supply which was vital to the economic and strategic viability of Western Europe.[4] Lebanon contained no significant oil resources and was itself not strategically vital. But the administration believed that U.S. actions toward Lebanon would have an impact on both Nasser's ambitions and the resolve of pro-West, anti-communist governments in the Middle East.

After his ascension to the presidency in 1952, Camille Chamoun attracted the support of U.S. and British officials by backing Western objectives in the Middle East despite mounting pressure from Arab nationalists in Lebanon, Egypt, and Syria who insisted on a middle path in the Cold War and vigorous opposition to the state of Israel.[5] Chamoun's moderate public stands on the Baghdad Pact and Israel stemmed from his own cultural and political identity, but they also represented successful moves to draw U.S. support against the intensifying opposition of pro-Nasser elements.[6] By the spring of 1956, aggregate pressure from Chamoun, the British, the U. S. Joint Chiefs of Staff (JCS), and the U.S. Embassy in Beirut began to move Eisenhower and Secretary of State John Foster Dulles toward modest economic aid and sales of military equipment to Lebanon.[7]

The Anglo-French-Israeli attack on Egypt in October 1956 launched the United States through the final stages of a process that had begun with the Truman Doctrine in 1947. Before October of 1956, "the United States had relied on Great Britain as the chief bulwark against Soviet intervention in the Middle East." But in a matter of hours, as Secretary Dulles put it, "that bulwark had been swept away."[8] It was apparent to Eisenhower and Dulles that, as a result of the crisis, the United States must take over the Western commitment to guard the vital region against Soviet encroachment. The administration's attempt to invigorate U.S. policy toward the Middle East culminated on 1 January 1957 when President Eisenhower called a meeting with congressional leaders to announce his intention to submit to the House and the Senate a resolution authorizing him to undertake economic and military assistance programs to help nations in the Middle East maintain their national independence. The resolution would further permit the president to use the armed forces of the United States to "secure and protect the territorial integrity and political independence of [Middle Eastern] nations, requesting such aid, against overt armed aggression from any nation controlled by International Communism."[9] Eisenhower explained to the assembled lawmakers that, "given the present impossibility of France and Britain acting as a counterweight" to Soviet ambitions, "the existing vacuum" in the Middle East "must be filled by the United States before it is filled by Russia."[10] U.S. treaties with Turkey (NATO) and Pakistan (SEATO), together with the Baghdad Pact, helped secure parts of the region, but the Eisenhower Doctrine was intended to demonstrate America's commitment to guard the area stretching from the Arabian Peninsula to the Mediterranean coast and Egypt.[11] Eisenhower and Dulles asserted that the resolution would exert a positive "psychological impact on the area [of the Middle East] and upon the world."[12] In the aftermath of Suez, the Middle East became a major focus of America's containment policy.

During the Suez crisis, Chamoun shone in American eyes as the Arab leader most willing to publicly support a moderate Arab response consistent with the efforts of the United States and the United Nations to end the crisis.[13] He further improved his image in Washington by supporting the Eisenhower Doctrine "one hundred percent" (his was the only Arab government formally to endorse the resolution).[14] Chamoun thus placed his government in an ideal position to benefit from the expanded American commitment to the region. Following the enunciation of the Doctrine, the State Department began to approve grants (as opposed to sales) of arms to Lebanon, and once the House and Senate passed the resolution, the flood gates of U.S. material support opened on the Chamoun government.[15] A report from the Operations Coordinating Board (OCB) of the NSC in late July outlined the advantages of the new program of grant aid, particularly economic development aid, for Lebanon: "While U.S. actions in the Lebanon will be important for the effect they will have in Lebanon itself, they may in the long run have an equally important effect area-wide." According to the OCB, the aid program was intended to make Lebanon a showcase of "U.S.-Arab cooperation, the tangible benefits of which could be expected in the long run to stimulate more favorable attitudes toward the U.S. and U.S. policies *elsewhere* in the Arab world."[16] So, a policy shift that had begun with a crisis in Egypt bore fruit in Lebanon to make an impression on peoples across the Middle East. The unmistakably United States stance of the Chamoun government and its repeated complaints of interference from Cairo and Damascus helped to pull the U.S. to Lebanon's door, but following the adoption of the Eisenhower Doctrine, the administration leapt over the threshold on its own volition. The Eisenhower administration's increased material support further identified Chamoun in the eyes of the world as an ally of the U.S. So when an internal revolt, apparently fomented by Nasserist elements in the United Arab Republic (UAR), threatened Chamoun's government in 1958, the administration was faced with a choice between fulfilling his request for military intervention or demonstrating a lack of

commitment to protect friendly governments against forces hostile
to the West.

The months leading to the U.S. intervention in Lebanon in July
of 1958 provided an example of what Ernest May has termed, "the
pull from the periphery."[17] The Chamoun government wanted
U.S. diplomatic and material support against the elements that
opposed it. So in their communications with high U.S. officials,
Chamoun and his foreign minister, Charles Malik, portrayed their
domestic opposition as a product of interference from the same
elements in Egypt and Syria that opposed America's world
leadership and flirted with the Soviets.[18] In April, a revolt against
the rule of King Hussein in Jordan heightened fears in Washington
and Beirut surrounding the increasingly radical *Ba'athist*
government in Syria, which appeared to have fostered the
opposition to Hussein.[19] The merger of Egypt and Syria into the
United Arab Republic in February of 1958 increased the pressures
that threatened to destroy Lebanon's political cohesion, and the
merger made the Chamoun administration feel increasingly
surrounded by radical nationalist forces (Chamoun and Malik
detected an increased flow of arms and cadres from Syria and an
increase in hostile radio broadcasts directed from Egypt).[20] By
May of 1958, the atmosphere in Lebanon was highly volatile, and
the assassination of an opposition newspaper editor on May 8
sparked violent clashes between government police forces and rebel
bands in pockets around Lebanon.[21]

As soon as it appeared that the Chamoun government was
seriously threatened by armed opposition groups in Lebanon, the
question arose in the White House as to whether the United States
would intervene militarily to protect one of the most strongly pro-
West governments in the Arab Middle East. The Eisenhower
administration knew that Chamoun's refusal to disavow a second
term (the Lebanese Constitution precluded the tenure of
consecutive Presidential terms) was the major impetus behind the
Lebanese unrest. Furthermore, the administration believed that "it
would be best for Lebanon, for Chamoun and for [the] United
States if he stepped down from power."[22] But U.S. foreign policy
makers were convinced that the vital question was not whether the
rebellion against Chamoun was domestically inspired, or even what
course of action would best protect U.S. interests in Lebanon. The

crucial issue was that vital U.S. interests in the Middle East and across the world would suffer if the administration failed to come to the aid of an avowed friend whose regime *appeared* to be under attack from neutralist and communist-inspired elements. According to a National Intelligence Estimate, "if Chamoun's government . . . collapsed under the onslaught of anti-Western opposition elements, friends and enemies of the West alike would believe . . . that the U.S. had proved itself unwilling to come to the aid of its declared ally and friend, and that it had capitulated to Nasser. The governments of Middle East countries disposed toward cooperation with the West would be strongly influenced to revise their policies." Moreover, the "collapse of a pro-Western government, with no U.S. action, would almost certainly accelerate the activities of the UAR and its supporters in seeking to undermine anti-Nasser regimes."[23] Given its fear that radical nationalist and neutralist forces were on the verge of engulfing the governments that welcomed Western influence in the Middle East, the administration preferred appearing reactionary to seeming weak or uncommitted. At any rate, the administration realized that it could not avoid the charge of being reactionary, for its main objective in the Middle East was protecting a status quo that favored Western interests.[24] To intervene might turn people who were already ambivalent against the United States. But to stand aloof and allow Chamoun to fall would shake the confidence of pro-Western elements across the globe and embolden both Nasser and the Soviet Union.[25] In early May, Eisenhower and top officials in the State Department determined that, despite predictions of an adverse Arab reaction to U.S. military intervention in Lebanon, the United States had no alternative but to back Chamoun with force if he declared his intention to run for a second term and his government was consequently threatened.[26] What mattered most was not the impact of U.S. action on the internal political situation in Lebanon, but rather the psychological effect on pro-U.S. governments across the world.

High U.S. officials were under no illusion that military intervention would solve the internal problems of Lebanon. In fact, Dulles feared that U.S. intervention could set into motion a "train [of] indigenous trends [leading toward] Lebanon's ultimate territorial partition or truncation," and he predicted that "the

Lebanese government itself probably would not survive our
withdrawal." The Secretary conjectured further that the
governments of Jordan and Iraq would be "swept away" in a wave
of Arab nationalist fervor regardless of U.S. action.[27] President
Eisenhower told his closest foreign policy advisers that "he had
little, if any, enthusiasm for our intervening."[28] Although both
options, intervention and inaction, appeared undesirable, the
administration determined that intervention would at least
demonstrate American strength and commitment to the pro-West
governments of Iran, Turkey, and Pakistan, which formed a crucial
defensive barrier along the southern periphery of the Soviet
Union.[29] U.S. intervention might result in the loss of Lebanon,
Jordan, and Iraq to Arab nationalism, but Dulles thought those
countries were likely to be lost anyway. Besides, Eisenhower and
Dulles believed that they had to jeopardize U.S. interests in such
secondary states to broadcast an image of American resolve to the
governments of more strategically vital countries in the Middle
East.[30]

   In the early morning of 14 July 1958, a group of young army
officers led by Brigadier Abdel Karim Qassim carried out a *coup
d'état* in Iraq against the royal family and the government of Nuri
Said and proclaimed the establishment of the Republican
Government of Iraq. When news of the *coup* reached Beirut,
President Chamoun contacted Ambassador McClintock and
demanded "the 6th fleet here within 48 hours or else he would at
last know where he stood [in terms of] assurances of support from
[the] West."[31] At 9:30 in the morning, Secretary Dulles called a
meeting of all Department officers concerned with Iraq and
Lebanon, together with CIA Director Allen Dulles and the
Chairman of the Joint Chiefs of Staff, General Nathan F. Twining.
The assembled foreign policy makers did not ask whether the Iraqi
coup was connected to the revolt against Chamoun, nor did they try
to determine what impact the coup would have on the internal crisis
in Lebanon. Their concern was the effect the coup would have on
the expectations of pro-West governments in the Middle East and
worldwide. The assembled officials agreed that if the United States
failed to act, the "dependability of U.S. commitments for assistance
in the event of need would be brought into question throughout the
world."[32] In a meeting later that day, President Eisenhower made

the final decision that "we must move."[33] That afternoon, the President told assembled Congressmen that "if we do or if we don't go in, the consequences will be bad," but that "it was better if we took a strong position rather than a Munich-type position, if we are to avoid the crumbling of our whole security structure." To Democratic protests that the United States lacked sufficient evidence to determine that the civil disturbances in Lebanon were communist-inspired, Eisenhower responded that "the crucial question is what the victims believe. Chamoun believes it is Soviet communism that is causing him his trouble."[34] At any rate, there was little the Democratic lawmakers could do to halt the intervention. The Commander-In-Chief was acting within his constitutional authority in responding to a request for military assistance from the democratically-elected president of a foreign state.

On the evening of the fourteenth, the commander of the U.S. Naval forces in the Eastern Atlantic and the Mediterranean received the order to land Marines on the beaches of Beirut the following day (the United States eventually deployed 14,357 troops in Lebanon).[35] The British simultaneously sent forces to protect the government of King Hussein in Jordan.[36]

U.S. forces encountered few military difficulties in Lebanon. After some initial uncertainty, the Lebanese army proved acquiescent toward the presence of American troops, and the Marines were able to take control of the Beirut International Airport without any resistance. Ten days after the initial landing of the Marines, JCS Chairman Twining could report that the "situation in Lebanon was calm" and that "there had been no casualties from enemy action."[37] Chamoun, the British, and certain top U.S. military men pressured the Eisenhower administration to expand the military operation to root out Nasserist insurgents in Lebanon, Jordan, and possibly Iraq. But Eisenhower, Dulles, and most of the administration's top foreign policy advisers decided against "expanding the forces or area of deployment in Lebanon,"[38] for the Marines had proved America's commitment to stand behind pro-West governments resisting communist and Nasserist expansion the moment they landed in Beirut. (It is worth noting that the governments of the Northern Tier countries—Turkey, Iran, and Pakistan—sent a joint cable to President Eisenhower praising the dispatch of Marines to Lebanon as "bold and appropriate."[39]) As soon as the Marines established a secure position in Beirut, the administration's goal became creating a political situation in Lebanon that would allow the United States to proclaim its mission a success and enable U.S. troops to withdraw with honor before they became embroiled in the political turmoil of Lebanon and before the United States' reputation among nationalist-minded Arabs suffered irreparably.[40]

In late July, Deputy Undersecretary of State Robert Murphy, whom Eisenhower had sent to Beirut, got the various factions in Lebanon to accept General Chehab, the leader of the Lebanese army, as the next president; the Lebanese parliament elected Chehab to office on 31 July.[41] By the end of the first week of August, Ambassador McClintock believed that Chehab's behavior and the internal situation in Lebanon were encouraging enough to warrant a "phased withdrawal of U.S. forces."[42] On 21 August ten Arab states introduced to the General Assembly of the UN a resolution, pre-approved by the U.S., which called for "such practical arrangements as would . . . facilitate the early withdrawal of the foreign troops from" Lebanon and Jordan. The General Assembly passed the resolution with minimal discussion, and the United States and Britain began to withdraw their troops.[43]

Neither Chamoun nor the powerful leader of the *Phalanges* militia, Pierre Gemayel, was satisfied with the political compromise concluded in mid September. The limited objectives of the U.S. intervention left Chamoun bitter, and he was furious that the new cabinet included men such as Rachid Karame, whom he described as a "rebel from the barricades" who "had taken Syrian arms and money" and would now take orders from Nasser.[44] Although Chamoun was out of government, he and the Maronite militia possessed considerable influence, which they used to "mastermind" a strike of Christian industrial workers and shop owners beginning in late September.[45] It soon became clear that the former president would have to be offered concessions for the new government to survive. Consequently, the membership of the Karame cabinet was widened to include some loyalist, pro-Chamoun leaders, including Gemayel, and Chamoun gave signs of assuagement. On 16 October Secretary Dulles told the NSC that "the new stop-gap Cabinet has ended for the moment the strikes and violence of recent months," and the last of the U.S. troops were able to leave Lebanon on 25 October in an atmosphere of relative calm.[46]

While some historians have deemed the 1958 intervention "an excessive and wholly inappropriate use of force that in the long run harmed America's position in the region,"[47] I suspect that the intervention had little impact on U.S. relations with the Middle East. Because American troops never engaged rebel forces[48] and withdrew completely after three months, and because the United States allowed a government composed largely of opposition leaders to come to power instead of forcing a second term of Chamoun on the Lebanese people, the image of the United States did not significantly tarnish in the Middle East or elsewhere in the Third World.[49] Furthermore, the spread of Nasserism and neutralism did not accelerate as a result of the U.S. intervention. In fact, one consequence of the intervention was to reign in Nasser's efforts to destabilize the Lebanese government, for the crisis of 1958 taught him that Egyptian interference in Lebanese affairs attracted the thing he wanted least in his vicinity: Western troops.[50] Despite Dulles's earlier fears, no pro-Western, Middle Eastern governments fell as a direct result of the presence of U.S. and British troops in the Middle East.[51] Once Lebanese opposition leaders came into official power in the government, many of them committed themselves to maintaining Lebanon's independence against all foreign powers, including the UAR, and both Saeb Salaam and Rashid Karame assumed a reasoned and moderate attitude toward the United States.[52] Without overstating the case, I would argue that the intervention was a short-term success, largely because its goals were so limited. The administration demonstrated the credibility it held so vital without instigating the dire consequences that Eisenhower, Dulles, and U.S. military planners had feared. But the fact remains that the ill-conceived Eisenhower Doctrine had led the administration to over-commit U.S. prestige in a country that held very little importance for U.S. security.[53] It appears that Eisenhower and Dulles, with the help of officials such as Robert Murphy and a healthy dose of luck, managed to extract the United States from a noose they themselves had tied.[54]

Reluctant Activism in Costa Rica

Throughout most of the 1950s, top policy makers in the Eisenhower administration supported pro-U.S., anti-communist dictators in Central America while opposing more democratic, progressive governments (in Guatemala, for instance).[55] Nevertheless, the administration tolerated and even protected the democratic, leftist government of José Figueres in Costa Rica. Understanding the Costa Rican anomaly requires appreciating the extent to which Washington's preoccupation with appearances on the global stage shaped its relations with Costa Rica. Whereas the Eisenhower administration intervened in Lebanon to project an image of anti-communist resolve, it intervened on behalf of the Figueres government in 1955 to prevent any further damage to America's reputation as a force for democracy and to bolster the image of the Organization of American States (OAS), whose credibility helped to exclude overseas meddling from the affairs of the Western Hemisphere.

When Eisenhower took office in January of 1953, officials in the State Department and many influential American liberals were already familiar with the pro-U.S., anti-communist background of José Figueres Ferrer, who was then a candidate for the Costa Rican presidency.[56] But most members of the U.S. government were poorly informed on Costa Rican affairs, and many officials in both Congress and the Executive were reluctant to abandon their suspicion that Don Pepe (Figueres's popular nickname) harbored pro-communist sympathies.[57] Furthermore, it was common knowledge that on 16 December 1947, Figueres and other revolutionary leaders of the Democratic Left had signed the Caribbean Pact, by which they agreed to fight together to liberate their respective countries from dictatorship.[58] Department officials feared that if Figueres became president of Costa Rica, he would lead a campaign against Central American dictators, most of whom enjoyed friendly relations with the U.S. government.[59] The administration therefore viewed President Figueres as a potential threat to the envelope of hemispheric stability that blocked communist penetration and created a fertile environment for U.S. capital investment.[60]

For the first two years of Figueres's presidency, he and U.S. policy makers viewed one another through the lens of Guatemala.

In 1953 and 1954, Figueres watched and learned as the heavy hand of the United States came down on the Guatemalan president, Jacobo Arbenz, who had dared to nationalize land belonging to the powerful United Fruit Company (UFCO) and to court Guatemalan communists.[61] The U.S. campaign against Arbenz offered a gruesome lesson for Figueres in the limits of Washington's tolerance for independently-minded governments in Central America, and Don Pepe shaped his policies accordingly.[62] The Guatemalan crisis created a series of tests through which Figueres demonstrated his willingness to exclude communist influence, accommodate American private capital, and support U.S. anti-communist policies. By passing these tests, Figueres secured official U.S. toleration of his government.

By 26 July 1953, the date of José Figueres's election as president, relations between the U.S. and Guatemala had grown extremely tense, and the State Department was watching closely to see if Figueres would follow Arbenz's example and threaten UFCO's large capital investment in Costa Rica. Don Pepe had never explicitly threatened to nationalize UFCO property. But during the campaign, he had publicly promised to bring the company into line with his economic policies and to work for its eventual withdrawal from the country.[63] Figueres was adamant that the present arrangement, in which the company paid the Costa Rican government less than 20 percent of the profits it garnered from holdings in Costa Rica, must change. In April, months before his presidential term began, Figueres had presented the U.S. Embassy with his draft of a revised contract between UFCO and the Costa Rican government.[64] The revisions would increase the government's revenues from UFCO's profits, but more importantly, the new contract would assert Costa Rican control over all internal affairs of the country, even in the company's "Banana Zone."[65]

Department officials believed that UFCO's position rested "on a perfectly valid contract which is not demonstrably unfair to Costa Rica." But Secretary Dulles did not want to exert pressure on UFCO's behalf unless Figueres proved unreasonable and negotiations broke down.[66] As it happened, Don Pepe demonstrated that he was prepared to negotiate reasonably and with a degree of flexibility. After a meeting with Figueres in February of 1954, Embassy officials reported that Don Pepe's "reasoned

attitude . . . contrasted greatly with that of a few months ago."[67]
Figueres's flexibility at the negotiating table was partly an
outgrowth of his belief that, though the final goal was "an ending
of discriminations in favor of United Fruit Company," the "period
of transition would continue for some years."[68] But the main
reason behind Figueres's careful, moderate approach to UFCO was
undoubtedly the example that Guatemala provided of the fate of
Central American governments which threatened U.S. business
interests. Events in Guatemala throughout 1953 and the first half of
1954 were stark and ever-present reminders to the *figueristas* that
they should keep their dealings with UFCO within pro-American,
pro-U.S. business bounds.[69] Nevertheless, the terms of new
contract, which the parties signed on 4 June 1954, were testament
to Figueres's success as a negotiator.[70]

Figueres's successful negotiations with UFCO during the height
of Guatemala's conflict with the company led to praise for Don
Pepe in the U.S. Senate.[71] But officials in the State Department
were still not inclined to embrace Figueres as a friend; the
favorable outcome of the UFCO negotiations simply removed one
of the factors which could have led the administration to oppose
Figueres.[72] The Eisenhower administration's mounting campaign
against the Arbenz government in Guatemala loomed ahead as a
potential disaster for relations between the United States and the
new administration in Costa Rica. But over the first half of 1954,
Figueres demonstrated that he would not stand in the way of
Washington's anti-communist crusade in Guatemala.

From virtually the beginning of Eisenhower's presidency,
Figueres proved receptive to U.S. denunciations of Arbenz;
however, he voiced strong opposition to any anti-Arbenz plots that
included Anastasio Somoza of Nicaragua.[73] A *coup* organized
around Somoza would not only increase the dictator's strength in
the region, but also most likely install an authoritarian regime in
Guatemala. Although Figueres had no qualms about coups and
revolutions, he saw them as justified only when they replaced
dictatorship with democracy, as he believed the Costa Rican
revolution had done in 1948. While visiting Washington in May of
1953, Don Pepe lobbied UFCO officials for funds to back a
Figueres-led revolution to replace the communist-tainted
government in Guatemala with a pro-U.S. democracy. The UFCO

executives rebuffed Figueres,[74] but the meetings in Washington nevertheless revealed that Figueres had little sympathy for Arbenz and few objections to his overthrow.[75]

The Eisenhower administration began to coordinate its campaign against Arbenz in the weeks leading to the Tenth International Conference of American States, which was to be held in Caracas, Venezuela in March of 1954. Dulles planned to go to Caracas himself "to achieve adoption of a resolution which will lay ground work for subsequent positive action against Guatemala by the Organization of American States."[76] Figueres did not object to the anti-communist resolution, but he vehemently opposed holding the conference in Venezuela, whose President, Marcos Pérez Jiménez, he labeled a ruthless dictator. With the support of the exiled Venezuelan leader, Rómulo Betancourt, who was living under Figueres's protection in San José, Figueres decided to boycott the conference unless Pérez Jiménez released his political prisoners.[77] Although no other members of the OAS seconded Figueres's call for moral action, Don Pepe declared that Costa Rica's absence alone would call "attention to the long-abandoned problem of internal democracy in Latin America."[78]

Figueres wanted there to be no confusion as to the reasons for his proposing to boycott the conference. He knew that his opponents would seek to portray the boycott as a challenge to the Eisenhower administration's crusade against communism. So, in an open letter, Figueres explained that Costa Rica "will agree to any resolutions that come of this conference—pro-human rights, and pro-West, and pro-United States;" the Costa Rican boycott was solely a protest against Pérez Jiménez.[79] But democracies were rare in Latin America; anti-communist ones were even rarer, and the State Department feared that the anti-communist resolution would lack legitimacy if the only Latin Americans present to support it were dictators.[80] The U.S. Ambassador in San José, Robert Hill, expressed to Figueres in "most energetic terms" the disappointment felt in the United States toward Costa Rica's action at a time when the U.S. "needed support," and he warned Figueres that the reaction in the U.S. might be "harmful" to Costa Rica.[81] Despite the Department's pressure, and despite signs that the Costa Rican public opposed the boycott, Figueres held his ground, and Costa Rica did not attend the conference.[82] Assistant Secretary of

State R. Richard Rubottom said later that the administration was "embarrassed" by Costa Rica's absence, and Figueres recalled that "Mr. Dulles was furious."[83] Dulles had not had much personal involvement with Costa Rican affairs before March of 1954, and the boycott served as a sour introduction to José Figueres. But the Department already viewed Figueres as a regional troublemaker and an opportunist, and since Figueres left no room for doubt as to his support for the anti-communist resolution, there was nothing in Figueres's actions to change the prevailing estimation of Don Pepe in the Eisenhower administration.[84] Though no one in the State Department in mid-1954 proposed that the United States lavish praise and support on Figueres, the Department did not recommended opposition to his government.

In the case of PB SUCCESS, the CIA's plot to overthrow Arbenz through an exile invasion from Nicaragua, the Eisenhower administration would not have tolerated any interference from Figueres.[85] Don Pepe knew an American crusade when he saw one, and he knew that the only consequence should he try to stand in the way would be sharp U.S. recriminations against his fledgling administration. So to a large extent, Figueres swallowed the indignation and bitterness he felt toward the United States for giving Somoza a central role in the invasion of Guatemala that began on 18 June 1954. Following Arbenz's fall, the United States compensated Figueres for his acquiescence by signing a mutual defense pact with Costa Rica.[86]

By the late summer of 1954, Figueres had cleared several of the obstacles which could have blocked U.S. toleration of his administration. With the renegotiation of the UFCO contract, Figueres assured Washington that, unlike Arbenz, his policies would not be detrimental to U.S. business interests. With his general acquiescence in U.S. actions against Arbenz (and despite his boycott of the Caracas conference), Don Pepe showed the Eisenhower administration that he was no threat to its anti-communist objectives in the hemisphere. The administration still viewed Figueres as a potential threat to regional stability, and State Department officials had little regard for his character. But Don Pepe had shaken off any appearance of pro-communist sympathies and established himself in the eyes of the Eisenhower administration as a man to be tolerated.

Figueres proved reasonable in dealing with UFCO and acquiescent in Guatemalan matters partly because his government faced a dangerous external threat in mid 1954, and Don Pepe felt he needed U.S. support.[87] The Venezuelan dictator, Pérez Jiménez, was infuriated by Costa Rica's boycott of the Caracas conference because it broadcasted his regime's horrible record on human rights.[88] In April, Somoza's agents had uncovered a Figueres-backed plot to assassinate the Nicaraguan dictator.[89] So by late spring of 1954, both Somoza and Pérez Jiménez had strong reasons to attack Don Pepe. Sometime in late spring or early summer, the two dictators "entered into an anti-Figueres conspiracy" with the Costa Rican ex-President, Raphael Angel Calderón Guardia, to invade Costa Rica from Nicaragua.[90] In late June, Somoza sent his army to the Nicaraguan-Costa Rican border, and by mid-summer, rumors were rampant in San José that an invasion was imminent.[91]

The Eisenhower administration did not deliberate long before deciding to intervene on Costa Rica's behalf in the event of an invasion. Aside from treaty obligations,[92] the U.S. Embassy in San José recognized that "if shooting occurred," the U.S. "would be blamed for not forestalling these events, in view of Costa Rica's lack of an army." Furthermore, the embassy predicted that if the dictators succeeded in toppling Figueres, anti-American propaganda would assert that the U.S. had once again contracted its regional henchmen to silence a democratic critic of U.S. policies, and the resulting anti-U.S. opprobrium would ripple across the Third World.[93] Dulles agreed with the Embassy's assessment, and he instructed the ambassador to tell Figueres "that the United States would step in should Costa Rica be invaded."[94]

Despite the Department's diplomatic efforts and the withdrawal of Nicaraguan troops from the border in mid-July, November brought signs that an invasion was once again imminent.[95] In response to the renewed threat, the administration rerouted five F-84 Thunder jets to the Panama Canal Zone in order to provide a "psychological" deterrent against aggression in the region.[96] Tensions again subsided during the holiday season, but in early January of 1955, an invasion appeared more likely than ever.[97] The Department had decided the previous July that it desired to "prevent the violent overthrow of the present lawfully elected Government of Costa Rica."[98] The question in January was how far the United States was willing to go. The Figueres administration would have preferred "direct U.S. action," such as the dispatch of American destroyers to Costa Rican waters and overflights of Costa Rican territory by U.S. Air Force fighter-jets.[99] But the Department repeatedly insisted that Costa Rica "resort to the procedures of the OAS for inter-American peace rather than . . . request unilateral U.S. action."[100] The Eisenhower administration was not inclined to open itself up to charges of interventionism and incur the enmity of Figueres's enemies in the region by taking unilateral military action to protect Costa Rica. Instead, the U.S. strove to take actions within the multilateral, juridical framework of the OAS. Following Washington's suggestion, the Costa Rican government outlined a complaint which it submitted to the OAS on 8 January.[101]

On 11 January the long-awaited invasion of Costa Rica finally began when a force of a few hundred men crossed the border from Nicaragua and seized a small town sixty-nine kilometers northwest of San José.[102] The Costa Rican ambassador immediately asked Holland for U.S. military assistance under Article 3 of the Rio Treaty, but the Department hoped that the OAS would act quickly and decisively enough to obviate any unilateral U.S. military response.[103] The attitude of the U.S. government toward the threat to Costa Rica had not changed since the previous July. But now that the threat was dire and immediate, policy-makers began to speak more urgently about the need to protect the viability of the inter-American system.[104] The whole impetus behind Article 51 of the UN Charter and the creation of the OAS had been the desire of the United States to exclude overseas, and particularly communist, powers from the affairs of the Western Hemisphere. As Dulles put it in a meeting of the National Security Council on January 13, an important part of the U.S. effort to coordinate a vigorous OAS reaction to the Costa Rican crisis "was a desire to prevent the United Nations from meddling in the situation, as several members of the UN would be only too glad to do."[105] Furthermore, if the OAS failed to protect Costa Rica, Latin Americans might be less inclined in the future to refer their disputes to any multilateral organization. In that case, the U.S. would be forced to intervene unilaterally to preserve stability, exposing itself to charges of imperialism.

Despite discussions of protecting the stability of the region and the efficacy of the OAS as an instrument of U.S. leadership, the administration never lost sight of a vital, though less tangible, interest at stake in Costa Rica: America's image on the global stage. A barrage of telegrams, press reports, and entreaties from U.S. missions abroad ensured that Dulles and other policy makers involved did not neglect the conclusion they had reached months earlier: that a failure to rescue Figueres would deal the United States a stinging propaganda defeat which the country's image could not afford so soon after the Guatemalan coup. In a meeting of the National Security Council on 13 January the director of the CIA, Allen W. Dulles, referred to the "present revolution" in Costa Rica as "the most publicized of any Latin American revolution in history."[106] The remark revealed that the administration was impressed by the scale of the world-wide media reaction, which largely portrayed the situation as an attempt by militarist, reactionary elements to crush a defenseless democracy.[107] On 12 January a flood of telegrams entreating President Eisenhower, Secretary Dulles, and Assistant Secretary Holland to protect the Costa Rican government began to flow to the White House and the State Department from influential American liberals both in and out of government,[108] and by the following day, U.S. officials were already detecting condemnation from vocal elements in Latin America and overseas.[109] The Ambassador in Belgrade appealed directly to the Department's fears when he reported that, given the developments in Costa Rica and the widespread suspicion of American complicity in Arbenz's overthrow the previous year, the "Yugoslav leadership [is] capable [of] drawing conclusions which could make [the] U.S. task here more difficult."[110] Most significant to the Department was the public interest noted in countries normally friendly to the United States. The London Embassy echoed the desires of U.S. representatives world-wide when it "urgently" requested guidance from the Department "to prevent [a] possible hardening of opinion, as occurred during [the] Guatemala crisis, which once rooted, makes general acceptance [of] United States views infinitely more difficult [to] achieve."[111] Evidently, audiences across the globe saw the crisis as a test of U.S. good faith. Because the administration had anticipated just such a reaction, U.S. officials could respond by 13 January with confident assurances that the United States was taking decisive action through the OAS to protect the Costa Rican government.[112]

In the early morning of 16 January the Council of the OAS approved a resolution, submitted by the U.S., which called on the member states to offer military assistance to the Costa Rican government.[113] By dawn, four U.S. Air Force P-51 Mustang fighters were airborne and *en route* to San José, where they were turned over to the Costa Rican government at token cost.[114] The U.S. planes had a decisive effect on the conflict, for the invaders' main military advantage had been their air force. Within a week, the P-51's and their Costa Rican pilots destroyed or grounded all rebel aircraft.[115] Consequently, a U.S. official in Costa Rica was able to report by 22 January that the "rebels are already apparently crossing into Nicaragua where they will presumably be interned."[116] An OAS Investigating Committee achieved Costa Rican and Nicaraguan agreement on a neutral zone running the length of their shared border and extending three miles into each country. Although skirmishes between *Guardia Civil* units and pockets of rebels erupted sporadically for weeks to come and tensions would persist for years,[117] the threat to the Costa Rican government was over.[118] Following the dispatch of U.S. planes to Costa Rica and the apparent triumph of the Figueres government, U.S. embassies abroad confirmed that the administration's actions had forestalled a wave of criticism that had begun to rise around the world.[119] The administration was pleased with the outcome of the conflict. According to a report prepared by the Operations Coordinating Board (OCB) in August, the "successful action of the OAS in the Costa Rican situation not only enhanced the prestige of the OAS" and the U.S. in Latin America, it also confounded communist propagandists.[120] The administration had supported Figueres's government in order to protect the United States' image in the world and to safeguard the juridical system on which U.S. hegemony in the region rested.

As soon as the threat to the Costa Rican government passed, the top objective for U.S. policy makers became the restoration of regional stability. The administration was not inclined to censure the aggressors, who comprised most of the United States' solid friends in Central America. Furthermore, U.S. officials believed that Figueres's foreign meddling, culminating in the April 1954 plot to assassinate Somoza, was largely responsible for the crisis. Dulles and Holland believed that the OAS had already "served notice on all who might henceforth contemplate intervention;" they therefore "proposed prompt overtures" to the governments involved so that the "investigation and fact findings" of the OAS could be halted before they reach a conclusion that "destroyed all possibility [of a] reconciliation."[121] The Department desired a personal meeting of reconciliation between Figueres and Somoza to end the conflict once and for all. But Figueres vehemently opposed this idea, holding that a personal meeting between the two presidents would give the impression that their "personal relationship" had caused the conflict (this was precisely the Department's impression). After separate visits to San José by Adolf Berle and Vice President Richard Nixon both failed to secure Figueres's compliance, the administration decided to settle for public statements released by the two presidents "to the effect that neither would try to overthrow the other."[122] Figueres was grateful for U.S. aid in thwarting the invasion, but he resented the administration's attitude following the crisis. He had hoped that Costa Rica's triumph would lead to a reaffirmation of democratic government and non-aggression. Instead, the only thing affirmed was the Eisenhower administration's tendency to favor dictators in Central America.[123] Although Figueres did agree to drop the case against Nicaragua in the OAS, he had no intention of feigning friendship with Somoza. By April of 1955, he was again making public statements to the effect that the only way to establish the "political and social equilibrium" the United States frequently spoke of was to clear the region of dictatorships.[124] In May, the U.S. Embassy remarked that his "recent uncompromising speeches" before the Costa Rican National Congress were "reminiscent of his high-riding days before he got into trouble in April, 1954."[125] Evidently, the United States did not succeed in pressuring Figueres to abandon his convictions and become a docile hemispheric citizen.

Neither Costa Rica nor Lebanon held much on-the-ground importance to the United States and there was no history of close U.S. diplomatic involvement in either country. Therefore, Washington took little heed of the internal political complexities of these countries and viewed them largely as means toward the administration's psychological-strategic ends. In Costa Rica this meant intervening on behalf of the Figueres regime to ensure the credibility of American democracy in the region. But like Chamoun, Figueres, encountered the limits of U.S. support just when it seemed to reach a dramatic height. Although both leaders were initially gratified by Washington's military response to their calls for help, they grew bitter in the months following the initial American interventions, for both men discovered that the Eisenhower administration's priorities had little to do with their own goals. In fact, the objectives behind both U.S. military interventions had little to do with either Costa Rica or Lebanon. In both cases, the Eisenhower administration responded to a call for help to make the right impression on broader or more vital audiences. Once the administration determined that its actions had preserved America's image globally, it back-pedaled furiously to preserve a status quo that favored U.S. power. In the Middle East, this amounted to negotiating with Chamoun's opposition and accommodating Nasser's concerns. In Central America, this meant soothing the wounded pride of dictators and reigning in an aggressive democrat. Although the Eisenhower administration reluctantly intervened in countries that held little strategic interest, it tried to confine its actions to those that served broader, more vital ends on the global stage.

Defining Neutrality in Austria

As in the Lebanese and Costa Rican cases, the Eisenhower administration viewed Austria in the shadow of concerns with a more vital country (in this case, West Germany), and U.S. actions in Austria were chosen for their effect on a broad, international audience. But unlike Lebanon and Costa Rica, Austria possessed a strategic location which endowed the country with direct importance to the security of the Western Bloc. Because the administration viewed the security and continued Western alignment of Austria as vital to the West, policy makers on the National Security Council gave high priority to maintaining a close and cooperative relationship with Vienna. Furthermore, the fund of understanding and good will which had accrued between the United States and Austria during the occupation period worked to smooth Austro-American relations in the late 1950s. (This positive familiarity was lacking in Washington's relations with either Lebanon or Costa Rica.) Austria's direct importance to Western security, together with the mutual understanding between Vienna and Washington, explain why Austria fell less in the shadow of the Eisenhower administration's global-psychological priorities than did either Lebanon or Costa Rica and why the Austro-American relationship was the most steady and mutually beneficial of the three cases in this study.

In the spring of 1955, the Eisenhower administration believed that the Kremlin's rapid reversal on the Austrian State Treaty betrayed a Soviet plot to use a unified and independent, yet neutral, Austria to lure nations along the Western side of the Iron Curtain out of the Western collective security network.[126] In particular, Eisenhower and Dulles believed that the Soviets would use the Austrian example to foster public opposition in the Federal Republic of Germany to rearmament and membership in NATO.[127] U.S. policy makers feared that a neutral, independent, and unified Austria could provide the Soviet Union with powerful evidence that membership in NATO was the only thing separating the German people from reunification.[128] For years, the integration of West Germany into the defensive structure of Western Europe had been a central goal of American foreign policy. Therefore, Eisenhower and Dulles were committed to the development of a viable Austrian army and the maintenance Austria's conspicuous Western alignment in order to show the Germans and the rest of Europe that Austria's regained independence and national unity had no grounding in either demilitarization or nonalignment.[129]

Factors relating directly to Austria also fueled the Eisenhower administration's quest for a militarily strong, politically pro-West Austria. Given the country's crucial geostrategic position in Central Europe, its well-known pro-Western sympathies, and the massive amounts of money and effort which the United States had already invested in Austrian independence by 1955, U.S. policy makers believed that the loss of Austria to the Soviet sphere of influence would constitute a chilling strategic defeat (both in a military and a psychological sense) for the Western powers.[130] Therefore, the Eisenhower administration continued the long-standing American effort to maintain an "independent and stable Austria" capable of resisting "Communist pressures and subversion." By 1955, $1.4 billion in U.S. aid had reestablished Austria's economic stability, but the country's military security was by no means insured.[131] Consequently, the Eisenhower administration was committed to the development of an Austrian military force large enough to halt mid-sized incursions from its Eastern neighbors and provide an adequate psychological bulwark against Soviet "pressures and subversion."[132]

The Eisenhower administration acquiesced when Austrian leaders tabled an offer of military neutrality at the Berlin foreign ministers' meeting in late 1954 and during their trip to Moscow in April 1955.[133] But the administration insisted that the provisions of the State Treaty reestablishing Austrian national independence allow the Austrians to raise forces sufficient to preserve internal order and territorial integrity and that the treaty allow Austria to accept Western military equipment.[134] At the urging of the U.S. Ambassador in Vienna, Llewellyn Thompson, Austrian Chancellor Julius Raab asked the Soviets to eliminate the clause of the State Treaty that placed a ceiling on the size of the Austrian army. By mid-April 1955, the Soviets were in a mood to conclude the Treaty quickly, and they agreed to remove the size limit.[135] This revision made the prospect of Austrian neutrality more palatable for the Americans, because a neutrality model that allowed an army of unlimited size "could hardly be proposed by the Soviets as a model to be followed in Germany." Nevertheless, the Eisenhower administration wanted tangible proof to show the West Germans that Austria's fate was not relevant to their own and to show the U.S. Congress that the Austrians intended to shoulder the burdens associated with defending themselves against the communist East.[136]

In late May 1955, just days after the signing of the State Treaty, the U.S. expanded its program of military support for Austria (which the Truman administration had initiated covertly in 1951) by authorizing the transfer of $20 million in small arms and equipment from the stockpiles of U.S. occupation forces to the Austrian government.[137] Because the transfer was secret and because the Austrians had yet to tackle the problem of raising military personnel, the military issue was not yet exposed to the complications of Austria's coalition politics.[138] But when the occupation troops left Austria in late 1955, they took with them the unifying goal that had bred ten years of cooperation between the People's Party (ÖVP) and the Socialist Party (SPÖ), which composed Austria's coalition government. Increased partisanship was an inevitable consequence of Austria's regained independence, and since the development of a national army was one of the first divisive questions to face the independent Austrian state, the issue quickly became embroiled in coalition bickering.[139] The Socialists were concerned that the People's Party, whose narrow electoral victory in 1953 secured the chancellorship, not enjoy exclusive control over Austria's army, and Socialist Party leaders feared that if they failed to take up the anti-militarist banner, the issue might provide a "wedge" which the Austrian Communist Party could use to "win over from the Socialists a large proportion of the industrial working population."[140] Consequently, the Socialists advocated limiting the duration of military service to a paltry six months (the People's Party pressed for a one year minimum).[141] The U.S. Joint Chiefs of Staff believed that it would be difficult to establish a sizable, well trained army in a country with the modest population of Austria if mandatory service extended for only six months, and officials in the White House and State Department realized that maintaining America's large and expensive commitment to Austria's military build-up under the Mutual Security Act required convincing Congress that the Austrians were willing to do their part to support their own defense.[142] Six months of service hardly looked like a sacrifice.

The State Department registered its concerns regarding the duration of mandatory service through Ambassador Thompson in Vienna and the Austrian Ambassador, Karl Gruber, in Washington. But the Eisenhower administration did not attempt to coerce the Austrian government; U.S. officials realized that continuing to treat Austria like an occupied county would provoke a hostile reaction and perhaps drive the Austrians closer to the Soviets. The administration was not inclined to threaten withdrawal of military aid (as the Austrians well knew), for such action would jeopardize the establishment of Austria's defensive capability and might prompt the Austrians to accept substantial military aid from the Soviets. In addition, the administration did not want to take action which could hand the Socialists' electoral support in Austria over to the Communists. Ambassador Gruber's reassurance helped to convince U.S. officials that Austrian foot-dragging on the military issue stemmed not from a refusal to recognize the importance of Austria's defensive viability, but from the political foibles of a coalition government adjusting to independence.[143] In late July, the Austrian coalition came to an agreement based on a nine-month period of military service and on an ÖVP concession: although the military would be under the ultimate control of Raab, the Chancellor would consult Vice Chancellor Schärf (of the SPÖ) on all important policy questions involving the army.[144]

During the summer of 1955, haggling over the Austrian federal budget and delays of the final parliamentary vote on the military legislation distressed Department officials who were anxious that the Austrian army "be built up as rapidly as possible during the period between the entry into force of the Treaty and final withdrawal of occupation troops in order not to leave a military vacuum in Austria."[145] After a week-long deadlock at the end of August, the Austrian Parliament finally passed the Army law during a special session on 7 September but its budget was smaller than the Department had hoped.[146] Austrian defense remained an important U.S. objective, but there was little the Americans could do to determine the outcome of Austria's coalition wrangling. The administration resigned itself to the fact that "an effective Austrian defense force will require additional military assistance."[147]

By the end of 1955, U.S. and Austrian officials had established a pattern that would continue to the end of the Eisenhower administration. The United States continued its large-scale commitment to Austrian defense through authorizations for aid under section 401 of the Mutual Security Act. (The total value of U.S. military aid to Austria between the ratification of the State Treaty and September 1959 was approximately $91 million.)[148] Meanwhile, the Austrian government struggled toward the ultimate goal of a 65,000-man army, but budget difficulties and the short duration of military service continued to hold the Austrian army below U.S. force goals.[149] The Eisenhower administration was impatient to witness the development of a viable Austrian army, but this impatience rarely developed into resentment. For the most part, the Americans realized that the Austrians could not be ordered to do things, and U.S. officials recognized that the delays in the development in Austrian military strength stemmed not from lack of commitment to the nation's defense, but from complications arising from the rivalries within the Austrian coalition. There were exceptions to the generally calm approach of U.S. policy makers. In July 1959, responding to signs that the Austrians were poised to drastically cut the defense budget, Ambassador H. Freeman Matthews requested and received the Department's authorization to threaten to terminate United States military aid. But over the following few weeks, Austrian officials assured Matthews that "reductions were not really intended and talk thereof was only the result of political bargaining in the attempt to form a new government" following the recent elections.[150] Matthews's hard line reveals that the U.S. was sensitive to any developments which could hamper the Austrian military buildup. But, in general, policy makers in Washington trusted the Austrians' commitment to defending their country against Soviet pressures and communist military aggression, and the administration determined that the Austrians were making reasonable progress toward the "objective of a time-phased buildup to 65,000 men by October 1959."[151]

In late September 1958, Foreign Minister Leopold Figl announced that Austria was prepared to contribute to the United Nations Peace Force which Eisenhower had proposed following the U.S. intervention in Lebanon (Austria joined the UN on 16 December 1956).[152] United States officials were enormously satisfied by Figl's announcement, because it demonstrated before a global audience that Austria's declaration of neutrality had not precluded the development of a viable military defense force and, implicitly, that demilitarization had played no part in Austrian independence.[153]

Eisenhower and Dulles believed that Austria, like West Berlin, held "world-wide psychological importance as a symbol of resistance to Soviet subversion." In their view, the world was watching to see if Austria, free from foreign occupation and under the protection of neutrality, would begin to drift toward nonalignment in the Cold War. The administration feared that even slight shifts toward a more central orientation could open the way for the Kremlin "to use the Austrian example as an incentive to develop neutralism elsewhere."[154] Furthermore, seemingly harmless cases of acquiescence to Soviet and satellite pressures could be "the camel's nose under the tent," creating an opening for the eventual destruction of Austria's independence and ties to the West.[155] The Eisenhower administration therefore viewed with concern any Austrian actions that could be perceived as signs of increasing political or economic nonalignment. But at the same time, the level of understanding between Washington and Vienna mitigated the alarm with which United States officials viewed Chancellor Raab's more troubling policies and moderated the administration's response to the Austrian actions it opposed.

One of the first problems to develop between the U.S. and Austria after the signing of the State Treaty concerned Chancellor Raab's apparent desire to enter Austria into the Belgrade Danube Convention, which established shipping and navigation rights among the riparian states (Hungary, Czechoslovakia, Yugoslavia, Romania, and Bulgaria) of Eastern Europe. Despite the concern of some in Washington that Austria was succumbing to the pressures of geography and drifting toward economic integration with the communist bloc,[156] high State Department officials remained calm, rejecting a French proposal to "indicate to the Austrian Government that its adherence to the Belgrade Convention would be hard to reconcile with the policy of neutrality" unless it were balanced by Austria's admission to the Council of Europe. The Department believed that a "tit for tat" approach to Austrian neutrality might set a dangerous precedent which both the Soviets and the Austrians could use to graft economic and political meaning onto Austria's strictly military neutrality. Since the U.S. wanted to restrict Austria's neutrality to the narrowest military definition, it could not insist on a return "favor" every time the Austrians made some small step toward the East. Besides, Raab appeared only to be floating the idea; the Department did not predict "precipitate Austrian adherence" to the Belgrade Convention.[157]

U.S. officials reacted with greater concern when it was suddenly revealed in November 1955 that the leadership of the ÖVP in Lower Austria had agreed to accept a development loan from the Soviet Union. What alarmed the Department was the fact that the negotiations with the Soviets took place without the notification of U.S. officials, and that Chancellor Raab apparently advocated the loan as a demonstration of Austria's absolute neutrality. The Socialists were as shocked as the Americans. In their opinion, the loan threatened "a complete reorientation of Austrian foreign policy" in the direction of the Soviet Union, and the Socialists viewed the fact that Raab and the Lower Austrian officials had negotiated the loan in secret as a violation of the spirit of the coalition pact.[158] U.S. officials backed the Socialists' opposition with a stick-and-carrot approach: the administration induced the World Bank to notify the Austrian government that it would be "reluctant to participate in Soviet-funded projects" while simultaneously showing willingness to conclude a Public Law 480 agreement for economic development with Austria. When the Lower Austrian officials submitted the loan agreement to the Federal Cabinet, the Socialists united to defeat the proposal.[159] Department officials were alarmed by Chancellor Raab's handling of the loan issue, but they saw the decisive defeat of the loan as evidence that the Austrian people intended "to interpret [their] neutrality in a strict military sense rather than beyond the stipulations of the State Treaty."[160]

The United States faced other troubling developments in Austria in late 1955 and early 1956, and they all seemed to revolve around Raab. The chancellor blocked the Socialists' efforts to enter Austria into Council of Europe and thereby "give Austrian neutrality an unmistakably Western cast." In December, Raab delivered a radio address in which he called upon Austrian commentators and journalists to "observe neutrality in commenting upon Eastern as well as Western ideology." More ominously, the chancellor and his foreign minister began to show signs of supporting diplomatic recognition of Communist China. In late December 1955, Dulles cabled Ambassador Thompson expressing his concern that recent developments "could constitute . . . indications that . . . [the] Austrian Government [is] applying [its] neutrality policy beyond [the] area [of] military alliances and bases."[161] But Thompson responded that he did not believe that recent Austrian developments were "as significant" as Dulles had indicated. The ambassador pointed out that matters such as the Soviet loan had their "roots in domestic issues" such as the ongoing rivalry between the two major parties. Although the prospect of Austria's recognition of the People's Republic presented a "more serious problem," Thompson argued that it should be viewed against Austria's secret approval of air transit rights across Tyrol for U.S. war planes. Furthermore, Thompson was reassured by the obviously pro-Western and staunchly anti-communist line of the Austrian press and a large majority of Austrian politicians, and he held up the defeat of the Soviet loan proposal in January as further evidence that the Austrian people would not allow themselves to be dragged toward nonalignment by their "naïve" chancellor. [162]

The State Department took comfort in the approach of national elections, scheduled for the spring of 1956, because, as the Socialists believed, neutralism was "so unpopular among the Austrian public (and in Raab's own party)" that once the chancellor faced the prospect of elections, he would have to change his policy line or suffer defeat at the polls. [163] In March 1956, the embassy reported that the Socialists' predictions had been correct. [164] In the early spring of 1956, the Chancellor adopted a more overtly pro-Western public stance, supported the expulsion of the communist-dominated World Federation of Trade Unions, and even buckled to the pressure to enter Austria into the Council of Europe. [165]

The Austrian political events of late 1955 and early 1956 defined the way in which the Eisenhower administration would continue to view developments in post-State-Treaty Austria. First, concerns over the Soviet loan and other issues convinced U.S. policy makers of the need to remain alert to Austrian actions which could lead to increasing economic and political nonalignment. More importantly, though, events showed that the official Austrian positions which the United States found troubling were frequently outgrowths of domestic issues that had little connection to the growth of nonalignment. Furthermore, the defeat of the Soviet loan and the positive results of the call for early elections revealed that pressures *within* Austria were frequently sufficient to thwart the potentially dangerous moves of politicians like Raab.

In late 1955 and early 1956, Austrian policy makers probed the boundaries of Washington's tolerance for an independent Austrian agenda. But in late 1956, U.S. officials beamed with admiration and respect as the Austrians passed with highest marks a crucial test presented by events in neighboring Hungary. The Austrian government initially avoided official mention of the Hungarian uprising that began on 23 October but once the Soviet military crack-down began on 4 November the Austrian government unleashed harsh diplomatic protests against the Soviet Union and supported UN resolutions condemning Soviet actions.[166] The Austrian government decided to keep the eastern border open to the waves of Hungarians fleeing Soviet repression, despite the fact that, by 21 November the number of refugees in Austria exceeded 40,000 (more were coming at a rate of 5,000 per day).[167] The Eisenhower administration greatly appreciated the burden which Austria accepted during the refugee crisis as well as Austria's resolute determination to maintain "its right to grant asylum to all refugees" in the face of repeated accusations by communist governments that Austria was interfering in internal Hungarian affairs and violating its declared neutrality.[168] Both the White House and Congress agreed that Vienna's reaction "has furthered Austria's alignment with the West."[169] The Austrian reaction to the Hungarian crisis of late 1956 raised the levels of Austro-American cooperation and trust higher than at any point since late 1954 and established a wealth of good will that the tensions of 1958 diminished but could not extinguish.

From early 1957 until midsummer 1958, the major problems in the Austro-American relationship centered on the failure of the Austrian government to settle claims owed to British and American oil companies (under the Vienna Memorandum of 1955) and to World War II persecutees (under the State Treaty). After the re-establishment of Austrian independence, the Eisenhower administration allowed the Austrians a grace period to insure the stability of the coalition and the establishment of a strong army. The danger and euphoria of the Hungarian refugee crisis further suppressed the United States' inclination to raise delicate issues between the two governments, for issues regarding Austria's military status and Western alignment superseded financial claims in United States policy making.[170] But when the Austrians still had not settled certain categories of claims by September 1957, Department officials warned them that they were fueling the argument that the Austria took the U.S. for granted.[171] Despite its dissatisfaction, though, the Department did not threaten any specific repercussions.[172] Austria's failure to settle the claims contributed to the position of those within the Department who began to call for a tougher line toward Austria, but high officials did not begin to advocate a 'get-tough' policy until Chancellor Raab sparked deeper concerns regarding Austria's political alignment during his trip to Moscow in July 1958.

On 21 July 1958, Chancellor Raab arrived in Moscow to negotiate a lowering of Austria's continuing reparations payments to the Soviets. At the Moscow airport, before microphones and reporters, Raab stated that the State Treaty had been concluded "mainly thanks to the Soviet Union" and that "developments between the [Western] Allies" were responsible for the long postponement of Austrian liberation. As U.S. Ambassador to the Soviet Union, Llewellyn Thompson (who had recently been U.S. Ambassador to Austria) stood aghast a few feet away, Raab boasted that Austria had asserted its military neutrality against American pressures only a week earlier with a protest against the overflight of Austrian territory by U.S. military airplanes. Raab closed his statement with the assurance that Austrian neutrality "is not simply a limited but an unlimited neutrality."[173] It is difficult to imagine a statement more likely to alarm Washington than the one Raab made on the morning of the twenty-first. What most upset the Department was the fact that Raab's statement was ideally suited to be "rapidly exploited by Soviet propaganda."[174] All hope of forestalling a negative reaction in Washington was crushed the next day when Raab announced that Austria had decided to join the Belgrade Danube Convention, bragging that the decision had been an "Austrian initiative."[175] U.S. officials were furious because Foreign Minister Figl had promised to consult the State Department before Austria made a final decision to join the Convention and because, by making such a public announcement in Moscow, Raab was broadcasting Austria's entrance into the Convention as an indication of Vienna's drift to the East.[176]

Throughout the late summer and autumn of 1958, Austrian officials tried to mitigate the damage that Raab's statements had caused. But although they were willing to apologize for Raab's demeanor in Moscow and for Figl's failure to consult with the Department on Austria's admission to the Belgrade Convention, Austrian officials were reluctant to retract Raab's comments concerning overflights,[177] even though they knew that their actual response to the overflights in July had been more vague than defiant. (A careful look at the chronology of events in mid-July

1958 reveals that although the first eighteen U.S. planes that had passed over Tyrol en route to Lebanon did so without prior notification of the Austrian government, the Austrians nevertheless had been careful *not* to interfere with further U.S. overflights.[178]) The Eisenhower administration believed that the root of Raab's claim to have stood up to the United States on the overflights issue was his quest for further concessions from the Soviets on annual oil shipments.[179] But however innocent Raab's motivation, his statements read like neutralism when they appeared under headlines in hundreds of newspapers across the world. The Eisenhower administration believed that this sort of publicity undermined its efforts to convince the world that Austria's military neutrality did not carry with it any semblance of nonalignment.[180] Raab's Moscow trip led the new U.S. Ambassador to Austria, Freeman (Doc) Matthews, to press the Department for a harder line with Vienna. In particular, he believed there were times "when we should drag our feet a little" on economic and military aid to Austria.[181]

The behavior of several Austrian politicians in the late summer and early autumn seemed to add definition to Matthews's portrait of Austrian ingratitude. In September, Vice Chancellor Pittermann told the Ambassador, in reference to the outstanding claims of World War II persecutees and Soviet concessions on annual oil deliveries, that the impression was "gaining ground" in Austria that the Soviet government was "handing Austria ten million dollars a year through oil, while [the] Austrian Government is giving the [United States] five million dollars for former Nazi persecutees." Matthews felt that Pittermann was trying to manipulate the United States with his friendly advice, and the meeting cemented his belief that the Austrians took the United States for granted. He recommended that Dulles express indignation over Pittermann's statement in an upcoming meeting with Foreign Minister Figl.[182] But Dulles had been an observer of Austrian politics longer that Matthews, and the Secretary realized that Pittermann's statement was just another errant emission from Austria's coalition wrangling. Dulles rejected Matthews's proposal to raise the matter with Figl, explaining that Pittermann's statement was merely an attempt by a Socialist to throw a wrench into the chancellor's plan to settle the persecutee claims with a lump sum payment.[183] In late 1955,

Ambassador Thompson had counseled Dulles to be patient with the difficulties caused by Austrian domestic politics. In late 1958, Dulles instructed the new Ambassador to do the same. In early 1959, Matthews began to focus his frustration with the Austrians on their failure to settle the persecutee and Vienna Memorandum claims, and he lobbied with increasing insistence for delays in the release of counterpart (Marshall Plan) funds to Austria.[184] Finally, the aggregate frustrations regarding recent Austrian behavior led the Department to authorize a delay in the release of $33 million of counterpart funds during the winter of 1958-1959. It is significant, however, that the Department did not authorize "foot dragging" on the counterpart funds until after Dulles was no longer acting as Secretary of State.[185]

The delay in the release of counterpart funds did not achieve the desired effect in Austria. The word did circulate on the Austrian political cocktail party circuit and in the Austrian press that the United States was frustrated regarding the Vienna Memorandum, the persecutee claims, the Belgrade Convention, and the frequency of Austrian official visits to the Eastern Bloc.[186] But although the Viennese press declared that Austrian policy makers were largely at fault for the recent tensions between Vienna and Washington, many Austrian commentators asserted that the United States would have to grasp the fact that Austria was "an independent, neutral state, which cannot be treated like an occupied country even though it considers itself part of the Western community." Many Austrians accepted that they needed to act more like "friends" of the U.S., but they strongly resented being treated like "servants."[187] Following the tensions of 1958, Austrians began to insist that Washington judge them on the substance of their actions rather than on the myriad of ways which those actions could be distorted through Soviet propaganda and American paranoia. In mid-March 1959, Assistant Secretary Merchant and Undersecretary Dillon agreed that the Department's tactic had backfired, and they instructed Matthews to release the counterpart funds.[188]

Ambassador Matthews had taken offense at the notion that Austria did not afford the United States the proper deference and gratitude. But policy makers such as Dulles, Merchant, Dillon, and the officers of the West European desk at Foggy Bottom were less inclined to react with personal indignation to the wayward statements of Austrian politicians.[189] Given the large-scale (and CIA-backed) movement of Vienna's youth to turn the communist-inspired World Youth Festival (held in Vienna in the summer of 1959) into a pro-West event, and the increasing press and political attacks in Austria against Raab's foreign policy,[190] the West European Desk concluded "that we should not be concerned that there is a trend in Austria toward neutralism or toward a more sympathetic attitude toward the Soviet Union." The Department continued to oppose the bridge-building initiatives of Austrian politicians when they appeared to fuel the Soviet objective of spreading neutralism. But U.S. officials began to accept in the late 1950s that they could not expect from Austria "conduct as favorable to our interests as [that] of our NATO allies." The administration resolved to remain attentive to the continuing Western alignment of Austria, but to do so with "consideration" for Austria's domestic political complexity.[191]

From 1954 to 1959, Austria gained much and sacrificed little in its relationship with the United States. The Austrians shared Washington's desire to secure their country against Eastern Bloc aggression, and massive U.S. military aid made bearable the Americans' frequent urgings to accelerate the build-up. Strong cultural and ideological foundations fueled the Austrian commitment to the Hungarian refugees in 1956, and U.S. assistance helped maintain Austria's favorable attitude. Nevertheless, the Austrian reaction to the Hungarian crisis had a tremendous, positive impact on relations with Washington. In the late 1950s, the administration viewed with alarm Chancellor Raab's attempts to broadcast a nonaligned public image. But U.S. policy makers recognized that Raab's gestures existed in the field of public relations, not substantive policy, and they were confident that the staunchly pro-U.S. Austrian public would pull Raab back to the Western fold if he strayed too close to the Eastern precipice. Consequently, the administration continued to extend support toward Austria and restrain the heavy hand that the U.S. wielded elsewhere in the world.

Conclusion

Historical assessments of Eisenhower's foreign policy have reached the postrevisionist phase. A consensus of scholars now holds that Eisenhower and Dulles operated as a team, with the President securely and actively in command, and that both the President and his Secretary of State were capable, within administration circles, of thoughtfully, rationally, and accurately assessing developments such as Third World nationalism, nonalignment, and antagonism between communist states.[192] But Stephen Rabe, Robert Divine, Robert McMahon, and others point out that administration officials' "flexible and pragmatic private statements" on international developments had little effect on the substance of American diplomacy during the Eisenhower years. Although the administration evaluated world developments "in a perceptive, deliberate, even sophisticated manner," it nevertheless "pursued a narrowly anti-Communist foreign policy" that precluded an accommodation with those governments and groups reluctant to adhere to the polar, zero-sum framework of the East-West conflict.[193] The explanation for this failure lies with the consuming preoccupation of Eisenhower, Dulles, and other top U.S. officials with projecting images of steadfast anti-communism to vital audiences. The three cases in this study reveal that Washington's preoccupation with avoiding psychological setbacks on the battlefield of world opinion compelled U.S. policy makers to oppose all foreign developments, even in small nations like Lebanon, Costa Rica and Austria, that might be viewed elsewhere as a gain for international communism. Consequently, the Eisenhower administration often found itself opposing actions taken by foreign peoples even when those actions did not significantly threaten tangible U.S. geostrategic interests. Moreover, the Lebanese case reveals strikingly that the administration sometimes jeopardized U.S. interests in states of secondary importance in order to forestall psychological defeats in more vital theaters.

But the Austrian case shows that top policy makers in the Eisenhower administration (including the infamous Mr. Dulles) could, even when viewing a small country that lay squarely in the crossfire of U.S.-Soviet image-warfare, free their decision-making from the influence of knee-jerk anti-communism and world opinion. Because Washington deemed Austria's pro-West alignment as directly vital to Western security, U.S. policy makers gave high priority to maintaining a cooperative relationship with the Austrian government. Furthermore, Austria's direct geostrategic importance to the United States, together with the in-depth experience in Austrian affairs that U.S. officials had gained during the decade-long occupation, meant that the Eisenhower administration was greatly interested in and intimately familiar with the complexities of Austria's internal politics. Finally, because Washington held Austria's economic health, political stability, and military security to be important in their own right, the Eisenhower administration found that its fundamental goals in Austria corresponded closely with the basic aims of the Austrian people. For these reasons, and despite the fact that Raab's bridge-building agenda was as troubling to Washington as Figueres's anti-dictatorial crusade and Chamoun's political ambitions, Austria emerged from underneath Washington's preoccupation with global perceptions to enjoy a mutually beneficial relationship with the United States.

NOTES

1. This article was partly inspired by Robert McMahon, "Credibility and World Power: Exploring the Psychological Dimension in Postwar American Diplomacy," *Diplomatic History* 15 (1991): 455-471.

2. See John Lewis Gaddis, *The United States and the Origins of the Cold War* (New York: Columbia University Press, 1972), 460, Gaddis, *Strategies of Containment: A Critical Appraisal of Postwar American National Security Policy* (New York: Oxford University Press, 1982), 91-92, 102-103, 201-202.

3. See NSC 5501, Policy Paper Series [hereafter cited as PPS], National Security Council file [hereafter cited as NSC], Office of the Special Assistant for National Security Affairs file [hereafter cited as OSANSA], White House Office file [hereafter cited as WHO], Eisenhower Library, Abilene, Kansas [hereafter cited as Eisenhower Library].

4. Letter from Dulles to Eisenhower, 2 July 1958, WH - Meetings with President 1/1-6/30/1958 (3) folder, Dulles Papers, Eisenhower Library; Dulles before the Senate Foreign Relations Committee, 23 June 1958, *Foreign Relations of the United States 1958-1960*, Vol. XI (Washington, D.C.: Government Printing Office, 1988), 173-174 [hereafter cited as *FRUS 1958-1960*, XI, 173-4]; Memorandum of a Conversation [hereafter cited as MemoConv] at the White House, 15 July 1958, Eisenhower Diary Series

[hereafter cited as EDS], Ann Whitman File [hereafter cited as AWF], Eisenhower Library.

5. *Executive Sessions of the Senate Foreign Relations Committee* (Washington, DC: U.S. Government Printing Office) IX (1957), 11, fn. 1 [hereafter cited as *ESSFRC,* IX, 11, fn. 1]; NSC 5801/1, "Long-Range U.S. Policy Toward the Near East," 16 January 1958, NSC 5801/1 Pol Twd NE (2) folder, Box 23, PPS, NSC, OSANSA, WHO, Eisenhower Library, 15.

6. Michael C. Hudson, *The Precarious Republic: Modernization in Lebanon* (New York: Random House, 1965), 281-284; MemoConv between Foreign Minister Malik and President Eisenhower, 6 February 1957, Box 37, International Series [hereafter IS], AWF, Eisenhower Library.

7. Embassy in Beirut to Department of State, 21 January 1956, *FRUS 1955-1957,* XIII, 183-184; Heath to Assistant Secretary Allen, 26 January 1956, 611.83A/1-2356, Record Group 59, National Archives, Washington, D.C. [hereafter cited as appropriate file number, RG 59, NA]; Heath to Department of State, 1 March 1956, 783A.56/3-156, RG 59, NA; Report by the Joint Strategic Plans Committee (U.S. and Britain) to the JCS, 8 May 1956, *FRUS 1955-1957,* XIII, 188-189; Dulles to Embassy in Beirut, 25 May 1956, *FRUS 1955-1957,* XIII, 191-192, fn 4.

8. *ESSFRC,* IX (1957), iii.

9. "President Eisenhower's Message to Congress, 5 January 1957," M.S. Agwani, ed., *The Lebanese Crisis, 1958: A Documentary Study* (London: Asia Publishing House, 1965), 9-10. See also House Joint Resolution 117, *ESSFRC,* IX (1957), 763-769.

10. Summary Notes of Bipartisan Congressional Meeting, 1 January 1957, EDS, AWF, Eisenhower Library.

11. Dulles before the Committee, *ESSFRC,* IX (1957), 3-4.

12. Representative McCormack, Summary notes of Bipartisan Congressional Meeting, 1 January 1957, EDS, AWF, Eisenhower Library; Dulles before the Committee, 2 January 1957, *ESSFRC,* IX (1957), 6, 18.

13. Hudson, *The Precarious Republic,* 288-290.

14. Heath to Department of State, 13 January 1957, *FRUS 1955-1957*, XIII, 196; Michael Bishku, "The 1958 American Intervention in Lebanon: A Historical Assessment," *American-Arab Affairs* 31 (Winter 1989-1990):108.

15. Special Assistant to the President James P. Richards to Dulles, 16 March 1957, *FRUS 1955-1957*, XIII, 210-211; Richards before the Committee, 27 May 1957, *ESSFRC*, IX (1957).

16. "Operations Plan for the Lebanon (NSC 5428)," 31 July 1957, *FRUS 1955-1957*, XIII, 214-215, emphasis mine.

17. Lectures by Professor Ernest R. May at Harvard College, spring of 1993.

18. MemoConv between Dulles and Malik, 5 February 1957, 680.00/2-557, RG 59, NA.

19. Letter from Eisenhower to Chamoun, 15 April 1957, Box 37, IS, AWF, Eisenhower Library; Heath to Department of State, 29 August 1957, Box 9, Dulles/Herter Series [hereafter cited as D/HS], AWF, Eisenhower Library; MemoConv between Malik, Khouri, Rountree, and Rockwell, 17 October 1957, 783A.00/10-1757, RG 59, NA.

20. NSC 5801/1, "Long-Range U.S. Policy Toward the Near East," 16 January 1958, NSC 5801/1 Pol Twd NE (2) folder, Box 23, PPS, NSC, OSANSA, WHO, Eisenhower Library, 16.

21. Bishku, "The 1958 American Intervention in Lebanon," 110. Chamoun and Malik insisted that, were it not for the intervention of the UAR, Lebanon would not be descending into civil war. United Nations Security Council, *Official Records*, 13th year, Supplement for April, May, and June 1958, 33, 47.

22. Ambassador McClintock to Department of State, 21 February 1958, 783A.00/2-2158, RG 59, NA.

23. National Intelligence Estimate 36.4-58, 5 June 1958, *FRUS 1958-1960*, XI, 94-95.

24. NSC 5801/1, "Long-Range U.S. Policy Toward the Near East," 16 January 1958, NSC 5801/1 Pol Twd NE (1) folder, Box 23, PPS, NSC, OSANSA, WHO, Eisenhower Library, 1-2.

25. MemoConv between President Eisenhower and Secretary Dulles, 13 May 1958, "WH - Meetings with President 1/1 -6/30/1958 (2)" folder, Dulles Papers, Eisenhower Library; NSC 8801/1, 16 January 1958, NSC 5801/1 Pol Twd NE (2) folder, Box 23, PPS, NSC OSANSA, WHO, Eisenhower Library, 15. Eisenhower felt domestic pressure to act forcefully in Lebanon. He was especially concerned to maintain the support of right-wing, rabid anti-communists such as Senator William F. Knowland (R-California). Letter from Eisenhower to Hoffman, 23 June 1958, Administrative Series [hereafter cited as AS], AWF, Eisenhower Library.

26. MemoConv between Dulles and Eisenhower, 2 May 1958, "WH - Meetings with President 1/1-6/30/1958 (3)" folder, Dulles Papers, Eisenhower Library.

27. MemoTel Conv between Dulles and McClintock, 14 July 1958, IS, AWF, Eisenhower Library; MemoConv between Dulles, Rountree, Rockwell, and British officials, 18 June 1958, *FRUS 1958-1960*, XI, 154.

28. MemoConv between Eisenhower, Dulles, and others, 16 June 1958, *FRUS 1958-1960*, XI, 136.

29. MemoConv between Secretary Dulles, Allen Dulles, William Rountree, Henry Cabot Lodge, and others, 22 June 1958, *FRUS 1958-1960*, XI, 167.

30. MemoConv between Eisenhower, Dulles, and others, 15 June 1958, *FRUS 1958-1960*, XI, 137.

31. McClintock to Department of State, 14 July 1958, 783A.00/7-1458, RG 59, NA.

32. MemoConv at Department of State, 14 July 1958, *FRUS 1958-1960*, XI, 209-211. The Department had already received a demand for action "at once" from King Saud of Saudi Arabia, who stated that "if the United States and the United Kingdom do not act now they are finished as powers in the Mid-East." MemoConv at the White House, 14 July 1958, EDS, AWF, Eisenhower Library.

33. MemoConv at the White House, 14 July 1958, EDS, AWF, Eisenhower Library. A telegram from Ambassador McClintock on the afternoon of the fourteenth reflected the fact that the United States was not intervening to accomplish objectives within Lebanon. McClintock stated that, "so far as Lebanon alone is concerned," the U.S. Embassy could not discern the "need for so portentous a step" as armed intervention. The Ambassador affirmed

that "the decision on military intervention can only be taken in light of broader . . . political and strategic considerations affecting the entire Middle East."McClintock to Department of State, 14 July 1958, 783A.00/7-1458, RG 59, NA.

34. MemoConv at the White House, 14 July 1958, *FRUS, 1958-1960*, XI, 220, 224.

35. Chief of Naval Operations to the Commander in Chief, U.S. Naval Forces, Eastern Atlantic and Mediterranean, 14 July 1958, *FRUS 1958-1960*, XI, 231; Bishku, "The 1958 American Intervention in Lebanon," 106-119

36. Prime Minister Macmillan to President Eisenhower, 18 July 1958, IS, AWF, Eisenhower Library.

37. MemoConv, 373rd Meeting of the NSC, 24 July 1958, *FRUS 1958-1960*, XI, 385.

38. On July 19, in a telephone conversation with President Eisenhower, Dulles said, "we have to make clear to the [British that] we are not looking on this as a long-term operation. . . . Now the problem is to get out." MemoTelConv, 19 July 1958, *FRUS 1958-1960*, XI, 332. See also MemoConv at the White House, 20 July 1958, *FRUS 1958-1960*, XI, 348. The documentary evidence showing Eisenhower's resistance to British pressure to expand the mission in Lebanon disproves Peter Lyon's speculation that the "real reason" for the intervention "was the misplaced hope that Lebanon could serve as a base of operations against the new revolutionary regime in Iraq." Peter Lyon, *Eisenhower: Portrait of the Hero* (Boston: Little, Brown, 1974), 822-826. See also Robert J. McMahon, "Eisenhower and Third World Nationalism: A Critique of the Revisionists," *Political Science Quarterly* 101 (1986): 465-466.

39. The shah of Iran, the president of Pakistan, and the president of Turkey to President Eisenhower, 16 July 1958, "Turkey (2)" folder, Box 44, IS, AWF, Eisenhower Library.

40. MemoConv between Eisenhower and Dulles, 21 July 1958, Dulles Papers, Eisenhower Library.

41. Murphy to Department of State, 25 July 1958, *FRUS 1958-1960*, XI, 389; Murphy to Dulles, 30 July 1958, 783A.00/7-3058, RG 59, NA; Allen Dulles briefing the NSC, 31 July 1958, BNS, NSC, AWF, Eisenhower Library.

42. McClintock to Department of State, 6 August 1958, 783A.00/8-658, RG 59, NA.

43. United Nations General Assembly, *Official Records*, Third Emergency Special Session, Supplement No. 1 (A/3905), 1. Printed in *American Foreign Policy: Current Documents*, 1958, 1047-1048.

44. McClintock to the Department of State, 783A.00/10-258, RG 59, NA.

45. McClintock to Department of State, 1 October 1958, 783A.00/10-158, RG 59, NA.

46. See Bishku, "The 1958 American Intervention in Lebanon," 118.

47. Robert J. McMahon, "Eisenhower and Third World Nationalism: A Critique of the Revisionists," *Political Science Quarterly* 101 (1986), 465-466; Robert W. Stookey, *America and the Arab States: An Uneasy Encounter* (New York: Wiley, 1975), 148; Robert A. Divine, *Eisenhower and the Cold War* (New York: Oxford University Press, 1981), 101-104; Herbert Parmet, *Eisenhower and the American Crusades* (New York: Macmillan, 1972), 574. McMahon's and Stookey's assessments are highly critical, whereas Divine's and Parmet's are generally positive.

48. Bishku, "The 1958 American Intervention in Lebanon," 106. See also: Margaret M. Bodron, "U.S. Intervention in Lebanon—1958," *Military Review* 56 (February 1976): 74.

49. See Oral History Interview with Raymond A. Hare by John Luter, 16 June 1972, Washington, DC, Eisenhower Library, 21.

50. Ambassador Hare (Embassy in Cairo) to Department of State, 7 June 1958, 783A.00/6-758, RG 59, NA; Ambassador Hare to Department of State, 20 May 1958, *FRUS 1958-1960*, XI, 69; MemoConv, 366th Meeting of the National Security Council, 23 May 1958, BNS, NSC, AWF, Eisenhower Library; Dwight D. Eisenhower, *Waging Peace, 1956-1961* (Garden City, 1965), 290.

51. Special National Intelligence Estimate [hereafter cited as SNIE] 30-6-58, 28 October 1958, *FRUS 1958-1960*, XI, 617.

52. Acting Secretary of State Douglas Dillon to President Eisenhower, 21 September 1960, EDS, AWF, Eisenhower Library; Department Brief for the President, 21 September 1959, IS, AWF, Eisenhower Library.

53. I agree with Stephen Rabe's statement that "the practical effect of the Eisenhower Doctrine was to entangle the United States in intra-Arab politics." Stephen G. Rabe, "Eisenhower Revisionism: A Decade of Scholarship," *Diplomatic History* 17 (Winter 1993): 109.

54. See Stephen E. Ambrose, *Eisenhower, Vol. 2, The President* (New York, 1984), 626; Bishku, "The 1958 American Intervention in Lebanon," 106.

55. See: Interview with John C. Dreier by Philip A. Crowl, 24 May 1965, Washington, DC, Dulles Oral History Project, Seeley Mudd Library, Princeton University [hereafter cited as Dulles Oral History Project], 5; NSC 144/1, "United States Objectives and Courses of Action With Respect to Latin America," 18 March 1953, *FRUS, 1952-1954*, IV, 7; Stephen G. Rabe, *Eisenhower and Latin America* (Chapel Hill: The University of North Carolina Press, 1988), 87,177; Interview with José Figueres Ferrer by Professor Donald R. McCoy, 8 July 1970, San José, Cost Rica, Oral History 119, Truman Library, Independence, Missouri [hereafter cited as Truman Library], 32-35; Interview with Roy Richard Rubottom by Richard D. Challener, 12 June 1966, Dallas, Texas, Dulles Oral History Project, 17; Interview with Ambassador John Moors Cabot by Philip A. Crowl, 15 November 1965, Washington, DC, Dulles Oral History Project, 11.

56. Kyle Longley, "Resistance and Accommodation: The United States and the Nationalism of José Figueres, 1953-1957," *Diplomatic History* 18 (Winter 1994): 5; Adolf A. Berle, Jr., "Communist Thunder to the South," *New York Times Magazine,* 4 July 1954.

57. Letter from Assistant Secretary of State for Inter-American Affairs, Henry F. Holland, to U.S. Ambassador to the United Nations, Henry Cabot Lodge, 12 April 1954, *FRUS 1952-1954*, IV, 840; MemoTelConv between Burnett of the office of Senator Chavez and R.B. Moon of MID, 18 July 1957, 718.00/7-1857, RG 59, NA; Longley, "Resistance and Accommodation," 8; Richard H. Immerman, *The CIA in Guatemala: The Foreign Policy of Intervention* (Austin: University of Texas Press, 1982), 130.

58. Charles D. Ameringer, *Don Pepe: A Political Biography of José Figueres of Costa Rica* (Albuquerque: University of New Mexico Press, 1978), 40. See also: John Patrick Bell, *Crisis in Costa Rica: The 1948 Revolution* (Austin: University of Texas Press, 1971), 138, 156-157.

59. U.S. Embassy Attaché Alex A. Cohen to Department of State, 17 March 1953, 718.00/3-1753, RG 59, NA.

60. Ohmans to Leddy at MID, 24 April 1953, 718.00/4-2453, RG 59, NA;
Ambassador Philip B. Fleming to Department of State, 1 June 1953,
718.00/6-153, RG 59, NA.

61. See: Rabe, *Eisenhower and Latin America*, 58-59.

62. Longley, "Resistance and Accommodation," 15.

63. Ameringer, *Don Pepe*, 111. Interview with José Figueres Ferrer by
Donald R. McCoy, 8 July 1970, San José, Costa Rica, Oral History Interview
119, Truman Library, 22.

64. MemoConv between Vice Consul of the U.S. Embassy in San José,
Thomas A. Brady, and José Figueres, 14 April 1953, 718.00/4-1553, RG 59,
NA.

65. MemoConv between Mr. Stanley Posner and Mr. Reid of MID, 4 May
1953, 718.00/5-453, RG 59, NA.

66. Assistant Secretary of State for Inter-American Affairs John M. Cabot to
Deputy Assistant Secretary of State for Inter-American Affairs Robert F.
Woodward, 18 November 1953, *FRUS 1952-1954*, IV, 832-833; Interview
with John Davis Lodge by John T. Mason, Jr., New York, NY, 9 October
1967, Oral History 144, No. 2, Eisenhower Library.

67. Secretary of the U.S. Embassy C. Allan Stewart to Department of State,
4 December 1953, 718.00/12-453, RG 59, NA; Ambassador Hill to
Department of State, 28 December 1953, *FRUS 1952-1954*, IV 835.

68. MemoConv between President Figueres, Ambassador Hill, and First
Secretary Stewart, 6 February 1954, *FRUS 1952-54*, IV, 838-839.

69. Interview with José Figueres Ferrer by Professor Donald R. McCoy in
San José, 8 July 1970, Oral History Interview No. 119, Truman Library, 21;
Longley, "Resistance and Accommodation," 10, fn. 39.

70. Longley, "Resistance and Accommodation," 14-15; José Figueres, *Estos
Diez Anos* (San José: Imprenta Nacional, 1958), 11, quoted in Ameringer,
Don Pepe, 114-115.

71. Senator William J. Fulbright's speech in the Senate, 1 February 1954,
Congressional Record, 1954 (Washington DC: United States Government
Printing Office, 1954) [hereafter cited as CR], 1073; Senator Paul H. Douglas

to Secretary Dulles and Assistant Secretary Holland, 12 January 1955, 718.00/1-1255, RG 59, NA.

72. Hill to Department of State, 30 April 1954, 718.00/4-3054, RG 59, NA; Letter from Hill to Secretary Holland, 4 May 1954, 718.00/4-1954, RG 59, NA.

73. Diary entry, 31 March 1953, Berle Papers, Box 218, quoted in Longley,"Resistance and Accommodation," 17.

74. First Secretary of the U.S. Embassy in San José, Philip P. Williams, to Department of State, 2 June 1953, 718.00/6-253, RG 59,NA.

75. Given his reputation as a supporter of democratic processes, Figueres had to maintain the public appearance of supporting the Arbenz government's right to exist. Philip P. Williams to Department of State, 2 June 1953, 718.00/6-253, RG 59, NA.

76. Assistant Secretary Cabot to Secretary Dulles, 10 February 1954, *FRUS 1952-1954*, IV, 290.

77. Interview with José Figueres Ferrer by Professor Donald R. McCoy, 8 July 1970, San José, Costa Rica, Oral History Interview 119, Truman Library, 34.

78. "Costa Rica," *Hispanic American Report* 7 (February 1954), 16, quoted in Longley, "Resistance and Accommodation," 15.

79. Interview with José Figueres Ferrer by Professor Donald R. McCoy, 8 July 1970, Son José, Costa Rica, Oral History Interview 119, Truman Library, 34-35.

80. Longley, "Resistance and Accommodation," 16.

81. Ambassador Hill to Secretary Dulles, 19 February 1954, 718.00/2-1954, RG 59, NA.

82. C. Allan Stewart to Department of State, 26 February 1954, 718.00/2-2654, RG 59, NA.

83. Interview with Roy Richard Rubottom, Jr., by Richard D. Challener, 12 June 1966, Dallas, Texas, Dulles Oral History Project, Dulles Papers, 9; Interview with José Figueres Ferrer by Professor Donald R. McCoy, 8 July

1970, San José, Costa Rica, Oral History Interview 119, Truman Library, 34-35.

84. See: Letter from Holland to Lodge, 12 March 1954, *FRUS 1952-1954*, IV, 841.

85. MemoTelConv between Leddy of MID and Sam Baggett, vice president of UFCO, 7 June 1954, *FRUS 1952-1954*, IV, 844-845.

86. Ameringer, *Don Pepe*, 120; MemoConv between Ambassador Facio, Assistant Secretary Holland, and John Ohmans of MID, 27 April 1954, *FRUS 1952-1954*, IV, 843-844.

87. Memo from Ohmans to Holland, July 1954, *FRUS 1952-1954*, IV, 377-378.

88. Ameringer, *Don Pepe*, 119.

89. Longley, "Resistance and Accommodation," 18.

90. Ameringer, *Don Pepe*, 199.

91. Longley, "Resistance and Accommodation," 18; Stewart to Department of State, 1 July 1954, 718.00/7-154, RG 59, NA.

92. Article three of the Inter-American Treaty of Reciprocal Assistance (commonly referred to as the Rio Treaty) would oblige the U.S.,"in the event of an armed attack by any State on Costa Rica . . . to go immediately to the assistance of Costa Rica." Atwood and Neal to Assistant Secretary Holland, 22 July 1954, *FRUS 1952-1954*, IV, 377-378, emphasis in original.

93. First Secretary of the U.S. Embassy Stewart to Department of State, 1 July 1954, 718.00/7-154, RG 59, NA.

94. Dulles to U.S. Embassies in Guatemala City, San Salvador, Tegucigalpa, Managua, San José, Panama City, and Caracas, 9 July 1954, 718.00/7-954, RG 59, NA; First Secretary of the U.S. Embassy Stewart to Department of State, 1 July 1954, 718.00/7-154, RG 59, NA.

95. Leddy to Holland, 18 November 1954, *FRUS 1952-1954*, IV, 858.

96. JCS to Secretary of Defense Wilson, 26 November 1954, *FRUS 1952-1954*, IV, 863.

97. Ambassador Robert F. Woodward to Department of State, 3 January 1955, 718.00/1-355, RG 59, NA.

98. Holland to Leddy, 7 January 1955, 718.00/1-755, RG 59, NA.

99. MemoConv between MID Director Newbegin and Ambassador Facio, 26 November 1954, *FRUS 1952-1954*, IV, 864; MemoTelConv between Ambassador Facio and Holland, 8 January 1955, 718.00/1-885, RG 59, NA.

100. MemoConv between MID Director Newbegin and Ambassador Facio, 26 November 1954, *FRUS 1952-1954*, IV, 864; First Secretary of the Embassy in San José C. Allan Stewart to Department of State, 10 January 1955, 718.00/1-1055, RG 59, NA. The Department was especially inclined to promote the OAS as a forum for resolving the invasion crisis because it recognized that the Inter-American Treaty of Reciprocal Assistance of 1947 (Rio Treaty) would probably not provide adequate justification for U.S. intervention against the imminent invasion of Costa Rica. Given that the invasion force would probably consist of exiled Costa Ricans instead of regular army troops from a foreign state, and that any airplanes used against Costa Rica might be hard to identify as being Nicaraguan or Venezuelan, the attack would not be "clearly within the meaning of paragraph 1 of Article 3" of the Rio Treaty. Ambassador Woodward to Department of State, 3 January 1955, *FRUS 1955-1957*, VI, 581-582.

101. MemoTelConv between Ambassador Facio and Holland, 8 January 1955, 718.00/1-885, RG 59, NA.

102. MemoTel Conv between Holland and Woodward, 11 January 1955, *FRUS 1955-1957*, VI, 586.

103. MemoConv between Facio, Holland, and MID Director Newbegin, 11 January 1955, 718.00/1-1155, RG 59, NA.

104. Dreier to Holland, 15 January 1955, *FRUS 1955-1957*,VI, 601.

105. MemoConv of the 231st meeting of the NSC, 13 January 1955, *FRUS 1955-1957*, VI, 597.

106. Ibid., 596.

107. For a list of articles written about the crisis in January, 1955, see Longley, "Resistance and Accommodation." 23, fn. 114.

108. Representative Albert P. Morano to Dulles, 12 January 1955, 718.00/1-1255, RG 59, NA; Arthur M. Schlesinger, Jr. of Americans for Democratic Action to President Eisenhower, 12 January 1955, 718.00/1-1255, RG 59, NA; Senator Paul H. Douglas to Dulles and Holland, 12 January 1955, 718.00/1-1255, RG 59, NA; Norman Thomas, Chairman of the Post War World Council, to Dulles, 12 January 1955, Reel 37 (Box 96), Dulles Papers; Memo from Jack Ohmans to Dulles, 3 December 1954, 718.00/11-2754, RG 59, NA;

109. Secretary General of the Federation of Cuban Sugar Workers, José Luis Martínez Alvarez, to Eisenhower, 13 January 1955, 718.00/1-1355, RG 59, NA.

110. U.S. Ambassador in Belgrade to Secretary Dulles, 13 January 1955, 718.00/1-1355, RG 59, NA; Robert C. Martindale of the U.S. Consulate in Zagreb to Department of State, 21 January 1955, 718.00, RG 59, NA.

111. Ambassador Butterworth in London to Department of State, 12 January 1955, 718.00/1-1255, RG 59, NA.

112. Letter from Holland to Schlesinger , 2 February 1955, 718.00/1-1255, RG 59, NA; Letter from Assistant Secretary of State for Congressional Affairs Thurston B. Morton to Senator Douglas, 25 January 1955, 718.00/1-1255, RG 59, NA; MemoConv between Holland and Victor Reuther, 12 January 1955, 718.00/1-1255, RG 59, NA.

113. Mr. Cornic to Ambassador Mora, Chair of the OAS Council, 16 January 1955, 718.00/1-1555, RG 59, NA.

114. Ameringer, *Don Pepe*, 123; MemoTelConv between Holland and Woodward, 16 January 1955, 718.00/1-1655, RG 59, NA.

115. Dreier to Department of State, 18 January 1955, 718.00/1-1855, RG 59, NA.

116. Dreier to Department of State, 20 January 1955, *FRUS 1955-1957*, VI, 602.

117. OCB Progress Report on NSC 5613/1, "Policy Toward Latin America," 11 September 1955, NSC 5613/1 Pol Twd LA folder, Box 18, PPS, NSC, OSANSA, WHO, Eisenhower Library.

118. Longley, "Resistance and Accommodation," 25.

119. First Secretary of the U.S. Embassy in Belgrade, Edwin M.J. Kretzmann, to Department of State, 25 January 1955, 718.00/1-2555, RG 59, NA; Ambassador Hooker in Belgrade to Dulles, 17 January 1955, 718.00/1-1755, RG 59, NA; Ambassador White in Mexico City to Dulles, 21 January 1955, 718.00/1-2055, RG 59, NA; Counselor of the U.S. Embassy in Habana Carlos C. Hall to Department of State, 20 January 1955, 718.00/1-2055, RG 59, NA.

120. OCB progress report on NSC 5432/1, 10 August 1955, NSC 5432/1 Pol Twd LA folder , Box 13, PPS, NSC, OSANSA, WHO, Eisenhower Library. See also: NSC 5613/1, "U.S. Policy Toward Latin America," 25 September 1956, NSC 5613/1 Pol Twd LA folder, Box 18, PPS, NSC, OSANSA, WHO, Eisenhower Library.

121. Dulles to U.S. Ambassador in San José Woodward, 26 January 1955, 718.00/1-2655, RG 59, NA.

122. Holland to Woodward, 1 February 1955, 718.00/2-155, RG 59, NA; Berle to Department of State, 4 February 1955, 718.00/2-455, RG 59, NA; Woodward to Secretary Dulles, 15 February 1955, 718.00/2-1555, RG 59, NA; MemoConv 240th Meeting NSC, 10 March 1955, *FRUS 1955-1957*, VI, 616.

123. Ameringer, *Don Pepe*, 124-125; Interview with José Figueres Ferrer by Professor Donald R. McCoy in San José, 8 July 1970, Oral History Interview 119, Truman Library, 34-35.

124. Ohmans to Holland, 1 April 1955, 718.00/4-155, RG 59, NA.

125. Stewart to Department of State, 7 May 1955, RG 59, 718.00/5-655, NA.

126. Llewellyn Thompson to Secretary Dulles, 23 March 1955, *FRUS 1955-1957*, V, 13; Dulles before the Committee, 17 May 1955, *ESSFRC*, VII (1955), 509; MemoConv between Gruber and Department officials, 31 August 1955, 763.00/8-3155, RG 59, NA. See also: Gerald Stourzh, "The Origins of Austrian Neutrality," *Neutrality: Changing Concepts and Practices*, Alan T. Leonhard, ed. (Lanham, MD: University Press of America, 1988), 52-53; William B. Bader, *Austria Between East and West, 1945-1955*, (Stanford: Stanford University Press, 1966), 205-207.

127. "United States Policy on Neutrality - Department of State Press Release," 24 May 1955, Reel 37 (Box 96), Dulles Papers. See also Stourzh, "The Origins of Austrian Neutrality," 52; Bader, *Austria Between East and West*, 201. See especially Michael Gehler, "State Treaty and Neutrality: The

Austrian Solution in 1955 as a 'Model' for Germany?," *Contemporary Austrian Studies* 3 (1994): 39-78.

128. Conant to Dulles, 14 April 1955, 663.001/4-1455, RG 59, NA; Bader, *Austria Between East and West*, 206; Günter Bischof, "The Anglo-American Powers and Austrian Neutrality, 1953-1955, *Mitteilung des Österreichischen Staatsarchivs* 42 (1992), 375-376; Günter Bischof, "John Foster Dulles and Austrian Neutrality," *Proceedings of the John Foster Dulles Centennial Conference*, Princeton University, 1988, p. 19; 21-22; Deborah Welch Larson, "Crisis Prevention and the Austrian State Treaty," *International Organization* 41 (Winter 1987): 53-54; Hanspeter Neuhold, "The Permanent Neutrality of Austria," in *Neutrality and Nonalignment in Europe*, ed. Karl E. Birnbaum and Hanspeter Neuhold (Vienna: Wilhelm Braumüller Universitäts-Verlagsbuchhandlung, 1982), 51; Gerald Stourzh, "The Origins of Austrian Neutrality," 45.

129. Senator Humphrey in the Senate, 19 May 1955, CR, 1955: 6460. See also Oliver Rathkolb, "The Foreign Relations Between the U.S.A. and Austria in the Late 1950s," *Contemporary Austrian Studies* 3 (1994): 24-38; this is a short version of Rathkolb's much longer study "Grossmachtpolitik gegenüber Österreich 1952/53-1961/62 im U.S. Entscheidungsprozess," Habilitationsschrift, Vienna 1993, which covers some of the same issues that are discussed here in much greater detail.

130. NSC 164/1, 14 October 1953, *FRUS 1952-1954*, VII, pt. 2, 1914. On Austria as a "secret ally" of the West, see Günter Bischof, "Österreich - ein 'geheimer Verbündeter' des Westens: Wirtschafts- und sicherheitspolitische Fragen der Integration aus der Sicht der USA," in Michael Gehler and Rolf Steininger, eds., *Österreich und die europäische Integration 1945-1993* (Vienna-Cologne-Weimar: Böhlau, 1993), 425-450.

131. NSC 5603, "U.S. Policy Toward Austria," 23 March 1956, NSC 5603 Pol Twd Austria folder, Box 17, PPS, NSC, OSANSA, WHO, Eisenhower Library, 4-5.

132. OCB Progress Report on NSC 164/1, 14 December 1955, *FRUS 1955-1957*, XXVI, 25.

133. MemoConv between Ambassador Gruber and WE desk officers, 4 April 1955, *FRUS 1955-1957*, V 31; Ambassador Thompson to Department of State, 18, 21 and 28 April 1955, *FRUS 1955-1957*, V 45-46, 55, 60.

134. MemoConv 245th Meeting NSC, 21 April 1955, *FRUS 1955-1957*, V, 52; Bischof, "The Anglo-American Powers and Austrian Neutrality," 356-357.

135. Thompson to Department of State, 21 April 1955, *FRUS 1955-1957*, V, 55.

136. MemoConv between Ambassador Karl Gruber and WE officers, 24 May 1955, 611.63/5-2455, RG 59, NA. See also Gehler, "Austrian Solution as a 'Model' for Germany?"

137. Special Assistant for Mutual Security Affairs (Nolting) to Assistant Secretary of Defense for International Security Affairs (Hensel), 25 May 1955, *FRUS 1955-1957*, XXVI, 1-2. See also Rathkolb, "U.S.-Austrian Relations in the Late 1950s."

138. MemoConv between Ambassador Gruber and Department officials, 26 May 1955, 611.63/5-2655, RG 59,NA.

139. NSC 5603, 23 March 1956, NSC 5603 Pol Twd Austria folder, Box 17, PPS, NSC, OSANSA, WHO, Eisenhower Library, 2-4; MemoConv between Gruber and WE officials, 12 July 1955, 763.00/7-1255, RG 59, NA.

140. Minister-Counselor of U.S. Embassy James K. Penfield to Department of State, 14 March 1956, 763.00/3-1456, RG 59, NA.

141. Ambassador Thompson to Department of State, 28 June 1955, *FRUS 1955-1957*, XXVI, 11-12; MemoConv between Ambassador Gruber, Counselor of the Austrian Embassy Ernst Lemberger, and Messrs. West, Wolf, and Compton of WE, 7 July 1955, 763.00/7-755, RG 59, NA.

142. Dulles before the Committee, 17 May 1955, *ESSFRC*, VII (1955), 500.

143. MemoConv between Gruber, Lemberger, and officials of WE, 7 July 1955, 763.00/7-755, RG 59, NA.

144. Minister-Counselor of U.S. Embassy James K. Penfield to Department of State, 14 March 1956, 763.00/3-1456, RG 59, NA.

145. MemoConv between Gruber, Lemberger, and officials of WE, 21 July 1955, 763.00/7-2155, RG 59, NA.

146. Counselor of Embassy in Vienna Richard H. Davis to Department of State, 763.00/9-955, RG 59, NA.

147. OCB Progress Report on NSC 164/1, 14 December 1955, *FRUS 1955-1957*, XXVI, 25.

148. OCB Progress Report on NSC 5603, 1 September 1959, *FRUS 1958-1960*, IX, 774.

149. OCB Progress Report on NSC 164/1, 14 December 1955, *FRUS 1955-1957*, XXVI, 25; OCB Progress Report on NSC 5603, 24 April 1957, NSC 5603 Pol Twd Austria folder, Box 17, PPS, NSC, OSANSA, WHO, Eisenhower Library, 2-3; OCB Progress Report on NSC 5603, 29 January 1958, NSC 5603 Pol Twd Austria folder, Box 17, PPS, NSC, OSANSA, WHO, Eisenhower Library.

150. Matthews to Department of State, 15 July 1959, *FRUS 1958-1960*, IX, 807-808 (Quote from fn. 1 on 808).

151. OCB Progress Report on NSC 5603, 22 October 1958, NSC 5603 Pol Twd Austria folder, Box 17, PPS, NSC, OSANSA, WHO, Eisenhower Library, 1. With the delivery of U.S. military equipment authorized for fiscal year 1959, the Austrians completed the build-up of their army to the agreed level of 65,000 troops. OCB Progress Report on NSC 5603, 23 November 1959, *FRUS 1958-1960*, IX, 817-821.

152. Acting Secretary of State Herter to U.S. Embassy in Vienna, 25 September 1958, *FRUS 1958-1960*, IX, 787.

153. MemoConv between Foreign Minister Figl, Secretary General of the Austrian Foreign Office Fuchs, Austrian Ambassador Platzer, and Assistant Secreatry of State for European Affairs Burke Elbrick, 26 September 1958, 763.00/9-2658, RG 59, NA.

154. NSC 5603, 23 March 1956, NSC 5603 Pol Twd Austria folder, Box 17, PPS, NSC, OSANSA, WHO, Eisenhower Library, 1-2; G.F. Muller to Edgar Allen (WE), 15 June 1955, 763.00/6-1555, RG 59, NA.

155. MemoConv between Gruber and Merchant, 23 September 1955, 763.00/9-2355, RG 59, NA.

156. See: Representative Feighan in the House, 19 May 1955, *CR*, 1955, 6691.

157. Letter from Minister-Counselor of U.S. Embassy, James K. Penfield to Department of State, 2 August 1955, 763.00/8-255, RG 59, NA; MemoConv between Dulles, W. Barbour, and S. Waugh, 5 August 1955, 763.00/8-555, RG 59, NA.

158. Minister-Counselor of U.S. Embassy, James K. Penfield, to Department of State, 14 March 1956, 763.00/3-1456, RG 59, NA.

159. The P.L. 480 agreement was concluded on February 7, 1956. Editorial Note, *FRUS 1955-1957*, XXVI, 31-32.

160. James Penfield to Department of State, 6 March 1955, 863.10/3-656, RG 59, NA.

161. Dulles to Thompson, 29 December 1955, 763.00/12-2955, RG 59, NA.

162. Thompson to Department of State, 31 December 1955, 763.00/12-3155, RG 59, NA.

163. F.E. Maestrone of the Consulate in Salzburg to Department of State, 7 February 1956, 763.00/2-756, RG 59, NA.

164. Minister-Counselor of U.S. Embassy, James K. Penfield, to Department of State, 14 March 1956, 763.00/3-1456, RG 59, NA.

165. OCB Progress Report on NSC 5603, 17 October 1956, NSC 5603 Pol Twd Austria folder, Box 17, PPS, NSC, OSANSA, WHO, 1-2; MemoConv between Gruber and Department officials, 763.00/3-156, RG 59, NA.

166. See: Resolution 1005 (ES-11), Dusan J. Djonovich, comp.ed., *United Nations Resolutions,* Series I, *Resolutions Adopted by the General Assembly*, Vol. V (1954-1956), 250-251.

167. MemoConv between Foreign Minister Figl, Ambassador Gruber, and Department officials, 21 November 1956, 763.00/11-2156, RG 59, NA; OCB Progress Report on NSC 5603, 17 October 1956, NSC 5603 Pol Twd Austria folder, Box 17, PPS, NSC, OSANSA, WHO, Eisenhower Library, 5.

168. In mid December 1956, Eisenhower sent Vice President Nixon to Austria to demonstrate official U.S. support for Austria in the crisis. Editorial Note, *FRUS 1955-1957*, XXVI, 47. The Austrian government appeared to throw more defiance in the face of the communist bloc on February 2, when it expelled from Vienna the World Peace Council after labeling the

organization a communist front. Thompson to Department of State, 9 November 1956, *FRUS 1955-1957*, XXVI, 45-46; OCB Progress Report on NSC 5603, 24 April 1957, NSC 5603 Pol Twd Austria, Box 17, PPS, NSC, OSANSA, WHO, Eisenhower Library, 1.

169. OCB Progress Report on NSC 5603, 24 April 1957, NSC 5603 Pol Twd Austria, Box 17, PPS, NSC, OSANSA, WHO, 1. U.S. See also: Representative Sikes in the House, 3 January 1957, CR, 1957, 50.

170. OCB progress report on NSC 5603, 24 April 1957, NSC 5603 Pol Twd Austria folder, Box 17, PPS, NSC, OSANSA, WHO, Eisenhower Library, 2.

171. For more information on the persecutee claims, see: J. Wesley Jones (EUR) to Dulles, 3 January 1958, 611.63/1-358, RG 59, NA; Bischof, *Between Responsibility and Rehabilitation*, 1-78; Donald R. Whitmah and Edgar L. Erickson, *The American Occupation of Austria: Planning and Early Years* (Westport, CT: Greenwood Press, 1985), 3-20, 117-268. For detailed background on the Vienna Memorandum, see: "Department of State Memo—Background Information on the Vienna Memorandum," 14 March 1957, 611.63/3-1457, RG 59, NA.

172. Deputy Assistant Secretary of State for European Affairs, Burke C. Elbrick, to Dulles, 23 September 1957, *FRUS 1955-1957*, 50-52.

173. Matthews to Department of State, 28 July 1958, *FRUS 1958-1960*, IX, 772; U.S. Ambassador to Moscow, Llewellyn Thompson, to Department of State, 24 July 1958, 611.63/7-2458, RG 59,NA.

174. MemoConv between Ambassador Platzer, Director Haymerle, and Deputy Assistant Secretary Jandrey, 8 December 1958, 611.63/12-858, RG 59, NA.

175. McBride (WE) to Assistant Secretary Merchant, 12 December 1958, 611.63/12-1258, RG 59, NA.

176. Jandrey to Dulles, 30 July 1958, 611.63/7-3058, RG 59, NA; Ambassador Matthews to Dulles, 24 October 1958, 611.63/10-2458, RG 59, NA.

177. MemoConv between Foreign Minister Figl and Assistant Secretary Elbrick, 26 September 1958, 763.00/9-2658, RG 59, NA; Thompson to Department of State, 31 December 1955, 763.00/12-3155, RG 59, NA; Matthews to Dulles, 24 October 1958, 611.63/10-2458, RG 59, NA.

178. MemoConv, Meeting of the JCS, 16 May 1958, *FRUS 1958-1960*, XI, 59; Thompson to Department of State, 31 December 1955, 763.00/12-3155, RG 59, NA; OCB Progress Report on NSC 164/1, 14 December 1955, *FRUS 1955-1957*, XXVI, 26; MemoConv between Counselor of U.S. Embassy James K. Penfield, General Arnold, Chancellor Raab, and Vice Chancellor Schärf, 16 July 1955, *FRUS 1955-1957*, XXVI, 16-17; MemoConv, Meeting of the JCS, 16 May 1958, *FRUS 1958-1960*, XI, 59; Matthews to Dulles, 24 October 1958, 611.63/10-2458, RG 59, NA; Jandrey to Dulles, 30 July 1958, 611.63/7-3058, RG 59, NA; OCB Progress Report on NSC 5603, 1 September 1958, *FRUS 1958-1960*, IX, 780-781; Matthews to Dulles, 24 October 1958, 611.63/10-2458, RG 59, NA; MemoConv between Ambassador Platzer, Director Haymerle, and Deputy Assistant Secretary Jandrey, 8 December 1958, 611.63/12-858, RG 59, NA; MemoConv between Figl and Elbrick, 26 September 1958, 763.00/9-2658, RG 59, NA; MemoConv between Ambassador Platzer, Director Haymerle, and Deputy Assistant Secretary Jandrey, 8 December 1958, 611.63/12-858, RG 59, NA; Letter from W. Tapley Bennett, Jr., Counselor for Political Affairs, U.S. Embassy, to Frederick L. Chapin, Acting Austria Desk Officer, 9 October 1958, 763.00/10-958, RG 59, NA; MemoConv between Ambassador Platzer, Miss Harvey (WE), and Mr. Chapin (WE), 763.00/10-958, RG 59, NA; McBride (WE) to Assistant Secretary Merchant, 12 December 1958, 611.63/12-1258, RG 59, NA; MemoConv between Ambassador Platzer, Director Haymerle, and Deputy Assistant Secretary Jandrey, 8 December 1958, 611.63/12-858, RG 59, NA; Letter from W. Tapley Bennett, Jr., Counselor for Political Affairs, U.S. Embassy, to Frederick L. Chapin, Acting Austria Desk Officer, 9 October, 1958, 763.00/10-958, RG 59, NA; MemoConv between Ambassador Platzer, Miss Harvey (WE), and Mr. Chapin (WE), 763.00/10-958, RG 59, NA; McBride (WE) to Assistant Secretary Merchant, 12 December 1958, 611.63/12-1258, RG 59, NA; OCB Progress Report on NSC 5603, 1 September 1958, *FRUS 1958-1960*, IX, 780-781; McBride (WE) to Assistant Secretary Merchant, 12 December 1958, 611.63/12-1258, RG 59, NA.

179. OCB Progress Report on NSC 5603, 1 September 1958, *FRUS 1958-1960*, IX, 780-781; McBride (WE) to Assistant Secretary Merchant, 12 December 1958, 611.63/12-1258, RG 59, NA.

180. OCB progress report NSC 5603, *FRUS 1958-1960*, IX, 774-779.

181. Letter from Matthews to Elbrick, 17 September 1958, *FRUS 1958-1960*, IX, 782-784; Matthews to Department of State, 5 December 1958, 763.00/12-58, RG 59, NA.

182. Matthews toDulles, 12 September 1958, 763.00/9-1258, RG 59, NA.

183. Dulles to Matthews, 28 September 1958, 763.00/9-1258, RG 59, NA.

184. Director of ICA James H. Smith to Undersecretary of State for Economic Affairs, C. Douglas Dillon, 25 January 1959, *FRUS 1958-1960*, IX, 800. See also Rathkolb, "U.S.-Austrian Relations in the Late 1950s."

185. Counselor of Embassy W. Tapley Bennett, Jr., to Department of State, 12 February 1959, 611.63/2-1259, RG 59, NA.

186. "Points of Dissatisfaction," *Die Wochen-Presse,* 13 November 1958 (Quoted in 611.63/12-1658, RG 59, NA); Counselor of Embassy W. Tapley Bennett, Jr., to Department of State, 19 December 1958, 611.63/12-1958, RG 59, NA.

187. Counselor of Embassy W. Tapley Bennett, Jr., to Department of State, 12 February 1959, 611.63/2-1259, RG 59, NA.

188. Merchant to Dillon, 30 March 1959, 763.5-MSP/3-3059, RG 59, NA; Assistant Secretary Merchant to Undersecretary Dillon, *FRUS 1958-1960*, IX, 806-807.

189. OCB Progress Report on NSC 5603, 22 October 1958, NSC 5603 Pol Twd Austria folder, Box 17, PPS, NSC, OSANSA, WHO, Eisenhower Library, 6.

190. "C.I.A. Subsidized Festival Trips," *NYT*, 20 February 1967, 33:1; OCB Progress Report on NSC 5603, 23 November 1959, *FRUS 1958-1960*, IX, 819.

191. McBride (WE) to Merchant, 12 December 1958, 611.63/12-1258, RG 59, NA.; MemoConv between Minister-Counselor of U.S. Embassy Jandrey and Austrian Foreign Office Director Haymerle, *FRUS 1958-1960*, IX, 796; OCB Progress Report on NSC 5603, 23 November 1959, *FRUS 1958-1960*, IX, 817.

192. Richard H. Immerman, "Confessions of an Eisenhower Revisionist," *Diplomatic History* 14 (1990): 319-342; See also H.W. Brands, *The Specter of Neutralism: The United States and the Emergence of the Third World, 1947-1960* (New York: Columbia University Press) and Günter Bischof and Stephen E. Ambrose, eds., *Eisenhower: A Centenary Assessment* (Baton Rouge-London: Louisiana State University Press, 1995).

193. Robert A. Divine, "John Foster Dulles: What You See Is What You Get," *Diplomatic History* 15 (Spring 1991), 278-279, 284-285; Rabe, "Eisenhower Revisionism," 113-114; McMahon, "Eisenhower and Third World Nationalism," 457; Gaddis, *Strategies of Containment*, 163; Dennis Merrill, "America Encounters the Third World," *Diplomatic History* 16 (Spring 1992): 328

FORUM

The 'New Right' in Austria

Introduction - "What's right?"

Günter Bischof

"Vienna must not become Chicago"
Jörg Haider

In the 1994 summer issue of the prestigious journal *Foreign Affairs*, the Harvard historian Charles S. Maier has perceptively discerned a current "moral crisis of democracy." Marked by a feeling of disorientation and a broad distrust of political representatives, this open-ended moral crisis leads to *Politikverdrossenheit*. It gives political outsiders opportunity "to capitalize on the perceived defects and corruption of 'the system'." It presents what Maier terms "territorial populists" with the opportunity to "promise to restore a sense of identity and to repatriate decisions to a cohesive community on a familiar home territory." Such territorial populism easily skids to familiar right-wing motifs such "an appeal to ethnic exclusiveness, the desire to reinvigorate the national unit, the contempt for the existing parliamentary class." Among this new right some admire the interwar fascist dictators and so it may turn into what Maier calls "a retro-right." This larger comparative perspective of a moral crisis of western democracy sounds familiar to the observer of Austrian politics and provides crucial insights to figure out "Haiderism" and the current political climate.[1]

In the spring of 1994 the Feuilleton section of the influential conservative German daily *Frankfurter Allgemeine Zeitung* (*FAZ*) unleashed an interesting debate on "What's right?" in post-unification Germany. What is the state of German conservatism after the fall of the Berlin Wall and the unification of the two Germanys? How did the historic earthquake of 1989/90 shake up the political landscape and reshuffle the political spectrum where the Left is in decline and the Right (especially a more radical and extreme Right) on the rise? The issues at the center of the debate were: 1) Germany's new position in Europe/Central Europe in general and the closeness of its Western integration (*Westbindung*) in particular; 2) both the locus and focus of German nationalism, patriotism and identity after unification; 3) closely linked to the issue of the "German nation," its future as a backward-looking homogeneous German society or a progressive, cosmopolitan multicultural one; and 4) what's called the "*Sonderweg*" of German history, particularly the centrality of National Socialism and Auschwitz in twentieth-century German history as well as the feasibility of "historicizing" the National Socialist era and the horrendous crimes committed by the Third Reich.[2]

Austrian trends are influenced by the larger political arena and often parallel, follow in the footsteps of, or are overshadowed by German discourses. Therefore it seemed worthwhile and profitable to ask such questions in the Austrian context as well. Of course, I realize that Austria is not Germany. Austria did not experience an earthquake of the proportion of Germany's unification battles. Yet sea changes in the international arena such as the collapse of the Soviet Union and communism in Eastern Europe, the unification of Germany, the end of the Cold War confrontation and the ongoing process of increasing European integration have affected Austria's geostrategic position in the center of Europe as profoundly as that of her larger neighbor to the North.[3] Also, many of the vital issues aggravating the political arena in post-unification Germany are visible to a larger or lesser extent in Austria as well: the rise of the mercurial populist Jörg Haider; the breakup of the old "party system"—the post-World War II ÖVP/SPÖ grand coalition "duopoly" and the emergence of a more diffuse party spectrum (the "Third Republic" as Haider has christened it, straining to intimate the end of an era); the debate over the depth of Haider's and his party's ties to right-wing extremism; xenophobia and the highly emotional public debate over immigration/asylum, and multiculturalism unleashed or abused by Haider; the future of Austrian neutrality and national security and its relationship to the ongoing process of European integration; and a series of grisly letter bomb attacks against public officials by hitherto unidentified right-wing extremists, most recently resumed by the craven bomb planting killing four gypsies in Burgenland.[4]

Haider's notoriety and seemingly inexorable meteoric rise to political prominence with the attendant repercussions in Austrian politics, along with the right-wing terrorism mentioned above, have driven the "What's right?" issue home to Austrians. A more rigorous intellectual discussion has ensued. *CAS* has been in the forefront of this debate with its analytical comparison of Haider and the American political maverick David Duke.[5] The landmark publication of the *Handbuch des österreichischen Rechtsextremismus* by the Dokumentationsarchiv des österreichischen Widerstandes in 1993 (see the review by the noted Oxford scholar Peter Pulzer in this volume), visibly placing Haider in the camp of the right-wing extremists by superimposing his image over the nationalist German *Reichkriegsflagge*, added much-needed factual fuel to the controversial Haider debate. The *Handbuch* took particular care in defining right-wing extremism vis-à-vis conservatism. A scholarly symposium scrutinizing how Austria and the two Germanys mastered, or failed to master, the difficult legacies of World War II (namely National Socialism, Anti-Semitism and the Holocaust)[6], organized in the scenic environment of Schloß Leopoldskron outside of Salzburg (of *Sound of Music* fame), dealt with the historical roots of the contemporary new Right.[7] The potential explosiveness of these issues was brought home to the conference participants when the intense discussions in the serene premises of the *Schloß* were shattered by a bomb threat.[8]

This coincided with the contentious U.S. debate unleashed by the highly respected Columbia historian Alan Brinkley over the failure of mainstream American scholarship to take American Conservatism seriously and being content "with a set of paradigms in which conservatism plays so small a role." Brinkley charged that it was the problem of American scholarship "of finding a suitable place for the Right—for its intellectual traditions and its social and political movements—within our historiographical concerns." Apart from the fact that he gives considerable prominence to the emigrè Austrian economist Friedrich A. Hayek[9] and his 1944 treatise *The Road to Serfdom*, which became a "political and even programmatic bible" to postwar American conservatives, what Brinkley has to say about the "fundamentalist Right" and its debate on "values" is highly relevant for understanding Haider's new firebrand populism, which often seems like a cheap version of American models.[10]

There are, then, a set of issues cropping up in international "What's right?" debates that should not be ignored in Austria.

Austrian conservatism surely is as much a stepchild of academic research in Austrian academe as it is in the U.S. And as Brinkley is suggesting for the U.S.—and Max Riedlsperger in his essay in this FORUM for Austria—ignoring conservatism, and the hard-to-determine transitions to its more extreme right fringes, has much to do with the specific predilections of dominant and domineering liberal (in the case of Austria leftist) scholars in the world of academe.

These are issues that need to be rigorously explored—not only by government leaders but also by intellectuals and the general public. The Austrian people should not simply be content to let the government determine the future direction of their country in time honored Josephinian tradition. Austria's relationship with the West,[11] the character and the homogeneity of its nationhood and identity, and the difficult problem of mastering its World War II past are vital issues of concern to everyone. Instead, the future of neutrality is often debated with extreme emotions and not as part of a realistic discussion of Austria's future options for national security in a dramatically changing international environment. In a similar fashion, the Austrian decision to join the European Union in 1994 and the attendant plebiscite as well as the current discussion over the feasibility of joining NATO have hardly seen a broad national "great debate" as would be the case with public opinion formation in more mature western democracies. Instead, the government is handing down these decisions to the people in time-honored fashion as the people are assumed not to comprehend.

After World War II, Austrian governments never were interested in initiating a serious debate about the role of Austrians in the war. Instead they have perpetrated the myth that Austria was a "victim" of German annexation and occupation until today. The role Austrians played in National Socialism and the Holocaust was simply ignored or historicized by the founding fathers of the Second Republic and most Austrians never felt guilty or responsible for war crimes committed with their help by the Third Reich. Only recently have Chancellor Franz Vranitzky and President Thomas Klestil, in speeches given in Israel, admitted that Austrians were also perpetrators of war crimes in the killing machine of the Third Reich; these statements were not welcomed by the majority of the population at home who still savor the victim's mythology.[12]

It is this egregious failure to master its World War II past that is also seen by two of the authors in this FORUM as instrumental in helping prepare the ground for the new Right. *Richard Mitten* and *Walter Manoschek* demonstrate how the founding fathers in both the SPÖ and the ÖVP failed to take denazification of Austrian society seriously and outdid each other in advocating amnesty for the "little Nazis" in their fierce competition for voters. They also see a continuity in anti-Semitism in Austrian elites from the pre- to the postwar period. In his study of contemporary right-wing extremism in Europe, Geoffrey Harris sees precisely both this early abandonment of denazification in Germany and Austria and the continuity of racist ideas such as anti-Semitism as having allowed for a continuity of fascist personnel and ideology that prepared the soil for a resurgence of the new Right in the 1980s.[13] The failure to master the past by all parties, then, constitutes one historical root of the contemporary Right in Austria.

But there are also much older and deeper ideological roots of new Right doctrine in the *mentalitè* of the Austrian elites as *Michael Gehler* shows in his essay on the student fraternities. Particularly the German nationalist *Burschenschaften*, which broke with liberalism in the later nineteenth century, cultivated the extreme forms of racist anti-Semitism that directly led to the Holocaust in the sense that these people joined the SS killing machine in droves (Adolf Eichmann only being the most prominent example). After the war these same *Burschenschaften* did not distance themselves from National Socialism and the war crimes of their brethren. Instead they castigated Allied "reeducation" and Westernization and often became active in the FPÖ. Haider, of course, and much of the current FPÖ leadership were socialized after the war in this right extremist milieu.[14] And as *Reinhold Gärtner* shows here and elsewhere, these are often the people that write, publish and read the more extreme right-wing press such as the *Aula*, with its racist, xenophobic and revisionist tracts.[15] Historical revisionism—the outright purging of an embarrassing past—and the overcoming of what Weißmann calls the "*Schuldmetaphysik*" and the "black legend" of World War II history is also very prominent on the program of Haider and the FPÖ.[16] The *Aula* and extreme right go a decisive step further and are part and parcel of the "international of Holocaust deniers."[17]

Who, then, is Jörg Haider and how far on the right is he? This seems to be the central question of the "What's right" debate in Austria. The authors of the *Handbuch des Rechtsextremismus* have concluded that "the ideas of Jörg Haider and his core group dominating the FPÖ are unquestionably on the extreme right." They

285

add: "the FPÖ . . . has become an authoritarian *Führer* party cut in the cloth of Jörg Haider; people with an extreme right-wing nationalist ideology dominate it; they do not clearly distance themselves from National Socialism and keep a few liberals in their ranks for camouflage and fooling the public."[18] Is he a "Yuppie fascist,"[19] a "Crypto-neo-fascist,"[20] "a political chameleon hiding his real origins and objectives,"[21] a rabble-rousing "conservative populist"[22] à la Silvio Berlusconi, a "territorial populist" along Maier's analysis, or only a shrewd Ross Perot type for that matter?

   Max Riedlsperger thinks so in his FORUM essay. From his less alarmist Californian perspective, where a very tough anti-immigration ballot vote gained a clear majority recently, he sees Haider's FPÖ as a "libertarian New Right protest party." Haider's regionalist anti-statism, his protest against the shameless governmental corruption by the entrenched Austrian party system, his leadership in the popular immigration and asylum issue, his empowerment of people through more direct electronic democracy, and the moral values debate he unleashed, do not strike Riedlsperger as particularly extremist. The same issues, often addressed more radically than by Haider, seem to be daily fare of the new Republican Congress in Washington and Governor Pete Wilson of California—a likely 1996 presidential contender. The Left beating Haider over the head with the old "Nazi" bludgeon, Riedlsperger avers, is only an "exaggerated obsession of the old parties with the past." Or is it rather a case of bad conscience by a younger generation of leaders, given the failure of the "founding fathers" to deal honestly with Austria's World War II past and hide behind the victim's myth? From this more sanguine perspective, Haider's inexorable rise to power as the leader of a very successful protest party of the new—*not* extreme—Right seems inevitable.

   Peter Pulzer offers a solution to resolve the debate over the "Haider phenomenon." He suggests that Brigitte Bailer and Wolfgang Neugebauer. the principal authors of the *Handbuch des östereichischen Rechtsextremismus*, are "hypnotized by the neo-Nazism of the [FPÖ] cadres" from the right and not sufficiently cognizant of Haider's populist vote-fetching skills—his wide popular appeal in Austria. The authors of the *Handbuch* never resolved this dysfunction between the cadres' outdated and unpopular revisionist agenda and Haider's popularity, suggests Pulzer and adds: "Is the FPÖ a genuine party of the extreme right, as claimed by the contributors [of the *Handbuch*], or an exceptionally effective post-Fascist populist movement, led by a demagogue who has tapped a vein of alienation with the existing interest articulators, rather in the manner of Gianfranco Fini's *Allianza Nazionale?*" Unless Austrian intellectuals come to accept this dichotomy and place the "Haider phenomenon" within a broader comparative framework, they will never understand the realignment of the Austrian party system under way as both Riedlsperger and Pulzer argue from their more detached Anglo-American perspective. Surely Haider's appeal is bound to grow at a time when the old coalition faces painful and highly unpopular budget-cutting decisions.

NOTES

1. Charles S. Maier, "Democracy and Its Discontents," *Foreign Affairs*, 73/4 (1994): 48-64.

2. Starting the *FAZ* series on 18 April 1994 with Brigitte Seebacher-Brandt, the contentious widow of Willy Brandt, the "What's right?" column in the following days and weeks featured a number of prominent intellectuals such as the upstart new conservative Karlheinz Weißmann on the Right (22 April 1994)—for a change not the *spiritus rector* of the new Right in Germany Ernst Nolte himself—via more centrist Kohl staffers such as Michael Mertes and Hubertus von Morr (20 April 1994), to historian Hans-Ulrich Wehler on the Left (6 May 1994). For a critical, somewhat condescending, analysis of the debate, see Norbert Seitz, "Die 'What's right?'"-Debatte: Das zaghafte Herantasten an eine zivile Rechte," in *Aus Politik und Zeitgeschichte* B10/95 (3 March 1995), 23-27. On the central historiographic concern of "historicizing" National Socialism, see Martin Broszat's 1985 essay "Plädoyer für eine Historisierung des Nationalsozialismus," in his thoughtful collection *Nach Hitler: Der schwierige Umgang mit unserer Geschichte* (Munich: dtv, 1988), 266-81.

3. See, for example, the topical essays in *Austria in the New Europe*, in *Contemporary Austrian Studies* 1 (1993); Oliver Rathkolb, Georg Schmid, Gernot Heiß, eds., *Österreich und Deutschlands Grösse: Ein schlampiges Verhältnis* (Salzburg: Otto Müller, 1990); Nicholas X. Rizopoulos, ed., *Sea Changes: American Foreign Policy in a World Transformed* (New York-London: Council on Foreign Relations Press, 1990).

4. Alan Cowell, "Attack on Austrian Gypsies Deepens Fear of Neo-Nazis," *New York Times*, 21 February 1995, 1, 5.

5. Anton Pelinka and Susan Howell, "Duke and Haider: Right Wing Politics in Comparison," in *Contemporary Austrian Studies* 2 (1994): 152-71.

6. On the most incisive analysis of German *Vergangenheitsbewältigung*, with some Austrian comparisons, see Charles S. Maier, *The Unmasterable Past: History, Holocaust, and German National Identity* (Cambridge, MA: Harvard University Press, 1988).

7. The conference *"Differenzen in der Bearbeitung des Nationalsozialismus, des Antisemitismus und des Holocaust in Österreich, in der Bundesrepublik Deutschland und der DDR"* took place 6-9 November 1993 and was organized by Albert Lichtblau of the University of Salzburg. I am much indebted to Dr. Lichtblau for permitting the English publication of the Gehler, Gärtner, Manoschek and Mitten papers in this FORUM. The Salzburg papers are published by Werner Bergmann, Rainer Erb, and Albert Lichtblau, eds., *Schwieriges Erbe: Der Umgang mit Nationalsozialismus und Antisemitimus in Österreich, der DDR und der Bundesrepublik Deutschland* (Frankfurt: Campus, 1994). See also Rolf Steininger and Ingrid Böhler, eds., *Der Umgang mit dem Holocaust: Europa - USA - Israel* (Vienna-Cologne-Weimar: Böhlau, 1994).

8. I heard oral accounts of the bomb scare from Gerhard Botz and Jonathan Petropoulos, who were present.

9. Ironically Von Hayek's ideas seem to have a following in the FPÖ and are reprinted in the right-wing *Aula*, see *Handbuch des Rechtsextremismus*, 278, 438.

10. See the *AHR Forum*, Alan Brinkley, "The Problem of American Conservatism," with responses by Susan M. Yohn and Leo P. Ribuffo in *American Historical Review* 99 (April 1994): 409-52 (quotations 410, 414, 416).

11. Austria's difficult, and at times surreptitious, postwar relationship with the process of Western European integration has only recently seen a first attempt at serious history. See Michael Gehler and Rolf Steininger, eds., *Österreich und die europäische Integration 1945-1993* (Vienna-Cologne-Weimar: Böhlau, 1993), and Alan Milward's review in this volume.

12. See, for example, Anton Pelinka and Erika Weinzierl, eds., *Das große Tabu: Österreichs Umgang mit seiner Vergangenheit* (Vienna: Edition S, 1987); Heidemarie Uhl, *Zwischen Versöhnung und Verstörung: Eine Kontroverse um Österreichs historische Identität fünfzig Jahre nach dem 'Anschluß'* (Vienna-Cologne-Weimar: Böhlau, 1992); Günter Bischof, "Die Instrumentalisierung der Moskauer Erklärung nach dem 2. Weltkreig," in *Zeitgeschichte* 20 (1993): 345-66.

13. Geoffrey Harris, *The Dark Side of Europe: The Extreme Right Today* (Edinburgh: Edinburgh University Press, 1994), esp. ch. 1.

14. See Markus Perner and Klaus Zellhofer "Österreichs Burschenschaften als akademische Vorfeldorganisation des Rechtsextremismus," in *Handbuch des Rechtsextremismus*, 270-78 and *passim*.

15. Reinhold Gärtner, "Die Aula," ibid., 278-96.

16. See Uhl, *Zwischen Versöhnung und Verstörung*, 418-37; for Weißmann's "*Schuldmetaphysik*," see *FAZ*, 22 April 1994, 33.

17. The term "*Internationale der Auswitzleugner*" has been coined by Georg Stefan Troller. See his wonderfully sensitive "Abschied von einem Freund: Brief an Axel Corti," *Süddeutsche Zeitung*, 11-12 June 1994, 41. The tight international network of historical revisionism is described in Brigitte Bailer, "Internationale Verbindungen und Zusammenhänge," in *Handbuch*, 530-36; see also the very useful small handbook on the revisionists' favorite lies and myths by Wolfgang Benz, ed., *Legenden, Lügen, Vorurteile: Ein Wörterbuch zur Zeitgeschichte* (Munich: dtv, 1992).

18. For these conclusions see the long and factually dense essay by Brigitte Bailer and Wolfgang Neugebauer, "Die FPÖ: Vom Liberalismus zum Rechtsextremismus," in *Handbuch des Rechtsextremismus*, 357-494 (quotations 403, 462).

19. "Europe's New Right," *Newsweek*, 27 April 1992, 32.

20. Simon Wiesenthal quoted in Craig R. Whitney, "In Europe, the Right also Rises," *New York Times*, 14 November 1994.

21. Harris, *The Dark Side of Europe*, 181.

22. *New York Times*, 14 November 1994 (see note 16).

Student Corporations in Austria and the Right: A Historical Outline

Michael Gehler

This essay deals with the historical development of student fraternities in Austria from the nineteenth to the twentieth century. It points out the change from an early democratic to a bourgeois-liberal and finally conservative-reactionary attitude. In the course of this development Catholic fraternities experienced several ideological changes, from legitimist loyalty to the Habsburg dynasty before 1918 to German national Anschluß attitudes in the early 1920s and the authoritarian "fatherland philosophy" of the corporate state initiated by Dollfuss and Schuschnigg in the 1930s. In contrast, the *Burschenschafen* showed a clear line of development in the direction of pan-German and racially motivated nationalism, after having shed their early liberal and radically democratic positions from the middle of the nineteenth century onwards. Their direction was characterized by an increasing radicalization.

Student fraternities developed at medieval universities (Bologna, Padua, Vienna, Prague, Leipzig) where students (*"scholares"*) were grouped as *"nationes,"* and regional and national patriotism started to form. During their studies, it was almost obligatory for students to join the *"nationes,"* although these associations did not entail a bond for life, as is the case for the type of fraternities discussed in this essay. Life in the student dormitories, the so-called *"Bursen"*—which gave rise to the name *"Bursche"* referring to a senior member of a fraternity, and the later fraternity of the *"Burschenschaft"*—was dominated by strict discipline.

"Burschenschaften" came into existence at middle-German universities. The political and military events of the French Revolution (1789) and the involvement of large parts of the

population in the war had led to increased patriotism in German-speaking areas. New thought and behavior patterns had come into existence as part of the fight against the Napoleonic regime. The *fête* on the Wartburg (1817) was an articulation of protest against the German Confederation (*Deutscher Bund*), a loose association of thirty-nine states. However, the rigorous execution of the Carlsbad Decrees (1819) by Metternich's regime contributed to the persecution and dissolution of the *Burschenschaft* movement, which was considered "revolutionary." Only later, during the revolutionary years of 1848 and 1849, which saw an increased politicization of the students, did it become possible for fraternities to form. The focus of these societies, however, remained on social get-togethers, literature, art, and gymnastics.

Fixed rituals became standard in the fraternities from the mid-nineteenth century onwards, where seven principles characteristically played a role:

1. Admission into the fraternity, i.e. a trial, novice, and initiation period characterized by a step-by-step integration with certain prescriptions, a progressively formed bond (integration society).
2. The use of specific clothing with the colors of the fraternity, which makes integration possible via colors, images, and signs (symbolic society).
3. Duels and adherence to dueling rituals, representing attacks on the physical integrity of a person that, as a rule, ended in a bloody way (society of "blood brothers").
4. The codes of behavior with standard and repetitively used rituals, as well as singing and drinking customs to support the maintenance of discipline (ritual society).
5. Hierarchical structure and internal differentiation, with more alumni members (*"Alte Herren"*) than active students (hierarchical society).
6. Ideological identification through asserting common values, such as character strength, loyalty, commitment to lifelong allegiance, accepting the principle of dueling (or in some fraternities the rejection of dueling), preservation of values, tradition and religion, care of German culture and civilization, as well as love of the fatherland, including the

acknowledgment of the forefathers' achievements (ideological society).
7. Lifelong membership (lifelong allegiance).

These fraternities' principles of lifelong allegiance have always had socio-psychological consequences. It has been and still is normal for members in the community of young and old to use the informal personal pronoun "*du*" with one another, which establishes personal ties among members. Conflicts are generally avoided and the overall tendency has been one of adaptation. As a result, it has always been difficult if not impossible for members of the fraternity critically to confront the organization's past. Given this background, certain personal and ideological continuities can be detected.

The ideological positions that the *Burschenschaften* upheld were directly connected with the principle of fighting duels, which led the members to a strong common identity and ideological strength. Dueling rituals were—because of the ban by the state and the Church (threat of excommunication and strict rejection on the part of the Catholic bourgeoisie)—socially and politically stigmatized and therefore "interesting" and "attractive." The "educational value" of the duel consisted in strengthening self-control in difficult situations, increasing endurance and tolerance to bodily pain, improving personal courage and enhancing will power. Dueling also helped individuals to become progressively insensitive to pain and misery inflicted on others and habitually ready to attack another person and violate the physical integrity of the opponent in the duel. (The terms "cut down" and "disable" are used.) The quasi-legality of the dueling ritual—according to the logic of the "dueling" fraternities, an integral component of their world— guaranteed a violent solution to problems and voluntary injuries in a framework removed from generally accepted moral and ethical values, that is to say, unsanctioned.

By 1848, early democratic consciousness had shifted from moderate constitutionalism to republican radicalism. In the following period, the nationalist idea became more important than the love for political liberty, a development that went hand in hand with the establishment of bourgeois society. From the 1870s onwards, fraternities, encouraged by the German victory against France, embraced the conservative dueling conception and increasingly advocated ideas of German nationalism. The concept of a unified German national state became for the *Burschenschaften* more important than a liberal state based on principles of freedom and liberty. This movement went hand in hand with opposition to liberalism, an economically motivated rejection of Jews, and racially induced anti-Semitism. In terms of color symbolism, the flag black-red-gold changed to black-white-red.

The paradigmatic ideological and political changes were paralleled by the successive economic and social establishment of the originally revolutionary *Burschenschaften*, whose alumni members had meanwhile acquired well-paid positions in state and society. In the last two decades of the nineteenth century, the basic characteristics of fraternities—statutes, color symbols, mottos, Latinized names—became fixed and thus the organizations' formal and structural features were determined. This process was concurrent with the strengthening position of bourgeois forms of life and the corresponding claims for power. As a consequence, the duel too was seen as a manifestation of bourgeois identity.

In this phase of their ideological development, the fraternities focused on being the basis of a lifelong bond. Along with increasingly obvious social and political changes (the emancipation of the workers movement, the "battle for civilization," i.e. "*Kulturkampf*," and the problem of the nationalities) and their firmly established ideologies, the fraternities became more and more political, despite their claims to the contrary. Following the ideas of Georg Ritter von Schönerer, the Austrian *Burschenschaften* pursued a pro-Prussian, German national direction that included only the German areas of Austria as a part of a future German Reich; this policy meant a radical break with liberalism. Their predominantly racially motivated anti-Semitism was connected with a fervent anti-clericalism and anti-ultramontanism. The attitude of the corps regarding the German question was much less clearly defined. Their ideological inclination comprised pan-Germanic and legitimist tendencies, as well as loyalty to the Austrian emperor and the Habsburg dynasty.

At the end of the nineteenth century, the anti-Semitic ideology of the *Burschenschaften* pushed the confessional aspect of the fraternities into the background. In 1879, the Viennese *Burschenschaft Libertas* integrated the principle of Aryan birth into their statutes. In 1896 several *Burschenschaften*—united in the "Military Associations of the Eastern March" (*Wehrhafte Vereine der Ostmark*)—committed to the principle of Waidhofen ("*Waidhofener Prinzip*"), which had its origin in Florian Albrecht, a member of the *Burschenschaft Germania* in Innsbruck, and which denied Jews the right to satisfaction, that is, to defend one's honor with the saber. This position can be understood as a reaction to the creation of Jewish dueling fraternities in Vienna, which in turn was an answer to the growing anti-Semitism among students. The principle of Waidhofen socially stigmatized Jews. From this point onwards, not only were the members of Jewish fraternities ostracized, but the Jewish members of the *Burschenschaften* were ostracized and expelled (Theodor Herzl, Victor Adler, Heinrich Friedjung).

The Catholic fraternities identified with the movement of political Catholicism, that is, the social-reformist ideas of the Christian social mayor of Vienna Karl Lueger. In contrast, the dueling *Burschenschaften* progressively leaned towards Schönerer's pan-Germanic ideology. Thus, two camps confronted each other: the Catholic camp, the *Cartell Verband* (CV), which embraced the Austrian-specific attitude towards a "Greater Germany," legitimism, loyalty to the Habsburg dynasty, and Catholicism and the camp of the national fraternities, especially the *Burschenschaften*, which championed German nationalism, anti-Papism, and racial anti-Semitism. There were, however, ideological contact points between the two camps, such as moderate anti-Semitism, the fight against social democracy, and the stance against non-Germanic elements in the conflict of the nationalities. The conflict between "liberal" national and "clerical" fraternities derived not only from ideological differences but also from the struggle for power and influence at the universities. But the common experience in the front lines during the First World War (1914-1918) narrowed the political-ideological gap between Catholic and national students and university graduates, and even laid the spiritual and ideological basis for the time after the war.

Although it is easy to surmise that the change from early democratic to a radically German-national ideology made the *Burschenschaften* susceptible to National Socialist propaganda, the direction of Catholic fraternities is not as easy to discern. Strong ambivalence existed within the Catholic fraternities vis-a-vis their former loyalty to Austria and the Habsburg dynasty. After 1918, they were clear proponents of pan-Germanism and the integration of Austria into the German Reich (*Anschlußbewegung*). Until 1932, Catholic students and dueling national students worked together in the "German-Aryan" German Students' League, the "*Deutsche Studentenschaft*" (DSt), fighting together against Marxism. In 1931, National Socialist students had assumed the leadership in the DSt, thus acting as forerunners of the general development to follow two years later. This anticipation of the political seizure of power was characteristic of the 1930s, as was the fact that in the inter-war period, the percentage of fraternity members among students (50-60 percent) was significantly higher than after 1945. Additionally, more Austrian students were members of the NSDAP than their counterparts in the German Reich. From 1934 onwards, the conflict between Hitlerite Germany and the authoritarian "corporate" state of Austria brought about an additional polarization, which ended only in 1938 as a consequence of the Anschluß.

A 1990 study indicates the far-reaching affinity of fraternity members to the NSDAP as well as their involvement with specific National Socialist organizations. Membership in the NSDAP among members of dueling fraternities exceeded the figures of the average population by far. An almost equal proportion of both *Burschenschaften* and *Corps* (75 percent) had supported the illegal NSDAP. For the Catholic fraternities the picture was different. During the time of the Austrian "corporate state," they rejected the NSDAP on political and ideological grounds. After the Anschluß, however, a change occurred. A considerable proportion of the members (between 20 and 30 percent) were members of Hitler's party after 1938, but less for ideological than pragmatic and existential reasons. Approximately 17 percent of the National Socialists among the *Burschenschaften* became members of the stormtroopers ("*Sturmabteilung*" = SA), while 27.4 percent joined the blackshirt "*Schutzstaffel*" (SS). Something that is true of students from all fraternities: the upper and lower middle class formed the main recruitment basis for the NSDAP. These results confirm the recently criticized hypothesis of the "runaway bourgeois" as the recruitment basis for fascism for National Socialist students.

In contrast to the national fraternities, the majority of the Catholic ones had supported the authoritarian regime of Engelbert Dollfuss (member of the CV Franco Bavaria-Vienna) and Kurt Schuschnigg (member of the CV Austria-Innsbruck). Until 1938, a great number of them stood for the "Christian-German corporate" state that emphasized romanticism, a return to the importance of agriculture and a nostalgia for the Habsburg empire, as well as advocating an independent Austria. Since the CV societies in the German Reich (later abolished) drifted more and more in the direction of National Socialism, the Austrian fraternities jointly left the common league on 5 July 1933 and formed the ÖCV. Despite a friendship treaty signed after 1945, this breach has continued until today. The Catholic fraternities were not only formally against the NSDAP but also opposed National Socialism on ideological grounds, something that was difficult since the willingness to maintain a democratic form of government did not exist; sometimes their militant anti-Marxism was more pronounced than their opposition to National Socialism. Therefore, the tradition that sees CV members predominantly as victims of National Socialism in Austria (1938-1945) represents only one side of history. Before that period, the members of the league had been accomplices and active agents of the elimination of democracy in Austria; for example, they were involved with the suppression of the 12 February 1934 uprising and the dissolution of the Social Democratic party.

For the national, pan-Germanic ideology, dueling national students did everything, including sacrificing their beloved fraternity. It is a tragic and ironic fact that with their active support of National Socialism's ascension to power, the *Burschenschaften* brought about the end of their principle of lifelong allegiance. The new tendencies in the German Reich to make everything uniform (*"Gleichschaltung"*) and dissolve particular fraternities did not prevent the fraternity members in Austria from supporting National Socialist ideology. Therefore, the dissolution of the "national" fraternities in the summer of 1938 was—in contrast to the dissolved and forbidden CV—staged as "voluntary" self-dissolution which was rationalized by explaining that the aim and ideal pursued for decades, the pan-German solution (*"großdeutsche Volksgemeinschaft"*), had been accomplished and that therefore the "national" fraternities seemed to lack a legitimate reason for existence. This line of argumentation also shows the degree to which they had become ideological and political bodies. The ideology of a pan-Germanic fatherland had priority over the all-male society of friends.

While the *Burschenschaften* in part showed inhuman and radical reactions, the *Corps* tolerated "half-Jews" or Jewish members in their societies. From the end of the nineteenth century onwards, however, German-national ideology had increasingly fascinated and completely absorbed the dueling fraternities. They underwent a development during which even their core philosophy of lifelong allegiance was to fall victim to the totalitarian ideology of National Socialism. Before the fraternities were finally dissolved, "half-Jewish" members who had been overlooked or partly tolerated and members who were related to or had contact with Jews were expelled. Since the National Socialist laws were adopted throughout Austria, in spring 1938 the principle of Waidhofen finally triumphed over lifelong friendship and the allegiance to an all-male society.

In the interwar years, the duels and dueling rituals functioned both as para-military compensation for the general compulsory military service which no longer existed as well as for the armies that were limited in size both in Austria and Germany. It is not a coincidence that during the Nazi era the ideological and political esteem for manly duels increased. Despite the special place of the duel from 1938 onwards, the principle of unconditional satisfaction was interpreted as positive. It remains to be analyzed to what degree the "saber blows" and "bloody fights" from student times were continued in the violent excesses of the destructive war of the National Socialists. Detailed biographies of Austrian dueling students such as Dr. Ernst Kaltenbrunner (*Burschenschaft* Arminia-Graz), Dr. Ferdinand von Sammern-Frankenegg (*Sängerschaft* Skalden-Innsbruck), Dr. Irmfried Eberl (*Burschenschaft* Germania-Innsbruck), Dr. Walter Pfrimer (*Burschenschaft* Ostmark-Graz) or Hanns Rauter (*Corps* Vandalia-Graz) might be able to verify this hypothesis.

While the Catholic fraternities partly tried to break with their "German" and National Socialist past in Austria and Germany and by 1945 had dissociated themselves from their national counterparts, national fraternities, particularly the ones situated in Austria, dealt with their National Socialist past differently. Even after the Nuremberg trials, the *Burschenschaft* Arminia in Graz felt allegiance to their member Ernst Kaltenbrunner, who was found guilty in Nuremberg and executed. Similarly, the first commander of the extermination camp of Treblinka and "specialist" in euthanasia, Irmfried Eberl, is still listed among the alumni members of the

Burschenschaft Germania Innsbruck. Eberl had committed suicide in 1948, but a posthumous expulsion was never considered. The *Burschenschaft* Suevia in Innsbruck considered the lawyer Dr. Gerhard Lausegger a honorable alumni member, whose accident in Argentina in 1967 was severely regretted. Lausegger was the speaker of the fraternity in 1937, the chairman of the Innsbruck Association of Dueling Fraternities for two years, and the leader of a commando that killed the head of the Jewish community in Innsbruck on the night of 9-10 November 1938—the Crystal Night. The motto of the *Burschenschaft* Germania, "through purity to unity," was, at least, reinterpreted in a general moral sense after 1945.

The developmental tendencies of fraternities in Germany after 1945 show a different picture, where a process of renewed democratization set in faster than in Austrian fraternities. In general, the German members of *Burschenschaften* showed a positive attitude towards the Federal Republic of Germany, which was founded as a successor of but also in contrast to the Third Reich. The majority of them also accepted Germany's integration into the West and the NATO philosophy connected with this. Conversely, the Austrian *Burschenschaften* criticized this development as "Americanization," "Westernization," and "reeductation" and rejected the idea of the "Austrian nation," a concept revived by the Second Republic after 1945. Likewise, even today they renounce the Austrian National Holiday. This rejection is epitomized by a statement made by the FPÖ politician and right-wing populist Jörg Haider (*Burschenschaft* Silvania-Vienna) who termed the Austrian nation an "ideological monstrosity."

Over and over again, the CV has emphasized the achievements of its fraternities as a "bastion in the fight against National Socialism," leaving untouched the right-wing conservative and in part right-wing extremist aspects of its history, which include involvement in the semi-fascist Austrian militia movement (the *Heimwehr*) and collaboration in the establishment of the anti-democratic corporate state. These aspects were, for example, expressed in leaving intact various honorary memberships such as that of August Rohling (professor of theology in Prague and author of the racist and anti-Semitic book *The Talmudic Jew*) in the Innsbruck-based CV fraternity Austria. The esteem, admiration and glorification of the authoritarian dictators Dollfuss and Schuschnigg among CV members round off this picture. However, it has to be said that recently a clear tendency of a more objective and critical treatment of this topic can be observed. It is interesting to note that the ÖCV incorporated the commitment to democracy into its statutes as late as 1967. Before 1918, the motto was for the "Throne and Altar," while in the time between 1933 and 1938, members were committed to the "corporate" state under "Christian" leadership. After 1945 allegiance was, logically, shifted to the new Christian-democratic politicians Leopold Figl and Julius Raab, who before 1938 had held important positions in the authoritarian Austrian Militia Movement (*Heimwehr*).

The continuity in this orientation towards authority seems plausible, but it is also marked by breaks. Until the late 1960s, a great number of members were committed to "German culture and civilization," an attitude expressed even in some of the statutes. It would, however, be totally wrong to place the CV and the *Burschenschaften* on the same ideological level. The latter had, since the *Kulturkampf* progressively removed themselves from the loyalty to the state and had become "politically" active for a pan-Germanic ideology, while the CV showed a much larger ideological spectrum. Later, in the 1970s and 1980s, a partly strong movement to separate the fraternities from ideological questions set in. The CV became an open association, even if they have never been able to shed the image of being a "patronage" society. Ideological aspects have, in this case, totally moved into the background.

In many ways, the 1960s brought about an activation of the right-wing extremist ideological potential, with events in both foreign and domestic policy developing their own logic. One of those events was the Eichmann trial in Jerusalem, which was considered an injustice by the Austrian *Burschenschaften*, namely a kidnapping to administer the law. Other items included the South Tyrol question, which became critical because of bombing attempts in the early 1960s, and the events of 1965 surrounding the neonational attitudes of the university professor Taras Borodajkewycz (former member of CV Norica-Vienna), which led to a radicalization of the political climate. These events provoked reactions from the "national" camp and led to right-wing extremist and neo-Nazi activities which manifested themselves in many ways.

Anti-Semitism continues to play a role after 1945. Even if it was less openly articulated than before the Second World War, it still lived on as a movement beneath the surface. Anti-Semitism was entrenched among many of the alumni members and was not critically analyzed by the student members. Not only was it possible for leading proponents of anti-Semitism of the pre- and inter-war years to remain members in the fraternities; they were still considered role models. Examples include Schönerer, the founder of racial anti-Semitism in Austria in the *Burschenschaft* Germania-Innsbruck; Anton Jerzabek, Christian social member of Parliament and leader of the League of Anti-Semites in the *Burschenschaft* Olympia-Vienna; Emmerich Czermak, chairman of the teachers' appointment committee for Lower Austria, minister of education (1929-1932), and chairman of the Austrian CV Association of Alumni Members in the CV Nordgau Vienna. In his book *The Settlement of the Jewish Question* the latter had, years before the Anschluß, advocated a Madagascar plan for solving the Jewish question in Europe. Another example was Leopold Kunschak (CV Norica-Vienna), the chairman of the Christian-Socialist Workmen's Association and militant anti-Semite, after 1945 honorary chairman of the ÖVP and president of the Austrian Parliament (*Nationalrat*) from 1945 to 1953.

It would be wrong to say that all fraternities or *Burschenschaften* can be called anti-Semitic and right wing. In particular one has to differentiate between such *Burschenschaften* and Austrian and German fraternities. In the late 1950s the Liberation Committee for South Tyrol (BAS - *Befreiungsausschuß für Südtirol*) was founded, in which an Assistant Professor of the University of Innsbruck, Norbert Burger, *Burschenschaft* Olympia-Vienna, participated. The South Tyrol question was considered a national cause and the fight for South Tyrol's self-determination was, from that point onwards, one of the priorities of national fraternities—quite true to their tradition. Activities for "Germans in borderland areas," for example for the Carinthians or Upper Silesians in the 1920s, corresponded to their self-image. In this connection, it is characteristic of the Austrian situation that a Borodajkewycz affair did occur and that the "'68 Movement" can, at least in part, be observed. Conversely, in Germany, the already reestablished fraternities withdrew to their fraternity houses instead of participating in the critical discussions at the universities. With the defeat of the national fraternities in the Borodajkewycz case (the incriminated professor was retired)—something that must not necessarily be interpreted as breach

with right-wing continuities—and the signing of the South Tyrol
Package in 1969, a decline in active right-wing extremism can be
observed. However, right-wing ideological thinking continued in the
fraternities and in their superstructure, the Ring of Liberal Students
(*Ring Freiheitlicher Studenten*—RFS).

The Austrian *Burschenschaften* considered the German
fraternities as too "reeducated" and loyal to the Federal Republic of
Germany. On 15 July 1961 the "Union of the *Burschenschaften*"
(*Burschenschaftliche Gemeinschaft* - BG) was founded in the house
of the *Burschenschaft* Danubia in Munich, mostly because of the
disappointment over the DB's (*Deutsche Burschenschaft*) rejecting a
merger of German and Austrian *Burschenschaften*. The BG formed
a common platform with the German *Burschenschaften* in Austria
(DBÖ), whose forty fraternities from that point onwards can be
considered as a "right-wing cadre school for the universities." In the
BG's conception, Germany exists in the boundaries of 1 September
1939, including all territories that were—neglecting the right of self-
determination—annexed after 1919 (e.g. Alsace-Lorraine, the
southern part of Styria, northern Silesia). This ideology of retaliation
and revanchism has repeatedly been encouraged and enforced by the
Austrian *Burschenschaften*.

The events of the years 1989 and 1990 in connection with the
end of SED socialism and Germany's reunification pleased a great
number of *Burschenschaften*, since they had for years kept the
German question alive and had emphasized the importance of
national considerations. German unity confirmed their anti-Marxist
theories and gave a new impetus for political action. The radical
changes inside Germany led to numerous activities, such as
investments of the DB in the former GDR to conquer "middle
Germany." For instance, old fraternity houses were renovated,
societies that in part existed in the GDR before the reunification were
activated, and new fraternities were founded. Anticipation of career
positions on the one hand and the hope for new members and
rejuvenation on the other seemed to mirror the hopes and
expectations of the new members from the ex-GDR and the DB. In
this case, ideological positions seem capable of encompassing a
broader basis.

The historical development of fraternities illustrates the change
from an early democratic to a bourgeois-liberal and finally a

conservative-reactionary attitude. In the course of their development, Catholic fraternities experienced several ideological changes, for instance from their legitimist loyalty to the Habsburg dynasty before 1918 to German national and Anschluß endeavors of the 1920s and the authoritarian "fatherland philosophy" of the Austrian corporate state. In contrast, the *Burschenschaften* showed a clear line of development in the direction of German and racially motivated nationalism, after having shed their early liberal and radically democratic positions from the middle of the nineteenth century onwards. This direction of ideological movement was less characterized by fluctuations than by an increasing radicalization.

FURTHER LITERATURE

Wolfgang Benz, ed., *Rechtsextremismus in der Bundesrepublik: Voraussetzungen, Zusammenhänge, Wirkungen*, rev. ed. (Frankfurt/Main: Fischer, 1992).

Hans Endlich, Rolf Grix, Klaus Willberg, *Extremismus, Radikalismus, Demagogie von rechts: Entwicklungen und Bestandsaufnahme* in Geschichte und Politik-Unterrichtsmaterialien, ed. Hans Endlich (Frankfurt/Main: Verlag Moritz Diesterweg, 1990).

Ute Frevert, *Ehrenmänner: Das Duell in der bürgerlichen Gesellschaft* (Munich: C.H. Beck, 1991).

Rainer Fromm/Barbara Kernbach, . . . *und morgen die ganze Welt? Rechtsextreme Publizistik in Westeuropa* (Marburg: Schüren Presseverlag, 1994).

Michael Gehler, "Antisemitismo studentesco all' Università di Innsbruck dalle origini al 1938: Un contributo storico sull' antisemitismo in Austria," in *Materiali di Lavoro. Rivista di studi storici* (Rovereto, 1988): 43-81.

_____, "Entstehungs-, Organisations- und Wirkungsgeschichte der österreichischen Studentenvereine unter besonderer Berücksichtigung des Vormärz (1815-1848)," in *Jahrbuch 4 der Hambach Gesellschaft* 1992/93, ed. Hambach-Gesellschaft für historische Forschung und politische Bildung (Neustadt an der Weinstraße 1993): 37-67.

_____, "Geschichte der österreichischen Studentenvereine von den Anfängen bis 1918," in *Österreichisches Parteienlexikon*, ed. Anton Pelinka, Helmut Reinalter (Thaur: Kulturverlag, 1995).

_____, "Korporationsstudenten und Nationalsozialismus in Österreich. Eine quantifizierende Untersuchung," *Geschichte und Gesellschaft* 20 (1994): 1-28.

_____, "Männer im Lebensbund: Studentenvereine im 19. und 20. Jh. unter besonderer Berücksichtigung der österreichischen Entwicklung," *Zeitgeschichte* 21 (February 1994): 45-66.

_____, "Die Studenten der Universität Innsbruck und die Anschlußbewegung 1918-1938, in *Tyrol und der Anschluß: Voraussetzungen, Entwicklungen, Rahmenbedingungen 1918-1938*, ed. Thomas Albrich, Klaus Eisterer, Rolf Steininger (Innsbruck: Haymon, 1988), 75-112.

_____, "Neuere Literatur zur Geschichte der Universitäten, Wissenschaften, Studenten und Korporationen in Deutschland und Österreich unter besonderer Berücksichtigung der Jahre 1918-1945," *Archiv für Sozialgeschichte* 34 (1994): 300-332.

_____, "Rechtskonservativismus, Rechtsextremismus und Neonazismus. Zur Rolle der Studentenverbindungen nach 1945 unter besonderer Berücksichtigung der österreichischen Bünde," in: *Differenzen im Umgang mit Nationalsozialismus, Antisemitismus und Holocaust in der Bundesrepublik, DDR und Österreich*, ed. Werner Bergmann, Rainer Erb, Albert Lichtblau (Frankfurt: Campus, 1995).

Michael Gehler, *Studenten und Politik: Der Kampf um die Vorherrschaft an der Universität Innsbruck 1918-1938* (Innsbruck: Haymon, 1990).

Handbuch des Österreichischen Rechtsextremismus, ed. Stiftung Dokumentationsarchiv des österreichischen Widerstandes (Vienna: Deuticke, 1994).

Ingo Hasselbach/Winfried Bonengel, *Die Abrechnung: Ein Neonazi steigt aus* (Berlin: Aufbau-Verlag, 1993).

Eckhard Jesse, *Politischer Rechtsextremismus in Deutschland und Europa* (München: Brönner & Daentler KG, 1993).

Wolfgang Kowalsky/Wolfgang Schröder, eds., *Rechtsextremismus: Einführung und Forschungsbilanz* (Opladen: Westdeutscher Verlag, 1994).

Hans-Helmuth Knütter, *Die Faschismus-Keule: Das letzte Aufgebot der deutschen Linken* (Berlin: Ullstein Verlag, 1993).

Hans-Uwe Otto/Roland Merten, eds., *Rechtsradikale Gewalt im vereinten Deutschland: Jugend im gesellschaftlichen Umbruch* (Opladen: Leske Verlag + Budrich, 1993).

Gerhard Paul, ed., *Hitlers Schatten verblaßt: Die Normalisierung des Rechtsextremismus* (2nd ed., Bonn: Verlag J.H.W. Dietz Nachf., 1990).

Friedbert Pflüger, *Deutschland driftet. Die Konservative Revolution entdeckt ihre Kinder* (Düsseldorf: ECON Verlag, 1994).

Wolfgang Purtscheller, ed., *Die Ordnung, die sie meinen: "Neue Rechte" in Österreich* (Vienna: Picus Verlag, 1994).

Wolfgang Purtscheller, *Aufbruch des Völkischen: Das braune Netzwerk*, (Vienna: Picus Verlag, 1993).

Manfred Sicking/Alexander Lohe, eds., *Die Bedrohung der Demokratie von rechts: Wiederkehr der Vergangenheit?* (Köln: Bund-Verlag, 1993).

Helmut Wohnout, "Rechtsextremismus, Rechtspopulismus und ihre Rückwirkungen auf das österreichische politische System: Eine Untersuchung unter besonderer Berücksichtigung der Rolle der FPÖ," in *Österreichisches Jahrbuch für Politik* 1993, ed. Andreas Khol, Günther Ofner, Alfred Stirnemann (Vienna-Munich: Oldenbourg, 1994): 381-400.

Ulrich Wank, ed., *Der neue alte Rechtsradikalismus* (Munich: Piper, 1993).

Right-Wing Press in Austria

Reinhold Gärtner

"Right-wing," "new Right," and "extreme Right" are terms that scholarship has a hard time defining with any precision. In everyday discourse they are used with notorious abandon. I will nevertheless try to present a qualifying framework in which these terms are being used here. The "right-wing" is essentially anti-democratic and favors "natural elites." "Natural" here means a homogenous society in which the weak are expendable and all foreigners and aliens unwanted. "Natural" also means that the behavior and attitudes of a society's members are predetermined by the traditional gene pool; no alternative behavior or views are acceptable.

Another feature of the new Right is the stress on "ethno-pluralism," which means that all peoples should live in and—above all—stay in their countries. Thus slogans like "German for Germans" or "Tyrol for Tyroleans" take turns with "Turkey for Turks" or "Asia for Asians." The new Right takes it for granted that peoples are still homogeneous groups who have been living in their territories for ages. They do not take into account that these groups are continuously changing, and above all they ignore the fact that one can find this homogeneity almost nowhere. Even the defining characteristics of a certain group are unclear: on the one hand, it is impossible to be "German" if your parents or grandparents were not; on the other hand, people with names like Pawkowicz (FPÖ Wien), Andronik (FPÖ Villach), Barcaba (FPÖ Oberösterreich), Bukovnik (FPÖ Kärnten), Cladrowa (FPÖ Graz), Canori (FPÖ Klagenfurt), Cermak (FPÖ Steiermark)—to name just a few—consider themselves members of "*deutsche Volks-und Kulturgemeinschaft.*" Thus, one's blood functions as a pretext for exclusion if one wants to keep his or her identity and it is not decisive if one considers himself or herself as "German."

"Right-wing" also means a network of authors, publications, seminars and meetings in which various participants try to establish their view of reality. These are by no means in every case right-wing extremists; we do indeed find many conservatives and even leftists among them, who—more or less consciously—act as useful vehicles for the transfer of extreme thoughts and ideologies.

In general, it is difficult to distinguish exactly between "extreme" and "new Right." The difference is not in basic tenets but rather in degrees: for example, the extreme Right generally denies the Holocaust and the new Right admits the Holocaust in relative terms. But even this distinction seems to be vanishing. Another criterion is the support of violence. On the one hand, many representatives of the new Right have condemned the attacks against foreigners (especially in Germany) in recent years, but, on the other hand, they have been quite straightforward in their verbal attacks against foreigners.

As far as the media are concerned, we find a few curiosities in Austria, such as the influence of the Austrian tabloid *Kronen Zeitung*. This paper reaches some 2.4 million people every day and is a "tabloid" in the strictest sense: small size, low quality, emotion instead of information, defamation instead of serious articles. Above all, it features two journalists who pander to the Right by focusing on anti-Semitism, xenophobia, discrimination against minorities and the like. Moreover, only a few quality papers have a wide distribution. *Der Standard, Die Presse* and *Salzburger Nachrichten* are quality papers that try to cover not only certain regions but the whole of Austria. It would be interesting to analyze these big Austrian dailies with regard to elements of right-wing ideology. In addition to the dailies, right-wing monthly and quarterly magazines exert some influence. A few papers—for example *Bundesturnzeitung* (paper of *ÖTB-Österreichischer Turnerbund* with some 70,000 members) and *Der Kärntner* (paper of *KHD-Kärntner Heimatdienst*)—reach tens of thousands of their members. A special paper is *Aula*, magazine of "*Freiheitliche Akademikerverbände*," the clubs of academics with close connections to FPÖ.

Der Standard and *Kronen Zeitung*

Der Standard is one of the papers which not only show no connections to the Right but which try to give steady information about the extreme Right, its activities and its representatives. But we do find a few examples of what one could call lack of sensitivity even in papers like *Der Standard*. In February 1993, *Der Standard* published an enthusiastic review on a recent book of Gerd-Klaus Kaltenbrunner, one of the prominent and important representatives of the new Right who publishes in various extreme Right papers. This Kaltenbrunner, an Austrian with German domicile, is a permanent author for papers like *criticon, Nation und Europa, Deutschland in Geschichte und Gegenwart* or *Junges Forum* and is one of the prime examples of the grey area between the Right and conservatism.

Asked why this review was published, *Der Standard* made no response. This is not to imply that *Der Standard* has any connections to the extreme or to the new Right. But even papers like *Der Standard* sometimes have problems with actors from the Right and demonstrate a lack of discerning sensitivity.

Another example in *Der Standard* was more serious. In summer 1992, when Carinthia's political and social elite wanted to celebrate the 100th anniversary of Hans Steinacher's birthday, Anton Pelinka wrote about Steinacher's National Socialist-past. Pelinka's article was published in *Der Standard,* as were the reactions to his commentary. Among those whose articles were published was a certain Helmut Golowitsch, former member of RFS (*Ring Freiheitlicher Studenten*) and NDP (*Nationaldemokratische Partei*), speaker at the AfP (*Aktionsgemeinschaft für demokratische Politik*) and one who in the late 1970s distributed leaflets questioning the Holocaust. *Der Standard* in these cases did not print reactions on the Kaltenbrunner review and gave space to representatives of the extreme Right.

In May 1992, Richard Nimmerrichter—alias "Staberl"—wrote about "*Methoden eines Massenmordes*" ("Methods of Mass Murder") in the *Kronen Zeitung*. He pointed out that only relatively few Jews were killed in gas chambers; most of them, Staberl argued, were beaten, frozen or starved to death. All in all, the Jews had been in a situation comparable to POWs in Russian camps. Official response to this article was small: though Austria's Jewish community protested, there was no reaction by court or public prosecutors. The protest of Austria's press council fell on deaf ears. Nimmerrichter knew what he was writing about. Only a month earlier, in April 1992, Gert Honsik, one of Austria's main Auschwitz-deniers was sentenced to prison, and in the course of the legal proceedings the Viennese contemporary historian Gerhard Jagschitz emphasized what everyone knew—that the mass murder of the Jews had been committed by National Socialists.

Right-Wing Press in Austria

If we take a closer look at Austria's right-wing press, we find, as mentioned above, quite a few extreme papers: *Sieg* and *Halt* are the best know among them. Both papers are extremely anti-Semitic and racist and favor National Socialism. And both are distributed illegally. The editors of both papers, Walter Ochensberger and Gert Honsik, were given prison sentences a few years ago.

Apart from Gottfried Küssel, Ochensberger and Honsik are Austria's best known neo-Nazis. In 1961, Honsik threw a firebomb at the Parliament in Vienna. In 1976 he was elected to the federal committee of NDP and in the same year was sentenced to prison for 15 months. In 1986, legal proceedings against Honsik were initiated ("*NS-Wiederbetätigung*") and, finally, in 1992 he was given prison sentences in Austria (18 months) and in Bavaria (12 months, suspended, with probation). Honsik fled to Spain. In the course of these legal proceedings, Professor Gerhard Jagschitz was asked to write the expert's report mentioned above.

Like Honsik, Ochensberger was member of NDP, and legal proceedings against him were initiated. As mentioned above, Ochensberger was also sentenced to prison, but only after having been judged "not guilty" in earlier trials. Ochensberger, like Honsik, fled from Austria, but in 1993 he was arrested in Germany and extradited to Austria. If anything is amusing in these cases, it is that Ochensberger, who is not only hostile to foreigners but actively supports hatred against foreigners, applied for political asylum in Germany.

One could list many other papers—like *Kommentare zum Zeitgeschehen, Fakten* or *Der Volkstreue*—which belong to this group of extreme right-wing publications but are mainly distributed among supporters. A few right-wing papers specialize on cultural topics, "culture" in this context meaning "German nationalism" (e.g. *Eckartbote*).

The *Aula*

There are reasons for analyzing the *Aula* as an extreme example of right-wing papers. First, it was founded in 1951, and thus has a long tradition. Second, the *Aula* gives examples of many views of both the extreme and moderate Right. Third, as mentioned above, the *Aula*—since October 1991 *das freiheitliche Magazin*—shows close connections to the FPÖ, including FPÖ politicians as authors, FPÖ advertisements and frequent articles on the FPÖ.

FPÖ politicians as authors are prominent party members like Jörg Haider, Andreas Mölzer, Rainer Pawkowicz or John Gudenus as well as small supporters and politicians like Walter Neuner, an FPÖ member of the district council of Grambach near Graz. FPÖ politicians are also important interview partners for the *Aula*; in 1993 six out of 13 interviewed persons were FPÖ politicians (Pawkowicz, Dillersberger, Schöfnagel, Haider, Grasser, and again Pawkowicz).

FPÖ advertisements can be found, especially before elections, on both the national and regional level. And we can find quite a few advertisements from FPÖ-politicians for their businesses, like Elmar Dirnberger, Walter Sucher, Erich Slupetzky or Dietmar Sulzberger. In 1977, Elmar Dirnberger, head of *Magnum Immobilien* (real estate), was a member of the extreme Right student group ANR (*Aktion Neue Rechte*) and at the same time a member of the Vienna FPÖ executive committee, Walter Sucher, managing director of GEFFA (*Gesellschaft für Finanzierungsvermittlung und Anlageberatung*), is also head of *Ring volkstreuer Verbände*, a small extreme Right group. Erich Slupetzky, an FPÖ candidate in Linz in 1991, until 1945 was a leader of the *Hitler Jugend* and after 1945 involved in the so called "Soucek Affair." Finally, Sulzberger in the 1970s was a member of the extreme Right NDP and ran as an FPÖ candidate in Vienna in 1991.

Since the Haider takeover in 1986, the *Aula* has been almost enthusiastic in its reports on the FPÖ. Either in publishing basic party documents like the *Lorenzener Erklärung*, a collection of basic FPÖ statements, the *"FPÖ Resolution zur Ausländerfrage"* or in commenting favorably on FPÖ policies. In 1994, however, the sympathies seem to have become somewhat strained because—at least in public—Haider makes clear that German nationalism is not the main FPÖ issue. German nationalism is one of the central tenets of the *Aula* and its éminence grise (or rather brown), Andreas Mölzer.

In general, the *Aula* is clear-cut in both its statements and its style: death-penalty for people with *"kriminelle Defektgene"* (criminal deficiency genes, whatever that means); crude attacks on minorities like gypsies or homosexuals; racist arguments against foreigners and frequent anti-Semitic remarks. Examples of the *Aula* ideology are found in what the new Right calls "Ethnopluralism," what one could call "racism" in the attempts to deny the Holocaust.

In 1992 Andreas Mölzer, former editor-in-chief of *Aula*, used the term *"Umvolkung"* for the first time in public. *Umvolkung* is a term difficult to translate; it means that in the long run the genes of the indigenous population might be changed or, as someone put it, in course of time we might become "niggers with slit eyes." That this term *Umvolkung* was used by the Nazis was certainly no hindrance for Mölzer's using it too. In the *Aula* we find this term appearing again and again after 1989 while the *Aula* has been presenting (pseudo)scientific evidence for the *"Umvolkung"* of the Austrian population.

Since 1989, comments on the topic of "foreigners" have been increasing. Initially comments were grounded less in biological reasoning than they have been since. More and more often we read that foreigners have too many children and that instead of having foreigners and their children in Austria, Austrian men and women should try to produce more genuine Austrians. Meanwhile, we also find more and more arguments about the impossibility of integration. Foreigners, the *Aula* argues, simply cannot be integrated, especially if they are from non-European (third world) countries. And foreigners remain foreigners even if they are no longer foreigners: having become Austrian citizens, former Turks, Poles or Egyptians remain Turks, Poles or Egyptians. The *Aula*, though, seems to argue as some Austrian politicians do: the so-called *Aufenthaltsgesetz* points out that the yearly rates of visas have to be fixed according to the number of foreigners who are already in Austria. And in Austria we still have—and will continue to have—*jus sanguinis* instead of the *jus soli*: being born in Austria does not convey Austrian citizen's rights and privileges.

The most preeminent example of new Right thinking is the denial of the Holocaust. If someone like the Auschwitz-denier David Irving is not permitted to speak publicly in Austria, the *Aula* smells an attack on freedom of speech. The *Aula* charges that in Austria historical events cannot be discussed if they are not seen along the lines of "Allied propaganda." Those who discuss these events are threatened with court or even convicted and fined. Irving is one example; remarks about the numbers of Jews killed in gas chambers being too high or that the "six million" Jews killed in the Holocaust is a biblical standard-number, are others.

In 1994 the so called "Lüftl-Report" provided much grist for the *Aula* mill. A few years ago, Walter Lüftl, former head of Austria's Chamber of Engineers, published a report on the gas chambers, in which he said that according to laws of nature, killing people in the way it was claimed in Auschwitz would be impossible and that in Mauthausen no one was killed in the gas chamber. The *Aula* evidence is the "Lüftl report," published in the *Journal of Historical Review* of the American Institute for Historical Review, which has close connections to neo-Nazi organizations. Investigations were abandoned in June 1994 and the *Aula* commended this as a milestone on the path to truth.

In general, the *Aula* has been—especially since 1986—moving into the center of Austria's right-wing extremism. In its political tenets and its organizational structures, the *Aula* serves as a link between FPÖ and all extra-parliamentary attempts of German nationalism and right-wing extremism. According to Brigitte Bailer and Wolfgang Neugebauer, the *Aula* represents the German national and extreme Right milieu in Austria (apart from the younger militant skinhead neo-Nazism).

The Others

Bailer and Neugebauer find the extreme Austrian Right in milieus such as

* political and organizational fringe groups;
* veteran organizations;
* cultural or/and sport organizations;
* organizations with political and ideological integration.

Though the *Aula* is the most widely read right-wing paper in Austria, there are many others which are Right or extreme Right, and some of them—especially *Sieg* and *Halt*—can be qualified as "neo-Nazi." Both politically and organizationally unimportant fringe papers are the *National-Konservative Nachrichten, Mitteilungen: Freundeskreis der Stiftung soziales Friedenswerk zur Förderung begabter Jugend* or *Der Volkssozialist*. Publications of veterans organizations are papers like *Mitteilungen: Wohlfahrtsverband der Glasenbacher*. The *Glasenbacher* are former inmates of the postwar American Nazi internment camp Glasenbach near Salzburg (Nazi officials and war criminals); *Prinz Eugen - Kampforgan des VÖK* (VÖK - *Verband österreichischer Kameradschaften)*, or *Die Kameradschaft*, paper of *Kameradschaft IV*, a veterans organization of former Waffen-SS members.

Cultural and/or sport organizations publish papers such as *Lot und Waage* (edited by the *"Alpenländischer Kulturverband Südmark"*); *Bundesturnzeitung* (edited by the ÖTB - *"Österreichischer Turnerbund"*); *Der Völkerfreund* (edited by the *"Österreichische Gesellschaft der Völkerfreunde"*), or *Huttenbriefe für Volkstum Kultur, Wahrheit und Recht* (edited by the DKEG - *"Deutsches Kulturwerk europäischen Geistes, Österreich"*).

Kommentare zum Zeitgeschehen is the monthly of AfP (*"Arbeitsgemeinschaft für demokratische Politik"*), a heavily misleading name. Formally, the AfP is a political party with revisionist and partly neo-Nazist tendencies. In *Kommentare zum Zeitgeschehen* one can find advertisements for publications that deny the Holocaust; even though the AfP does not have many members, it shows connections to groups, persons and publications of the extreme Right in Austria as well as in other countries. The AfP is also organizer of "political academies." The list of speakers in these gatherings is like reading the *"Who's Who"* of the extreme Right, which does not prevent FPÖ politicians from appearing as speakers too.

Another important paper is *Eckartbote - Monatszeitschrift für deutsche Kultur*. Its publisher *"Österreichische Landsmannschaft"* (ÖLM), is an extreme right-wing organization with considerable activities, especially in right-wing publishing. The head of ÖLM is the FPÖ politician Helmut Kowarik while other FPÖ politicians such as Barbara Schöfnagel are members of the board. In general, Austria's right-wing press is not widely read, but those papers that show close connections to the FPÖ seem to have at least some influence on the party line.

Another part of what one could call right-wing is the role of Austria's most widely read tabloids, especially of *Kronen Zeitung* and *täglich alles*. In 1992/93 the FPÖ announced a referendum called *"Österreich zuerst"* ("Austria first"). The general idea of this referendum was to minimize the foreigners' chances of coming to Austria and—for those who were in the country already—of staying in Austria. A recent study showed the connections between mass media and Austria's alien policy: fear of foreigners was remarkably higher among those who were reading *Kronen Zeitung* and/or *täglich alles* than among readers of other newspapers:

Table 1:   Greater than average xenophobia and (exclusive)
           newspaper readerships (dichotomized)

Percent	Greater than average fear of foreigners
Total population	32
Krone/Täglich Alles readership	46
Readers of other dailies	21
Krone/Täglich Alles readers below age of 50	43
Readers of other dailies below 50	17
Krone/Täglich Alles readers over 50	50
Readers of other dailies over 50	29
Krone/Täglich Alles readers with primary/secondary education	48
Readers of other dailies with primary/secondary education	25
Krone/Täglich Alles readers with university education	25
Readers of other dailies with university education	15

Source: Fessel+GFK Public Opinion Polls
            Life-Style 1992 - Political Orientation
            in: Plasser and Ulram, *Ausländerangst* (1992), 19

Asked whether foreigners in Austria were the reason for the difficulties of Austrian employees and a threat to our way of living, most readers of the *Kronen Zeitung* and *täglich alles* said "yes."

Another survey shows that xenophobia (*"Ausländerangst"*), consent to authoritarianism and upset about politics is far above average among readers of *Kronen Zeitung* and *täglich alles*:

Table 2:   Political Fears and Xenophobia in Newspaper Readerships

Classified as percentage	Newspaper types				
	Austrian total	Prestige	Tab I	Regional	Tab II*
Authoritarian core	4	2	2	3	4
Potentially Authorit.	44	20	31	40	51
Xenophobic core	32	16	21	25	43
German nationalist core	10	5	7	11	9
Potentially German Nat.	24	11	17	26	24
Anti-Party** Core	23	18	17	21	37

*   4 percent of all regular tabloid readers are considered to be hard-core authoritarian

** = *"parteiverdrossen"*

Prestige papers	=	*Die Presse, Der Standard*
Tab(loid) I	=	*Kurier*
Regional	=	Regional newspapers
Tab(loid) II	=	*Kronenzeitung, täglich alles*

Source: Bruckmüller, *Österreichbewusstsein im Wandel* (1994), 88

Maximilian Gottschlich, professor at the University of Vienna, compared the role of tabloids with political thrillers: a good thriller is relaxing because it eases the tension which it produced. Haider and the tabloids are acting in the same manner. First, they load national feelings with negative emotions; then they present easy solutions with Haider.

Fritz Hausjell of the University of Vienna presented a few theses about the connection of mass media to fear of foreigners and right-wing extremism: first, the mass media unconsciously prepare the basis for these emotions by following the principles of reporting, e.g. the principle of giving priority to the exceptional—in this case Turkish speed maniacs, Hungarian swindlers or Polish thieves. This leads to the widespread opinion that foreigners in general have a greater propensity for crimes than Austrians. Second, some papers openly support right-wing extremism by consciously hallmarking foreigners or by exaggeration. In April 1991, the Austrian borders were opened for Poles, and *Der Standard* wrote of some 20,000 Poles coming to Austria, *Die Presse* and *Kurier* of some 50,000 and 100,000 respectively, and in the *Kronen Zeitung* the number of Poles amounted to 500,000; *Kronen Zeitung* called it "an invasion." Third, daily reports are usually oriented towards events and—unlike quality papers—tabloids do not present thorough analyses of these events. And if they pretend to offer analysis, it can be like the *Kronen Zeitung's* Nimmerichter quoted above in "Methods of Mass Murder." Finally, we find more and more competition among mass media, encouraging papers like *Kronen Zeitung* and *täglich alles* to favor sensationalism. These things are true in other countries, as well. But with *Kronen Zeitung* and *täglich alles*, the Austrian media landscape has two dominant tabloids that reach almost half of all Austrian readers.

FURTHER LITERATURE

Wolfgang Benz, *Rechtsextremismus in Deutschland. Voraussetzungen, Zusammenhänge, Wirkungen* (Frankfurt/Main: Fischer Verlag, 1994).

Ernst Bruckmüller, *Österreichbewußtsein im Wandel. Identität und Selbstverständnis in den 90er Jahren* (Vienna: Signum Verlag, 1994).

Dokumentationsarchiv des Österreichischen Widerstandes, ed., *Handbuch des österreichischen Rechtsextremismus* (Vienna: Deuticke, 1993).

Rainer Fromm and Barbara Kernbach, *. . . und morgen die ganze Welt? Rechtsextreme Publizistik in Westeuropa* (Marburg: Schuren, 1994).

"Gesellschaft für politische Auklärung/DÖW," *Strategien gegen den Rechtsextremismus* (Innsbruck, 1994).

Wolfgang Gessenharter, *Kippt die Republik? Die Neue Rechte und ihre Unterstützung durch Politik und Medien* (Munich: Knaur, 1994).

Wolfgang Kowalsky and Wolfgang Schroeder, *Rechtsextremismus. Einführung und Forschungsbilanz* (Opladen: Westdeutscher Verlag, 1994).

Astrid Lange, *Was die Rechten lesen. Fünfzig rechtsxtreme Zeitschriften. Ziele, Inhalte, Taktik* (Munich: Beck, 1993).

Fritz Plasser and Peter A. Ulram, *Ausländerangst als parteien- und medienpolitisches Problem*, unpublished manuscript, Vienna, 1992.

Wolfgang Purtscheller, *Die Ordnung, die sie meinen. "Neue Rechte" in Österreich* (Vienna: Picus,1994).

_____, *Aufbruch der Völkischen. Das braune Neztwerk* (Vienna: Picus, 1993).

How the Austrian People's Party Dealt with the Holocaust, Anti-Semitism and National Socialism after 1945

"The Jews of Austria will be able to prove their noble sentiments directly to our entire people."[1]

Walter Manoschek

The Founding Myth of the Second Republic

The founding myth of the Second Republic was based upon the Austrian interpretation of the Moscow Declaration which had been agreed upon by the Foreign Ministers of the three Allied powers on 30 October 1943.[2] This tersely worded and, at the same time, equivocal statement maintained:

a) that Austria was the first free country to fall victim to Hitler's policy of aggression;

b) that Germany's occupation of Austria is considered null and void;

c) that Austria indeed bears an inescapable responsibility for its participation in the war on the side of Hitler's Germany.[3]

The declaration, conceived by the Allies as a call to arms on the dormant Austrian resistance movement, was reinterpreted in 1945, based upon pragmatic political considerations by the three founding political parties in Austria (ÖVP, SPÖ and KPÖ), into a program-legitimizing statement of principles for the national rebirth of Austria, and subsumed within the formula of the "occupation of Austria" which brought enormous benefits from the point of view of international law. The occupation theory proceeds from the assumption that Austria, despite its annexation by and incorporation into the Third Reich, continued to exist as a lawful state. Only its capacity to contract as an sovereign nation had been lost through the occupation. Therefore, based upon international law, responsibility could neither accrue to Austria stemming from its participation in the war, nor could it be regarded as a successor state to the Third Reich.[4]

Out of this international legal construction, the "self-infantilization"[5] of the "first victim of National Socialist expansion policy" could now be established as a basis for the state and built upon further. While, in the Federal Republic of Germany, the assumption of the status of legal successor to the Third Reich brought with it, along with the claim upon the reunification of Germany, the burden of responsibility for the National Socialist regime, the occupation theory was promoted in Austria to a magic formula which served, not only as a diplomatic guideline for the *Staatsvertrag* negotiations with the Allies, but also as a barrier to ward off the reparation and indemnification claims of Jewish victims[6] and—in the long term, surely the most significant factor—as a legitimizing point of departure in the Austrian process of nation building following 1945.

A clear expression of the integrating effect of this national political formula is the fact that the conflict over historical interpretation which took place in the Second Republic between the ÖVP and the SPÖ concerned itself, not with the period of Nazi domination, but rather with the time between 1933 and 1938. At the date of the annexation (12 March 1938), conflicting lines of interpretation cease. In its place emerged a homogenous, identity-endowing view of history which was subjected to only partial erosion by occasional foreign policy necessities.

ÖVP and National Socialism

The assessment of Austria's role as the first victim of Nazi Germany was equally shared by the three founding parties of the Second Republic (ÖVP, SPÖ and KPÖ) and was ultimately successfully prevailed upon the occupation powers: on the very evening before the signing of the Austrian *Staatsvertrag* in May 1955, ÖVP Foreign Minister Leopold Figl succeeded in compelling the signatories to delete the clause on the subject of Austria's joint responsibility for World War II and, thereby, officially established Austria's postwar status as a victim of National Socialism.[7] Even more remarkable is a passage from a radio speech by ÖVP

Chancellor Julius Raab on the day of the signing of the *Staatsvertrag* (15 May 1955), in which he solemnly declaimed: "Let this now be a symbol that, after ten years, Austria is liberated again."[8]

The ÖVP historical conceptualization regarding the period of Nazi domination was assembled before the beginning of the Second Republic from a conglomerate of set pieces from history, international law and the philosophy of history. Austrofascism from 1933-34 until March 1938 was stylized as the heroic struggle against National Socialism; the annexation in March 1938 was interpreted exclusively as an occupation through the use of force by Nazi Germany which had, indeed, been furthered by the appeasement policy of the western powers;[9] Austria's participation in the system of Nazi domination from 1938 to 1945 was disavowed with the stereotypical international legal formulation of the occupation of Austria, and National Socialist ideology and the form of its regime was—in vehement distinction to Germany—apodictically characterized as "contrary to the essence of Austria."

This attitude was clearly expressed in a programmatic article entitled "We and National Socialism" in the November 1945 issue of *Österreichische Monatshefte*, the theoretical organ of the ÖVP:

> We protest . . . in the strongest possible terms, against the assertion—regardless of whether made within Austria or from abroad—that the majority of Austrians ever really favored National Socialism. If this had been the case, our tiny land would never have been able to defend itself for five years [Author's Note: the reference is to 1933-38] against the unrestrained, ten-fold numerical superiority of the Third Reich . . . . There is no idea or movement that is more antithetical to the innermost Austrian essence than National Socialism . . . . The eternal righteousness, that ultimately presides over all peoples, has kept Austria from sharing the fate of the Third Reich. While this thousand-year Reich disappeared like a phantom in smoke and mist after 12 years of existence, Austria has . . . risen again out of the ashes of this war. This is, amid all the misery and destruction, a victory of the Austrian spirit and the Austrian people.[10]

Nor did the ÖVP undertake a revision of these patriotic myths in the 1980s during the discussion of Austria's historic identity. In a comprehensive analysis of the historic-political discourse within Austrian print media on the occasion of the *"Gedenkjahr* 1988," Heidemarie Uhl comes to the following conclusion: "The glorifying view of the past, becoming at times a patriotic pathos which rejects any criticism of the victim theory, is the generally accepted stance of the ÖVP."[11]

Consequently, even in the *"Gedenkjahr* 1988," oversaturated with historical reportage, the period 1938 to 1945 constituted for ÖVP print media "no topic for historic representation."[12] This phase of history was "consistently by-passed or mentioned only in connection with resistance."[13]

The ÖVP and its Anti-Semitic Heritage

That such a conception of history precludes an analytical confrontation with National Socialist extermination of Jews in general and Austrian involvement in particular is quite obvious. In equating anti-Semitism with National Socialist persecution of Jews, the ÖVP succeeded, moreover, in evading a confrontation with its own genuinely anti-Semitic heritage. The Catholic-Austrian anti-Semitism of the ÖVP's Christian socialist predecessor party could be marginalized before the backdrop of National Socialist death camps. The political anti-Semitism of the Christian Socialist party (after 1933-34, the Austrofascist regime) was an integral component of the party's ideology.[14] The demands for discrimination against and exclusion of Jews, for the introduction of a "numerus clausus" in institutions of learning and in public service, for the ban on the recruitment of Jews by the Austrian army were not just radical verbal forms of anti-Semitism.[15] They also had their concrete expression in the numerous bills proposed in Parliament by Christian socialist representatives that had as their goal the legal relegation of Jews to the status of second-class citizens.[16] The anti-Semitic dichotomy "Jewish"-"German (nationalist)" was explicitly inscribed in the program of the Christian Socialist party, remaining valid from 1926 until the dissolution of the party in 1934: "As a nationalistically oriented party, the Christian Socialist party demands the cultivation of the German [sic!] way of life and opposes the predominance of the undermining Jewish influence upon spiritual and economic life."[17]

A comparative analysis of the Catholic daily press in Germany and Austria in the years before the National Socialist seizure of power in Germany clearly shows what an important place anti-Semitism had assumed within the political culture of the Christian socialist camp: While in the German Catholic press, articles which can be classified as anti-Jewish were marginal, in Christian socialist newspapers in Austria, they made up approximately 50 percent of all statements on the subject, while statements in these newspapers tending to be positive, pro-Jewish are completely absent. In the Catholic press in Germany before 1933, the reportage on the subject of Jews was for the most part neutral, with those articles tending to be pro-Jewish roughly balanced out by those tending to be anti-Jewish.[18]

The extent to which Christian socialist anti-Semitism was identical in its objectives with the Jewish policy of the early National Socialist regime can be seen in an article commissioned in 1933 by the Christian Socialist party and written by its chairman, Emmerich Czermak. Czermak called for—a few months after the National Socialists had assumed power in Germany—the "partial solution to the Jewish question" by means of compulsory emigration of Jews to Palestine and Madagascar, and registered with satisfaction the fact that the National Socialists in Germany placed "the highest value upon impeding the continued existence of Jews in Germany" and "want, in all seriousness, to remove them entirely from German territory, to force them to pack their bags."[19] The political rivalry and competition of the emerging Austrofascism with National Socialism thus by no means precluded a common view in the "Jewish question"—the National Socialist, anti-Semitic propaganda rag *Stürmer*, for example, found that Czermak's article had to be taken seriously, above all because Czermak was a leading member of the Christian Socialist party.[20]

Often dismissed as innocuous, "Christian socialist anti-Semitism, labeled as merely economic, ethnic and confessional, cannot be separated from its racist preconceptions."[21] As an interpretational model of social reality, Christian socialist anti-Semitism differed "neither in its depiction of the foe nor in its essential function from völkisch-anticlerical anti-Semitism."[22] In the weeks following the annexation in the spring of 1938, this native Austrian hate for Jews was coupled with the racist, völkisch state ideology of National Socialism and led to pogrom-like anti-Semitic rioting the likes of which had not been seen in Germany.[23]

ÖVP and Anti-Semitism after 1945

In contrast to Germany, the general political background conditions in postwar Austria permitted an "externalization of the preconditions, content and consequences of National Socialism."[24] The "nation building process" made possible by the political power relationships among the Allied occupation powers demanded the constitution and development of a national identity whose most essential element was its clear demarcation from Germany and, in particular, from the seven years of collective "greater German history." While in postwar Germany, the treatment of Jews became the "touchstone of genuine democratic convictions" or even a sheer "categorical imperative,"[25] it sufficed in Austria to prohibit the resurrection of the political anti-Semitism of the interwar period.

By no means, though, did this imply that the ÖVP's policies would be free of anti-Semitism. In the person of former concentration camp prisoner and ÖVP founder Leopold Kunschak, "this true Austrian patriot and genuine democrat,"[26] as his fellow party member Felix Hurdes characterized him in 1945, the personal continuity of Christian socialist anti-Semitism remained in effect at the beginning of the Second Republic. Even then, as president of the national assembly, Kunschak saw no grounds for denying the anti-Semitism which had already been his political practice in the First Republic: in December 1945 before a crowd of thousands protesting the presence of Jewish-Polish "displaced persons," Kunschak declared "he had always been an anti-Semite and continued to be one. Jews, neither domestic nor foreign, had any business in Austria."[27]

Undisguised anti-Semitic statements of this kind remained, at least in public, the exception within the political discourse. The extermination carried out in the name of this policy had placed a taboo upon the open acknowledgment of anti-Semitism. The discussion of Jewish subjects was generally avoided in the ÖVP. "The 'Jewish question' in postwar Austria (amounted to) a story of silence"[28] in the ÖVP as well. This fundamental strategy of avoidance was abandoned only when concrete political motivations demanded that an explicit or implicit position be taken on a Jewish issue.

A 1946 discussion in the ÖVP's theoretical organ exemplifies the contextual shift that placed the question of the Jews in Austria after the Holocaust into an exclusively material context of the so-called reparations payments is provided by a discussion carried on in the

ÖVP's theoretical organ in 1946. In an article entitled "The Jewish Question," Artur Rosenberg pointed out that

> . . . those atrocities would never have been possible if a portion of the population had not actively taken part in them and if a great number of people had not hidden behind a wall of non-involvement. Out of indifference to the stranger and to the obligation and responsibility of human beings for what took place, they turned away their eyes or, simply out of a lack of integrity and courage as citizens, they buckled under . . . . After a time such as this, it cannot suffice to attempt to find the solution to the Jewish question in the avoidance of its discussion . . . . The sense of responsibility for what has happened must be aroused in everyone—in those who actively took part, as well as in those whose tacit complicity made it possible. These are moral reparations. It is the decisive one. From this alone can flow material reparations which possesses value and durability . . . . It is not enough to deny the existences of a Jewish question in order to simply make it go away.[29]

With this, Rosenberg had touched a sore spot. In a footnote, the editors characterized the essay cautiously "as a first important contribution to the discussion of such a multifaceted complex of issues, without endorsing the exposition in all its details."[30] Three months later, in May 1946, the topic was taken up again—though not as an "important contribution," but rather as a short gloss. The article, signed only with the initials W.O., first alludes indirectly to the general conformity of opinion between the ÖVP and the SPÖ in the treatment of the Jewish question, whereby the author makes reference to an article in the social democratic *Arbeiter Zeitung*. In it, a "special treatment of the Jews" (sic!) was rejected based on the argument that "it is a disputed contention that the Jews had the highest priority in the Nazi order of persecution." The Jews were thus victims of equal rank; to accord them a special legal or financial status "would only serve to revive racism with completely reversed premises." In harmony with his coalition partner, the author in the ÖVP organ concurred that "as in the view taken above . . . it seems to be generally acknowledged that the suffering of Jewry throughout Europe has a certain amount of truth to it." Not content to leave it at that, he closes by issuing an blatant threat: "The Jews of Austria will be able to prove their noble sentiments directly to our entire people through the temperate behavior that they display to us. With a great deal of tact and a consciousness of their responsibilities, and with little noise and propaganda, the work at hand must be attended to if the centuries-old mean instincts of the masses are not to be reawakened, as is now taking place in Hungary and Poland. When we finally reach the point when the question of the momentary victor and vanquished no longer must be asked, then we will know that we have the last round of a long, calamitous dispute behind us."[31]

With the demand for "temperate behavior" as proof of "noble (Jewish) sentiments," the author's insinuation was to the deliberations then in process over a law governing the restitution of property and assets confiscated during the time of National Socialism, which most directly affected that portion of the population defined as Jewish by the Nuremberg racial laws.[32] This disciplinary admonishment was even more infamous in light of the fact that the restitution laws contained no provision for financial payments by the state,[33] but rather only mandated the return to their rightful owner of assets robbed by the National Socialists.

A completely different tone, though, was struck by the ÖVP organ when addressing the former National Socialists. After the ÖVP was unsuccessful in achieving its demand to grant voting rights to simple NSDAP members for the first national assembly elections in December 1945, these future potential voters were courted with the greatest deference:

Not everyone who was a member or candidate for membership in the NSDAP can be regarded as a true National Socialist . . . . Certainly, these people can not be labeled as heroes and martyrs, but to indiscriminately defame them and to exclude them from normal economic and civic life is contrary to the general interest . . . . Another chapter is the question of reparations and the equitable distribution of the burdens and sacrifices caused by National Socialism . . . . Just as we, party members and candidates for membership who are not personally incriminated, are prepared to show understanding, so must we demand of you in this issue of reparations and burdens the greatest understanding . . . . These burdens include not only financial payments, but also material and personal sacrifices of all kinds, which have resulted from the current extraordinary circumstances. No party member should consider it unjust, for example, that, when someone is required to give up all or a part of his housing, a party member and not a concentration camp prisoner or Nazi victim should be called upon first. He will loyally accept claims of this kind by those who suffered under the Nazis and by victims of the bombing. This has nothing to do with the personal defamation of unincriminated party members; rather, it is a purely objective question of fairness and equity.[34]

The sympathy for the *Ariseur*, so clearly evoked as early as 1945, quickly developed in the following year into a partisanship for the legal claims of former National Socialists. The ÖVP provincial party convention in Salzburg declared the subject of "reparations" to be a matter of the highest priority—indeed, not reparations for Jews, but for former National Socialists. The catalog of demands read: "We call for reparations for those who have been punished for political reasons, and especially for those retirees today eking out a meager existence on unlawfully reduced pensions."[35] With their view aimed at the ballots to be cast by former NSDAP members who would again have the right to vote in the 1949 national assembly elections, the ÖVP from the end of 1948 openly supported the *Ariseure*, who had banded together in an "Association of Those Affected by Restitution."[36]

In 1955, the election issue of the ÖVP newspaper in Linz summed up the party's good works on behalf of the National Socialists: under the leadership of the ÖVP, the sanctions against National Socialists had been de facto lifted much earlier than in the other Austrian provinces; the dismissal of National Socialist government officials was rescinded as early as 1947, they received credit for their time out of office, and the pay cuts they suffered due to loss of seniority were made up by personal stipends through administrative channels; Allied decrees, in particular the objections against laws benefiting Nazis, were informally circumvented and the question of illegality was resolved "in the most favorable sense" for the National Socialists.[37]

In the following decades as well, the subject of "reparations" served repeatedly as an occasion for anti-Semitic imputations. When, in 1966, a report appeared in a publication of the World Jewish Congress on the subject of the revival of anti-Semitism in Austria, the ÖVP-aligned *Oberösterreichische Nachrichten* commented: "The demand to raise and expand reparations payments to the victims of Nazism casts a peculiar light over this entire peculiar report . . . . Is, in this one demand, the significance of all the other demands to be found?"[38] Former ÖVP Foreign Minister Karl Gruber was still beating this drum more than twenty years later, when he implied that the attacks by Waldheim's Jewish opponents were merely an expression of the desire for additional "reparations payments."[39]

The ÖVP and the Emigrants

The ÖVP endeavored, particularly during election campaigns, to accentuate its image as the party of Austrian patriotism. An ÖVP brochure from 1954 resorted to a literary style along the lines of the "world Jewish conspiracy" to harangue against the "subversive hegemony of the emigrants" in the SPÖ, which, led by "Dr. Wilhelm Rosenzweig, age 45, born . . . near Tarnapol, Hebrew . . . and the SPÖ emigrant clique under the leadership of Dr. Oskar Pollak . . . resorting to their power-grabbing methods . . . which seem positively talmudistic."[40]

The ÖVP had also quickly learned how to bring well-targeted anti-Semitic codes into play. As early as the 1945 election campaign, Leopold Figl, top candidate on the ÖVP ticket, characterized the emigrants as those who had "found it more comfortable to sit in their club chairs than to suffer for Austria."[41] In the 1949 campaign, the first in which the parties were competing for the votes of the former National Socialists, leading ÖVP politician and later Chancellor Alfons Gorbach, himself severely wounded in combat on the front in World War I and a concentration camp prisoner during the Nazi period, fought for the veterans' votes with a clear comparison: "Nowhere, during the events of the recent past, was there so much genuine decency, so much selfless performance of duty as there was among the soldiers of this war . . . . The emigrant gentlemen can spread all the moralistic poison they want; those individuals out on the battlefield who withstood the severest test of their manhood know better what decency is than those who scampered to safety overseas at the first sign of trouble . . . . I say that the emigrants have no right to an opinion in the question of the National Socialists."[42]

With the entry of Kreisky upon the political stage, the ÖVP's anti-Semitic attacks were shifted to him personally. Thus, on the occasion of the provincial assembly elections in Styria in 1961, Heribert Pölzl, top ÖVP candidate in eastern Styria, attacked then Foreign Minister Kreisky by name with the following words: "He almost believes that if he [Kreisky] emigrated to Israel, he could become foreign minister there within ten years."[43] In the 1971 national assembly election campaign, the ÖVP put up posters advertising their top candidate Josef Klaus as "A True Austrian." Even the CSU Academy in Munich interpreted this poster as anti-Semitic: "The pointed style of representation and the text 'A True Austrian' awake associations of Kreisky's Jewish heritage and emigration . . . . Since the attack does not openly and directly address Kreisky . . . the viewer does not clearly notice that possibly residual subliminal anti-Semitism is meant to be activated here."[44] The ÖVP leadership in Styria, however, pointed out the "educational" objective of the poster: "We certainly did not wish to disparage anyone personally on racial or religious grounds, but we did want to very clearly portray the differences between the ÖVP and its candidates compared to the other parties. It is a fraud and a deception of the public to blur these differences or to even deny their existence."[45] And in the next election campaign as well, Burgenland ÖVP chief Soronics again posed the by now stereotypical question: "Who is the better patriot—the man who remained in Austria or the one who abandoned Austria?"[46] It hardly needs to be emphasized that these anti-Semitic utterances led to neither resignations nor any other political consequences for ÖVP politicians.[47]

The list of examples cited here could easily have been much longer[48] to bolster the thesis that the ÖVP after 1945, though not following suit with the anti-Semitic platform of its predecessor party from the interwar era, understood quite well how to instrumentalize anti-Semitic stereotypes for party and political campaign purposes. Anti-Semitic prejudices were not only used covertly by the ÖVP during the Second Republic; rather, they were quite openly used as a weapon aimed at specific political targets.

A First Attempt at Philo-Semitism

The Austrian-Jewish relationship can not be considered as the standard measure for the democratic character of the political culture in this land. For almost fifty years, this relationship could remain undefined and restricted by a taboo. In contrast to the Federal Republic of Germany, there arose no political or social necessity for the development of a philo-Semitism, either in public discourse or in the practice of rituals of remembrance. The attempts at public ritualizing appeared correspondingly awkward and, thereby, even more deceptive. Using the example of the message of salutation of leading ÖVP politicians on the occasion of the Jewish New Year celebration of the year 5721 (1960 by Christian reckoning), several elements of a specific Austrian philo-Semitic habitus[49] can be deciphered.

The Jews as a Part of the Austrian "Victims Collective"

As a former concentration camp prisoner, ÖVP national Chairman Alfons Gorbach referred most directly to the ostensibly mutual fate shared by "the Austrians" and the Jews during National Socialism: "What I went through during those hard times in the concentration camp, suffering bitterly together with members of the Jewish people, is something that is never forgotten, but extends beyond the narrow limits of barbed wire. And it remains to this day when all of us Austrians, regardless of heritage or religion, are working together to build a better future . . . . And we must still continue to carry on today, under the burden of this vanquished political regime."[50]

Jewish Fellow Citizens versus the Jewish People

While Gorbach declared Austrian Jews to be an integral component of the "Austrian Victims Collective," ÖVP General Secretary Hermann Withalm referred unmistakably to the difference between the (Christian) "Austrian people" and their, in a legal sense, equal "Jewish fellow citizens": "On the occasion of a pilgrimage to the Holy Land, I had the opportunity in Israel to gain a first hand impression of the enormous industriousness and will to work shown by your people. I saw for myself the truly imposing effort to build up this young state and I would like to express to you my highest esteem . . . . And likewise, I have repeatedly seen to my great satisfaction that our Jewish fellow citizens since the year 1945 have contributed mightily to the reconstruction of our Austrian fatherland."[51] In Withalm's case, the Austrian Jews were unambiguously relegated to the role of a "guest people."

The "Good" Jews

As in the case of the ÖVP general secretary, ÖVP Chancellor Julius Raab emphasized his satisfaction with the positive behavior of the Austrian Jews after 1945. He also sent along his best wishes to "our fellow citizens of the Jewish faith" and hoped "that the coming year would bring, for all Austrians, peaceful and steady development of our cultural and economic life, in consideration of our work since 1945, to which the members of the Jewish community in all fields and walks of life have so meritoriously contributed."[52]

Fifteen years previously, the ÖVP's theoretical organ had demanded "temperate behavior" on the part of Austrian Jews. The high marks that were passed out by ÖVP politicians in 1960 to the Austrian Jews can well be taken as a sign that they were quite satisfied with that behavior and that the Jews were well on their way to proving "their noble sentiments to our entire people." With this background in mind, the lines written in 1956 by a member of the Jewish community on the subject of the Austrian-Jewish relationship take on a poignant clarity: "In stillness and in silence, the Jews of Austria are rejected, shunted aside and forced into a social and spiritual isolation. There is no loud, to say nothing of rabid, anti-Semitism, no riots, but there is a 'wall of coldness' which can hardly be broken through. In Austria today, no one really gives the slightest concern to cultivating good relations with the Jews, to impart to them a feeling of inner moral security within the lap of Austrian democracy."[53]

Thirty years after this summing up of the state of affairs, during the course of the presidential campaign of ÖVP candidate Kurt Waldheim, the Austrian-Jewish relationship suddenly turned politically virulent. Under the watchful eyes of the world public, Austria's dealings with its National Socialist past and its current relations to the Jews became a barometer for the real democratic convictions and maturity of this land. While the ÖVP in its entirety continued to hold fast to the historical myth of "the first victim of National Socialism," it was Kurt Waldheim himself who pointed out to the Austrian Jews their place within the Austrian society, a conceptualization which did not go beyond constitutionally guaranteed basic civil rights: "Our Jewish fellow citizens have an unrestricted right to a life of peace, respect and equality within our midst."[54]

NOTES

1. *Österreichische Monatshefte*, Organ der ÖVP-Bundespartei Leitung, June 1946.

2. A synopsis rich in material on the interpretation of the Moscow Declaration by the "founding fathers" of the Second Republic is provided by Günter Bischof, "Die Instrumentalisierung der Moskauer Erklärung nach dem 2. Weltkrieg," *Zeitgeschichte* 20 (November/December 1993): 345-66.

3. The document is reprinted in Gerald Stourzh, *Geschichte des Staatsvertrages 1945-1955: Österreichs Weg zur Neutralität* (3rd ed., Graz-Vienna-Cologne: Styria, 1985), 214.

4. See also Stephan Verosta, *Die internationale Stellung Österreichs: Eine Sammlung von Erklärungen und Dokumenten aus den Jahren 1938 bis 1947* (Vienna: Manz, 1947), 1-8.

5. Ernst Hanisch coined this term. See Ernst Hanisch, "Gab es einen spezifisch österreichischen Widerstand?" *Zeitgeschichte* 12 (September/October 1985): 340.

6. See also Robert Knight, "Ich bin dafür, die Sache in die Länge zu ziehen": *Die Wortprotokolle der österreichischen Bundesregierung von 1945 bis 1952. Über die Entschädigung der Juden* (Frankfurt am Main: Athäneum 1988); Brigitte Bailer, *Wiedergutmachung—Kein Thema: Österreich und die Opfer des Nationalsozialismus* (Vienna: Löcker, 1993).

7. Lonnie R. Johnson, "Die österreiche Nation, die Moskauer Deklaration und die völkerrechtliche Argumentation," *Jahrbuch des Dokumentationsarchivs des österreichen Widerstandes (1988)*: 49-50.

8. Quoted from Susanne Breuss, Karin Liebhart, Andreas Pribersky, "Österreiche Nation, österreiches Nationalbewußtsein und österreichische Identität, " in *Handbuch des österreichischen Rechtsextremismus*, ed. Dokumentationsarchiv des österreichischen Widerstandes (1st ed., Vienna: Deuticke, 1993), 547.

9. See, for example, the statement of ÖVP Chancellor Leopold Figl during the *Staatsvertrag* negotiations in London in January 1947, in which he characterized Austria as a victim of this policy of appeasement since, following the annexation, a "military reaction by the major powers completely failed to materialize and they managed to mount only a weak diplomatic response," in Eva-Marie Csáky, *Der Weg zur Freiheit und Neutralität: Dokumente zur österreichen Außenpolitik* (Vienna: Österreichische Gesellschaft für Außenpolitik und internationale Beziehungen, 1980), Documents 52, 123.

10. Carl Hollenburg, "Wir und der Nationalsozialismus," *Österreichische Monatshefte* 1 (November 1945): 10.

11. Heidemarie Uhl, *Zwischen Versöhnung und Verstörung: Eine Kontroverse um Österreichs historische Identität fünfzig Jahre nach dem "Anschluß"* (Vienna-Cologne-Weimar: Böhlau, 1992), 72.

12. Uhl's résumé of the reportage of the three ÖVP Bundesländer newspapers *Neue Volkszeitung Kärnten, Salzburger Volkszeitung* and *Neue Tiroler Zeitung*, Uhl, *Versöhnung*, 386.

13. Evaluation of the ÖVP organ *Neues Volksblatt*, Uhl, *Versöhnung*, 359.

14. On the history of Catholic-Christian socialist anti-Semitism during the Habsburg monarchy, see Peter Pulzer, *Die Entstehung des politischen Antisemitismus in Deutschland und Österreich 1867 bis 1914* (Gütersloh: Mohn, 1966).

15. A headline in the *Reichspost*, the official organ of the Christian Socialist party, read: "Jewish republic or German republic—the fateful question of the present and the future," *Reichspost*, 26 September 1919.

16. See Anton Staudinger, "Katholischer Antisemitismus in der ersten Republik", in *Eine zerstörte Kultur: Jüdisches Leben und Antisemitismus in Wien seit dem 19. Jahrhundert*, ed. Gerhard Botz, Ivar Oxaal and Michael Pollak (Buchloe: dvo, 1990), 247-270.

17. Quoted from Klaus Berchtold , ed., *Österreichische Parteiprogramme 1866-1966* (Vienna: Verlag für Geschichte und Politik, 1967), 376.

18. Walter Hannot, *Die Judenfrage in der katholischen Tagespresse Deutschlands und Österreichs 1923-1933* (Mainz: Matthias-Grünewald-Verlag, 1990), 283.

19. Emmerich Czermak, "Verständigung mit dem Judentum?" in *Ordnung in der Judenfrage*, ed. Nikolaus Hovorka (Vienna-Leipzig: Reinhold-Verlag, 1933), 55.

20. *Stürmer*, 11 November, 1933.

21. Staudinger, "Katholischer Antisemitismus," 251.

22. Ibid., 269.

23. Hans Safrian, Hans Witek, eds., *Und keiner war dabei: Dokumente des alltäglichen Antisemitismus in Wien 1938* (Vienna: Picus, 1988).

24. Rainer Lepsius, quoted in Werner Bergmann, Rainer Erb, *Antisemitismus in der Bundesrepublik Deutschland: Ergebnisse der empirischen Forschung von 1946-1989* (Opladen: Leske + Budrich, 1991), 301.

25. Frank Stern, *Im Anfang war Auschwitz: Antisemitismus und Philosemitismus im deutschen Nachkrieg* (Gerlingen: Bleicher, 1991), 84.

26. Felix Hurdes, "Wie die ÖVP entstand," in *Österreichische Monatshefte* 1 (October 1945): 5.

27. Quoted by Oliver Rathkolb, "Zur Kontinuität antisemitischer und rassistischer Vorurteile in Österreich 1945-1950," in *Zeitgeschichte* 16 (May 1989): 168.

28. Richard Mitten, "Die 'Judenfrage' im Nachkriegsösterreich: Probleme der Forschung," *Zeitgeschichte* 19 (November/December 1992): 357.

29. Artur Rosenberg, "Die jüdische Frage," in *Österreichische Monatshefte* 1 (March 1946): 226-28.

30. Ibid., 226.

31. W.O., "Zur jüdischen Frage," in *Österreichische Monatshefte* 1 (June 1946): 397.

32. On the subject of the domestic and foreign policy background of the restitution laws, see Robert Knight, "Ich bin dafür, die Sache in die Länge zu ziehen"; Robert Knight, "Restitution and Legitimacy in Post-War Austria 1945-1953," in *Leo Baeck Year Book 36* (1991): 425; Brigitte Bailer, "Ohne den Staat damit weiter zu belasten . . . : Bemerkungen zur österreichischen Rückstellungsgesetzgebung," *Zeitgeschichte* 20 (November/Dezember 1993): 367-381.

33. The ÖVP representative and later Minister of Trade Ernst Kolb succinctly expressed the basic attitude of the ÖVP: "Austria has nothing to indemnify, because it hasn't done any wrong," Ernst Kolb, *Stenographisches Protokoll der 14. Sitzung des Nationalrates der Republik Österreich, V. Gesetzgebungsperiode*, 15.5.1946, quoted by Bailer, "Ohne den Staat damit weiter zu belasten," 368.

34. Carl Hollenburg, "Wir und der Nationalsozialismus," in *Österreichische Monatshefte* 1 (November 1945): 10.

35. Protokoll des. 2 Landesparteitages der ÖVP-Salzburg vom 8.11.1946, in Franz Schausberger, Friedrich Steinkellner, eds., *Protokolle der Landesparteitage der Salzburger Volkspartei: Band 1* (1945-1951) (Salzburg: IT-Verlag, 1986), 26-27.

36. Bailer, "Ohne den Staat weiter zu belasten", 372-73.

37. *Heimatruf. Wahlzeitung der ÖVP-Linz*, 17 October 1955.

38. *Oberösterreichische Nachrichten*, 17 September 1966.

39. Karl Gruber, *Meine Partei ist Österreich* (Vienna-Munich: Amalthea, 1988), 328-29.

40. ÖVP-Broschüre, *Die SPÖ und ihr Rosenzweig.* The author gratefully acknowledges Wolfgang C. Müller who made this brochure available.

41. *Das Kleine Volksblatt*, 22 November 1945.

42. Quoted in Manfried Rauchensteiner, *Die Zwei: Die Große Koalition in Österreich 1945 bis 1955* (Graz-Vienna-Cologne: Bundesverlag, 1979), 134-35.

43. Quoted in *Die Gemeinde*, 24 March 1961.

44. Quoted by John Bunzl, Bernd Marin, *Antisemitismus in Österreich: Sozialhistorische und soziologische Studien* (Innsbruck: Inn-Verlag, 1983), 79.

45. Quoted in *Neue Zeit*, 7 February 1970.

46. Quoted in *Arbeiter Zeitung* 2 June 1974.

47. A partial exception was the resignation of Michael Graff as ÖVP general secretary after his statement: "As long as it can't be proven that he (Waldheim) strangled six Jews with his own hands, there's no problem," quoted by *Neue AZ*, 16 November 1987. Graff, however, continued on as an ÖVP representative in the national assembly and the judicial speaker of his party.

48. For an historical analysis of anti-Semitic statements by, among others, ÖVP functionaries during the course of the Waldheim affair, see Ruth Wodak, Peter Novak, Johanna Pelikan, Helmut Gruber, Rudolf de Cillia, Richard Mitten, *"Wir sind alle unschuldige Täter": Diskurshistorische Studien zum Nachkriegsantisemitismus* (Frankfurt am Main: Suhrkamp, 1990); see also Richard Mitten, *The Politics of Antisemitic Prejudice: The Waldheim Phenomenon in Austria* (Boulder-San Francisco-Oxford: Westview, 1992), 198-246.

49. The term "habitus" is used here, following the work of Stern, as a concept "with whose help, the forms of mediation between, on the one hand, social and political realities, and individual mental, linguistic, attitudinal and behavioral forms of reaction on the other, can be interpreted," Stern, *Im Anfang war Auschwitz*, 357-58.

50. *Iskult-Pressenachrichten*, 165 (1960), 5.

51. Ibid., 10. Italicized by the author.

52. Ibid., 3.

53. From an address before the general assembly of the Bundesverband der Israelitischen Kultusgemeinden Österreichs on 17 June, 1956, quoted by *Iskult-Pressenachrichten* 67 (1956), Supplement.

54. Kurt Waldheim, "Gemeinsam für Österreich", speech on 21 May 1986 in Vienna, quoted by Walter Schwimmer, "Zum Vorwurf des Antisemitismus im Wahlkampf", in *Die Kampagne: Kurt Waldheim—Opfer oder Täter? Hintergründe und Szenen eines Falles von Medienjustiz*, ed. Andreas Khol, Theodor Faulhaber, Günther Ofner, (Munich-Berlin: Herbig, 1987), 323.

The Social Democratic *"mémoire volontaire"* and Coming to Terms with the Legacy of National Socialism in Austria

Richard Mitten*

During an official visit to Israel in June 1993, Austrian Chancellor Franz Vranitzky delivered a widely acclaimed speech upon receiving an honorary doctorate from the Hebrew University of Jerusalem. In this address, Vranitzky rejected the notion of "collective guilt" (though to my knowledge no one had made such a charge), but acknowledged an Austrian "collective responsibility," which he defined as "the responsibility of each and every one of us to remember and to seek justice." The social democratic chancellor also reiterated in Israel a motif he had initially embraced in a speech in 1988 commemorating the fiftieth anniversary of Austria's anschluss with Nazi Germany: "[We Austrians] admit to all that has happened in our history and to the deeds of all Austrians, be they good or bad. Just as we claim credit for our good deeds we must beg forgiveness for the evil ones—the forgiveness of those who survived and of the descendants of those who perished."

Though the enthusiasm in Israel over Chancellor Vranitzky's moving words was extensive and genuine, it was not universal.

* This essay is a shortened and slightly revised version of "'Die Sühne . . . möglichst milde zu gestalten': Die sozialdemokratische 'Bearbeitung' des Nationalsozialismus und des Antisemitismus in Österreich," in Werner Bergman, Rainer Erb and Albert Lichtblau, eds., *Schwieriges Erbe. Der Umgang mit Nationalsozialismus und Antisemitismus in Österreich, der DDR und der Bundesrepublik Deutschland.* Frankfurt: Campus-Verlag, 1994 (forthcoming), which contains the evidence and references for all source material quoted here.

During a radio program arranged to inform the public about the historical significance of the Austrian chancellor's visit, an Israeli historian fielded phone-in questions from listeners. The prevailing genial and favorable ambience of this particular program was broken by a discordant question from one caller, who wanted to know "the difference, in shekels, between guilt and responsibility."

This anecdote seems worth mentioning not only because of its irony, but also because it shows the difficulties that subjects like the Holocaust have presented to social democratic politicians in the Austrian Second Republic. Indeed, not only does the social democrats' post-World War II role as a pillar of the Second Republic constitute the most significant contrast to their experience in the First Republic; this new role has also influenced the ways in which Austrian social democracy has come to terms with the legacies of national socialism, anti-Semitism, and the Holocaust.

In this essay I will argue that social democratic interpretations of certainhistorical events or periods (in particular, the histories of the First Republic and of Austria under the Nazi dictatorship) have made possible, or even privileged, a particular conception of how to come to terms with Nazism, anti-Semitism and the Holocaust. Since I assume that there is no single "national socialist past" or even "past" in general, which need only be acknowledged to be reconciled—the fact that Vranitzky felt obliged to reassure his audience that Austrians admitted "to all that has happened in [their] past," is politically revealing, though theoretically naïve—I argue further that a distinctively social democratic coming to terms with the heritage of anti-Semitism and national socialism must consist of the elements of historical consciousness, or historical memory, that can be shared and accepted by the core constituency (in this case members and sympathizers of the SPÖ) as a legitimate and meaningful portrayal of these historical events or periods. This specific social democratic memory, I argue finally, has retained its ideological salience down to the present day, at least for the party faithful, even while governmental responsibilities and the exigencies of international politics have favored the adoption by politically prominent social democrats of a more anodyne consensual remembrance more consonant with the statesmanlike duties they perform today.

Four features of Austrian social democracy before 1934 are indispensable to understanding the framework within which a given social democratic reading of the experience of national socialism or the history of anti-Semitism could even make sense. Together, these four aspects form an allusive reservoir of historical knowledge upon which postwar social democratic leaders drew, as well as a moral fundament upon which the normative aspects of a coming to terms with the Nazi past could be constructed.

First, although the Austro-Marxist leadership of the Social Democratic party in the First Republic designated itself as neither Bolshevik nor reformist (in the sense of its sister party in Germany, the SPD), the Austrian party itself was widely viewed as being on the far left. The goal of the party, according to the Linz program of 1926, remained "the victory over the capitalist, and the construction of a socialist social system," but the social democrats nonetheless pledged themselves to achieving this goal "by means of universal suffrage." The famous passage of the party program which warned that the "working class [might be] forced to employ dictatorial methods to break the resistance of the bourgeoisie," should it attempt to prevent forcibly the party's taking power after winning it by democratic means, was portrayed in Christian social propaganda as a social democratic threat to establish a Soviet-style dictatorship of the proletariat. Such political and ideological conflicts fostered the increasing polarization between the social democrats and the governing Christian socials in the First Republic, which culminated in the civil war of February 1934. It is possible to bracket the question of the accuracy of this portrayal of the social democrats. The point to emphasize is that from the perspective of the right wing inside the SPÖ, the defeat in February 1934 could be plausibly traced, at least in part, to the confrontational and ostensibly uncompromising politics which was identified with the inter-war leadership of Otto Bauer. The greater part of the leadership cadre that supported Bauer was driven from Austria for clearly political reasons; many were later forced to flee the Ostmark for clearly racial reasons, and if not, were deported to concentration camps. In any event, the left-wing leadership of the inter-war period did not survive the Nazi dictatorship. In the SPÖ of the Second Republic, their place was for the most part taken by an alternative leadership cadre, one that had belonged to the more moderate, non-Jewish right wing of the party represented by Karl Renner.

This latter element leads directly to our second point about the Social Democratic party in the First Republic, namely its complex relationship towards anti-Semitism. In terms of its theoretical self-conception, Austrian social democracy opposed discriminatory acts against Jews as Jews and was free of any taint of anti-Jewish prejudice. However, concepts of race and nation shared by some social democratic theories bore a close enough resemblance to racial theories with an extreme right-wing provenance to accommodate a more conspicuously anti-Semitic take. For example, orthodox Marxist conceptions held anti-Semitism to be an ordinary consequence of capitalist development. Thus, the rhetoric of anti-Semitism—Ferdinand Kronawetter's "socialism of fools"—was not infrequently viewed as a confused, but on balance positive sign of anti-capitalist consciousness. Austrian social democrats were also not above pandering to prevalent negative stereotypes about "Jewish capital," either to embarrass their Christian social political enemies for defending this "Jewish capital," or to appeal to workers to fight the common class enemy. This indifferent attitude led the social democratic leadership seriously to misjudge the danger of anti-Semitism in Austrian culture; all the more, as the Jewish leaders of the party who tolerated this attitude did their best to downplay their own Jewish heritage, in a futile and misguided attempt to spare the party criticism that it represented only Jewish special pleading.

Third, the history of their support of an anschluss with Germany even into the Nazi period presented the social democrats in the Second Republic with an infelicitous political patrimony bound to encumber a coming to terms with the national socialist past. The Linz Program, as is well-known, considered "the joining [anschluss] of German-Austria to the German Empire a necessary conclusion of the national revolution of 1918." The Social Democratic party congress in 1933 decided—in view of the Nazis' rise to power—to remove this plank from its program. But Karl Renner's famous "I am voting yes" declaration before to the plebiscite affirming the anschluss in April 1938, as well as Otto Bauer's article in *Der Kampf* the following June, in which he characterized as "reactionary" the "slogan of the re-establishment of the independence of Austria," both weighed heavily on Austrian social democracy in the postwar period.

According to his memoirs, even as late as spring 1943, the idea of rescinding the anschluss came to Adolf Schärf, a future president of independent Austria, suddenly "like an illumination" during a discussion with the visiting German social democrat Wilhelm Leuschner. The social democrats have promoted the popular legend that it was they who pronounced the anschluss idea finally dead; the party's long prior advocacy of the idea, however, would occasionally come back to haunt it in the succeeding years of the Second Republic.

By far the most significant element of social democratic history for coming to terms with National Socialism after the war—and our fourth point—was the experience and, more important, the memory of the years 1934 to 1938, i.e., of the civil war and of the Austro-fascist dictatorship. In its basic outlines—and I am oversimplifying somewhat for brevity's sake—Austro-Marxist theory held fascism to be a symptom of the crisis of capitalism, and emphasized the structural similarities between national socialism and Austro-fascism. Any conception that viewed national socialism as but the German variant of European fascism would necessarily consider Nazi policies towards the Jews as a lower-order phenomenon. Similarly, an analysis which argued that a fascist dictatorship was the ultimate means employed by the bourgeoisie to prevent the working class, through its elected representatives, the social democrats, from "taking power in the democratic republic," would accord Nazi racial policies at best epiphenomenal significance in relation to the determining element of class. Both these aspects of the analysis of fascism had political and pedagogical implications for dealing with the legacy of national socialism. If anti-Semitism is seen as an inessential concomitant of capitalist society, and *a fortiori* if it is not viewed as a constitutive feature of National Socialism, then it is not clear why (or even how) one would justify historically or theoretically any autonomous significance, or even any explicit sensitivity towards the social psychological phenomenon of anti-Jewish prejudice.

These four themes represent a condensed version of the historical legacy with which social democrats, along with the former Christian socials and the Communists, went about their task of establishing and leading a post-Nazi democratic Second Republic. The given military-political framework, together with the putative lessons taught by the *Lagerstraße*, could not but reinforce the already strong political predilection of the national leaders of the SPÖ—above all Karl Renner, Adolf Schärf and Oskar Helmer—towards close collaboration with the other anti-fascist parties in the interests of Austrian independence. As both interlocutors and representatives of the Austrians—with responsibilities to both the Austrians themselves and to the Allied occupying powers—the new government's main tasks were to execute orders of the Allied Council while consolidating and extending the sovereignty of the Austrian state and government as much as possible. One such mission was the eradication of the National Socialist "spirit" [Geist] in Austria, specifically, carrying out de-Nazification in line with perceived Allied wishes (which, however, were not always identical or even consistent). The social democratic founding fathers of the Second Republic could pursue such tasks with aplomb, as they believed themselves unconstrained by any contrary ideological burdens. However, leaders such as Renner, Schärf and Helmer were not only Austrian statesmen, they were also social democratic politicians, even though of a new type. The cooperation with the ÖVP and the communists, which abetted the carrying out of national political objectives, was sometimes difficult to reconcile with the conflicting partisan political aims of these very coalition partners.

De-Nazification in Austria was never limited to the prosecution of seriously incriminated Nazis, but was also explicitly aimed at eliminating the national socialist spirit from Austrian society, a rather more nebulous endeavor altogether. The difficulties which might have arisen with respect to this latter, administratively more elusive task, were allayed to a certain degree by the occupation authorities' tendency to equate the removal of the Nazi spirit with the "de-Prussianization"—i.e., the removal of influences identified with the German state—of Austria. De-Nazification in this broader sense thus came more or less to be equated with the combating of "Pan-Germanism." At the same time, the Allies viewed the anti-democratic features of national socialism as those representing the most onerous legacy and which most needed to be overcome in order to build a stable democratic republic. This coincidence was particularly propitious for the Second Republic's founding fathers: not only could they dissociate themselves from (Nazi) Germany by means of a non-partisan cultivation of Austria's cultural distinctness; they were spared altogether the plight of examining the specifically Austrian roots of national socialism.

The social democrats in the provisional government and then in the first elected coalition government after November 1945 took full advantage of the opportunities this constellation presented. After all, it was Schärf who had first proposed the passage of the first de-Nazification law approved by the Austrian provisional government, the *Verbotsgesetz*, according to which "illegal" Nazis were to be punished for "high treason." "Among the National Socialists," Schärf had argued, "there was a distinction made between those who had been prepared to commit the crime of treason against the Austrian state, and those who had not, in other words, those whose joining the NSDAP did not contravene Austrian interests. Naturally, those who should be considered traitors are those who had been active in the National Socialist party prior to the anschluss, thus essentially [those who were referred to] even during the period of the Third Reich as illegals. Since the National Socialist party, as everyone knows, introduced a new registration procedure for its Austrian membership after the anschluss, and the individual membership application, signed by the applicant, played an important role [in the procedure], there is a list of people in the registration catalogue of the national socialists who boasted of their treason against Austria with their own signature." However, by the time the social democrats assumed government responsibility, even the severity of the punishment foreseen by Schärf for the "illegals" had been moderated considerably. In an address to employees in the presidential office, for example, Renner vowed "to keep the punishment within the bounds of the law and to make it as mild as possible."

This emphasis on the guilt of the "illegal" Nazis was matched by the leniency promised rank-and-file Nazis or fellow travelers. On the one hand, this conviction corresponded to the social democrats' indulgently realistic explanation of the possibilities of independent individual action during the Nazi dictatorship. "Let us not forget," argued Ernst Koref, socialist member of Parliament and mayor of Linz, "that the whole of modern technology was put into service of uninhibited propaganda methods. Thus, if one examines the question soberly, it is not surprising that many people who at the time were unaware of the true nature of national socialism fell into the trap of the Pied Piper of Munich." The understanding accorded the "little Nazis" by the party's political analysis was reinforced by the pragmatic consideration that, as Renner put it, "there is almost no family, also no socialist family—and I use this word for social democrats and communists—that did not have a member or relative who went along with the national socialists."

Soon, however, even this relatively mild recipe for de-Nazification had to be abandoned, as it became clear to the Socialists that no votes were to be won through the vigorous pursuit of the "treasonous" Nazis. On the contrary: all parties, including the SPÖ, tried to outdo the others in the vigor of their advocacy of an amnesty for the "little Nazis," and in their opposition to the revisions the Allies were demanding in the national socialist law that the Austrian parliament had passed in 1946. The 1947 "Action Program" of the SPÖ did demand the "punishment of fascist and National Socialist crimes," but the very same paragraph contained the call for the "integration of the former fellow travelers of both fascist parties into the community of citizens."

The formulation of the problem in this program is significant, for it illustrates quite well the conflicting demands placed upon on people like Schärf in their roles as social democratic statesmen and Social Democratic party leaders. Indeed, only in the context of the political debate about Austro-fascism can one truly speak of a specifically social democratic coming to terms with national socialism.

The experience of February 1934 and the Austro-fascist interlude could serve as a party political trope in a variety of ways. The trauma of February 1934 provided a general explanatory nostrum to account for the ease with which the anschluss was achieved. "The majority of the nation [Volk]," Renner stated in April 1945, "had become indifferent towards the state, and the minority, which had been dressed up as so-called estates [Stände], was naturally too weak to offer resistance. The consequence of this was that Hitler had it easy. Do not think that the working class has forgotten what was done to it." A few years later, Rupert Zechtl, social democratic member of Parliament, offered a similar, though somewhat less polemical view of Austro-fascism as having paved the way for national socialism: "Austro-fascism exploited the desperate economic situation of

hundreds of thousands, in order to deliver the decisive blow to a
democracy which it hated. Material want led to intellectual and
psychological confusion. . . . Democracy in Austria was decimated
and in just a few weeks [after the February 1934 civil war] was
liquidated. All democratic bastions were systematically destroyed.
Victorious Austro-fascism bears the tragic responsibility of having
been the trailblazer for national socialism."

Similarly, the Austro-fascist past of certain ÖVP leaders was
recalled tactically to cast doubts on the individual's democratic
reliability, and to validate the social democrats' own constitutional
credentials in an idiom both provocative and familiar. During the
run-off election for Austrian president in 1951 between Heinrich
Gleissner of the ÖVP and Theodor Körner, the socialist mayor of
Vienna, then Vice-Chancellor Adolf Schärf was quoted in the party
paper as asking "[w]hat guarantee does democracy in Austria have
with Gleissner? Did he not break an oath sworn to the democratic
constitution once already? As a member of the government of
Dollfuss and as the provincial governor of Upper Austria [who was]
installed in an authoritarian manner, is he not guilty and
co-responsible for the incarceration of thousands and tens of
thousands of [his] political opponents? His democratic convictions
only appeared, like lilies of the valley, in the spring of 1945. Who
can give Austria a guarantee that Dr. Gleissner will not once
again—for the umpteenth time—revise his evaluation of democracy?"

Whether the social democrats tacitly alluded to the criminal
nature of the Austro-fascist regime, recalled the embitterment or
indifference of the working class towards the authoritarian
dictatorship, or impugned the democratic credentials of former
Christian social politicians, certain implications for any possible
social democratic coming to terms with the national socialist legacy
seem to follow. How could a social democratic politician credibly
justify imposing an atonement fine, not to mention a more severe
punishment, on broad sections of the population, indeed, how was
such a punishment of former Nazis even conceivable from a social
democratic perspective, if the "crimes" of the Austrian fascist
dictatorship remained unpunished, and ostensible "criminals" like
Julius Raab, Gleissner, and others not only did not suffer any
criminal penalties or political disabilities, but were entitled to enjoy
the highest honors of the Second Republic and were sitting with the

comrades in the same government? I do not wish to argue either that this somewhat cynical approach was the only possible one for Austrian social democracy, or that an alternative social democratic vision of dealing with the Nazi past—drawing on equally potent party antecedents—might even contradict this particular view. I do wish to argue, however, that we are ill served if we underestimate the legitimating power of the realpolitische dimension of the social democratic reading of the Nazi past. Viewed from this perspective, neither the willingness of the SPÖ to recruit former Nazis after 1945 nor Bruno Kreisky's indifference to the Nazi pasts of not fewer than five ministers in his first government should seem particularly surprising.

The trauma of February also significantly influenced the social democratic take on the history of anti-Semitism in Austria. Inasmuch as the dominant social democratic theory of fascism viewed anti-Semitism as an epiphenomenon of capitalist society or even as primitive anti-capitalism, the combating of anti-Jewish stereotypes or prejudices as such would seem not to require, and was not accorded, any independent significance in either the party's program or in politics. On this point, the analyses of the Western Allies, in particular the United States, did not diverge from that of the Austrian social democrats. It would also have been rather odd if the representatives of a democratic country whose own armed forces were racially segregated until 1948 had viewed the combating of ethnic or racial prejudice as constitutive in principle of a democratic political culture.

However, without pressure from the Allies to the contrary, the leading politicians of the Second Republic—including the social democrats—dissolved anti-Semitism as such into Nazi persecution and the attempted extermination of the Jews *tout court*. This conflation had obvious and politically advantageous implications: the status of non-Nazi anti-Semitism before 1938 could be trivialized or defined out of existence, while the Second Republic's explicit repudiation of Nazi racial policies was seen to refute accusations of residual anti-Semitic prejudice into post-Nazi democratic Austria. Moreover, since anti-Semitism was more or less equated with the Nazis' attempted extermination of the Jews, the founding fathers of the Second Republic could evince their genuine anti-Nazi credentials to underscore their personal abhorrence of anti-Jewish sentiment in the post-Second World War era and in some cases to deny its very existence.

Chancellor Leopold Figl from the People's Party, for example, in an interview with the *Shanghai Echo* in 1947, felt it "foolish to deny that Nazi racial propaganda [had] found an echo among some Austrians." However, "when they saw the means by which anti-Semitism was implemented, they were cured. One could safely say that the sympathy with the persecuted Jews eradicated anti-Semitism in Austria. I don't think this question will ever acquire even the slightest significance." Similarly, Theodor Körner, social democratic mayor of Vienna, pilloried (unnamed) newspaper accounts of the "fairy tale" that "after the defeat of national socialism and after the secession from Germany, Austria is still prone to anti-Semitism." "I often have the impression," he wrote in the socialist *Arbeiter-Zeitung*, "that what is involved in these reports is a conscious and deliberate agitation, unleashed just before and during the negotiations of the great powers over a new state treaty with Austria, in order to make us look bad in the eyes of international public opinion and to influence Austria's future fate. Of course, "Körner emphasized, "not one word of these horror stories is true." He wanted, he wrote, to make clear once and for all "that apart from the violent outrages [Ausschreitungen] organized by the Nazis during the period of their rule over Austria, there had never been pogroms against Jews in Vienna." Moreover, "Vienna had never witnessed anti-Semitic outrages of the kind found in other countries, even long before the founding of national socialism was even on the agenda, for the Viennese is a cosmopolitan and thus from the word go not an anti-Semite. Anti-Semitic tendencies are completely foreign to him now as well. Stories about such things are [either] conscious lies or mindless drivel."

In the Second Republic, coming to terms with the history of anti-Semitism in Austria necessarily included the question of the restitution of "Aryanized" property, as well as the more amorphous notion of *Wiedergutmachung*, or compensation beyond the mere restoration of identifiable tangible goods and property. In this connection as well, the memory of February 1934 played a significant role. For apart from any prejudice against Jews which might have influenced the actions of individual ministers (and there is no doubt that individual SPÖ ministers in the coalition government were prejudiced to greater or lesser extents), social democratic memory of the suppression of the party and the trade unions following the civil war provided several moral arguments which could be seen to undercut claims made against the Second Republic with regard to this particular legacy of national socialism. Exemplary of this attitude are Renner's remarks during a meeting of the Cabinet in May 1945: "It would be entirely incomprehensible if every small Jewish businessman or peddler were compensated for his loss, but that there would be no legal remedy for the losses of an entire class and a movement to which 46 percent of the population belonged, which had the accumulated results of their diligent saving and organizational work simply taken away without punishment and [without] compensation. . . . I could not continue to serve tainted by the fact that I had considered the rights of 7 percent of the population sacrosanct, that I had helped enact a special law, but that I had not protected the rights of another, and far greater, part."

The recently published transcripts of the council of ministers reveal a deep-seated cynicism of all three "anti-fascist" parties on the question of *Wiedergutmachung*. The official version of Austria's status as a victim of Nazi Germany, which emphasized above all the elimination of the state of Austria after the anschluss, served as a justification for delaying restitution payments to victims or their descendants, and for keeping those payments approved as small as possible, presumably for economic reasons. However, I would maintain that, in terms of domestic politics, one ought to broaden the applicability of the "victim thesis" beyond the anschluss itself. The arguments Renner advanced need not be seen simply as justifications contrived for the particular occasion and for a particular constituency, which were in turn traceable to anti-Jewish attitudes. On the contrary, they possessed an irrefutable logic which corresponded to the views of most non-Jewish Austrians in the immediate postwar period, and probably correspond to them now. More than that: his remarks delineate the boundaries of the social democratic contingent in the pan-Austrian community of victims, in which no one—and certainly not the Jews—were accorded any privileged status.

Though the above remarks have dealt primarily with the early years of the Second Republic, they are in my view of more than mere historical interest. The way in which the social democrats came to terms with the legacy of national socialism and anti-Semitism in these years determined the conceptual and ideological framework for two generations and more. Indeed, many of the argumentation strategies to be employed by social democratic politicians in the Kreisky-Peter-Wiesenthal affair in the 1970s and the Waldheim affair in the 1980s were foreshadowed in these earlier debates. In fact, I would argue, as late as 1988, the fiftieth anniversary of the anschluss was commemorated by the *Arbeiter-Zeitung's* legatee *A-Z/Tagblatt* in ways that would have been entirely comprehensible to Renner and Schärf. Even fifty years after the event, those Austrian social democrats without governmental responsibility still felt obliged to parry inconvenient allusions to the party's well-known tradition of support for the idea of an anschluss with Germany, while driving home the role of the Christian socials as gravediggers of the democratic First Republic and that of the Austro-fascists as trailblazers of national socialism.

Official commemoration in Western-style democratic states (but not only there) consists of the public propagation of an consensual interpretation of an historical event that also suggests a moral which can be seen to be relevant for the contemporary political culture. In 1988, being against the anschluss of 1938 was far less problematic than commemorating it officially. For any historical interpretation that goes beyond the mere repudiation of Austria's loss of independence must necessarily address the milestones which led to the peaceful incorporation of Austria into the Third Reich. The Second Republic, and the values it purports to enshrine, however, prescribe the normative conceptual and political idiom in which such a commemoration will have to be expressed, if it is to remain consensual. During the fiftieth anniversary commemorations in 1988, social democrats with high political positions sedulously attempted to fulfill their statesmanlike responsibilities in presenting a safely non-controversial reading of the events leading up to the anschluss, even while their paper representing the party's editorial line continued the old polemics. Because of Waldheim's international isolation, Chancellor Vranitzky in effect not only assumed the representative functions abroad assigned the president by the constitution; in 1988, two years into the Waldheim presidency, this meant in addition assuming a role as integrative figure which the embattled incumbent Austrian president could not reasonably fulfill.

As a consequence of the Waldheim affair, and the attendant publicity given to contemporary Austrian history in its train, moral sensibilities—in both Western historical scholarship and in public life generally—have become far different from those prevailing in 1945. It is fair to ask, however, just what the heightened moral sensibilities have brought us, apart from additional scholarly publications. For even if the contemporary Austrian government—particularly its social democratic chancellor—exhibits far more sensitivity towards the feelings of Austrian Holocaust survivors and their descendants (which cannot be doubted), it is nonetheless noteworthy that international pressure requires nothing more, and domestic political imperative will tolerate nothing more, than that the principal change in Austria's attitude, though genuine, remain in the realm of public pronouncement rather than major financial commitment.

To return to the radio call-in show we mentioned at the beginning: I will not hazard an answer, not even a guess, as to the difference, in shekels, between a verbal commitment to recognize the deeds of history, and the restitution which an admission of guilt would presumably enjoin. Nonetheless, our Israeli wit astutely recognized both that the difference could be measured in shekels, and that in 1993 the price was apparently right. Moral responsibility, it seems, revealed itself as an Austrian bargain of a lifetime.

FURTHER LITERATURE

Martin von Amerongen, Bruno Kreisky, und seine unbewältigte Vergangenheit, Graz, 1977.

Robert Knight, ed., "Ich bin dafür, die Sache in die Länge zu ziehen. Die Wortprotokolle der österreichischen Bundesregierung von 1945 bis 1952 über die Entschädigung dder Juden (Vienna, 1988).

Richard Mitten, The Politics of Anti-Semitic Prejudice. The Waldheim Phenomenon in Austria (Boulder, Colorado, 1992).

Helmut Konrad (Hrsg.), Sozialdemokratie und Anschluß. Historische Wurzeln, Anschluß 1918 und 1938, Nachwirkungen (Vienna, 1978).

Richard Mitten, *The Eyes of the Beholder: Allied Wartime Attitudes and the Delimiting of the "Jewish Question" for Postwar Austria*, Tel Aviv Jahrbuch für deutsche Geschichte XXIII/1994, 345-370.

Richard Mitten, Die "Judenfrage"im Nachkriegsösterreich. Probleme der Forschung, Zietgeschichte, 13, 1992, S. 365-367.

Karl Renner, *Österreich von der Ersten bis zum Zweiten Republik* (Vienna, 1953).

Erwin Scharf, *Ich darf nicht schweigen* (Vienna, 1948).

Adolf Schärf, *Österreichs Erneuerung 1945-1955* (Vienna, 1955).

Kurt Shell, *The Transformation of Austrian Socialism* (New York, 1962).

Dieter Stiefel, *Entnazifizierung in Österreich* (Vienna, Munich and Zurich, 1981)

Robert Wistrich, *Socialism and the Jews. The Delimmas of Assimilation in Germany and Austria* (East Brunswick, New Jersey and London, 1982).

Ruth Wodak, Florian Menz, Richard Mitten and Frank Stern, *Die Sprachen der Vergangenheiten. Staatliches Gedenken in österreichischen und deutschen Medien* (Frankfurt, 1994).

Rugh Wodak, Peter Nowak, Johanna Pelikan, Helmut Gruber, Rudolf de Cilla and Richard Mitten, "Wir sind alle unschuldige Täter!" Studien zum Nachkriegsantisemitismus (Frankfurt, 1990).

The FPÖ and the Right

Max Riedlsperger

When I received the invitation to contribute to this forum, I was, coincidentally, reading the lead essay by Alan Brinkley in an *American Historical Review* forum on American conservatism. As I began to formulate thoughts for my own essay, I was struck by the similarities and differences in the scholarly attention to the Right in the United States that Brinkley noted and my own perceptions regarding the treatment of the Austrian Freedom Party (FPÖ), the party of the "new Right," in Austria. Brinkley notes a general ignoring of the Right in the United States, which he attributes to the dominance of historians who have seen twentieth-century American political and cultural history as the story of ". . . the triumph of the progressive-liberal state and of the cosmopolitan sensibility that has accompanied and to a large degree supported it." The Right thus remains ". . . particularly baffling to many of those historians who (as most do) stand outside it and try to make sense of it." The problem, for Brinkley, is to find ". . . a suitable place for the Right—for its intellectual traditions and its social and political movements—within our historiographical concerns."

As in the United States, most currently active Austrian scholars stand outside the Right, but unlike their American counterparts, they have no trouble finding a place for the parties of the third or German-national camp or *Lager* from which the FPÖ emerged—and that is on the extreme Right. For example, in September 1986, only days after Jörg Haider was elected Chairman in a convention showdown with the liberal Norbert Steger, the news magazine *profil* ran a cartoon depicting Haider in Carinthian folkdress, standing before a painting showing another, brown-shirted Jörg Haider strangling his predecessor while wearing a red armband with a partially obscured black insignia on a circular white field. Paralleling the striking success of the FPÖ since 1986 has been a corresponding flood of articles and books comparing Haider with Hitler. *Haiders Kampf* discusses whether the FPÖ chairman can be considered a fascist, a neo-Nazi and a right-extremist with the conclusion implied by its unsubtle title. More recently, the strongly leftist *Dokumentationsarchiv des österreichischen Widerstandes*, which proudly claims to have established the standards for analyzing the Right, tried to give visual emphasis to the content of its new *Handbuch des Österreichischen Rechtsextremismus* by making Jörg Haider its coverboy pictured against a background of the World War I *Reichskriegsflagge*, which has become the symbol of German neo-Nazis.

To accept this view of Haider and his FPÖ is to believe that the continuing string of FPÖ electoral successes, which at this writing extends to sixteen *Landtag* elections and two federal elections, is due to growing neo-Nazi and right-extremism sentiment. To be sure, right-extremism, German-nationalist nostalgia and even neo-Nazism have been part of the political scene in Austria since the founding of the Second Republic, but have been the most marginal factors in electoral behavior.

For purposes of this essay, the contemporary FPÖ will be identified with the Right. It is, however, a new Right that is closer to the "Libertarians," "Moralists" and "Enterprisers" of the United States Right as defined by a recent study of the Times Mirror Center for the People & the Press, than it is to the traditional, Christian-conservative Right or the National Socialist extreme Right of the Austrian past. As in the United States, the dominant political trend over the past decade has been the growth of an antipolitics and antigovernment mood. Unlike the United States where antipolitics, antigovernment sentiment has usually been expressed by nonvoting, the existence of a long, if weak third party tradition in Austria has permitted the FPÖ to become the main vehicle of protest. It is, therefore, the thesis of this essay that the upsurge of the FPÖ since 1986 has much more to do with the growth of political protest and with the collapse of the traditional political *Lager* that has made many more people susceptible to its populist appeal, than with linkages between a Nazi past and a putatively right-extremist drift in the electorate today.

How the FPÖ, which has its roots in revolution on behalf of individual rights and German unification in the nineteenth century, became identified with the extreme Right has to do with the ultimate conflict between the liberal and nationalist ideologies upon which the third *Lager* was based. After 1866, when "German-Austria" was excluded from Bismarck's "small Germany," the national-liberal *Lager*, while retaining its emphasis on individual achievement, freedom of expression and anticlericalism, became stridently nationalistic and decidedly illiberal towards other nationalities and ethnic groups. When the Third Reich, under the leadership of Austria's most famous immigrant, then offered its parties the prospect of inclusion, they went over wholesale to National Socialism, thus casting a shadow that lingers over the FPÖ as their heir. To understand the continuing stigmatization of the FPÖ a half-century after the fall of National Socialism, it is necessary briefly to examine the history of the national-liberal *Lager* in the Second Republic.

In 1945, what Adam Wandruszka once described as the "naturally, or divinely ordained" division of the Austrian political structure into three *Lager* seemed at an end. When the Second Republic was founded, it was based on a partnership between the elites of the Peoples' Party (ÖVP) and the Socialist Party (SPÖ) devised to overcome the differences between their predecessors that had undermined democracy in the First Republic. They were only the contemporary iterations of the Christian conservative and socialist *Lager*, which in the nineteenth century had vertically integrated the still pre-modern elements of Austrian society into discrete and mutually hostile pillars. Despite their commitment to cooperate, neither major party trusted the other sufficiently to risk allowing it sole responsibility for governing. Thus they devised a unique kind of coalition government, known as *Proporz*, in which each received counter-balancing positions in the government, the bureaucracy, public and semi-public industries and corporate bodies in proportion to its representation in Parliament. Watching over each other at every level of public service, the elites of the two parties learned to cooperate horizontally across the cleavages between their two pillars while continuing to mobilize party loyalty downward within their respective *Lager* by appealing to traditional ideological values and exploiting historic prejudices.

One of the consequences of this *consociational* approach to building democracy was the development of what amounted to a new *bi-Lager* ideology. Founded by men and women of both coalition parties who had been persecuted during the Third Reich, one thing they were agreed upon was antifascism. German nationalism, even the idea of a nonpolitical *Kulturnation*, was equated with Nazism and the concept of an Austrian nation was made a *sine qua non* of loyalty to the state. While the *consociational* approach of the ÖVP-SPÖ coalition succeeded in stabilizing the Second Republic in the difficult period following the war, the traditional trifurcation of the Austrian political structure soon reasserted itself. Initially, the ideas that had animated the constituents of national-liberal *Lager* had no more appeal. Nevertheless, a protest movement soon began to form based on the anger of former Nazis guilty of no crimes other than their party membership and who felt themselves too severely punished by the de-Nazification laws of the coalition. They were joined by non-Catholic bourgeoisie and farmers and non-Marxist workers whose continuing hostility towards the ideological legacies of the coalition parties made them susceptible to a new, third party movement. Herbert Kraus, whose Research Institute polls showed as much as 30 percent of the electorate uncommitted to either of the *Lager* parties, thus decided in 1949 to launch the League of Independents (VdU) to create a centrist, liberal, third party alternative to the *"Demokratur"* of the ÖVP-SPÖ coalition.

In the parliamentary election of 1949 the VdU won the largest voter share for a third party until the Haider-led victory of 1990 and the VdU entered Parliament in hopes of becoming an alternative partner for either of the major parties. Indeed, the ÖVP on a number of occasions beginning in 1953 and the SPÖ at least once in the 1960s toyed with the possibility of forming a small coalition with the VdU or its successor, the FPÖ. Always, however, the anxiety among the founders of the Second Republic over having a major party in the opposition and their lack of confidence in the strength of the democracy they were building forced them back to *consociationalism*. The bitterness of their class struggle propaganda vis-à-vis each other was mitigated by the reality of their cooperation, but both defined themselves and the Second Republic *against* the ideology of the national-liberal *Lager*. Even after negotiating with the VdU and later the FPÖ about possible cooperation in secret, both parties continued to impute right-extremism to the FPÖ in public. Seen objectively, the programs of the VdU and later the FPÖ with regard to individual rights, *laissez faire* capitalism, and their regionalist, antistatist hostility towards Vienna are in fact reminiscent of the classic liberal tradition and can hardly be seen as Right in the traditional sense. Moreover, their rejection of private monopolies as well as socialized industry and support for a market economy and European integration were progressive by today's standards. But the insistence of the VdU and the FPÖ that Austria was a part of the German "ethnic and cultural community" and their support for unjustly or excessively punished former Nazis was enough to stigmatize them as Nazi parties reincarnate.

The pillars of pre-modern Austrian society had become skyscrapers of power of the socialist Left and the Christian conservative Right between which the tactics of *consociationalism* had built so many bridges that no light could penetrate to make the ground between them fertile for a liberal, centrist alternative. The VdU disintegrated with many of its supporters making their peace with one of the major parties which, after all, could provide them with the patronage necessary to find housing and jobs. Remaining was a hard core of German-nationals and others who, for various reasons, were unable to stomach that alternative and who then joined in the formation of the FPÖ under ex-National Socialist and Anschluß cabinet minister Anton Reinthaller in 1956.

Reinthaller, however, died less than two years later and was succeeded by the ex-*Waffen*-SS officer Friedrich Peter. Because he automatically had credibility with the German-nationalist Right and war veterans, Peter was able, as he explained to me in an interview, ". . . to again pick up the thread of that which in Austria was broken at the end of the last century—namely the further development of liberalism." This process was accelerated in the 1970s under the pressure of a young group of Peter's proteges who ultimately won acceptance into the Liberal International in 1979, the election of their own Norbert Steger as chairman in 1980, and finally, governmental responsibility in coalition with the SPÖ in 1983.

This escape from the right-wing ghetto could not have occurred without a significant change in the Austrian political landscape. Although the major parties continued to practice the politics of ideological and class division, the Austrian electorate came to accept the basic democratic principle that a change of government from one party to another would not throw the country into civil war. This became evident in 1966 when the ÖVP captured enough of that block of uncommitted voters, identified twenty years before by VdU-founder Herbert Kraus, to govern alone. In 1970, enough of these voters shifted to the SPÖ to permit Bruno Kreisky to build a minority government based on a *quid pro quo* with the liberalizing FPÖ. Had the FPÖ not made the crucial error of rejecting the possibility of a coalition with the SPÖ before the election, perhaps in partnership with the "Sun King" Kreisky, it might have finally received the light long blocked by the shadows of *consociationalism* to permit a strong liberal party to mature. Ironically, despite Kreisky's support and encouragement for Peter, his successful refashioning of the SPÖ as a "catchall" party captured the block of uncommitted voters that the FPÖ needed to become a significant political force. At the same time that the FPÖ was attempting to cultivate an image of itself as a progressive, liberal party, the ÖVP also sought to shed its Christian conservative image and move towards the Left to become a Peoples' Party, not just in name. By the mid-1980s there was such a crowding of the political Center that adherents of all parties were increasingly unable to define themselves as either Right or Left. Ideology as a factor in voting behavior dramatically declined as did identification with a *Lager* and therefore party loyalty.

Although not anticipated, the federal Parliament *(Nationalrat)* election of 23 November 1986 turned out to be a watershed in the political history of the Second Republic. Four months before, however, the only change that seemed likely was the transformation of Austria from a two-and-a-half party system to a two-party system. As a very much junior partner in the social-liberal coalition, the FPÖ had gained no "government bonus" among centrist, middle-class voters for permitting the continuation of socialist rule, and *profil* turned its Chairman, Vice Chancellor Steger, into a laughing-stock by derisively calling him *"der Umfaller."* Polls in the summer showed the party's potential vote at between 1 and 2 percent. Increasingly its right-nationalist voters were, as the party's liberals quipped, to be found "in the central cemetery" and only one in three of the younger generation raised in German-nationalist families indicated a preference for the FPÖ.

It was in this pitiful circumstance that German-nationalist and socially very conservative party functionaries from Carinthia formed the "Lorenzener Circle" to find a way to save the FPÖ from extinction. They saw their Carinthian Party Chairman, Jörg Haider, as the only salvation and joined with other party dissidents, principally from Upper Austria, Styria and Salzburg to overthrow Steger and his liberal Viennese establishment. When they were successful at the September party convention in Innsbruck, Chancellor Vranitzky declared an end to the Social-Liberal coalition and called for elections.

Although the Austrian political landscape had been described for years as among the most stable in the world, the incremental changes accompanying the end of *consociationalism*, the erosion of the *Lager* and the rise of post-modern political alienation had caused enormous energy to build up in the tectonic plates that underlay it. Thus when Haider defiantly led his party into opposition, he found a reservoir of voters to whom his aggressive, right-populism automatically appealed. As Anton Pelinka has explained, in a stable democracy in which opposition no longer threatened the system, a new "bonus" had emerged for those who could express the frustration and anger of the voters. This was confirmed in the results of the *Nationalrat* election, which gave the new, protest-oriented FPÖ a 9.7 percent voter share. Plasser, Ulram and Grausgruber found negative voting, the candidates and above all the personality of Haider to have been the overwhelming determinants in the choice of voters for the FPÖ. Ties to or identification with party were of no significance and issues even had a negative correlation. The total absence of German-nationalist tones from the FPÖ campaign, the high degree of voter mobility, the relative youth of FPÖ voters and the fact that 27 percent of the FPÖ voters had switched over from the ÖVP and 23 percent from SPÖ do not support assumptions that the FPÖ victory was due to the recrudesence of right-extremism typically identified with Haider. In the nine years since, the FPÖ has parlayed this victory as the party of protest with the opportunity offered by the ÖVP's surrender of the right side of the political spectrum into an unbroken string of election victories and in three of the nine states, the status of the second largest party. New and even more emotional issues were introduced into the ferment of political protest in the wake of the "change" in Eastern Europe and the Balkans after 1990.

In the period from 1987 to 1990, the FPÖ added victories in seven consecutive state Parliament *(Landtag)* elections to its 1986 success. A survey of the party literature and the coverage of these elections in the major print media reveals that the FPÖ campaigns primarily focused on problems that could be laid at the door of the federal government, e.g. unemployment, corruption, scandals, the need to privatize state-owned enterprises, lower taxes, fewer regulations on business and individuals and only in select cases on state issues. These are the same conservative issues that Margaret Thatcher, Helmut Kohl and Ronald Reagan had exploited so effectively and now seem to be serving the resurrection of the Republican party against the putative "leftist liberalism" of Bill Clinton. The new support for the FPÖ substantially came from middle class public workers and service sector employees who could no longer express their objections to the social-welfare state by voting for the ÖVP; there were also defections of skilled workers and members of the intellectual middle classes who had previously been won over by the Kreisky "catchall" strategy. Above all, FPÖ voters are young and therefore less likely to be influenced by lingering *Lager* loyalty. Since the FPÖ growth in popularity parallels its shift from a centrist to a relatively rightist position, one could assume that there has been a shift to the Right among the voters has occurred. Surprisingly however, those who identify themselves with the Right have dropped from 52 percent in 1976 to 30 percent in 1992. The explanation for this contradiction I believe lies in the protest nature of the FPÖ electorate mobilized by Haider.

Born 26 January 1950, Jörg Haider is a child of the Second Republic and began his political career with the FPÖ associated with the young, liberal reformers of the 1970s. These origins make questionable the pro-Nazi label his critics try to pin on him. Much of his support comes from his own generation and younger, who know little of the past and have even less interest in conquering it. This is not to suggest that these younger voters are uneducated; a 1993 poll by Fritz Plasser shows that among voters under thirty, who hold a *Matura* and students in institutions of higher education, the FPÖ, along with the other two opposition parties, enjoys support only slightly lower than that for each of the two coalition parties. Indeed, I suspect that the constant drumbeat charging Haider with pro-Nazi sentiment has backfired with these Generation X-ers who see the charges as an exaggerated obsession of the "old parties" with the past.

For example, when Haider championed the cause of German-speaking parents to establish German-only instruction for their children in the region of Carinthia where bilingual education was mandated, he was accused of secretly wanting to return to the Nazi policy of forced deportation or of creating a modern system of apartheid. Many Austrians, however, saw the desire to eliminate the time-consuming bilingual instruction for German-speakers as legitimate and the charges as typical leftist hyperbole. An even more striking example of public indifference to charges of right-extremism came in response to what was purported to be a speech by Haider praising the employment policy of the Third Reich. The stimulus for the incident came in June of 1991 when Haider, as the head of the governing coalition in Carinthia, was addressing the matter of welfare reform in a speech before the *Landtag*. Less extreme than California Governor, Pete Wilson, who demands the elimination of welfare benefits "for those who won't work," Haider merely proposed that benefits be cut. Interrupting, the SPÖ fraction leader shouted that this was akin to the forced labor of the Third Reich, to which Haider responded, "No, that wasn't so in the Third Reich, because in the Third Reich there was a proper employment policy *(ordentliche Beschäftigungspolitik)*, which your government in Vienna can't even manage." A charitable interpretation of Haider's retort might be to see it as a "Freudian slip" by the son of a man who as an Austrian Legionnaire had seen the apparent successes of the Labor Service and the Labor Front in the mid-1930's and had supported Anschluß as a means of bringing prosperity to Austria. The next speaker, from the ÖVP, put the "so successful labor policy" of the Third Reich in perspective by reminding Governor Haider of its ends and consequences, but then returned to the debate on economic policy, likewise criticizing socialist welfare policy. Later, Haider expressed his regrets for the remark and stated that he had not intended any positive comparison of the labor policy of the Third Reich relative to that of the Austrian Republic. The matter might have gone no further had not the SPÖ used the incident to enlist ÖVP support for a vote of no confidence against Haider in return for Socialist support of its chairman as governor. The media was delighted with new evidence with which again to tar Haider with the brush of Nazism; the

Chancellor threatened legal action and even within the FPÖ, future presidential candidate Heide Schmidt and others strongly criticized their chairman. Haider's popularity in *profil*'s "Politicians' Hit Parade" went from 47 percent to 33 percent. Nevertheless, in a *Landtag* election in Burgenland only two weeks after the incident, the FPÖ improved by 30 percent its first-ever election success of 1987, winning over voters in approximately equal numbers from both major parties, even though its share of the overall vote fell 2 to 4 percent below expectations. Although the Haider "comment" was one of the major themes in the campaign, and although only 16 percent in a poll saw the FPÖ as having been successful since first entering the *Landtag* four years before, 40 percent considered its representation there as an advantage. Before and after polls illustrate that the Haider "comment" had a negative effect on the FPÖ results; nevertheless, the primary motives for voting for the FPÖ continued to be protest against the two major parties and their candidates. In a country-wide poll on Haider's "comment," 42 percent regarded the media's reaction as exaggerated, 44 percent did not see it as damaging to Austria's reputation and a full one-third even felt that it was an acceptable statement of the facts, which seems to sustain my argument about the "back-fire" effect of the charges of right-extremism.

Beginning in 1990, the "change" in Eastern Europe and the Balkans brought new issues that have worked to the benefit of the FPÖ at a time when its merely protest appeal might have flattened out, and when its enemies might have had new opportunities to label it right-extremist. The most important of these is immigration, which is linked in the public mind with increases in crime and unemployment, inadequate housing and excessive taxes. It surfaced in the October 1990 *Nationalrat* election and was particularly potent in Vienna where legal and illegal immigrants and asylum-seekers were the most numerous. There the local FPÖ's exhortation, "Vienna must not become Chicago," played not very subtly on anxieties, but if anything in a less racist manner than the ÖVP's "Vienna for the Viennese." The tactics succeeded and the FPÖ passed the ÖVP as the second largest party in 5 of 23 Viennese working-class precincts. The Left again saw right-extremism and links to National Socialism, but the results in the remainder of the country which increased the FPÖ voter share to 16.6 percent were actually in keeping with the trend in

361

the state elections since 1986 before immigration exploded as an issue. In a post-election survey of seven electoral motives, protest dominated, with the FPÖ's stance on foreigners ranked at number four, the only one remotely right-extremist in nature.

In the fall of 1991, *Landtag* elections in Styria, Upper Austria and Vienna as well as Viennese municipal elections gave the FPÖ ideal opportunities to harvest support based on its now well-established "opposition bonus" and the new anxiety about the flood of immigration and asylum-seekers. Jörg Haider helicoptered to rallies everywhere elections were being held preaching his gospel of protest and exploiting anger against the inaction of the coalition on immigration. In Styria, the FPÖ more than tripled its vote to 15.4 percent, with about half of its new voters coming from the ÖVP, about 36 percent from the SPÖ and the remainder voting for the FPÖ rather than abstaining as they had in 1986. Two weeks later in Upper Austria, the FPÖ improved even on its Styrian success, jumping to 17.7 percent, with big gains in the previously safe precincts of both parties illustrating the strength of its "opposition bonus." Striking however, and beginning a trend that has grown ever since, was the extremely high shift of working-class voters to the FPÖ, apparently attracted by the party's stance on immigration, unemployment and welfare fraud. In both elections, because of Haider's virtually constant presence in the campaigns, the FPÖ victories have to be seen, in part, as a repudiation of his ousting as governor of Carinthia by the major parties following his "labor policy" remark only three months before.

In the 10 November Vienna elections, the three burning issues were housing, transportation and foreigners, all of which were tailor-made for the FPÖ appeal to protest. The waiting list for public housing had stood at 20,000 for years despite increased budgets for construction, and anger at allocation of finished units according to party membership had grown increasingly strong. Critical attention was also focused on the SPÖ-led municipal government for the subway construction program which had just been cited by the General Accounting Office for mismanagement and cost overruns. But the issue that had many people on edge was caused by the influx of over 240,000 legal immigrants and probably 100,000 illegal immigrants into Vienna in just the past two years. The FPÖ in particular focused on the schools where in some districts it claimed

75-80 percent of the children were non-German-speaking and demanded that special classes be established for them so as to not harm the learning of native-speakers. Not very obliquely, the opponents of the FPÖ warned of the return of "racist tones" of yesteryear, but almost 40 percent of the population identified immigration as a serious contemporary problem. The FPÖ came to be soon as the most competent party to deal with the foreigner issue, a factor that was cited as decisive for every third FPÖ voter, particularly among defectors from the SPÖ. Motives that can be summarized as protest remained the dominant factor behind the FPÖ success, with nothing to indicate nostalgic sympathy for German-national, fascist or National Socialist themes. Even Haider, who is so often portrayed as a "brown shirt" in modern guise, was among the least cited reasons for switching to the FPÖ. The consequences of the election were stunning for Vienna. For the first time during the Second Republic, the SPÖ slipped below the 50 percent mark and the FPÖ climbed from 9.7 percent in 1987 to 22.5 percent, tripling its number of seats in the city council and making it the second largest party represented. Even more apparent than in Upper Austria, the FPÖ had won over 26 percent of the working class and 35 percent of all skilled workers.

Late in 1992, the FPÖ attempted to parlay the credibility it had gained on the immigration issue in the Viennese elections of the previous year into mass political support with its people's initiative, "Austria first." The first of its twelve points proposed to add a statement to the Federal Constitution declaring that Austria was not a classic country of immigration. Other points demanded legislation to deal with the problems posed by non-German-speaking children in the schools, to require identity cards to document the legitimacy of foreigners for employment, public health and welfare services, the restriction of public housing to Austrian citizens and increased funding to combat crime and secure the borders against illegal immigration. A Gallup Poll showed 1.68 million in agreement with the principles of the initiative, 1.34 million who "would happily sign," and .84 million who were certain they would sign. When, however, a high-profile immigrants' rights group called SOS-Fellow Human Being *(SOS-Mitmensch)* formed, the SPÖ seized upon its campaign as a way to discredit the FPÖ that was threatening its own previously dominant position among the working class. It is ironic that less than two years later, another SOS campaign ("Save Our State") was conducted in California, but this time in opposition to immigration. Although the California SOS organization was virtually invisible and had little money for advertising, Republican Governor Peter Wilson made the SOS-initiative, Proposition 187, a centerpiece of his victorious reelection campaign, along with toughness on crime and enforcement of the death penalty. In his first term in office Wilson, along with most Republicans and not a few Democrats, had proposed virtually all of the measures foreseen in "Austria first" to deal with the exploding problem of illegal immigration. Specifically, Proposition 187 provides that illegal immigrants shall be denied public education, health and welfare benefits and require agencies to report those without documentation. Despite efforts similar to those of *SOS-Mitmensch* by the mainstream media and by public education and health professionals to portray the initiative as immoral and implicitly racist, it passed with an enormous 59+ percent majority, attesting to the currency and universality of the problem and not to some peculiarly Austrian xenophobia. In late 1992-1993, however, the climate in Austria was different from California in November 1994. At precisely this time, anti-foreigner demonstrations and murders were causing the world to question whether Germany had really conquered its Nazi past. Against this background, the SOS campaign skillfully turned attention from the immigration issues actually addressed by "Austria first" and portrayed it as a racist, anti-foreigner crusade against industrious and indispensable guest workers and helpless refugees fleeing poverty, political repression and civil war by a party that "everyone knew" was tinged with brown. Unlike Californians, Austrians could not hide their support of "Austria first" in the secrecy of the voting booth. When confronted with having openly to sign their names on the initiative, less than half of those who felt they would "certainly sign" actually did. But, although the media declared "Austria first" a flop, the initiative had its effect as the SPÖ cynically began to try to outmaneuver the FPÖ for the future by formulating a highly restrictive residency law for foreigners to the outrage of its erstwhile *SOS-Mitmensch* allies. Heide Schmidt, now third president of the *Nationalrat*, used the opportunity to defect from the FPÖ, forming the Liberal Forum with a handful of other dissidents. The media congratulated Austria for having exonerated itself from the shame of its recent drift to the Right and declared

Haider politically dead. Like Mark Twain, he might have responded: "the reports of my death have been greatly exaggerated."

In March, 1994, just over a year later, the FPÖ again extended its record of election victories since 1986 in three *Landtag* elections. In Carinthia it hurdled to 33.28 percent and to within one seat of parity with the SPÖ whose status as the largest party was threatened by a loss of 8.54 percent. In Salzburg, both major parties lost, while the FPÖ gained another 3.14 percent and two more seats with almost 20 percent of the vote. Only in Tyrol, where the ÖVP distanced itself from the federal leadership in Vienna and ran an FPÖ-style populist campaign was the improvement only marginal, with a .61 percent gain to 16.17 percent and a one more seat in the *Landtag*. Post-election polls again showed protest to be the dominant factor: 79 percent said they voted for the FPÖ because it expressed their grievances and because the SPÖ/ÖVP was in control; 57 percent said they wanted to send the SPÖ/ÖVP a message, and 54 percent agreed with the FPÖ's critical stance against the recently negotiated treaty for entry into the European Union (EU). Sixty-three percent were motivated by Haider and the party's other lead candidates, some certainly because of his defense of the German-national tradition, but others just as certainly for his aggressive personification of protest. The fear of a flood of immigration that motivated 63 percent of FPÖ voters certainly indicates the less liberal attitudes of the Right, but to attribute it to an unconquered past seems a fabrication that fails to recognize that racism and xenophobia are modern phenomena not necessarily linked to National Socialism.

Only three months after the euphoria of the March *Landtag* election victories, the FPÖ's position on the EU treaty was rejected by a massive 66.34 percent "yes" vote. This time, *profil* editorialized, the people sent Haider "a message." The FPÖ, which had been accused of right-extremist, Anschluß sentiment when it supported membership in the EEC in the late 1950s, was now accused of anti-democratic right-extremism for opposing entry into its successor, the EU. Again, as after the "Austria first" campaign, Haider dropped into the cellar of the "Politicians' Hit Parade" with only a 17 percent favorable rating, and the FPÖ in general hit its lowest level since the 1986. But "Europhoria" did not last long, and in a poll two months later at the beginning of the 1994 *Nationalrat* campaign, Haider, although still the lowest in the "Politicians' Hit Parade," had nevertheless recovered seven points and the FPÖ was projected at least to match its 1990 vote of 16.6 percent.

As if to mimic the 1994 Republican mid-term election campaign in the United States and most particularly the gubernatorial campaign in California, the FPÖ made crime, immigration and moral values the dominant issues. To emphasize the crime issue, Haider selected, as second on the FPÖ candidate list, a woman jurist and former ÖVP member who expressed her concern about crime and immigration and who implied her personal belief in the death penalty. As a judge, *profil* wrote that she had been known for her competence, objectivity, credibility, openness and freedom from cynicism, but when introduced as an FPÖ candidate, characterized her crime position as concern about *"Blut und Banden"* and criticized her statement that "life in prison must mean life" as simplistic. With the ÖVP committed, "without any ifs, ands or buts," to continuing in coalition with the SPÖ, the moral Right had no other place to go than to the FPÖ.

In his book, *Die Freiheit die ich meine*, Haider stakes his claim for their support citing the social-welfare state and moral-free materialism as the source of the modern malaise. A good example of what is wrong with modern society, he contends, is what has happened to the family, substantially because materialism has driven mothers to work. Taking on the feminists, Haider proposed tax incentives to permit mothers to remain home and raise their children and for those who must or want to work, he proposed more day-care centers unrestricted by class or party membership. In reaction, one critic drew the inevitable parallel with the Nazi policy of *"Kinder, Kirche, Küche"* and accused him of anti-foreigner racism for wanting to encourage the birthrate of Austrians. These ideological waters were, however, considerably muddied in the summer of 1994 by the wife of the SPÖ chancellor, who, in an interview with *profil*, touted "family values" and criticized mothers who put their children in day-care at seven in the morning ". . . in order to earn maybe four- or five-thousand shillings." The SPÖ was embarrassed and feminists exploded in rage, but a poll showed the public split virtually evenly on her views. By extension then, it can be inferred that close to half the public does not see the views of Haider and the FPÖ on this issue as reminiscent of National Socialism. In Austria, as in the United States, the moral values movement appears to be becoming mainstream, thereby seeming to repudiate the charge that the FPÖ's interpretation of these views is extreme, relative to contemporary public opinion.

There is much in the FPÖ's emergence as successful protest party of the Right to compare with the contemporary mood in the United States. There has been " . . . a disconnect between the political elite and the rank-and file . . . . The dam has broken and people feel they can express these feelings that are kind of pent up." This observation about the United States by political scientist Peter Skerry is even more applicable to Austria where the elites of the ruling parties can no longer rule *consociationally*, dividing the spoils of power proportionally among themselves while mobilizing their respective masses by appeals to *Lager* mentality. The disillusionment with politics and government that was already apparent in public opinion polls by the beginning of the 1980s had reduced the ruling SPÖ from solid, absolute majorities after 1971 to an historic low of 34.92 percent in the parliamentary election of 1994, almost eight points below its previous historic low in 1990. The ÖVP, which was able to maintain itself as a respectable major party with over 40 percent of the vote in federal elections throughout its twenty years out of government, dropped to 32.1 percent in 1990 after four years as junior partner to the SPÖ, and its promise in 1994 to continue the coalition for the next legislative period cast even more of its erstwhile supporters into the opposition, leaving it with a scant 27.67 percent. The FPÖ, on the other hand, added six points to its already historic high in 1990 to win 22.50 percent of the vote and with forty-two seats in the *Nationalrat* at least a mathematical possibility of forming a governing coalition with the ÖVP, within which the desire to end the coalition with the "Reds" is strong and the hunger for the chancellorship compelling.

The voter protest that produced this debacle for the incumbent SPÖ-ÖVP coalition parallels the surliness in the United States electorate that was responsible for the success of the Perot presidential campaign in 1992 and which is evidenced in the strong, anti-incumbent mood in mid-term elections a month after the latest FPÖ victory. In the United States, the new Right populism has been difficult for the primarily liberal scholarly community to fathom, because, as Brinkley notes, scholars of the Left have equated the masses with ideals that are democratic and progressive and

". . . found it difficult to acknowledge that they could emerge from the Right." Austrian scholars know about mass movements from the Right, but find it difficult to understand that such a movement is not somehow linked to National Socialism or aimed at achieving its goals.

If the criterion for defining the FPÖ as a party of the Right is opposition to the modern Austrian state that was built on Christian-conservative corporatism and social democracy and maintained by the "social partnership" based on *Proporz*, the designation is accurate. Its goals are radical because Haider dreams of replacing what he regards as the obsolete representative democracy of the Second Republic with a plebiscitary democracy. In this "Third Republic," Haider would introduce the direct election of mayors and state governors and, like Ross Perot and now Newt Gingrich, would empower the people, armed with the tools of modern telecommunications, to direct a government elected by citizens' movements, not parties, to recover the traditional values of the community that have been ignored or eroded by the social-liberalism of /the establishment. Like the American Libertarians, he believes in a radical reduction of government in all areas, for "only in an order where there is freedom, can freedom flourish and the worth of the individual be insured." As an American liberal, I can share the sentiments of Haider's Austrian critics who despair at their failure to retain the loyalty of the masses for an activist state as the means of achieving a more socially just society. When, however, they find the seeds of totalitarianism in Haider's ideas for a "Third Republic," as a resident of California where Haider's dreams are a reality and support for the death penalty a political necessity, I can only sardonically laugh.

FURTHER LITERATURE

Jörg Haider, *Die Freiheit die Ich Meine. Das Ende Des Proporzstaates. Pläydoyer Für die Dritte Republik* (Berlin: Ullstein, 1993).

Handbuch des österreichischen Rechtsextremismus, ed. Dokumentationsarchiv des österreichischen Widerstandes (Vienna: Deuticke, 1993).

Herbert Kraus, *Untragbare Objektivität: Politische Erinnerungen 1917 Bis 1987* (Vienna-Munich: Amalthea Verlag, 1988).

Kurt Richard Luther and Wolfgang C. Müller, eds., *Politics in Austria: Still a Case of Consociationalism?* (London: Frank Cass, 1992).

Anton Pelinka and Fritz Plasser, *The Austrian Party System* (Boulder-San Francisco-London: Westview Press, 1989).

Kurt Piringer, *Die Geschichte der Freiheitlichen: Beitrat der Dritten Kraft zur österreichischen Politik* (Vienna: Orac Verlag, 1982).

Viktor Reimann, *Die Dritte Kraft in Österreich* (Vienna: Verlag Fritz Molden, 1980).

Max Riedlsperger, "FPÖ: Liberal or Nazi?" in *Conquering the Past: Austrian Nazism Yesterday & Today*, ed. Francis Parkinson (Detroit: Wayne State University Press, 1989): 257-78.

_____, "Heil Haider! The Revitalization of the Austrian Freedom Party Since 1986." *Politics and Society in Germany, Austria and Switzerland* 4 (Summer 1992): 18-58.

_____, *The Lingering Shadow of Nazism: The Austrian Independent Party Movement Since 1945* in East European Monographs (New York: Columbia University Press, 1978).

Hans-Henning Scharsach, *Haiders Kampf* (Vienna: Verlag Orac, 1992).

Handbuch des Österreichischen Rechtsextremismus, Stiftung Dokumentationsarchiv des österreichischen Widerstandes (Vienna: Deuticke, 1993).

Peter Pulzer

Austria occupies an important place in the history of the European radical Right. This applies not so much to that movement's ideology which, as Isaiah Berlin has pointed out, has its origins in the anti-revolutionary reaction in France, associated with the philosophy of Joseph de Maistre. It does, however, apply to the political organization of the radical Right and the attempts at practical implementation of its program, beginning in the 1880s. This movement had its origins in the weakness of Austrian liberalism, the inability of the post-1867 monarchy to accommodate the claims of the competing nationalities and the peculiar structure of the Austrian professional and business bourgeoisie, with its strong Jewish component. This radical Right, whether in the pre-First World War period or between the wars, had two prongs—a Catholic-conservative one and a pan-German-racist one. For most of the period up to 1938 the Catholic-conservative component was the numerically stronger and the politically more influential, whereas the pan-German-racist was the more extreme and more inclined to resort to violence. The two prongs shared some of their enemies—parliamentary government, liberal pluralism, cosmopolitanism and Jews—but they were also periodically extremely hostile to each other. There were times when they constituted recognizably separate *Lager*, as in Adam Wandruszka's scheme, and others when they overlapped, as in the *Heimwehr* movements at the end of the First Republic and in the various "christlich-national" tendencies both before and after 1914.

What is striking about the analysis of the present-day Austrian extreme Right is that it is devoted almost entirely to the relics of the "third *Lager*," i.e. the "liberal-national," pan-German and neo-Nazi Right. The reader therefore automatically asks two questions to which the volume does not really give satisfactory answers: what has happened to the Catholic-conservative radical Right? and what is the future of a "third *Lager*" ideology which seems to be appealing to a small and diminishing segment of the population? On the first question a certain amount of impressionistic guess-work is possible. Little seems to remain within the Catholic-conservative *Lager* of the populist demagogy of which Karl Lueger was such a master; of the "no mercy" doctrine of Monsignor Seipel; of the Korneuburg Oath, which regarded Italian fascism as its model and one of whose chief authors was the post-1945 chancellor, Julius Raab; or of the anti-parliamentary "corporate state" of Dollfuss and Schuschnigg. Occasionally reminders of the old Christian-social original sin erupt, as during the Waldheim presidential campaign in 1986, but in the main the ÖVP has been converted to the rules of the democratic game, as has the Austrian Catholic Church. No doubt the experience of the Anschluß played its part in this conversion; so no doubt did opportunism. But it cannot be doubted that the Christian-conservative *Lager*'s radical Right legacy is a thing of the past and a study of the stages by which it disengaged itself from this would be instructive.

That leaves us with the problem of the FPÖ, of the neo-Nazi and *völkisch* sub-culture and the connection between the two. But here again we meet a paradox. The student of comparative politics would have no difficulty in accounting for the rise of the FPÖ since Jörg Haider took over its leadership. The components of a common-sense explanation would be the new leader's rhetorical skills, the poor image of the coalition parties and the self-enrichment attitudes of many of their functionaries, and above all fear of immigration and its (real or imagined) attendant evils, such as pressure on social services or the threat to law and order. Similarly, anyone familiar with the recent history of Central Europe could account without difficulty for the survival of the *völkisch* sub-culture in Austria. He could cite the ideological fragmentation of the Habsburg Monarchy and the First Republic, the Austrian origins of National Socialism, the crisis of national identity between 1918 and 1938, the success of the Third

Reich in mobilizing a significant proportion of Austrians for its activities, and the resentment of these people at events since 1945.

So far so good. What is less evident is why these two tendencies should have merged in recent years and whether the merger explains the FPÖ's electoral success. The most useful clues to answering this conundrum are contained in the long historical sketch of the FPÖ by Brigitte Bailer and Wolfgang Neugebauer and in the detailed information, compiled by the same authors, in the exhaustive sections on extreme organizations and activists and the organizations and persons associated with extremism. From these it is clear, firstly that many persons active in the extremist scene were implicated in engineering Haider's seizure of power in the FPÖ at the Innsbruck congress of 1986; secondly that, following the rather cool relationship between the extremist scene and the FPÖ during that party's "liberal" phase under Friedrich Peter and Norbert Steger, the two have now become fully reconciled; and thirdly that many of the functionaries of what would otherwise be insignificant sectarian conventicles now hold cadre positions in the FPÖ. The best-known example of the promotion of figures from the neo-Nazi fringe to central party offices is Andreas Mölzer, now head of the FPÖ's political academy. The outcome of this process is, as the authors point out, that the FPÖ is now an explicitly extremist party, as opposed to merely a party containing extremists. The formidable evidence collected in this volume explains the function of the extremist cadres in holding the party together organizationally, but says nothing about their function in expanding its electorate. The cadres may, indeed, be dysfunctional in this respect. Their ideological obsessions, which are concerned with re-writing the history of the Second (and in some cases the First) World War, with denying the Holocaust and disputing the existence of an Austrian nation, have a strictly limited—and declining—public appeal. Indeed, in its public rhetoric the FPÖ has largely abandoned the emphasis on pan-Germanism and replaced it with the slogan "Austria First," especially in the context of its anti-immigration drive. Yet this major ideological switch is only cursorily mentioned and discussed in this book, as if the authors were hypnotised by the neo-Nazism of the cadres.

The unsolved problem here is one that political analysts are familiar with, namely the relationship between the belief-systems of party activists and the motivations of their voters. My criticism of this aspect of the book is not that the authors fail to solve the problem, but that they appear in large part to be unaware of it. The contribution that comes closest to dealing with it is Anton Pelinka's chapter on the major parties and extremism. He reminds us that both SPÖ and ÖVP had an interest in mobilizing the ex-Nazi vote and therefore in a conspiracy of silence about Austrian collusion with the Third Reich; that this resulted in, among other unfavorable consequences, the inadequate transmission of democratic values and therefore in a significant residue of anti-democratic attitudes among the supporters of parties whose leadership and official commitments are democratic. The general decline in party loyalty has made it all the easier for the FPÖ to expand its base. Between 1983 and 1994 the FPÖ's electorate has more than quadrupled, from 5 to 22.5 percent. Is this *because* of the party's more extreme ideological profile or *in spite* of it? The book's authors appear to have no individual or collective views on this question.

The difficulties in assimilating the concept of the extreme Right to the question of the FPÖ's success emerges most clearly in Willibald Holzer's essay, nearly a hundred pages long, on the definition and explanation of the extreme Right phenomenon. It is the most ambitious contribution to the volume, but also one of the less satisfactory. It has considerable merits, however. Unlike many of the other contributors, Holzer does not identify the Austrian extreme Right exclusively with *völkisch* pan-Germanism. Like Pelinka, he stresses that individual "extremist" attitudes are widely distributed throughout the population (and not only in Austria), well beyond the strictly defined extremist fringe. But in two respects it is unsatisfactory: in its analysis of the individual psychology of the extremist and in its socio-economic explanation of the attractiveness of the extreme Right. The principal psychological characteristics that Holzer identifies are "aggressive-authoritarian orientations" and "a dichotomised view of the world" with a search for enemies and scapegoats (pp. 77, 52). It would be difficult to dispute this, though it surely applies to extremism *per se*, rather than specifically to extremism of the Right. On the Right it is combined with ethnocentric evocation of tradition, social homogeneity and *Volksgemeinschaft*. But which is the more significant factor: the mentality or its ideological objectives, when we consider that the mentality is compatible with quite different ideological objectives? Then there is the question of the relationship between the contemporary extreme Right and modernity. More than once Holzer describes those attracted to the extreme Right as "modernisation losers" (e.g. p. 37); as persons incapable of responding to the challenges of modern economic life by calling on innovative and flexible techniques and therefore "structurally threatened in their status expectations and life-chances" (p. 88). On the one hand, Holzer regards this kind of response to global modernization tendencies as irrational (p. 35), on the other, he quotes Habermas, with apparent approval, to the effect that it is these tendencies that are "the real sources of crisis in society" (p. 23), i.e., that it is the process of global modernization that is itself irrational. The proposition that it is the modernization losers who feed the extreme Right is repeatedly asserted and is indeed an old and familiar one, but how valid is it? Investigation of those who commit violence against foreigners in Germany suggest no consistent pattern of economic deprivation. Holzer's claim that it is the "social impact of the patterns of industrial modernization" that bring about "the origins, intensification and activation of extreme right orientation" (p. 86) assumes that the frustrations experienced by the right-wing extremist must have objective causes. The claim is all the more dubious since the programmatic response of the extreme Right parties points, according the evidence of the book, away from its traditional anti-liberal corporatism and in the direction of economic modernization. A significant part of the FPÖ's appeal is to "achievement-oriented persons, who simply want to be left in peace by the state" (p. 346) and Holzer himself confirms that "modern Right extremists . . . are meanwhile as good as totally absorbed by the modern economic and property constitution" (p. 47).

Given the seriousness of the subject addressed by this book and its ambitious claims, it is only right that one should judge it by the standards the authors and editors set themselves. The factual information it contains is formidable and well-arranged. It includes, incidentally, welcome evidence that the Austrian authorities are, however belatedly, cracking down on the more vicious of the hate-mongers. What remains unresolved is the apparent paradox that the more the FPÖ is taken over by extreme Right cadres the more successful it is in invading the center ground of politics. Is the FPÖ a genuine party of the extreme Right, as claimed by the contributors, or an exceptionally effective post-Fascist populist movement, led by a demagogue who has tapped a vein of alienation with the existing interest articulators, rather in the manner of Gianfranco Fini's *Allianza Nazionale*? I hope a new edition will address this puzzle.

Michael Gehler and Rolf Steininger, eds., *Österreich und die Europäische Integration 1945-1993. Aspekte einer wechselvollen Entwicklung* (Vienna: Böhlau Verlag, 1993)

Alan S. Milward

The collective volume by the Institut für Zeitgeschichte of Innsbruck University, marks a first attempt to narrate and analyze from what few documentary sources are available the long story of Austria's attempts to associate itself with the European Community. The central difficulty is that Austrian foreign ministry records remain closed. The two core narrative chapters by Florian Weiss and Stephan Hamel have to make do with such records from economic ministries as have been opened, public state papers, some information from political party papers, as well as newspapers and the like. Other contributors use whatever materials they can get hold of to try to fulfill the editors' laudable aim to make the volume as comprehensive as possible. On the whole, the volume is a success and does provide a compendium of what is known of the complex relationship between Austria and the Community. There is nothing here from the newly opened State Department files relating to the proposed expansion of the Community in 1961-3, but the chapters were probably written too early for that. Nor is there anything new from Soviet archives. Nevertheless, this is a useful interim report which will not be replaced for some time.

The immediate relevance of the work to current research is the light it throws on the assumption that extension of the Community, or association with it, depended after 1961 on the United Kingdom's success in winning membership. Austria's negotiations for association, which would have been almost full membership, took little account of de Gaulle's veto against the United Kingdom in 1963. Even more striking is that these negotiations were pursued in spite of repeated unambiguous Soviet assertions that a treaty of association would be regarded, in the words of the memorandum of 30 September 1964, as "a turning-point in Austria's announced policy of permanent neutrality" and, perhaps even more serious in Russian eyes, "a de facto implementation of the economic union with the German Federal Republic forbidden by the State Treaty."

Had the United States been more positive in its support for Austrian links with the EEC, this reaction might be more easily explained. Günter Bischof gives an accurate account of American attitudes, but to this should be added what can now be gathered from the release of the State Department files on the British application. It was the view of the Kennedy Administration that, commerically, neutrals should fend for themselves because they were free riders on the Western alliance. No matter how strong Washington's sympathy for its "secret ally," it could not be seen to be doing more in the negotiations for Austria than it was prepared to do for the other neutrals. Furthermore, the Americans wanted to limit the Community to countries for which political union was the goal, and for Austria it could not be. Behind these immediate problems in Washington lay anxieties about what Austria's "permanent neutrality" really meant.

The explicit Soviet comparison was with Switzerland, and so was that made by those Austrian politicians who were themselves uneasy about the approach to the Community. Of the other neutrals, only Ireland was prepared to contemplate full membership. Yet in the 1960s Austria was in the extraordinary situation that 46 to 50 percent of its exports by value went to a market which discriminated against it, and this was the driving force behind the search for "association." Austria was prepared to make large economic concessions for an arrangement that would be acceptable to the Community and might not in the end prove unacceptable to Moscow.

In July 1960 Austria offered to harmonize its tariff with the common external tariff of the EEC and to apply identical commercial rules to goods coming from third countries. With the collapse of Britain's negotiations, something both more and less than this move was needed; by summer 1966 it had been agreed to recommend to the EEC Ministerial Council that Austria should enter into a complete customs union for trade in manufactures while there should be preferences for trade in agricultural products. By the end of 1966, a four-year timetable for the implementation of this program had been accepted by the European Commission. On the day the EEC Ministerial Council first considered this, the Six-Day War broke out. Three weeks later, four Italian soldiers were blown up by South Tyrolean terrorists. The negotiations died. We have no available record of whether they could have succeeded. As several contributors point out, de Gaulle was opposed to Austrian association on these terms. Like the Soviets, he thought association was a step towards German unification. But of the attitude of the other member-states we are, in detail, still ignorant.

Later in the volume Gregor Leitner discusses Austrian-Community relationships in the 1980s. At what point French and Soviet attitudes relaxed is unclear. But after the collapse of the DDR, Austrian membership in the European Union became wholly subordinate to the issue of Germany's unification. With the whole of Germany in the European Union, Austria's accession, ironically, is now a guarantee to Russia and France that Austria remains a separate state.

Of the other contributors, Fritz Breuss provides a useful overview based on integration theory of the economic relationships between Austria and the Community, although as always, such analyses cannot capture the allegedly dynamic effects of reducing barriers to trade between the two areas. Michael Gehler traces the evolution of thinking about European integration before 1960 in the Österreichische Volkspartei. Rolf Steininger analyzes the moment of decision-making in London when the United Kingdom concluded that EFTA would not serve its purpose of so limiting the EEC as to persuade Germany to abandon it for a wider set of commercial arrangements. Thomas Angerer uses French foreign ministry papers to say something about France's attitude to Austria in the 1950s. France's constant concern was to multilateralise the Austrian question. As the Austrian economy in the 1950s came increasingly under German influence, the commercial separation between the two countries which the Treaty of Rome marked was evidently far from unwelcome in Paris, but France did not wish to appear the sole state to forbid Austrian membership in the EEC. Neither did it wish so to alienate Austria that Vienna should conduct its business with Brussels solely through Bonn. This may suggest that when French foreign ministry papers for the 1960s are opened, French policy will appear more ambivalent than it does by merely interpreting de Gaulle's rather brutal statements.

The first British application will come to be seen as a very divisive event for the other EFTA member-states. Henceforward, discrimination in international trade would be the accepted rule, and for the smaller west European states outside the EEC responses would vary widely. There is much left to discover, but this useful volume points the way to a wider history of European integration than the current literature, dominated as it is by French, German and British points of view. Sweden and Switzerland, unhelpfully for Austrian governments in the 1960s, regarded the EEC as a non-neutral, commercially undesirable organization. Norway was prepared to consider joining on terms which were unacceptable not merely to the Six, but which even the British government could not support. Denmark was ready to join, but only if the British market came with it. Ireland was ready to join to escape from the British market. Portugal's response was to unite its empire in the Portuguese Single Market. Thus fragmented by the British, EFTA was of little comfort or stability to Austria. Nor was it evident that if things changed in the EEC and Britain did join, anybody in London or Brussels would care about Austria's problems any more than they had in 1961-3.

Austria's version of *"sauve qui peut"* was the equally divisive negotiations of the 1960s, which delayed a clear definition of neutrality and left investors and exporters in a state of prolonged uncertainty caused by the effect of the failure of the negotiations for association on the Austrian economy. This book should surely be eagerly read in Oslo. Alternatively, the editors might consider asking the same team to write a book of the same format in ten years time. Not only would we then have a better test of how much membership of the Community/Union did actually matter, but most of the speculation opened by this study could probably be ended by the release of archival materials.

Klaus Fiesinger, *Ballhausplatz-Diplomatie 1945-1949* (Munich: tuduv Verlag 1993).

Michael Gehler, ed., *Karl Gruber: Reden und Dokumente 1945-1953* (Vienna: Böhlau Verlag 1994).

Wolfgang Krieger

How was the Austrian foreign office re-established after the war? What were the new Austria's policies toward her neighbors? These two questions are the focus of Klaus Fiesinger's *Ballhausplatz-Diplomatie*. They deserve a good deal of attention because Austrian foreign policy played a crucial role in the re-creation of Austrian nationhood.

The Ballhausplatz—once the home of Klemens von Metternich, later the office of the Austrian chancellors and their foreign office—was in shambles in April 1945. So was Austria's diplomatic machinery after a full third of its staff had offered their services to the Nazis. Fiesinger describes its re-establishment after the war in some detail, though little is said about the crucial denazification issue and about the extent to which personnel selections may have been made along party political lines.

Only twice does the author hint at the importance of party politics in this context. One reference suggests that the socialists (SPÖ) may have tried to get some of their people hired in that otherwise conservative-led (ÖVP) department. The other quotes Karl Gruber, Austria's foreign secretary until 1953, who told the author that he never discussed the great issues of foreign policy with his diplomats. "That was done in the party." But this hint is ignored and for the rest of the book, Austrian foreign policy is a matter of the Ballhausplatz diplomats and their secretary. Even the chancellor is barely mentioned. Was there no need to explore further the roles of the political parties in a democracy as literally partisan as Austria's?

Before dealing with any of the bilateral relationships between Austria and her neighbors, it is essential to understand the fundamentals on which Vienna's policies were built.

Unlike that of Germany, the Austrian leadership essentially sought—and largely managed—to return to the *status quo ante*, that is before the Anschluß of 1938. The guiding assumption was that Austria had been the first victim of Nazi aggression, had not been a state actor during the war and therefore bore no responsibility for Axis policies. The Austrian contribution in manpower at every level of the Nazi system never enters into the equation. (Nor does Fiesinger belabor the point. Even the 10 April 1938 Anschluß referendum, with its very large majority voting in favor, is never mentioned.) Now, in 1945, with Germany in ruins and given the promises of the 1943 Moscow Declaration, Austria would be recreated as an independent state. And what better proof of her national independence than to show that the new Austria could do what had been denied to the First Republic, namely to define her relations with her neighbors!

The Renner and Figl governments were extremely lucky, and they made excellent use of their opportunities. Contrary to the post-1918 period, the international climate after 1945 worked in favor of Austria's traditionally precarious position on the borderline of the Slavic and the Germanic worlds. Literally from the day when the European Axis front collapsed, in April 1945, the Austrians had a single national government, and since November 1945 they even had a freely elected one. Under the second Allied control agreement of June 1946 the Austrians could pass legislation and conduct their own diplomacy subject only to a unanimous Allied veto, which meant unimpeded by a lone Soviet "nyet." Economically, there was of course much hardship, not the least because of the ways in which the Soviets exploited their occupation zone. But Austria received much Allied help, too—per capita about ten times as much in Marshall Plan aid as did Western Germany!

Yet Austria's early foreign policy was by no means an unqualified success. After the highly promising June 1946 Allied agreement, it was to take another nine years for Austria to become fully independent of any Allied interference or military presence. The chief reason was of course Soviet intransigence, ostensibly tied to the issue of German investment property in the Soviet zone. In fact, however, Austria's situation was simply one of the pawns which the Kremlin left on the European chess board as a sign that the game of remaking Europe was still on. And Vienna could do precious little to change the minds in Moscow.

The South Tyrol was the first issue which Vienna's diplomats fully threw themselves into. In retrospect it is difficult to believe that they sincerely believed they could rescind the provisions of the 1919 peace treaty which had awarded a large part of the German-speaking Tyrol to Italy. True, the Austrians could argue with some justification that the principle of national self-determination had been violated in 1919, that Italy's security was hardly enhanced by the Brenner borderline, and that the forced Italianization of the South Tyroleans had left a legacy of hatred which might upset Italy's political stability in the future. But where would a new border be drawn? What would be the effect on the Italian body politic? What would be the implications for Italy's border dispute around Trieste? And were the moral claims of Italy's new democracy, based on nearly two years of anti-fascist and anti-Nazi fighting, of no value? In comparison, what moral weight did the Allies accord to Austria's self-portrayal as a mere victim of Nazism?

Unfortunately, Fiesinger makes little effort to understand the American and British, or indeed the Italian, positions on South Tyrol. They were not simply Cold War calculations as he claims. It is also doubtful that things would have gone very differently if the Ballhausplatz had been up to speed in September 1945 when the Allied Council of Foreign Ministers decided that Austria would only be allowed "minor changes" of her 1937 borders. Naturally this is a convenient explanation for the retired Gruber and his former staff members whom Fiesinger interviewed. But it overlooks a whole lot of other considerations, such as those relating to Italy, which Fiesinger never seriously considers.

For all his nationalist rhetoric as a leading politician of the Austrian People's Party, and a Tyrolean at that, Gruber adjusted quickly and, in September 1946, struck a deal with Italian foreign minister Alice De Gasperi. It held out the promise of cultural and economic minority rights for the South Tyroleans, indeed "autonomous legislative and executive regional power" for their region. It expressed the hope of close ties with Austria. And above all it had the qualities of an international treaty inasmuch as it became an annex of the Italian peace treaty of 1947. Thus, all signatory powers took a certain amount of responsibility for the improvement of the region's conditions and Austria could legitimately involve herself in what would otherwise have remained an internal Italian affair. That was a huge improvement, though it would take four decades before De Gasperi's promises were fully implemented.

Quite rightly, Fiesinger points out that roles were reversed concerning Austria's borders with Czechoslovakia, and Yugoslavia. Here it was the other side that claimed rectifications, either to restore old territorial connections or to "free" non-German minorities. Of the latter type, the Yugoslav border region was particularly touchy, because in a 1920 plebiscite a large minority of 41 percent had voted against Austria. Thereafter Slovenian ceased to be an official language and bilingual signs were removed. Later the Nazis stepped up Austria's already tough Germanization policies, and, during the war, the Slovenian minority fought particularly hard in the anti-Nazi resistance. Again it was the British and Americans who stuck to the 1937 borders by refusing to reopen the old Pandorra's box of ethnic claims. In May 1945 they literally forced Tito's troops out of Carinthia. In 1949, when Tito wished to be on his best behavior with the West, he buried his claims against Austria. Incidentally, on that issue Stalin seems to have been on Austria's side all along.

Relations with Prague were harder to fathom and are much less well explained by Fiesinger. The great disaster, from the viewpoint of Austria's "first victim" dogma, was that the Czechs made no distinction between Germans and Austrians when expelling millions of Sudeten ethnic Germans. In addition they demanded border changes which only made sense in military terms, giving important advantages to the Czechs. Now it was Vienna that stuck to the 1937 borders. Important issues, particularly those relating to Austrian property, remained unresolved until the detente era of the 1970s when full diplomatic relations were established and when Prague's foreign secretary came to Vienna for his first official visit in 1974.

By stark contrast, full diplomatic relations were reestablished with Hungary early on, although the communist take-over in Budapest made dealings as difficult as it did with other east European states. An Austrian request for the city of Ödenburg, ceded to Hungary under the name of Sopron in 1921, was dropped eventually. Perhaps it was "a strong conviction, weakly held"–to quote (out of context) from A.J.P. Taylor, the eminent historian of the Habsburg empire.

Then comes Austria's diplomacy toward Germany, of which little can be said except that it was narrowly focused on issues of social welfare, particularly repatriation issues, for years. This was because West Germany could not exchange ambassadors until 1955. But there was also a large element of psychology in this long period of non-relationship. Austria's identity as a separate state depended on a clear break with her German past. The years 1866 to 1945 had to be buried once and for all. Thus, at a 1950/51 GATT conference in Britain, Austrian and (west) German delegations met for the first time "officially."

The only surprise is a border issue fabricated by Gruber and other conservative politicians. They repeatedly laid claim to the Berchtesgaden and Rupertiwinkel districts (just to the west of Salzburg). And they did so for no better reason than geographical convenience and political propaganda. While Manfred Rauchensteiner, author of several very important books on post-1945 Austria, admits to the cynicism of this claim, Fiesinger dismisses it lightly. The hero was the old Austromarxist Karl Renner who, as chancellor in July 1945, vehemently opposed the claims as "in no way based on historic rights."

Little of interest can be said of Austria's relations with Switzerland and Liechtenstein. No problems existed, though one wonders if the old wish of the Vorarlberg population to join Switzerland—80 percent in a 1919 referendum—was mentioned at any stage by the diplomats. Fiesinger never raises the point.

If Fiesinger underrates party politics, the published papers of Karl Gruber, covering his years as foreign secretary, set the record straight. Here we have as much party politics, self-serving "first victim" propaganda, and foreign policy speeches for home consumption as anyone can stomach. In the early years, Gruber's speeches lash out against the "standardized Prussian" ("*dem preussischen Einheitsmenschen*"), who is clearly an Untermensch compared to the lofty Austrian. He gives soothing accounts of Austria's fate during the "alien" Nazi rule. Consequently the reborn Austria bears no war-guilt, no responsibility for the Holocaust. In fact, as Michael Gehler points out in his important introduction, Gruber never even mentions the Holocaust, by name or otherwise. And Gehler writes as someone who is preparing a biography of Gruber and has therefore surveyed a great deal more documents than could be included in this edition.

Gruber's biography has an unexplained blank from 1939 to March 1945 when he worked in Berlin as an electrical engineer, apparently undisturbed by the Nazis. Why, one wonders, given his own account that in 1938 he helped to purge Austria's telephone and telegraph services of their Nazi sympathizers and that he kept in touch with various resistance movements throughout the war? This information comes from Gruber's own curriculum vitae and from a 1991 Austrian state TV interview reproduced by Fiesinger. One hopes that Gehler will find the answer.

This edition of speeches and papers is a most welcome contribution to postwar Austrian history, carefully annotated and supplemented by a very detailed chronology. However, the bibliography might have included more non-German language works. Even the most important Cold War classics in English are missing, to say nothing about French, Italian and other scholarly works that deal with the many issues raised in this volume.

Gabriele Anderl and Walter Manoschek,
*Gescheiterte Flucht. Der jüdische 'Kladovo-
Transport' auf dem Weg nach Palestina, 1939-1942*
(Vienna: Verlag für Gesellschaftskritik, 1993).

Walter Manoschek, *'Serbien ist judenfrei:'*
Militärische Besatzungspolitik und
Judenvernichtung in Serbien 1941/42
(Munich: R. Oldenbourg, 1993).

Detlef K. Vogel

The first of these books describes the futile attempt of more than
a thousand Austrian, German, and Czechoslovakian Jews to escape
the Nazis. After suffering under anti-Semitic laws and pogroms in
their Austrian, German and Czechoslovak homelands, these Jews
decided to emigrate to Palestine. The British authorities there,
however, had reduced the immigration quota to a minimum, and the
only hope of getting to Palestine lay with the "Mossad," the secret
service branch of the Zionist workers' movement that helped save the
lives of more than 17,000 people from Central Europe. Sadly, the
plan to rescue another thousand Jews did not succeed. The effort
ended at the beginning of 1940 in the small Yugoslavian Danube
harbor of Kladovo. Only 200 of these refugees escaped before the
attack of German troops on Yugoslavia began. All others were caught
by the Germans in April 1941.

By this time, the Germans were not only determined to minimize
the rights of the Jewish minority and to confiscate their property;
now they intended to kill them all. The German occupation forces in
Yugoslavia took the men of the "Kladovo-Transport" hostage and

shot them as a reprisal for attacks by Yugoslav partisans. Of course, everybody knew that the Jewish refugees were in no way responsible for the acts of insurrection. They had been killed only because they were Jews. General Franz Böhme, as Territorial Commander of occupied Serbia, had ordered these atrocities, thereby launching the Holocaust in Yugoslavia. The women and children of the "Kladovo-Transport" were sent to concentration camps in the spring of 1942. They were later killed in so-called "gas-trucks," expressly constructed for this purpose.

Using letters, diaries, written interviews, and German documents, Anderl and Manoschek vividly describe the events that befell the people of the transport, from the decision to join the transport to the voyage on the Danube, the endless waiting in Yugoslav camps, and finally the grisly murders. The book includes numerous photographs and a detailed register of all persons of the "Kladovo-Transport," which should be helpful for further research.

Similar intensive new documentary research informs Manoschek's study of German occupation policy in Serbia. The author's main focus is the mass murder of Jews by the German armed forces, hitherto considered a taboo subject in historical research.

With General Franz Böhme's 1941 order, the military authorities in Yugoslavia initiated the slaughter of all Jewish citizens and all Jewish refugees in Serbia. It is both significant and tragic that the order to begin these atrocities did not come from the German high command in Berlin. About 50 to 60 percent of the Wehrmacht soldiers in Yugoslavia came from Austria because the German high command believed that Austrians were especially capable of dealing with the problems of an occupation policy in Southeastern Europe. As Manoschek explains, there was no active or even passive resistance to these murders among soldiers and officers. He suggests that this was the result of a very intensive anti-Semitic indoctrination decades before. We must not overlook, however, another reason soldiers obeyed the orders of their officers: in Yugoslavia, soldiers lived in far greater comfort and security than, for example, in Russia. Passivity or resistance could result in transfer to the Eastern front. Apart from describing the fate of the Jews in Serbia, Manoschek dedicates an important part of his book to the reality and structure of the German occupation policy. From the beginning, after the defeat of the Yugoslav armed forces in April 1941, the Germans built up a merciless occupation regime. After insurrection acts, for example, the chief of the high command, General Keitel, ordered 100 Yugoslavs shot for each dead and 50 for each wounded German soldier. Unable to seize the partisans responsible for their acts of insurrection, the Wehrmacht took hostages for retaliatory executions, first Jews and later uninvolved civilians.

To understand the events in Yugoslavia during World War II, says Manoschek, we must remember the broad tradition of hatred against the Serbian people in Germany and even more in Austria. This hatred originated before World War I when "*Serbien muß sterbien*" ("Serbia must die") was a widespread proverb. The behavior of the Germans in Yugoslavia found many imitators. Deportations and mass murder of ethnic minorities were committed all over the country, under the eyes of the German authorities.

Like Omer Bartov's book, Manoschek's book makes clear that the Wehrmacht was without doubt deeply involved with and coresponsible for the crimes of the Nazis. It shows how quite "normal" men became murderers under the influence of either anti-Semitic or anti-Slavic propaganda and popular tradition.

Ernst Bruckmüller, *Österreichbewußtsein im Wandel: Identität und Selbstverständnis in den 90er Jahren,* **Schriftenreihe des Zentrums für angewandte Politikforschung, Volume 4 (Vienna: Signum Verlag, 1994).**

William T. Bluhm

Austrians have systematically kept track of their developing national consciousness since the 1960s via opinion surveys, and since the 1980s, a number of monographs by Austrian scholars have appeared on the subject. (My *Building an Austrian Nation*, published in 1973, was a forerunner of this literature by an outsider.) *Österreichbewußtsein im Wandel* is the latest such study, the work of an historian using social science survey research to collect his empirical data. Bruckmüller's interpretation of the data from an historical perspective makes for a well-rounded and nuanced book.

In contrast to the confusion, conflict, and anomie of citizens of the First Republic, Second Republic Austrians have developed a solid national identity. Since 1964, Austrians in increasing numbers have been affirming that "Austrians are a nation." While in that year only 47 percent of respondents in a national survey were ready to make that affirmation, in 1993, 80 percent were prepared to do so. While an overwhelming majority of Austrians warmly greeted German reunification, 92 percent of them opposed a new Anschluß. Along with this, a 1989 poll showed Austrians ranked third (after the United States and Great Britain) in expressing great pride in their nationality (53 percent), with the French, Swiss and Germans following in the next three places. Bruckmüller attributes these findings largely to the positive experience of life in the Second Republic, which has been peaceful, secure, and prosperous. Loyalty to the state rests on its guarantee of individual rights, not on common cultural values. Austrians have thus abandoned the earlier Central European understanding of nationality as a cultural concept in favor of the Western idea of the political nation. This is the form of national identity that conforms best to liberal democratic political culture. Not surprisingly, therefore, survey research shows that 90 percent of Austrians today strongly affirm democratic norms. Only adherents of the Freedom Party (FPÖ) still favor the political "strong man."

In a time of modernization, which implies increasing individualization, along with the availability of an array of consumer goods from all over the world, Bruckmüller does not think it meaningful to undertake an empirical search from the marks of a specific Austrian "national character." Instead, he devotes two chapters to analyzing a package of common experiences and symbols in which Austrian national identity is embedded, and reviewing a bundle of collective self-images, concepts, clichés, and stereotypes that constitute a national mythology. The author thinks that the latter can be taken as an expression of role concepts for Austria. Common experiences that confirm the Austrian identity are the well-being, peace, and security of the Second Republic. Symbols such as the alpine landscape (with which foreigners also identify Austria) express, for Austrians, unchangeability and reliability, as well as a significant source of income. Other symbols derived from Habsburg times, some going back to the high middle ages, continue to have a partial value for national identity. Mariazell, the famed pilgrimage place, and the Abbey of Melk are examples. Central also to the Austrian mythology is the neutrality myth, which expresses Austrian acceptance of being a small state. While the currency of some traditional ideas such as "Catholic Austria" has declined, some very old self-images such as the *"Phäaken"* stereotype, which harks back to the medieval period, remain remarkably powerful.

Bruckmüller's positive findings about Austrians national identity are combined with anomalies. The author reports widespread political alienation, negative feelings about the army, the government of the day, Parliament, and the media. He also writes of the public's "enormous weariness with politics" (*"eine enorme Politikverdrossenheit"*). With these things go fear of foreigners and the rejection of "Western" standards. He also reports that the period of Nazi control of Austria has a relatively high number of positive connotations for Austrians. The author explains these attitudes as the result of the contradictory directions of Austrian history over the past one hundred years and by the continued influence of Austria's tradition of bureaucratic and authoritarian rule (*Obrigkeitsstaat*).

Bruckmüller devotes considerable space to Austrian attitudes to Europe. He finds that in comparison with other countries, Austrians have a thoroughly underdeveloped European consciousness. This is true not only among farmers and workers but also among professionals, business people, and entrepreneurs, and even among "green" sympathizers. The opposition to integration in Europe also appears to him to be emotionally based rather than grounded in reasoned opinions. Skepticism is greatest among the youth and the less educated, and it is connected to an obsessive attachment to the idea of Austrian neutrality. Bruckmüller explains these attitudes as a result of Austrians having twice suffered during the period 1918 to 1945 by being tied into a shattered imperial system. Only since 1945, through a policy of neutrality, has Austria prospered and found peace and a secure position in the world. He also sees skepticism about Europe as flowing from a basic lack of national self-confidence. But national self-esteem is essential to national openness to integration in larger associations, he tells us. And such openness is required by the increasingly international interlacing of economics, science, and culture. Bruckmüller also argues that strong national identity is entirely compatible with supranational integration.

In a chapter on Austrian sympathy and antipathy toward other peoples, both abroad and as minorities in Austria, the author reports a widespread fear of "foreigners" (ethnic minorities, especially Turks and southern Slavs) and of Jews. He is not sure whether the events surrounding the Waldheim affair produced a new wave of anti-Semitism in Austria or whether they gave continuing latent anti-Semitism a new social respectability. Along with this goes the Austrian's disinclination, in an international comparison to atone for Nazi crimes against the Jews. Bruckmüller might have attempted to relate this evidence of ethnocentrism to his analysis of Austrian lack of self-confidence.

Austria's problem of self-confidence Bruckmüller attributes to failure to come to terms with its contradictory history. It has eventuated in "bottled up self-hatred." "The way to world citizenship," he writes, "begins with clarity about one's identity." As therapy, the author recommends development of a national cultural canon that might help sew together the sundered and conflicting elements of the Austrian tradition. He also calls for changes in the program of public education, which for twenty years has emphasized generalized democratic lessons about issues of social justice, such as anti-feminism and apartheid, while excluding any attempt to build national consciousness in a context of an awareness of Austria's European relationships.

This is a frank, comprehensive, and objective study of the various dimensions of Austrian national consciousness. The author does not try to hide or disguise embarrassing realities. And his exposition is clear and engaging.

David F. Good, Margarete Grandner, Mary Jo Maynes, eds., *Women in Austria. Essays on Their Situation in the 20th Century* (Vienna-Cologne-Weimar: Böhlau Verlag: 1994).

Erika Thurner

This volume is the first result of a transatlantic discourse inaugurated with a symposium in 1991 at the University of Minnesota. Specialists in history, communications, literature, psychology, political science and economics from Austria, the United States, France and the Netherlands took part in the conference and contributed to this interdisciplinary collection. The common thematic denominator was women's living conditions and lifestyles (conceived both by and for women) in Austria from the early nineteenth century to the present. Three areas of concentration provided the general framework: the relationship of women to the state and to public life, the role of gender relationships in economic development and class structure as well as gender and identity.

The publication offers a multifaceted and richly colored depiction of the conditions of female existence and of gender-specific possibilities and limitations in Austria. The research and treatment of the topic are uneven, however. A few authors have broken new investigative ground, while others have served up previously published results. This does not necessarily constitute a shortcoming, since the inclusion of well-known research within a newly drawn thematic context—including a constructive discussion—may restructure and refocus modes of inquiry and thereby broaden research perspectives.

Most authors have attempted not only to elaborate characteristics peculiar to Austria but also to chart the course of developments in a larger European context. Thus, James C. Albisetti compares the upbringing of girls in German-speaking Austria at the turn of the century with that in the German Empire and in Switzerland to gain a relative perspective on the notion of a Austrian backwardness. Albisetti concerns himself with progressive-liberal education (pedagogic reform, higher education, access to universities, the high proportion of Jewish girls/women) via a highly segmented and comparative approach that examines the influence of the Catholic Church upon the educational system and the rearing of girls. Integrational possibilities for women and access to the public sphere of middle class society is treated by Pieter M. Judson as an example of German nationalist policy. In Germany, at the turn of the century, middle-class women were granted entry into certain realms of public life, although their access was limited by gender difference.

The range of topics encompassing gender-specific role attribution, inter-gender relationships and gender identity are taken up by Karen J. Jusek and Marie-Luise Angerer. Jusek analyses the views of Austrian feminists on the sexual autonomy of women in Vienna at the turn of the century. Her work shows, for example, that the ideas of early socialists on the subject of women's liberation have been accorded much stronger modern affirmation and acceptance than has previously been assumed. Marie-Luise Angerer investigates transitions in medicine with respect to the female body (from the end of the eighteenth to the beginning of the twentieth centuries)—woman as object, as a masculine field of research, as a projection screen for male conceptions. The articles by Jusek and Angerer convey the wide spectrum of the discussion of femininity and masculinity that took place at the turn of the century. Thereafter, to a certain extent, there occurred a conceptual narrowing and simplification in the question of gender roles and the social autonomy of women.

Two papers treat the subject of women and politics. Brigitta Zaar's investigation illuminates political goals and visions between 1890 and 1934, the period during which the struggle for equal political rights had its inception. Of particular interest, since it has received little academic attention, is the fact that there existed before 1918 a right to vote for women based on property ownership or income level, and that it was the discussions and attempts in the Lower Austrian provincial legislature to deprive tax-paying women of this right that set the women's suffrage movement in motion. Gerda Neyer treats opportunities and obstructions encountered by women in the Austrian Parliament since 1919 with a penetrating inquiry into the gender-differentiating ramifications of political structures and functions. She concludes that an increase in quantity—thus, quotas—cannot eliminate the de facto power gradient, as long as interlocking extra-parliamentary forces assure male dominance.

Women in the work force and in professional careers is the subject of three articles. While Gudrun Biffl uses statistical data to trace and analyze long-term trends in women's employment, tying her conclusions in to conditions of women's daily life (time budgeting of occupation and housework), Erna Appelt concentrates on the increasing presence of women in the service sector of the economy. The factor of Austrian backwardness is especially applicable to the national economy, as it was precisely this sluggish economic development that delayed the expansion of the service sector until the end of the nineteenth century. As women finally crashed the gates of previously all-male domains, the fragmentation of job fields and the institutionalization of gender-specific occupational models proceeded apace. The feminization of certain areas of employment, sanctioned by social devaluation, persists widely to this day. Erna Appelt handles this relatively short restructuring phase at the end of the nineteenth century, in which a gender-specific segregation relegated women to the service sector labor market, assuring the privileged positions for men.

Gertraud Diem-Wille uses methods of depth psychology to examine male and female professionals in management and top-level university positions, particularly with respect to self-image and gender-specific career planning. The age of the test group—40 to 52 years old, to a great extent children of the war and post-war generation—gave rise to a starkly defined interconnection between the personal life histories of the subjects and social phenomena of the parental generation. Independent of the biographical detailings of each individual situation, career motivations communicated through the parental home and environment were deeply marked by contemporary historical conditions.

"Women in the Ruins (*Trümmerfrauen*) of the Post-War Era," the topic taken up by Irene Bandhauer-Schöffmann and Ela Hornung, has constituted in the last decade—parallel to the complex of female guilt and responsibility for the terror and crimes of the Nazi regime—a central point of inquiry of feminist research in Germany. After a somewhat protracted delay, these questions are now being addressed in Austria. The methods of oral history practiced by Bandhauer-Schöffmann and Hornung in their project once again verify the fact that history as an element of the present is a component of political consciousness. Oral source material was gathered to gain first-hand knowledge in the elaboration of the continuities and breaks in the life stories of women. As a groundwork of the perception and processing of history in everyday life, oral recollections contain not only formed opinions but also retroactive interpretations. The biographical interviews with women from the most disparate social strata who had spent the post-war years in Vienna were carried out in the aftermath of the memorial year 1988 and the Waldheim affair. A majority of the women offered unprompted self-exculpations, claiming to have had no knowledge at the time of Nazi crimes; this reinterpretational endeavor is presumed to have flowed subliminally into the narrated recollections.

Oral history requires particularly critical evaluative and interpretational techniques. Furthermore, new approaches and methods can also expand upon the output from documentary sources. This is shown, for example, by Monika Bernold in her effort to identify gender-specific traces within autobiographical texts. Bernold has, along with Bandhauer-Schöffmann / Hornung, offered a key contribution to an emerging, but not yet complete, intellectual and cultural history of Austria at the turn of the century and in the early days of the Second Republic.

Once again, literature displays its power to enrich historical and social scientific research. It is much too seldom employed, both as a source and as a representational medium. With an analysis of Austrian literature of the 1980s by and about women, Klaus Zeyringer provides us with insights into gender relations and relationships. Through fiction written by and about women, we view portraits and depictions of moments in time which are not to be (mis)understood as an actual past or present, but which, nevertheless, can be decoded as a likeness or cipher of the real.

In closing, however, a few shortcomings must be pointed out, shortcomings under which such omnibus works striving toward an interdisciplinary approach so frequently suffer: isolated analyses are serially juxtaposed without the intended dovetailing of results and feedback linking structures to events is missing. The job of wrap-up and synthesis remains to a large extent the work of the reader. Certain lines of questioning are left over to subsequent papers to be analyzed, discussed and more comprehensively answered. Thus, for example, Zeyringer delivers a refinement and further development of the thematic issues, first raised by Bandhauer-Schöffmann and Hornung, of the division of roles within families and the unutilized emancipatory possibilities of temporarily empowered *Trümmerfrauen*. Austrian literature offers a glimpse into this behavioral pattern, whereby dominant mothers consistently carried on the child-rearing practices of the 'masculine system'; while others conveyed emancipatory messages by means of authoritarian measures and thus passed on a system of power and impotence. In Gertraud Diem-Wille's work on career women, as well, we find verification of the system-stabilizing parental work which mothers perform in the formation of (female) gender identity.

It is a source of particular irritation that in the American edition of a publication on the subject of women in twentieth-century Austria there is no separate chapter on National Socialism. At least in Bandhauer-Schöffmann and Hornung's essay, "From the Third Reich to the Second Republic," space is devoted to a discussion of the involvement of women in the Nazi regime. Questions concerning the effects of National Socialist policies on Austrian life and consciousness also emerge in other papers (Diem-Wille, Zeyringer). The victims' situation occupies a separate section of Zeyringer's literary analysis.

This is a fascinating book; its function of collecting and thematically arranging an assortment of the increasingly numerous contributions to women's studies is alone justification for its publication. The work is not a comprehensive history of women in Austria in the twentieth century. That is not its intent, and it is questionable whether such a project could ever come to fruition or should even be attempted. The contemporary tendencies which reject the isolated consideration of the conditions of female existence and historical concepts favoring a comparative approach to gender issues argue against an undertaking of this kind. The present volume is an interesting and successful effort to explore comparative paths that have been neglected until now. Expanding the scope of our inquiries beyond our own familiar territory, transcending both political boundaries and intellectual constraints, works to further the advance of understanding. The work has begun—we certainly look forward to its continuation.

H. Pierre Secher, *Bruno Kreisky, Chancellor of Austria: A Political Biography* (Pittsburgh: Dorrance Publishing, 1994)

Anton Pelinka

H. Pierre Secher was publishing on Austria's political system before political science even existed in Austria. His first article on "Coalition Government" in Austria dates from 1958, some years before the discipline was born in his native country. He belongs to the important group of social scientists who, like Austrian Paul Lazarsfeld, started successful careers in American academia and who, unlike the German social scientists, were not invited back to Austria in a systematic way after World War II. This neglect is one of the reasons for the slow development of the social sciences in Austria.

Secher is, understandably, fascinated by Bruno Kreisky. Based on many interviews with Kreisky's contemporaries, friends, and colleagues as well as on most of the important books, he describes the decisive phases of Kreisky's career: the young socialist with an educated, bourgeois, Jewish background; the prisoner of the authoritarian regime; the emigrant who had escaped narrowly; the diplomat who became one of a small number of prominent socialists whom the party called back from exile; the foreign minister; the leader of the opposition; and the chancellor.

Secher has done an excellent job concerning Kreisky as a person. Especially interested in Kreisky's complex attitude toward Jewish identity, he pictures Kreisky as the prototype of the "alienated Jew" (p. 202), who is against his will influenced by an identity forced upon him by his anti-Semitic environment. Kreisky is seen as a multifaceted personality who defies simplification.

Secher has done a less excellent job on many details about contemporary Austria. The biography contains numerous minor errors that a scholar more experienced in Austrian studies could have avoided. Some examples from one chapter only: Willy Lorenz has never been editor of the "very liberal,"Catholic weekly *Die Furche* (p. 173); Lorenz's editorship, begun in 1968, was the end of the liberal orientation of *Die Furche*. The installation of the extremely conservative Lorenz was meant to change the editorial policy completely. Kirchschläger was never a "loyal member of the SPÖ" (p. 175). Kreisky promoted Kirchschläger exactly because he was an independent. And more importantly, Kreisky's cabinet appointed in 1970, was by no means the first one after 1945 that consisted of former members of the Nazi party (p. 178); the ÖVP had already started the pattern of appointing former Nazi party members to cabinet ranks, Reinhard Kamitz being the most prominent case.

The strength of Secher's book is that it gives credit to all aspects of Kreisky's political life. Both the foreign and domestic policy aspects are integrated prominently. And Secher successfully mixes description with analysis. Despite the errors already mentioned, the book is a first attempt of writing a serious Kreisky biography and will be helpful for everyone who deals with Austrian contemporary history and politics. It is a "must" for all those specializing in Bruno Kreisky and nicely complements Volume II of *Contemporary Austrian Studies: The Kreisky Era in Austria.*

Anton Pelinka, Christian Schaller, and Paul Luif,
Ausweg EG? Innenpolitische Motive einer außen-
politischen Umorientierung
(Vienna: Böhlau Verlag, 1994).

Michael G. Huelshoff

Since its inception in 1958, the European Union (EU) has more
than doubled in size. By all accounts, it seems likely that the EU will
continue to grow, as the states of Central and Eastern Europe seek
membership. Despite the steady growth of the EU, however, there is
little theory that addresses the process of expansion of regional
organizations. This study is a welcome addition to the largely
nontheoretical literature on expansion. The authors lay out a model
based in the political culture of societies and explore the model in a
case study of the Austrian decision to join the EU. Despite its focus
upon a single case, the theoretical arguments presented here form a
solid body of testable hypotheses that will guide further study.

Pelinka, Schaller, and Luif focus upon the political changes
leading to the Austrian application for membership and its
negotiation, particularly the changes in Austrian political culture that
were necessary before the government could submit an application
for EU membership. The book is divided into three chapters: a
theoretical chapter, a chapter exploring the Austrian case in detail,
and a brief comparative chapter that places the Austrian case in the
broader, EFTA context, specifically, in the context of the Swedish
decision to negotiate EU membership.

In the introductory chapter, Pelinka argues that three factors
contributed to Austria's change of mind regarding the EU. These
factors include the collapse in public support for the two major
political parties, SPÖ and ÖVP (the "deconcentration" of the political

system), the weakening of Austria's social partnership, and the deregulation and privatization of the economy. He argues that Austria was "Westernized" from both below and above. Westernization from below included growing demands for access to European markets, deregulation of the economy, and privatization. This in turn led to an increase in political competition, as politicians sought to win votes among those in society demanding access to the EU beyond that afforded by the existing trade agreements and the European Economic Area.

Just as the prospects of political gain led politicians to re-evaluate their views of EU membership, political competition contributed to the deconcentration of voter support for the existing political parties and the social partnership they created. Additionally, the demands of the heads of major social and economic groups (business associations and to a lesser extent, trade unions) shifted toward EU membership. Economic elites, who feared falling behind the rapidly integrating EU during the mid- and late-1980s, began to call for change. Thus, pressures from below, both political and economic, generated pressures for change among elites, in this case, first and foremost from the relatively free market-minded pro-EU elements of the ÖVP.

Yet Austrian membership in the EU was not possible, as Pelinka notes, as long as the dominant political culture continued to embrace official Austrian neutrality. Neutrality was the cornerstone of postwar Austrian foreign policy, having been formally adopted by the Federal Parliament in October 1955. Emphasizing the social dimension of Austrian neutrality (the *"herrschende Lehre,"* as he puts it), Pelinka suggests that this key stumbling block was removed when the legal scholars Waldemar Hummer and Michael Schweitzer published their reinterpretation of the neutrality clauses of the Austrian constitution in 1987. (The report itself was commissioned by a pro-EU business association). With neutrality and EU membership no longer incompatible, the way was clear for Austria to submit its membership application in 1989.

Austria's slow drift toward a re-interpreted neutrality and EU membership carried with it unexpected political results. Some politicians attracted votes by championing EU membership (as did some by opposing membership, as the success of Haider's FPÖ in the last election suggests). Yet, Pelinka argues, all parties lost in terms of voter stability. Most politicians did not realize that increased economic competition would lead to increased political conflict, and hence to further deconcentration in Austrian politics. Additionally, contemplating EU membership also suggested the need for reform of Austria's social partnership and the expensive social programs the partnership had built over the years. The resulting cutbacks and decreasing benefits in the Austrian welfare state only accentuated political deconcentration, as disgruntled voters either switched parties or did not vote.

In the next chapter, Schaller explores in great detail the rise of the EU membership debate, beginning in the 1980s. After a brief review of background materials, he examines the public debates over membership, tracing the evolution of the debate through the ÖVP's initial membership proposal, its transformation into government policy, and finally the proposal's solidification in the membership application. At each point, Schaller goes to great lengths to recreate the debate, within the parties, government, and major social actors, and in the broader public. Schaller pays particular attention to the changing view of the ÖGB over membership. The chapter tries to answer a number of questions concerning how, why and when the Austrians decided to negotiate EU membership, and which actors played the most significant role in this process. Schaller is particularly interested in the extent to which politicians tried to improve their own careers via the membership issue. While Schaller also examines the role of public opinion in the membership debate, he claims that Austria's decision to join the EU was largely elite-driven. Schaller concludes with some thoughts concerning the implications of elite-led membership for democracy in Austria.

The final chapter expands the argument to other neutral, EFTA states, especially Sweden. Luif argues that the EU functioned as a *Rettungsanker* for the smaller, neutral states of Europe, especially as inflation and slow growth threatened the economies of Austria, Finland, Sweden, and Switzerland. With the end of the Cold War, neutrality was no longer as key an element of their foreign policies, and hence in the context of the economic problems, EU membership was attractive, at least to most elites.

There are but two minor weaknesses in the book. First, the authors are explicitly concerned with only the domestic elements of the Austrian decision to negotiate EU membership; hence, their argument cannot explain the timing of the Austrian decision to join the EU. The change in legal interpretation of Austrian neutrality is not sufficient to explain the timing. It seems likely that a more complete explanation could be found by linking domestic legal, political, and economic changes to changes in the international system. The Austrian government applied for EU membership only in the summer of 1989, after several years of "new thinking" in Soviet foreign policy, and shortly after it was clear that the Gorbachev government was tolerating reforms in Hungary and Poland. Hence, the model examined here remains incomplete. Of course, as the subtitle of the book clearly indicates, this is a study of the domestic dimensions of the Austrian case. Yet a complete analysis of Austria's decision to join the EU must take account of the international factors at work in this and the other cases of expansion. As scholars begin to analyze the move of Central and East European states toward EU membership, the international variables are likely to be significant.

Second, the book's effort to be fully comparative leaves important questions underdeveloped. The examination of other EFTA states is too short. The valuable insights that such an effort might generate are underexplored. While Luif takes the argument in a more political, economic, and foreign policy-oriented direction, which addresses in part my first comment, the balance with the first two chapters is lost. These are, however, minor weaknesses in an otherwise well-argued and detailed text.

Pelinka, Schaller, and Luif offer an important theoretical contribution to the literature on expansion of the EU. The hypotheses that guide this research will also inform further work on the expansion of regional organizations. The significance of this question is clear, as regional organizations as diverse as the EU and NAFTA expand their membership over the next two decades. The authors present a convincing case for careful examination of the domestic politics and political culture of prospective members of regional organizations.

Kurt Richard Luther and Wolfgang C. Müller, eds., *Politics in Austria: Still A Case of Consociationalism?* (London: Frank Cass, 1992)

*Max Riedlsperger**

For general readers as well as for students of comparative politics, the subtitle of this book poses a provocative question. This question is even more provocative, for those familiar with Austrian politics because it has long since been answered in the negative, indeed by some of this study's very contributors. Although this book masquerades behind a misleading title, it is not the first to do so; it is to be criticized only in that the foregone conclusion is not stated until the penultimate page.

The case for Austria as "an archetypal case of consociationalism" was made by Lehmbruch, Lijphart, Stiefbold and others in the late 1960s and 1970s as an explanation for the unusual stability of such a "pillarized" society. Actually, historian Adam Wandruszka had even earlier described many of the characteristics of what was later defined as consociationalism. In his 1954 study of Austria's political structure, he distinguishes three "naturally- or divinely-willed" *Lager*: the Catholic-conservative, the social democratic and the German-national. The word *Lager* itself implies the stark cleavages

* The editors of *CAS* would like to correct an error that slipped in at the final stage of preparing volume III in Innsbruck. We incorrectly credited Max Riedlsperger with the review of Wolfgang Mantl, ed., *Politik in Österreich. Die Zweite Republik: Bestand und Wandel* (Vienna: Böhlau, 1992), 295-98, when, in fact, Kurt R. Luther penned this review. Max Riedlsperger reviewed Luther's book printed here. We sincerely apologize to Professor Luther for this mix-up (Professor Riedlsperger did not mind).

that by the 1930s had made these alien subcultures into literally armed camps.

In their introductory chapter, editors Luther and Müller give a brief history of the development of the *Lager*. They move briefly on to define consociationalism and identify six characteristics of the Austrian version in its "classic phase" from 1945-1966. Unfortunately, the editors tend to equate *Lager* with party—a tendency shared by virtually all contemporary literature on Austrian politics. Although they recognize in their opening chapter that the parties were only the political representatives of their respective religious, socio-economic and ideological subcultures each surrounded by myriad auxiliary organizations, they then accept the usual usage of the word *Lager* as a synonym for party long after the vertical cleavages that created them had disappeared.

Politics in Austria benefits from a clear editorial plan that results in many fewer redundancies than are usually found in books with multiple authors. One chapter is devoted to each of the six characteristics identified in the introduction. The first, by prominent Austrian political scientists Fritz Plasser, Peter Ulram and Alfred Grausgruber, addresses "The Decline of '*Lager* Mentality' and the New Model of Electoral Competition" using abundant empirical data from as early as 1951 through the federal parliamentary election of 1990 to analyze the economic, religious, social, educational, political and demographic factors creating loyalty to the *Lager* and to trace the *Lagers'* decline as determinants of political behavior. It concludes with the identification of eight new categories of voters based on a cluster analysis of the political factors anticipated for the 1990s. A minor criticism is that the authors imply that low voter volatility was a constant characteristic of Austrian consociationalism "until the late 1970s" (p. 28). Haerpfer's use of the Pedersen index, however, shows 1949, 1956, 1966 and 1970 elections to have been quite volatile in the Austrian context, much more so than in any election from 1971 until 1986.

In the next chapter, English political scientist Kurt Luther describes how the elites of the coalition parties developed consociational techniques for vertically integrating the diverse levels of their respective *Lager* and for bridging the gap between the pillars upon which the success of the Second Republic depended. He provides useful statistics on party membership and its decline, describes their formal and informal auxiliary organizations and explains how they have appealed to values to mobilize their members. The remainder of the chapter is devoted to how consociational techniques worked in the electoral, parliamentary, governmental, corporate and bureaucratic arenas to ensure political stability and finally to how the decline of the *Lager* has created a process of change that is likely to continue. Luther provides evidence for my perception that the coalition parties retain at least remnants of their *Lager* character, thus alienating an electorate that has moved beyond this more primitive stage of democracy. This character helps explain the substantial decreases in voting and the remarkable rise of the populist FPÖ, which I have elsewhere in this volume discussed as the beneficiary of this process.

Next, Wolfgang Müller shifts the usual focus of politics from the parties and their leaders as the political actors to the institutions themselves. As the fear of civil war declined, which has held the two governing *Lager* parties in their consociational embrace, institutions such as the Parliament, the Constitutional Court, the Federal President, the Audit Office and the bureaucracy have gained freedom to develop their competencies in accordance with their constitutional mandates and with less regard for the party-political fallout their actions might have.

In "A Farewell to Corporatism," Peter Gerlich, well-known professor of political science at the University of Vienna, undertakes to explain "social partnership" which lay at the heart of Austria's consociational democracy after 1945. After quoting the truism that social partnership "cannot be explained to a foreigner, but need not be explained to a native," Gerlich, who edited the most exhaustive study of it in German, bravely sets about his task. He makes understandable the alphabet soup of chambers and commissions, how they interrelate with one another and function with the institutions of government and public administration. His chapter is, therefore, a must for anyone beginning a study of the politics of contemporary Austria. A chart, graphically presenting these complex interrelationships would, however, make this labyrinth of compulsory and voluntary interest groups easier to grasp. Gerlich concludes with a discussion of the growing dissatisfaction with these corporatist bodies and speculates that in an increasingly market-oriented and integrated European economy Austria will grow away from many of these remnants of its pre-modern, corporate tradition. The last two of the six topics around which the volume was structured are investigated by Salzburg political science professor Volkmar Lauber, "Changing Priorities in Austrian Economic Policy," and D. Mark Schultz, recent Oxford Ph.D. and European Analyst for the Royal Bank of Canada. Both chapters are informative and up-to-date, but lack the intimate relationship to the overall topic of the other chapters. Lauber discusses the development and contribution of "Austro-Keynsianism" to the political stabilization and remarkable economic growth of the Second Republic into the 1980s (the highest in OECD Europe). It concludes with a useful discussion of the recent reorientation of Austria's economic policy, which is only tenuously tied to the topic of consociationalism through its discussion of corporatism and then overlaps with Gerlich's discussion. Lauber argues that Austria's exposed position on the front line of the Cold War was an important factor in forcing the overarching cooperation upon which consociationalism was ultimately built and that the twin necessities of developing an export economy while protecting both domestic producers and workers further promoted cooperation between the *Lager.* Neutrality, which both *Lager* accepted as necessary for the preservation of unity and the restoration of sovereignty, thus became an important element in consociational cooperation. It was also perceived as incompatible with membership in the developing EEC, causing Austria to join in the formation of EFTA.

In the following chapter, Schultz focuses on Austria's gradual steps towards integration with the EC through its 1989 application for membership, but stopping short of the 1992 conclusion of the European Economic Area agreement. This is a useful survey, but requires evidence from specific debates, compromises and decisions to make the case that these foreign policy concerns were important causal factors in the development of Austria's particular style of consociationalism.

The volume concludes with an excellent short chapter by the editors summarizing the organizing principles and their contributors' discussions of them. Its title "Austrian Consociationalism: Victim of Its Own Success?" reveals the misleading character of the book's subtitle, concluding that the political subcultures have changed and that only the old *Lager* elites cling to the remnants of consociationalism which served their purpose by paving the way for a new and as yet not yet clearly evolved democracy. Appendices follow, including tables for federal parliamentary and presidential elections and cabinets since 1945 and an outstanding bibliography of English language sources which supplements the excellent end notes for each chapter.

Survey of Austrian Politics: 1994

Rainer Nick

Austria and the European Union

1994 marked the climax of Austria's efforts to become a full member of the European Union. Although the membership question has met with considerable political opposition in Austria, complex negotiations were started in June 1993, and intensive discussions about compromises on sensitive issues continued until 1994.

In early 1994 three main issues were still left to be resolved:

* The transit question: Austria and the EU differed on the issue of road transit traffic. Austria insisted on a restrictive and ecologically oriented traffic policy. The EU, on the other hand, wanted free and uninhibited traffic along the north-south and the east-west axes through Austria.
* Agriculture: Austria's agricultural interests clashed with those of more inexpensive production countries in the EU. Particularly critical points included production quotas and the amount and duration of subsidies.
* Acquisition of real property: Especially the western provinces—Tyrol, Vorarlberg, and Salzburg—feared that EU membership would result in substantial increases in the price of land suitable for building, an extremely scarce resource in these mountainous areas.

At the end of February, the discussion of controversial issues became increasingly dramatic. Agreement on transit traffic and agriculture, as well as on regional and structural policies, was reached literally at the last minute, only after extensive negotiations. The compromises regarding these controversial issues were as follows:

* On the extremely touchy question of transit traffic, Austria managed to preserve the existing contract. The basic aims of this contract were kept intact with modifications to be made only via Austria's agreement. However, the duration of the contract was shortened by one year.
* On the agricultural question, Austria had to agree to lower prices for agricultural products but achieved temporary national compensation payments.
* On structural and regional policy topic—a problem exacerbated by the question of secondary residences—the negotiation parties were able to agree on a five-year transition period.
* The emotional question of Austrian neutrality was resolved by means of ancillary legal measures. In principle, the Austrian Law of Neutrality, central to Austria's national identity, was kept intact.

It was important that the last-minute agreement made it possible to submit a body of contracts to the European Parliament. As a consequence, these contracts could be ratified prior to the new elections of the EU Parliament on 12 June. The European Parliament approved the applications for membership of all four applicants (Finland, Norway, Sweden, Austria). The Austrian Council of Ministers, the National Council, and the Federal Council agreed to the membership contract with the EU as well.

As a consequence of the negotiations for EU membership, the Austrian Constitution had to be amended, which generally requires a plebiscite. The date of the plebiscite was fixed for 12 June, the same day that the elections for the European Parliament were to take place in EU countries. At this point both supporters and opponents of Austrian EU membership had begun campaigning intensively.

The supporters of EU membership comprised parts of the population with higher levels of formal education, as well as people in urban areas and economically advantaged groups. All relevant business associations strongly advocated EU membership. As established in the coalition agreement, both governmental parties— SPÖ (Social-Democratic Party) and ÖVP (Austrian People's Party)—were for Austria's integration into the EU. Among the opposition parties, only the Liberal Forum (LIF) assumed a positive stance towards EU membership.

The central pillars of the political system, including the two largest parties, SPÖ and ÖVP, the social partners, the government, and the majority of the Parliament were positively inclined towards political and economic integration. Reasons for this support included economic considerations (since the Austrian and EU economy are strongly interlinked) as well as Austria's pronounced sense of stability and long-term security aims.

Opponents of EU membership recruited their followers mostly from among those groups who would be disadvantaged by Austrian EU membership. In addition to farmers and opponents of integration for ecological reasons (most of all in the western parts of Austria), opposition forces included right-wing populist groups whose concerns and fears were focused and articulated by the chairman of the FPÖ (Austrian Freedom Party), Jörg Haider. Issues like skepticism regarding the immigration of foreign workers into Austria, the fear of losing one's job, as well as the rejection of liberalization and modernization led to a broad and frequently contradictory alliance of groups against EU membership.

In a special party meeting, the FPÖ had decided to vote against the EU contract in Parliament. The party did not, however, make any official recommendation to the voters regarding the plebiscite, but this did not prevent Jörg Haider, the FPÖ party chairman, from speaking out against Austria's integration into the EU. The stance of the Green Party was ambivalent: a minority of the Green Party advocated membership in order to initiate democratic and ecological reforms from within the European Community. A majority within the official bodies of the Green Party, however, were against integration. The party perceived insufficient social and ecological policies, a lack of concern regarding Third World problems, and deficient democratic structures in the EU.

In the time between the final agreement in the negotiations and the plebiscite, a number of laws were passed to mitigate hardship for consumers, employees, and farmers on their way into the EU. With these methods, the government attempted to counter skepticism regarding EU integration. In the course of the EU campaign, the number of supporters continued to grow. Massive campaigning on the part of the government, compensation for the negative consequences of EU membership through cost-intensive measures, and the prospects of subsidies for structurally weak areas were effective against the highly emotional anti-EU campaign conducted by Jörg Haider and others.

Finally, on 12 June, 66 percent of all Austrians voted for integration into the European Union. Voter participation was critical for the outcome of the plebiscite. While a majority of voters were expected to support EU membership, the outcome would have been endangered by low voter turnout.

Table 1:   Survey of the Outcome of the EU Plebiscite

Voter turnout	81.27 %
Valid votes	99.08 %
Yes votes	66.39 %
No votes	33.61 %

Source: Compiled from official election data.

A socio-structural analysis of voting behavior shows that farmers as well as pronounced Green and FPÖ supporters voted against EU membership. Support for Austria's integration increased with the age of the voter—even if there was a majority of EU supporters in all age groups. The plebiscite was characterized by a large proportion of "late-deciders," a phenomenon which can also be perceived in Austrian elections. The rift between supporters and opponents cut along the lines of potential advantages and disadvantages of modernization, as well as between groups with above-average professional qualifications and those who expected personal job disadvantages from EU membership. An additional key factor was the regional distribution of EU support. Burgenland, the state that could expect most economic benefits from Austria's membership (high EU subsidies), was characterized by the largest proportion of "yes" votes. The lowest degree of EU support was found in Tyrol because of the problem of transit traffic and fears of a misguided structural policy in the agricultural sector. In summary, the Austrian population has, in a democratic way, clearly legitimized Austria's membership in the EU.

Table 2:   Results of the Plebiscite in the States

State	Proportion of "Yes" Votes in %	Proportion of "No" Votes in %	Voter Turnout in %
Vienna	65.8	34.2	71.5
Lower Austria	67.8	32.2	89.6
Upper Austria	65.3	34.7	84.5
Styria	68.7	31.3	79.6
Tyrol	56.4	43.3	76.5
Carinthia	68.0	32.0	81.0
Salzburg	64.8	35.1	81.2
Vorarlberg	66.4	33.6	79.0
Burgenland	74.6	25.4	93.4

Source: Compiled from official election data.

Finally, on 11 November the Austrian National Council ratified the EU membership contract with the necessary two-thirds majority. In addition to the governmental parties, the Liberal Forum and the Greens—as a sign of "respect for the results of the plebiscite"—voted for the ratification and thus the end of Austria's long-term endeavors for EU membership. After the vote on additional by-laws in the National and Federal Council in December, no obstacle remained to Austria's entry into the EU on 1 January 1995.

After elections for the National Council had taken place and the federal government was sworn in, debates started about who

Austria's delegates to EU institutions would be. Austria nominated one commissioner, Franz Fischler (up to this point agricultural minister) who assumed responsibility for agriculture in the EU Commission. Because in Austria elections to the European Parliament had not yet taken place, the seats allocated to Austria were distributed relative to party representation in the National Council. The respective personnel were recruited from representatives of the National and Federal Council.

1994: The Super-Election Year

Elections of State Diets

The "super-election" year of 1994, which included four State Diet elections, one EU plebiscite, municipal elections, Chamber of Labor elections, and National Council elections, commenced on 13 March with State Diet elections in three states. For several reasons, these elections had more than regional importance:

* More than one million Austrians were eligible to vote.
* The elections were held prior to the EU plebiscite.
* Despite the time lag, the "super-election Sunday" was expected to yield first data about voter behavior during the National Council elections in the fall.
* In Carinthia, Jörg Haider, the FPÖ chairman, ran for the office of governor of the state.
* The election results of the Liberal Forum were awaited with great interest.

On 13 March votes were cast in the states of Tyrol, Salzburg, and Carinthia. In the different states, various starting positions and electoral aims prevailed: in Tyrol and Salzburg the ÖVP wanted to maintain its position as strongest party and thus nominate the governor, while in Carinthia the ÖVP wanted to regain votes to support their claim for the governor's office.

The results of the elections to the State Diets from 13 March were spectacular in all respects. In Tyrol, the ÖVP managed to maintain its absolute majority (in terms of seats) against the competition of new parties. In Salzburg, the governor continued to be nominated by the ÖVP, despite a loss of votes. In Carinthia, the ÖVP once more became the second strongest party behind the SPÖ. A special characteristic of the elections in this state was the significant weakness of the Green Party: they did not get enough votes to be represented in the State Diet. The Liberal Forum was not able to repeat its success in the elections to the Lower Austrian State Diet. In all three states, the SPÖ had to face severe losses, which in Tyrol and Carinthia led to changes in the party leadership.

Table 3:   Elections to the Carinthian State Diet in 1989 and 1994

Party	Election Results 1994 in %	Number of Seats 1994	Election Results 1989 in %
SPÖ	37.4	14	46.0
ÖVP	23.8	9	21.0
FPÖ	33.3	13	29.0
Green Party	1.6	0	3.3
LIF	2.6	0	n.p.*

Source: Compiled from official election results.
* n.p. - no participation in the elections

Table 4:   Elections to the Salzburg State Diet in 1989
            and 1994

Party	Election Results 1994 in %	Number of Seats 1994	Election Results 1994 in %
SPÖ	27.1	11	31.3
ÖVP	38.6	14	44.8
FPÖ	19.5	8	16.4
Green Party	7.2	3	6.1
LIF	5.8	0	n.p.*

Source: Compiled from official election results.
* n.p. - no participation in the elections

Table 5:   Elections to the Tyrolean State Diet in 1989 and
            1994

Party	Election Results 1994 in %	Number of Seats 1994	Election Results 1989 in %
SPÖ	19.9	7	22.8
ÖVP	47.3	19	48.7
FPÖ	16.2	6	15.6
Green Party	10.6	4	8.3
LIF	3.3	0	n.p.*

Source: Compiled from official election results.
* n.p. - no participation in the elections

On the governmental level, the entry of the Green Party into the Tyrolean state government marked a significant novelty. Because of the distribution of seats, at this point all four parties in the State Diet are represented in the state government as well, which led to a discussion regarding the effectiveness of proportional governments at the state level. In Carinthia, the office of the Governor caused heated conflicts. A short-term agreement between the FPÖ and the ÖVP to appoint the ÖVP candidate Zernatto as governor represented a dangerous conflict potential and test of strength for the Grand Coalition of ÖVP and SPÖ on the federal level, especially with regard to the pending EU plebiscite. Finally, an agreement was reached between the ÖVP and SPÖ, and Christian Zernatto was elected governor of Carinthia.

While the State Diet elections of 13 March were clearly influenced by federal politics, the results cannot be explained without taking into account regional factors of influence, such as the image of top politicians, the electoral advantage given by the personality of the respective governor, or the specific political culture in the various regions. The topic of EU membership, which dominated the media landscape, was not a decisive factor in all states. Particularly in Carinthia, the elections to the State Diet did not foreshadow the EU plebiscite at all. In Tyrol, on the other hand, the EU issue played a significant role. The "Super-Sunday" clearly shows that the decrease in party ties parallels the trend of increased personalization and media orientation of political processes. The attractiveness of the top candidates was decisive for the election results. This is the only way that the absolute ÖVP majority in Tyrol and Vorarlberg can be explained.

The elections to the State Diet in the state of Vorarlberg were held on 18 September, three weeks before the National Council elections. As in Tyrol, the ÖVP was able to maintain its absolute majority of seats and only barely failed to receive the absolute majority of votes. In Vorarlberg, the SPÖ was reduced to the size of a small party: for the first time it received fewer votes than the FPÖ. The votes for the Liberal Forum did not suffice for a representation of this party in the State Diet, while the Green Party managed to stabilize its position. Overall, the election results reflect the political landscape of western Austria: the dominance of the ÖVP, the traditionally strong position of the FPÖ in Vorarlberg, and the structural weakness of the SPÖ. The reasons for this can be found in the socio-economic conditions (small and medium-sized crafts businesses, a third-sector economy based on tourism, an economically dominating position of family businesses) and the specific regional political culture. Particularly in Tyrol and Vorarlberg with their extremely popular governors the political developments of 1994 were totally different for the regional party branches of the ÖVP than those of the general ÖVP.

Table 6:   Elections to the Vorarlberg State Diet in 1989 and 1994

Party	Election Results 1994 in %	Number of Seats 1994	Election Results 1989 in %
SPÖ	16.26	6	21.3
ÖVP	49.91	20	51.0
FPÖ	18.44	7	16.1
Green Party	7.73	3	5.2
LIF	3.39	0	n.p.*

Source: compiled from official election results
* n.p. - no participation in the elections

The Elections to the Chamber of Labor
The campaign for the Chamber of Labor elections became extremely contentious in September. In a TV debate with Federal Chancellor Vranitzky, Jörg Haider publicly disclosed the salaries of certain Chamber of Labor directors, an event that received wide media coverage. As a consequence, the Chamber of Labor found itself under strong pressure to legitimize itself before the elections.

Compulsory membership in the Chamber of Labor was questioned, as was the overall profile of the institution. When the Chamber of Labor elections were finally held on 2 and 3 October, only 35 percent of the electorate went to the ballots. The organizations of the governmental parties, the social-democratic FSG (Faction of Socialist Unionists) and the Christian-democratic ÖAAB (Austrian Association of Workers and Employees) lost votes, while the workers associated with the FPÖ doubled their votes. Still, this did not affect the top positions of the organization: in Tyrol and Vorarlberg, the ÖAAB continued to nominate the president of the Chamber of Labor, while in the other states the FSG remained dominant.

Table 7:   Results of the Elections to the Chamber of Labor (ECL) in the Austrian States

State	ECL 94 FSG	ECL 94 ÖAAB	ECL 94 FA	ECL 89 FSG	ECL 89 ÖAAB	ECL 89 FA
Vienna	57.2	17.3	15.9	67	20.6	6.8
Lower Austria	56.3	29.1	10.4	61.2	31	5.1
Upper Austria	56.4	24.8	15.6	60.4	28.2	23.1
Styria	53.7	27.0	15.3	59.5	30.1	6.2
Tyrol	35.6	45.7	13.2	41.8	47.7	8.1
Carinthia	62.9	11.6	20.9	65.9	14.5	18.6
Salzburg	57.7	23.8	14.3	60.4	27.7	9.3
Vorarlberg	27.8	56.3	11.5	37.7	59.5	7.6
Burgenland	58.0	32.3	9.6	60.3	35.3	3.8

Source: Compiled from official data. All data in %.
Legend: FSG - Faction of Socialist Unionists
         ÖAAB - Austrian Association of Workers and Employees
         FA - Workers and employees associated with the Austrian Freedom Party

The results of the Chamber of Labor elections were a first sign of what was to be confirmed in the National Council elections. The SPÖ was losing more and more votes to the FPÖ, which more and more established itself as a "new protest-oriented workers' party." This result also had personnel consequences. The president of the Viennese Chamber of Labor, Heinz Vogler, had to resign under pressure exerted from the top SPÖ leadership.

The National Council Elections

Because of the large number of elections and a plebiscite in 1994, the parties found themselves campaigning continuously: the strategic positioning of the campaigning parties had already started before the State Diet elections in March and the EU plebiscite.

Some basic characteristics began to appear by the beginning of the year, such as the confrontation between Vranitzky and Haider, increased media importance, and highly personalized campaigns. Before the EU plebiscite, the issue of Austria's EU membership dominated discussions, but after 12 June the phase of intensive campaigning began. In the campaign for the National Council elections, the two governmental parties were not able to utilize the success of the EU plebiscite because of various petty fights concerning fields of competence and power.

The campaigning parties featured different initial positions and strategies.

* The two coalition parties were, most of all, interested in continuing their cooperation.
* The SPÖ's explicit aim was to prevent a coalition between ÖVP and FPÖ.
* The ÖVP wanted to exclude the possibility of a coalition in which it would not participate and thus aimed at a continuation of the Grand Coalition.
* The goal of the FPÖ was to win an "intermediary victory" to further Jörg Haider's aim to become federal chancellor in 1998.
* The explicit electoral aim of the Green Party was to prevent a two-thirds majority of the coalition parties.
* For the Liberal Forum as a new party, entry into the National Council was of prime importance.

A significant feature of the campaign was the extreme impact of the media and a highly personalized campaign focus. A significant example in this respect was the TV confrontation of the top party candidates. The one-on-one round-table confrontations and the media coverage they received had varied effects on electoral behavior. The opposition managed to define what was regarded an issue. The growing number of "late-deciders" and the increased significance of media image and emotional campaigning made the final phases of the campaign essential. After the election year of 1994 it should be clear that in Austria, as in other Western European and Northern American democracies, campaigns are predominantly fought and won on the TV screen. This means that a further personalization of political processes is pre-programmed.

The National Council Elections of 1994 were based on a new electoral law. Important new features included the establishment of forty-three regional electoral districts, as well as a modified ballot system. Voters could give preference votes on the regional level. The parties could nominate candidates on three levels, namely on the level of the regional electoral districts as well as on the state and federal level. The establishment of regional electoral districts was meant to strengthen the contact between representatives and citizens. In reality, however, only the strong parties had a chance to win seats on this level. As the results of the National Council elections show, only the SPÖ, ÖVP, and FPÖ managed to gain seats through the regional electoral districts. For the Green Party and the Liberal Forum the ballot system on the state and federal level was much more important.

The new election law resulted in modified recruiting processes of the parties. By far the most complex nomination process took place in the ÖVP, where open primary elections were made obligatory on the regional level. Primaries took place in the SPÖ as well. However, they were mostly organized as meetings for party members. The FPÖ carried out a nomination process that was primarily focused on media image and media presence. The party leadership utilized its strong position to introduce its preferred nominees. The Green Party tried to reach a compromise of intra-party principles and realized the necessity of personalized campaigns. The Liberal Forum followed the recruiting mechanisms of a classic "notables' party."

The nomination process for the candidates led to intra-party conflicts, particularly in the two governmental parties. The reason for this was that a loss of seats was predictable, which significantly limited the party leadership's room for action in terms of personnel nominations. Differences can also be observed with regard to the parties' campaign concepts. The SPÖ focused on Franz Vranitzky and counted on the electoral advantage of being the party with the current federal chancellor. Without an attractive top candidate, the ÖVP did not concentrate on a personalized campaign and rather tried to emphasize concepts such as "mother country" [Heimat] and its role as political center party. Jörg Haider expected support particularly from the protest potential of the electorate and strongly emphasized extreme positions. The Green Party shed its former reluctance to personalize campaigning and concentrated its efforts on its top female candidate. The Liberal Forum ran a program whose issues presented an alternative to Jörg Haider and fully counted on its popular female top candidate.

The results of the National Council elections from 9 October brought about massive changes in the Austrian party landscape.

Table 8:   Results of the National Council Elections (NCE) from 9 October 1994

Party	Votes NCE 94 in %	Seats NCE 94 in %	Votes NCE 90 in %	Seats NCE 90 in %
SPÖ	35.2	66	42.7	80
ÖVP	27.4	52	32.1	60
FPÖ	22.6	42	16.6	33
Green Party	7.0	13	4.8	10
LIF	5.8	10	n.p.*	n.p.*

Source: Compiled from official data.
* n.p. - no participation in the elections

National Council Elections in Austria

Analyses of the National Council elections indicate a far-reaching reorientation of party loyalties, an increasing number of mobile voters, as well as the emergence of new lines of tension and conflict in the Austrian party system. Overall, the election results show a break with three long-term developments in Austria.

* The election political status of SPÖ, ÖVP, and FPÖ has undergone substantial change. Now there are three center parties in Austria.
* The coalition government lost its two-thirds majority, which means that it can no longer pass constitutional laws alone.
* The Austrian party system is exposed to a rapid process of de-concentration. At no time before has voter participation been lower; at no time have SPÖ and ÖVP together received fewer votes.

Politically, 1994 was the year of women. Both the Green Party and the Liberal Forum ran their campaigns with female top candidates. The voting behavior of women was of special importance for the election results: The Green Party and the Liberal Forum owe their election success to a large extent to the votes of women.

The election results—particularly the coalition parties' loss of their two-thirds majority in the National Council—tend to make the National Council more important in Austrian politics. After the National Council elections, the SPÖ and ÖVP entered into coalition negotiations. Jörg Haider, the FPÖ party chairman, assured the ÖVP that he would "tolerate" an ÖVP minority government. For weeks the ÖVP and SPÖ discussed their future working program and list of ministers, and finally reached an agreement which focused on the consolidation of national finances. In terms of ministerial posts, personnel was shuffled but hardly any new faces appeared. In this respect, the SPÖ had to face difficulties within the party. Because of the budget savings that had been decided in the agreement, the unionists in the SPÖ threatened to boycott the coalition agreement.

On 29 November the Cabinet Vranitzky IV was sworn in. It consists of ten SPÖ and ten ÖVP representatives. The Ministry of Justice continues to be headed by a party-independent minister.

Chronology of 1994

Date	Select events
1 January	EEA (European Economic Area) agreement comes into force
1 March	Agreement between Austria and the EU concerning Austrian membership
13 March	State Diet elections in Tyrol, Salzburg, and Carinthia
24 April	Municipal Council elections in Innsbruck
12 June	Plebiscite about Austria's EU membership: 66 % of all Austrian say "yes" to Europe
1 July	Visit of Li Peng, the Chinese Prime Minister, in Austria accompanied by strong protests
6-9 July	CSCE conference in Vienna
22 August	Forum Alpach with the heads of state of all neighboring countries
24 August	Bomb attack in front of bilingual school in Klagenfurt
18 September	Elections to the State Diet in Vorarlberg
3 October	Chamber of Labor elections followed by Heinz Vogler's resignation as head of the Viennese Chamber of Labor
6 October	Series of letter bomb attacks
9 October	National Council elections
17 October	Gerhard Zeiler appointed new director of the ORF (Austrian Broadcasting Corporation)
23 October	Large meeting of German-national fraternities in Innsbruck accompanied by demonstrations
11 November	Ratification of the EU agreement in parliament
13 November	Federal President Klestil visits Israel
29 November	The new government is sworn in

FURTHER LITERATURE

Andreas Khol, Günther Ofner and Alfred Stirnemann, eds., *Österreichisches Jahrbuch für Politik 1993* (Vienna: Verlag für Geschichte und Politik, 1993).

Rainer Nick and Anton Pelinka, *Österreichs politische Landschaft* (Innsbruck: Haymon-Verlag, 1993).

Bundespressedienst des Bundeskanzleramtes, ed., *Der Österreichbericht*, vol. 45 (Vienna 1994).

Fritz Plasser, Peter A. Ulram, Erich Neuwirth and Franz Sommer, *Analyse der Nationalratswahl 1994. Muster, Wählerströme und Motive* (Vienna: Zentrum für angewandte Politikforschung and Fessel + GFK, 1994)

Fritz Plasser and Peter A. Ulram, *Wählerstrukturen und Entscheidungsmotive bei den Landtagswahlen am 13. März 1994 in Kärnten, Salzburg und Tyrol* (Vienna: Zentrum für angewandte Politikforschung and Fessel + GFK, 1994).

Fritz Plasser, Peter A. Ulram, Franz Sommer and Andreas Vretscha, *Analyse der EU-Volksabstimung vom 12. Juni 1994* (Vienna: Zentrum für angewandte Politikforschung and Fessel + GFK, 1994).

Der Standard

Die Presse

News

Profil

Salzburger Nachrichten

Wochenpresse

List of Authors

William T. Bluhm is professor emeritus of political science at the University of Rochester.

Lubomir Brokl is a senior fellow in the Institute of Sociology in the Czech Academy of Sciences.

Monika Cámbaliková is a research fellow at the Institute of Sociology, Slovak Academy of Sciences.

Reinhold Gärtner is an assistant professor of political science at the University of Innsbruck.

Michael Gehler is a fellow and a lecturer at the Institute of Contemporary History at the University of Innsbruck.

Birgitt Haller is a fellow at the Institute of Conflict Research in Vienna.

Michael G. Huelshoff is an associate professor of political science at the University of New Orleans; in the spring of 1995 he was a guest professor in the Institute of Politics of the University of Innsbruck.

Ferdinand Karlhofer is an assistant professor of political science at the University of Innsbruck.

Randall Kindley is a lecturer in political science and a research associate in the Center for Austrian Studies at the University of Minnesota in Minneapolis.

Bernhard Kittel is a research assistant at the Institutes of Political Science and Sociology at the University of Vienna.

Wolfgang Krieger is a senior policy analyst with the Stiftung Wissenschaft und Politik in Ebenhausen and a member of the History Department of the University of Munich.

Sándor Kurtán is a lecturer in political science at the Economics University in Budapest.

Igor Lukšič is an assistant professor in the Faculty of Social Sciences at the University of Ljubljana in Slovenia.

David McIntosh graduated *summa cum laude* in history from Harvard College and is a first year student at the Harvard Law School.

Walter Manoschek is an assistant professor of political science at the University of Vienna.

Zdenka Mansfeldova is a research fellow in the Institute of Sociology in the Czech Academy of Sciences.

Andrei S. Markovits is professor and chair, Board of Studies in Politics, at the University of California in Santa Cruz, and a senior associate at the Center for European Studies at Harvard University; in the spring of 1996 he will serve as a Fulbright Professor at the Institute of Politics of the University of Innsbruck.

Alan S. Milward is professor of economic history at the London School of Economics & Political Science.

Richard Mitten is a historian and an associate at the Center for International and Interdisciplinary Studies at the University of Vienna.

Rainer Nick is an assistant professor of political science at the University of Innsbruck.

Jonathan Petropoulos is an assistant professor of history at Loyola College in Maryland.

Peter G. J. Pulzer is a professor of history at All Soul's College at Oxford University.

Max Riedlsperger is professor of history at the California Polytechnic State University in San Luis Obispo.

Hans Seidel is retired from the Austrian Institute of Economic Research in Vienna and a former director of the Institute of Advanced Studies in Vienna; during the Kreisky administration he was a state secretary in the Ministry of Finance.

Emmerich Tálos is professor of political science at the University of Vienna.

Erika Thurner is an associate professor of history at the University of Linz and a guest professor in the of Institute Politics at the University of Innsbruck.

Detlef Vogel is a retired senior historian of the German Military History Office in Freiburg, Germany.